Review of International Studies

VOLUME 36 . SPECIAL ISSUE . 2010

CONTENTS

Review of International Studies

© British International Studies Association 2010

Subscriptions
Review of International Studies (ISSN 0260-2105) is published quarterly for the British International Studies Association in January, April, July and October by Cambridge University Press.

The subscription price (excluding VAT) of Volume 36, 2010, is £269 which includes print and electronic access (USA, Canada and Mexico US$469) for institutions, £50 (USA, Canada and Mexico US$75) for individuals which includes print only, ordering direct from the publishers and certifying that the journal is for their personal use. Single parts cost £58 (USA, Canada and Mexico US$90). The electronic-only price available to institutional subscribers is £235 (USA, Canada and Mexico US$380). EU subscribers (outside the UK) who are not registered for VAT should add VAT at their country's rate. VAT registered subscribers should provide their VAT registration number. Orders, which must be accompanied by payment, may be sent to any bookseller or subscription agent or to the publisher: Cambridge University Press, The Edinburgh Building, Shaftesbury Road, Cambridge CB2 8RU, UK. Orders from the USA, Canada and Mexico should be sent to Cambridge University Press, Journals Fulfillment Department, 100 Brook Hill Drive, West Nyack, New York 10994–2133, USA. Prices include delivery by air. Japanese prices for institutions are available from Kinokuniya Company Ltd, P.O. Box 55, Chitose, Tokyo 156, Japan.

Periodicals postage paid at New York, NY, and at additional mailing offices. POSTMASTER: Send address changes in USA, Canada and Mexico to *Review of International Studies*, Cambridge University Press, 100 Brook Hill Drive, West Nyack, New York 10994–2133, USA.

Notes for contributors

Manuscripts
The Editors welcome submission of material for consideration as a main article or as a review article. The length required for main articles is 9–12,000 words, including footnotes, and longer submissions will not normally be reviewed. Review articles should be about 4,000 words and replies about 2,000 words. These are also sent to independent referees. The *Review* is a refereed journal, and contributors should allow time for the process of refereeing to take place. **It is the author's responsibility to provide the editors with an accurate total word count for all articles on submission.**

Prospective authors should submit their manuscripts by electronic mail (RISsub@st-andrews.ac.uk) or on disk. Submission of manuscripts is now also online via the website: <**http://mc.manuscriptcentral.com/ris**>. Detailed instructions for submitting your manuscript online can be found at the submission website by clicking on the Instructions and Forms link in the top right hand of the screen; and then clicking on the Online Submission Instructions for Authors icon on the following page.

Manuscripts should be typed on one side of the paper only with generous margins and should be double spaced throughout. An abstract of 100 words plus a short biographical note (appropriate for Notes on Contributors) should accompany the manuscript. To guarantee anonymity, authors should include a title page without their names, and remove any reference to themselves from the manuscript.

When an article has been accepted for publication, the author **must** send a copy of the final version by e-mail attachment or on computer disk (IBM compatible PC) giving details of the word processing software used, and also one hard copy typescript. **The Editors reserve the right not to accept articles not presented in the house style, details of which are given below.**

References and notes
These should be amalgamated and signalled serially within each article by superscript numerals. References and notes should be at the foot of each page. References should give full biographical details, including place of publication **and** publisher, at first mention. Thereafter the author's surname and a short title should be used (not *op. cit.*). A cross-reference to the original citation, e.g. '(see n.4 above)', may also be added if the short title reference is not immediately clear. The title of an article should appear in single inverted commas; the title of a book or journal should be underlined. Main words should be 'first-letter' capitalised in article and book titles.

References and notes should be typed in the form of the following examples:
1. Lawrence Freedman, *The Evolution of Nuclear Strategy* (London: Macmillan, 1981), pp. 51–3.
2. Freedman, *Evolution of Nuclear Strategy*, p. 152.
3. Bruce Cumings, 'Japan and the Asian Periphery', in Melvyn P. Leffler and David S. Painter (eds.), *Origins of the Cold War* (London: Routledge, 1994), pp. 226–9.
4. *New York Times*, 13 May 1987.
5. Cumings, 'Japan', p. 216.
6. J. P. Cornford, 'The Illusion of Decision', *British Journal of Political Science,* 4:2 (1974), pp. 231–43.

Subheadings
Contributors are encouraged to include up to two levels of subheading in articles to provide 'signposts' for readers. They should be typed flush left with only the first word and any proper names capitalised.

General
First proofs may be read and corrected by contributors provided that they can give the editors a current address and can guarantee to return the corrected proofs, by airmail where appropriate, within three days of receiving them.

Contributors of accepted articles will be asked to assign their copyright, on certain conditions, to the British International Studies Association so that their interest may be safeguarded.

CAMBRIDGE UNIVERSITY PRESS
University Printing House, Cambridge CB2 8BS, United Kingdom
One Liberty Plaza, 20th Floor, New York, NY 10006, USA
477 Williamstown Road, Port Melbourne, VIC 3207, Australia
314-321, 3rd Floor, Plot 3, Splendor Forum, Jasola District Centre, New Delhi - 110025, India
03 Penang Road, #05-06/07, Visioncrest Commercial, Singapore 238467

Review of International Studies (2010), 36, 1–2
doi:10.1017/S0260210511000064   © 2010 British International Studies Association

Introduction: Evaluating global orders

NICHOLAS RENGGER

This is the final special issue of the *Review* under the Editorship of the team at St. Andrew's University.[1] In previous special issues we have investigated the critical turn in International Relations (IR) theory,[2] the politics of global communication[3] and the phenomenon of regionalism in contemporary IR.[4] For our final such issue we decided that we wanted to look, in rather more general compass, at conceptualisations of 'global order' *tout court*. That is to say, we wanted to look at the way in which we – all of us in this hugely contested and contestable field – imagine and evaluate both the 'orders' that make up what we often rather loosely refer to as '*the* global order', and the ways in which we do the evaluating.

Thus, in this special issue we look at a number of different ways of evaluating and assessing the global orders that characterise contemporary International Relations, both as it is conventionally understood (and practiced) and as it is variously and differently understood or imagined. We make no claim to exhaustiveness – indeed we doubt if an exhaustive understanding of the different ways we might imagine and evaluate global orders is possible – but we do hope that the various articles that collectively make up this special issue offer interesting and provocative 'evaluations' that can spark other such reflections in our readership.

We do not intend to list here or discuss the individual contributions – they will speak for themselves. While some of the chapters that follow have been specially commissioned for this issue – such as some of the responses to Louise Arbour's July 2008 article on the 'Responsibility to protect' and the discussion of David Miller's *National Responsibility and Global Justice* – others were submitted to the journal in the usual way and were selected for inclusion here because they seem to offer particular ways of 'evaluating' global orders that were interesting to reflect upon. Some reflect on a particular aspect of the contemporary global order (the role of the UN as an 'ideas entrepreneur', perhaps, or the problems and prospects of the 'liberal peace') others imagine a very different world order (that envisaged

---

[1] It has been a privilege and a pleasure to have been the custodians of the *Review* over the last five years. We thank all those who submitted articles to the *Review*, all of our referees without whom the job of the editorial team would be literally impossible and all of those at Cambridge University Press who work with such tireless efficiency to produce the journal. And we wish the new team every good fortune during their tenure.
[2] The 2007 special issue later published as Nicholas Rengger and Ben Thirkell-White (eds), *Critical International Relations Theory After twenty Five Years* (Cambridge: Cambridge University Press, 2007).
[3] The 2008 special issue, later published as Oliver Richmond, Alison Watson and Costas Constantinou (eds), *Global Communications and International Relations* (Cambridge: Cambridge University Press, 2008).
[4] The 2009 special issue later published as Rick Fawn (ed.), *Globalizing the Regional, Regionalizing the Global* (Cambridge: Cambridge University Press, 2009).

by ancient tradition, for example) but all make us think about how we might 'evaluate' global orders and what it is we do when we think of global order at all, in any context, and that was really our aim in this special issue.

While people will, of course, be inclined to agree with this or that article more than with some others, what these articles really constitute is an invitation to further dialogue. If we are to understand the complexities, opportunities and problems that constitute our increasingly global society, it is to such dialogue that we must look. And in that context the role of journals such as the *Review*, in facilitating such a dialogue is more important than ever. We look forward to seeing how the *Review* continues the dialogue in the years to come.

Review of International Studies (2010), *36*, 3–23   © *2010 British International Studies Association*
doi:10.1017/S026021051100009X

How United Nations ideas change history

THOMAS G. WEISS

Abstract. This article considers the United Nations (UN) as a creator and facilitator of innovative ideas in world politics. It thereby breathes new life into the world organisation's overlooked characteristics: the quality and diversity of its intellectual leadership, and its value-based framework for dealing with the global challenges of our times. The nature of UN ideas are examined – the good, the bad, and the ugly – while recognising that most have multiple origins and various carriers, and it continues by assessing impact. Three types of UN ideas – positive, normative, and instrumental – are discussed. Positive ideas are those resting on hard evidence, open to challenge and verifiable. Normative ideas are beliefs about what the world should look like. Instrumental (which some might label 'causal') ideas are often about what strategy will have what result or what tactic will achieve a desirable outcome, usually less verifiable and with a normative veneer. The article then examines nine UN ideas that changed the world, before illustrating the significance of this by examining two counterfactuals: a world without the world organisation and its ideas as well as with a more creative institution.

Thomas G. Weiss is Presidential Professor of Political Science and Director of the Ralph Bunche Institute for International Studies at The Graduate Center of The City University of New York and was President of the International Studies Association (2009–2010). His latest single-authored book is *What's Wrong with the United Nations and How to Fix It* (Cambridge: Polity, 2009).

Ideas are a main driving force in human progress and also one of the world organisation's most important contributions over the last six and a half decades, which is the central finding by the independent UN Intellectual History Project.[1] The project's seventeen volumes and oral history archive provide substantive accounts of the UN's work in major areas of economic and social thinking and action, as well as in related areas where the boundaries of peace and development intersect – namely, human security, human rights, preventive diplomacy, and global governance.[2]

This research has breathed new life into the UN's overlooked characteristics: the quality and diversity of its intellectual leadership, and its values-based

---

[1] This article draws on Richard Jolly, Louis Emmerij, and Thomas G. Weiss, *UN Ideas That Changed the World* (Bloomington: Indiana University Press, 2009).

[2] See S. Neil MacFarlane and Yuen Foong-Khong, *Human Security and the UN: A Critical History* (Bloomington: Indiana University Press, 2006) and Bertrand G. Ramcharan, *Preventive Diplomacy at the UN* (Bloomington: Indiana University Press, 2008). The project's volumes cited in this article are published by Indiana University Press with the exception of Thomas G. Weiss and Sam Daws (eds), *The Oxford Handbook on the United Nations* (Oxford: Oxford University Press, 2007). Full details are available at: {www.unhistory.org}.

framework for dealing with the global challenges of our times. The project's decade-long effort has explored areas omitted or undervalued in textbooks about the world organisation or units of the UN system – namely, the ideas, norms, and principles that permeate the world body's atmosphere. The results provide an argument that flies in the face of UN bashing, a favourite sport not just in Washington's Beltway but elsewhere. Unlike popular wisdom – graciously stimulated by the mass media – the UN is more than a rigid bureaucracy without sparkle, wit, or creativity. Nor is it merely a travelling circus, a talk shop, and paper-pusher. These perceptions and on-and-off-again tales of corruption sustain an unbalanced view even if elements of such criticism strike close to home on First Avenue in Manhattan. But we cannot judge a portrait about Boeing or Airbus that concentrates on its employees' globe-trotting, internet surfing, or wasting of resources without mentioning the quality of products, the bottom line, and plans for the future. A fair depiction of an enterprise or an international organisation is incomplete and misleading without a discussion of its goals and achievements, including intellectual leadership.

International organisations live or die, thrive or shrivel up, by the quality and relevance of the policy ideas that they put forward and sustain. It is essential to examine the good, the bad, and the ugly. This article begins by examining the nature of ideas, albeit recognising that most (especially those of the world body) have multiple origins and various carriers, and it continues by assessing their impact. Following a listing of nine UN ideas that have changed the world, the world body's under-appreciated role is illustrated by examining two counterfactuals: a world without the UN and its ideas as well as a more creative institution. The conclusion explores how to improve the UN's intellectual output and punch.

The nature of ideas

To most people, the UN is unitary; but the real organisation consists of three linked components that interact. Inis Claude long ago distinguished the arena for state decision-making, the First UN of member states,[3] from the Second UN of staff members and secretariat heads who are paid from assessed and voluntary budgets. The Third UN of non-governmental organisations (NGOs), experts, commissions, and academics is a more recent addition to analytical perspectives.[4] This broader embrace of what constitutes the world body is not only a more accurate reflection of reality but also crucial to understanding the itinerary of ideas. It is noteworthy that this history does not include the private, for-profit sector that has essentially been missing in action in relationship to the UN's past intellectual contributions. A foundation for a 'Fourth UN' has been laid with the Global Compact and other traditional ones like employers at the International Labour Organisation, which will certainly be a more substantial part of a future intellectual history.

---

[3] Inis L. Claude, Jr., *Swords Into Plowshares: The Problems and Prospects of International Organization* (New York: Random House, 1956), and 'Peace and Security: Prospective Roles for the Two UN', *Global Governance*, 2:3 (1996), pp. 289–98.

[4] Thomas G. Weiss, Tatiana Carayannis, and Richard Jolly, 'The "Third" UN', *Global Governance*, 15:1 (2009), pp. 123–42.

What do we – in this article, my use does not connote the 'royal we' but rather my close collaboration with Richard Jolly and Louis Emmerij that makes it hard to separate our collective responsibility for what follows – mean by ideas? Ideas are notions and beliefs held by individuals and institutions that influence their attitudes and actions, in this case, toward economic and social development. Such ideas mostly arise as the result of social interactions among people or groups within any of the three UN or among them. Often ideas take more definite shape over time, sometimes as the result of research, often through debate or challenges, other times through efforts to turn ideas into policy as well as experiment by putting them into practice.

Three types of UN ideas – *positive, normative,* and *causal* – are worth distinguishing. Positive ideas are those resting on hard evidence, open to challenge and verifiable. That the countries of the Development Assistance Committee (DAC) of the Organisation for Economic Cooperation and Development (OECD) spent about 0.3 per cent of their gross national income (GNI) on development assistance in 2009 is an example. Normative ideas are beliefs about what the world *should* look like. That these countries *ought* to implement the long-standing UN target of spending 0.7 per cent of the GNI on development assistance or that there should be a more equitable allocation of world resources are examples. Causal ideas are often about what strategy will have what result or what tactic will achieve a desirable outcome, usually less verifiable and with a normative veneer. At the UN, causal ideas often take an operational form – for instance, the calculation that over 0.5 per cent of GNI will be needed as official development assistance (ODA) to realise the Millennium Development Goals (MDGs). Causal ideas can be specific, but they usually are much less than full-blown theories.[5] For example, if we were to begin with the sweeping ethical proposition that the world should be more just, then the idea of a more equitable allocation of resources can be both a normative idea as well as one causal way to improve international justice.

UN ideas have set past and present international agendas within economic and social arenas and will do so for future ones. The lack of attention to the UN's role in generating or nurturing ideas is perplexing, as Ngaire Woods tells us: 'In short, ideas, whether economic or not, have been left out of analyses of international relations.'[6] Many political scientists are rediscovering the role of ideas in international policymaking. We say *rediscovering* because the study of ideas may be relatively new in analyses of international politics and organisations but is common bill-of-fare for historians, philosophers, students of literature, and economists – that is, analysts who see forces at work besides sovereign states selfishly calculating their interests.

The political science literature on the role of ideas that informs this inquiry can be grouped into three broad categories. The first is institutionalism – such as Judith Goldstein's and Robert Keohane's analyses of foreign policy[7] and Kathryn

[5] Morten Bøås and Desmond McNeill, *Global Institutions and Development: Framing the World?* (London: Routledge, 2004).
[6] Ngaire Woods, 'Economic Ideas and International Relations: Beyond Rational Neglect', *International Studies Quarterly*, 39 (1995), p. 164.
[7] Judith Goldstein and Robert O. Keohane (eds), *Ideas and Foreign Policy* (Ithaca, NY: Cornell University Press, 1993).

Sikkink's on developmentalism in Latin America[8] – and is concerned with how organisations shape the policy preferences of their members. Ideas can be particularly important for policymaking during periods of upheaval. In thinking about the end of World War II or of the Cold War or post-September 11th challenges, for instance, ideas provided a conceptual road map that can be used to understand changing preferences and definitions of vital interests for state and non-state actors alike. This approach helps to situate the dynamics at work among ideas, multilateral institutions, and national policies. It also enables us to begin thinking about how the UN influences elite and popular images, as well as how opinion-makers affect the world organisation.

The second category focuses on the approaches and interactions of various groups, including Peter Haas's epistemic communities,[9] Peter Hall's Keynesian economists,[10] Ernst B. Haas's purveyors of knowledge and power,[11] as well as Margaret Keck and Kathryn Sikkink's more amorphous transnational networks of activists.[12] These approaches examine the role of intellectuals in creating ideas, of technical experts in diffusing them and making them more concrete and scientifically grounded, and of all sorts of people in influencing the positions adopted by a wide range of actors, especially governments. The UN's Intergovernmental Panel on Climate Change (IPCC) is a powerful recent illustration of such influence because the network of world-class volunteer scientists from several disciplines translate scientific findings into the language comprehensible by policymakers.

Networks of experts influence a broad spectrum of international politics through their ability to interact with policymakers irrespective of location and national boundaries. Researchers working on climate change or HIV/AIDS, for instance, can have an impact on policy by clarifying an issue from which decision-makers may explore what is in the interests of their administrations. Researchers also can help to frame the debate on a particular issue, thus narrowing the acceptable range of bargaining in international negotiations. They can introduce standards for action. These networks can help provide justifications for alternatives, and often build national or international coalitions to support chosen policies and to advocate for change. In many ways, efforts by the Intergovernmental Panel on Climate Change to shed light on human impact on the natural environment borrow from Thomas Kuhn's often-cited work on the nature of scientific revolutions.[13]

[8] Kathryn Sikkink, *Ideas and Institutions: Developmentalism in Argentina and Brazil* (Ithaca, NY: Cornell University Press, 1991).
[9] Peter M. Haas, 'Introduction: Epistemic Communities and International Policy Coordination', *International Organization*, 46:1 (1992), pp. 1–36; and Peter M. Haas, Robert O. Keohane and Marc A. Levy (eds), *Institutions for the Earth: Sources of Effective International Environmental Protection* (Cambridge, MA: MIT Press, 1992).
[10] Peter A. Hall (ed.), *The Political Power of Economic Ideas: Keynesianism Across Nations* (Princeton, NJ: Princeton University Press, 1989).
[11] Ernst B. Haas, *When Knowledge is Power: Three Models of Change in International Organizations* (Los Angeles: University of California Press, 1994); and see Peter M. Haas and Ernst B. Haas, 'Learning to Learn: Improving International Governance', *Global Governance*, 1:3 (1995), pp. 55–284.
[12] Margaret Keck and Kathryn Sikkink, *Activists Beyond Borders: Advocacy Networks in International Politics* (Ithaca, NY: Cornell University Press, 1998).
[13] Thomas S. Kuhn, *The Structure of Scientific Revolutions,* 2nd edition (Chicago: University of Chicago Press, 1970).

The third category consists of so-called constructivists such as Alexander Wendt[14] and John G. Ruggie.[15] They seek to determine the potential for individuals, especially members of governments and international institutions, to be active agents for change rather than robots whose behaviour merely reflects previous theories and accumulated experience. Also relevant are the critical approaches of those influenced by Antonio Gramsci and the Italian school of Marxism, such as Robert Cox and his followers.[16] They, however, view the work of all organisations, including the UN, as heavily determined by material conditions and supportive of the *status quo*.

Irrespective of how one weighs the value of these three bodies of literature, individuals and organisations and their ideas matter. The UN system has spawned or nurtured a large number of individuals who have called into question conventional wisdom as well as reinforced it. Indeed, the very definition of what passes for 'conventional' at a particular point in time in various regions of the world is part of the puzzle that we have only begun to address.

In addition, numerous questions typically circulate about the importance of ideas. First, which comes first, the idea or policy and action? Most approaches do not explain the sources of ideas but rather their effects. They rarely explain how ideas emerge or change, with the exception of pointing to technological innovations. By ignoring where ideas come from and how they change, cause and effect are uncertain. Do ideas shape policy, or do they merely serve, after the fact, as a convenient justification for a policy or a decision? Or does policy push existing ideas forward, and perhaps even generate new ones that may emerge in response to that policy or action? Quentin Skinner raised these issues forty years ago: '[T]he social context, it is said, helps to cause the formation and change of ideas; but the ideas in turn help to cause the formation and change of the social context. Thus the historian ends up presenting himself with nothing better that the time-honored puzzle about the chicken and the egg.'[17] We are agnostic and eclectic.

Second, are ideas mere products, or do they have a life of their own? For us, it is the latter; and our volumes have tried to trace the trajectory of ideas within the UN and examine how individual leadership, coalitions, and national and international bureaucratic rivalries within the UN have generated, nurtured, distorted, and implemented particular ideas. At the same time, it is crucial to discern whether and how ideas, in and of themselves, have helped to shape policy outcomes at the UN.[18]

Third, should an idea be analysed in light of the historical and social context within which it emerged and evolved? For our part, we argue that economic and social ideas at the UN cannot be properly understood if examined on their own,

---

[14] Alexander Wendt, *Social Theory of International Politics* (Cambridge: Cambridge University Press, 1999).

[15] John G. Ruggie, *Constructing the World Polity* (New York: Routledge, 1998).

[16] See, for example, Robert W. Cox (ed.), *The New Realism: Perspectives on Multilateralism and World Order* (New York: St. Martin's, 1997); Robert W. Cox, with Timothy J. Sinclair, *Approaches to World Order* (Cambridge: Cambridge University Press, 1996); and Quentin Hoare and Geoffrey N. Smith (eds) and trans., *Selections From the Prison Notebooks of Antonio Gramsci* (London: Lawrence and Wishart, 1971).

[17] Quentin E. Skinner, 'Meaning and Understanding in the History of Ideas', *History and Theory*, 8 (1969), p. 42.

[18] See Ramesh Thakur and Thomas G. Weiss, 'UN "Policy": An Argument with Three Illustrations', *International Studies Perspectives*, 10:2 (2009), pp. 18–35.

divorced from historical and social circumstances. The birth and survival of ideas within the UN – or their death and suppression – invariably reflect events and are contingent upon world politics and the global economy.

Fourth, when should one begin to trace the trajectory of a particular idea? Could anyone disagree with Woods that 'very few ideas are very new'?[19] At what point in its life or in which of its many possible incarnations should one begin to study an idea? Frederick Cooper and Randall Packard point out that post-war modernisation theory aimed to transform individuals from 'superstitious and status-oriented beings to rational and achievement-oriented beings'.[20] But the idea of creating a new person is far older than development theory. It could be traced back to the efforts of the earliest missionaries, the Enlightenment, Karl Marx, or, to God with Adam's rib in the Garden of Eden. We are agnostic about origins, which make little difference to determining impact.

Fifth, what about copyrights and patents? Analysts are still arguing whether Charles Darwin or Alfred Russel Wallace should be foremost credited with the theory of natural selection, and whether Alexander Graham Bell deserves credit for inventing the telephone because so many others were toying with the idea at about the same time. The difficulty of identifying a single individual or institution responsible for the creation of an idea is even more manifest in the complex world of multilateralism. An idea evolves and ownership becomes more widely shared through group processes. Within multilateral institutions, anonymous documents or ones ghost-written for organisational heads are the rule; and widespread ownership is a goal of deliberations.[21] Hence, it seems futile to undertake the type of historical analysis pioneered by A. O. Lovejoy who sought to trace an idea 'through all the provinces of history in which it appears'.[22] Rather, it is more pragmatic merely to pick up an idea at the time it intersected with the UN.

Sixth, what is the influence of ideas versus the carriers of ideas?[23] There is little consensus about which – in this case, the ideas or the key individuals from the three UNs – are more influential. Yet, Thomas Risse's framing seems on target, 'ideas do not float freely'.[24] Or for Sheri Bermann, ideas 'do not have any independent impact by themselves, as disembodied entities floating around in a polity'.[25] They need institutions, actors, and opportunities. This is particularly relevant for our treatment of experts and the outside-insiders of the Third UN, many of whom go through revolving doors with experiences in government, secretariats, and the private sector. It can be argued that the more influential the members of an expert group or the greater their access to governmental policymakers, the greater the odds that their ideas will be adopted, irrespective of

---

[19] Woods, 'Economic Ideas and International Relations', p. 168.

[20] Frederick Cooper and Randall Packard (eds), *International Development and the Social Sciences: Essays on the History and Politics of Knowledge* (Berkeley: University of California Press, 1997), p. 17.

[21] See Ramesh Thakur (ed.), *What Is Equitable Geographic Representation in the Twenty-first Century* (Tokyo: UN University, 1999).

[22] Arthur O. Lovejoy, *The Great Chain of Being* (New York: Torchbook, 1960).

[23] See Albert Yee, 'The Causal Effects of Ideas on Policies', *International Organization*, 50 (1996), pp. 69–108.

[24] Thomas Risse-Kappen, 'Ideas Do Not Float Freely: Transnational Coalitions, Domestic Structures, and the End of the Cold War', *International Organization*, 48:2 (1994), pp. 185–214.

[25] Sheri Bermann, *The Social Democratic Moment: Ideas and Politics in the Making of Interwar Europe* (Cambridge, MA: Harvard University Press, 1998), p. 22.

their inherent value. The impacts of ideas (for good or ill) presuppose agents, and at the UN they cannot be divorced from agency – which is one reason that we documented through oral histories the role of individuals in the evolution of international economic and social development.

In short, our comparative advantage is not as philosophers or patent attorneys. The important fact is that an idea exists and has entered into the arena of the UN. The bottom line results from analysing the evolution and impact of key ideas, especially how international economic and social concepts have been nurtured, refined, and applied under UN auspices. They exist, and they matter.

Assessing the impacts of UN ideas

It is essential to examine how UN ideas exert influence, and how and when they fall flat. The late Barbara Ward wrote: 'Ideas are the prime movers of history. Revolutions usually begin with ideas.'[26] Even more to the point, political theorist Daniel Philpott's study of sovereignty demonstrates that revolutions for even this building block of international studies too are driven primarily by the power of ideas.[27] For instance, we are in the midst of an upheaval in which state sovereignty is becoming more contingent on upholding basic human rights values, in which states have obligations and not just rights.

Ideas lead to action in many ways. While the process is rarely linear, the steps run from the creation of new idea to dissemination to decisions by policymakers to implementation and on to impact and results. We can observe how UN ideas exert influence:

- changing the ways that issues are perceived and the language used to describe them;
- framing agendas for action and definitions of self-interests;
- altering the ways that key groups perceive their interests – and thus altering the balance of forces pressing for action or resisting it; and
- being embedded in institutions, which thus adopt responsibility for carrying the idea forward and become a focus for accountability and monitoring.

The formulation of statistical norms and guidelines provides a concrete example of how the four ways usually operate simultaneously but not necessarily in tandem when setting standards. In *Quantifying the World*, the late Michael Ward traced the development in the early 1950s of the System of National Accounts (SNA), which provided guidelines that even today enable and encourage countries to calculate gross national product (GNP) and other core economic indicators in a standardised way – thereby providing an economic snapshot of economic performance. Agendas for economic policy and action are thus defined in country-after-country, which in turn has unleashed pressures for better use of economic resources as well as for more attention to social and other indicators. The SNA was embedded in

---

[26] Cited by Mahbub ul Haq, *Reflections on Human Development* (New York: Oxford University Press, 1995), p. 204.
[27] Daniel Philpott, *Revolutions in Sovereignty: How Ideas Shaped Modern International Relations* (Princeton, NJ: Princeton University Press, 2001).

the work of the UN Statistical Commission (UNSC) and UN Statistical Office (UNSO). Thus in all four ways, the UN's early work on the SNA has sustained its influence over the following decades. Ward concludes that 'the creation of a universally acknowledged statistical system and of a general framework guiding the collection and compilation of data according to recognised standards, both internationally and nationally, has been one of the great and mostly unsung successes of the UN Organization'.[28]

Another example is the formulation and adoption of goals for development. Since the launching of the First Development Decade in 1961, the world organisation has debated, adopted, promoted, supported, and monitored a succession of quantified and time-circumscribed goals, serving as both national and international guidelines for economic and social development. In total, some fifty such goals have been agreed, the first being for educational expansion and acceleration of economic growth. Later goals for subsequent decades have covered reductions in child mortality, improvements in human welfare, efforts in sustainable and equitable development, and support for these efforts by the expansion of development assistance. The most well-known probably are the so-called Millennium Development Goals (MDGs) for poverty reduction by the year 2015.

A review of performance shows that many such goals have had considerable impact, more than most people realise. The idea of setting objectives and standards is, of course, not new. But setting internationally agreed targets as a means to foster economic and social development is a singular UN achievement. The results have been far from complete successes but rarely total failures. A few, such as the goal in 1967 for the eradication of smallpox or in 1980 for a worldwide reduction of infant mortality and for increases in life expectancy, have registered resounding successes – 'complete achievement' in the case of small pox eradication and 'considerable achievement' in the other two.[29]

The most serious failures have been in sub-Saharan Africa and the least developed countries. The other weakest performances have been in levels of development aid among the industrialised countries of the global North. Except for Denmark, the Netherlands, Norway, and Sweden – and in the last few years, Luxembourg – developed countries have consistently failed to achieve the 0.7 target for concessional transfers to developing countries in general and fallen short of the specific targets for aid to the least developed countries. But even here, the existence of the goal helped bureaucrats and do-gooders in some countries striving to reach the target and also resulted in their putting pressure on or at least trying to embarrass their stingier Western partners.

We can assess the impact of UN ideas on goal setting. Have the goals altered the ways development is perceived? Here the answer changes over time. The early

---

[28] Michael Ward, *Quantifying the World: UN Contributions to Statistics* (Bloomington: Indiana University Press, 2004), p. 2.

[29] By the year 2000, 138 countries had brought infant mortality to below 120 and 124 countries had raised life expectancy to 60 years or more, two of the goals set in 1980. A full assessment of the achievements in relation to the fifty goals are found in 'The Record of Performance', in *UN Contributions to Development Thinking and Practice*, by Richard Jolly, Louis Emmerij, Dharam Ghai, and Frédéric Lapeyre (Bloomington: Indiana University Press, 2004), chap. 10. Differences among regional thinking can be found in Yves Berthelot (ed.), *Unity and Diversity in Development Ideas: Perspectives from the UN Regional Commissions* (Bloomington: Indiana University Press, 2004).

goals for education, set at meetings organised by the UN Educational, Scientific, and Cultural Organization (UNESCO) in the 1960s, were in part preaching to the converted – countries newly independent or about to be independent, already with demands for educational expansion high on their political agenda. The UNESCO goals for rapid expansion at all levels did not so much shift perceptions of development but helped give international legitimacy to national ambitions that might otherwise have been treated by colonial powers as unrealistic and even unjustified. The goals for economic expansion of the First Development Decade were certainly treated as over-ambitious when first set – even though, like educational goals, in many countries they were in fact exceeded.

Expectations about performance in the 1960s raised the stakes in later decades, and economic performance increasingly fell below the most ambitious economic targets. By the 1980s, UN economic goals were sidelined by the shift of economic power and influence to the Bretton Woods institutions, which introduced programmes of structural adjustment and stressed economic and financial targets at the country level rather than social outcomes. Given the disastrous declines in rates of economic growth and levels of economic performance that followed, it is startling that considerable improvements nonetheless took place in health, water, sanitation, and child mortality if not in education. These experiences, especially the failures of economic adjustment in the 1980s and early 1990s and the accusation that they were imposed from outside rather than adopted by countries themselves, accounts for the shift by industrialised countries and the Bretton Woods institutions (the World Bank and International Monetary Fund, IMF) in the late 1990s towards accepting outcome goals in general and the adoption of the MDGs in particular.

These illustrations show how UN goals have influenced the ways that development has been perceived and influenced agendas for action by governments and their aid agencies, by local and international NGOs, by foundations and corporations. Goals have also served over the years as a focus for mobilising coalitions of interested partners. This is clear with respect to the MDGs but other goals have also served the same purpose: for instance, goals for the expanding aid toward the 0.7 per cent target, for debt forgiveness, and for priorities for women and children.[30]

New ideas and priorities have also led to the creation of new institutions to emphasise previously ignored issues – UNCTAD for trade, UNIDO for industrial development, UNEP for sustainability, UNIFEM for gender, and so on. And new ideas have also led to new emphases within existing organisations, usually called 'mainstreaming' – the insertion of new thinking into existing institutions and programmes or significant restructuring of an existing institution to make room for a new idea.

Nonetheless, the generation and spread of ideas is a necessary but insufficient condition for meaningful change. Sometimes UN ideas have spread but often with too little effect. Why do some ideas gain traction while others do not? Morten Bøas and Desmond McNeill have analysed how ideas evolve as they move among

---

[30] See Olav Stokke, *The UN and Development: From Aid to Cooperation* (Bloomington: Indiana University Press, 2009); and Devaki Jain, *Women, Development, and the UN: A Sixty-Year Quest for Equality and Justice* (Bloomington: Indiana University Press, 2006).

international institutions. New ideas may spread, especially if they are gaining support from governments and the Third UN. But in doing so, they are likely to be adapted and modified by the institutions into which they are moving – to fit their existing priorities, programmes of work, and paradigms. As Bøas and McNeill demonstrate, the processes of adaptation, negation, and distortion of ideas to make them fit existing agendas has often lead to perceptions of change rather than to genuine transformation. Their analytical effort is called 'CANDID' – the Creation, Adoption, Negation and Distortion of Ideas in Development, which summarises the key elements of the process.[31]

Adopting more recent work by McNeill and Asunción Lera St. Clair about moral variables,[32] five factors seem pertinent in giving some ideas clout and largely sidelining others: international consensus and legitimacy; professional endorsement and interest; non-governmental support; and financial backing. The fifth – and perhaps the most important for the longer run and certainly the most criticised in anti-UN circles – is the extent to which the UN organisations or institutions in which the idea is embedded take responsibility and initiatives for implementation. Here, even a critical theorist like Robert Cox, who spent twenty-five years in the ILO, suggests that the very existence of new institutions could challenge the rigidity of existing norms. 'I guess the reason why new institutions are created', he states, 'is that those people who feel that the new idea is important are doubtful that they are going to be able to put it into action through the existing institutions. It is the rigidity of existing institutions that leads to the idea that if you want to start something new, you have to create another institution.'[33]

The UN has 192 member states and multiple moving parts, and it is rare that all five factors come together. Perhaps the main occasions were at the beginning, when the very idea of founding the world organisation stirred professional and non-governmental enthusiasm and received strong financial backing from the richest country in the world. At that juncture, the politics within deliberative bodies were less divisive. The Cold War was raging; but the West and, at the time, supportive partners in Latin America were very much on the same ideological page. Thereafter, the influx of newly independent states in Africa and Asia along with the evolution of Latin America away from a pro-American stance changed the dynamics, and the North-South divide made many ideas highly controversial, even toxic.

The creation of the SNA described above is a case where Cold War divides, though disruptive, were insufficient to prevent or even slow ideas and action. The staff of the Statistical Commission was mostly drawn from developed Western countries, including all the directors, and drew heavily on leading statisticians and economists. Not surprisingly – and most professionals would argue properly – the guidelines matched the priorities of industrialised rather than developing countries; and the priorities of market economies dominated those of the non-market economies of the Soviet bloc even though the UNSO published analyses on how comparisons could be made. Thus, backed by a dominant international majority

---

[31] Bøas and McNeill (eds), *Global Institutions and Development*.

[32] Desmond McNeill and Asunción Lera St. Clair, *Global Poverty, Ethics and Human Rights: The Role of Multilateral Organisations* (London: Routledge, 2009).

[33] Thomas G. Weiss, Tatiana Carayannis, Loius Emmerij, and Richard Jolly, *UN Voices: The Struggle for Development and Social Justice* (Bloomington: Indiana University Press, 2005), p. 420.

with professional and financial support, the proposed SNA spread rapidly ahead in most parts of the world.

Other ideas that arose within the UN have not had such backing, especially following the establishment of the Group of 77 in the lead-up to the first UNCTAD in 1964.[34] Work on trade policy, debt relief, transnational corporations, and the formulation of targets for aid and the needs of the least developed countries had little clout in spite of being derived from detailed analyses. Proposals were strongly backed by developing countries while the main developed countries distanced themselves. NGOs often provided support and, since the 1980s, increasingly so. But clout has been feeble because the main donor countries and, often, mainstream professional economists resisted.

The phenomenon of opposition or weak support for UN ideas on economic and social policy from the mainstream of the economics profession requires reflection. Even before the current crisis, many have thought of economics as the 'dismal science' whereas others regard it as social science royalty because of its robust theory, evidence base, and ever more sophisticated econometric techniques. Whatever one's bottom line, it is safe to say that mainstream development economists have mostly stuck to the tools and perspectives of neo-liberal analysis. Outside this mainstream, there has been a vocal professional minority, especially in developing countries and somewhat in Europe, as well as sometimes economists and social scientists working within other disciplines or multidisciplinary frameworks.

The Bretton Woods institutions mostly have navigated within this mainstream – to some, explained by their overlapping interests with those of industrialised countries that provide the bulk of the funding. Although all such generalisations present problems, it is fair to say that the UN has mostly approached development issues by swimming outside of mainstream economics, in part reflecting the political priorities and broader interests of the majority of its member states from the global South. Another important factor has been a much greater pressure of non-economic professions in many UN organisations – the medical professions in the World Health Organization (WHO), agriculturalists in the Food and Agricultural Organisation (FAO), labour experts in the International Labour Organization (ILO), a diversity of educationalists and other scientists in UNESCO, and professionals of a wide variety of backgrounds and country experience with children in UNICEF, of nutrition in the World Food Programme (WFP), and of development and management administration in the UN Development Programme (UNDP). This diversity has meant that the UN system as a whole has approached development from wider perspectives than the economists working for the Bretton Woods institutions.

At its best, the result of pulling together different professions has challenged received wisdom and improved thinking about international policy options. And sometimes, as with the UN's early economic work on the need for concessional finance for poorer countries and the proposals for the Special UN Fund for Economic Development (SUNFED), the world organisation's work persuaded more orthodox economists at the World Bank or the IMF to think again. But on

---

[34] See John Toye and Richard Toye, *The UN and Global Political Economy: Trade, Finance, and Development* (Bloomington: Indiana University Press, 2004). See also Tagi Sagafi-nejad in collaboration with John Dunning, *The UN and Transnational Corporations: From Code of Conduct to Global Compact* (Bloomington: Indiana University Press, 2008).

other occasions, as with *Adjustment with a Human Face* for which UNICEF and the Economic Commission for Africa clamoured in the 1980s, adoption by the Bretton Woods institutions has been slow and lukewarm.[35]

Nine UN ideas that changed the world

Space here does not permit doing more than enumerating the nine ideas in which UN efforts have altered the ways that global issues are perceived and addressed. The argument in *UN Ideas That Changed the World* draws on the evidence from one or more of the commissioned volumes. Hopefully the chapter titles provide a sufficient flavour to whet the reader's appetite to examine, or even buy, the project's volumes about these significant ideas: 'Human Rights: From Aspiration to Implementation'; 'Gender and Women's Rights: From Empowerment to Equality'; 'Development Policies: From National and Regional Perspectives to Beyond'; 'International Economic Relations: From National Interests to Global Solidarity'; 'Development Ideologies: From Planning to Markets'; 'Social Development: From Sectoral to Integrated Perspectives'; 'Sustainability: From Protecting the Environment to Preserving Ecological Systems'; 'Peace and Human Security: From States to Individuals'; and 'Human Development: From Narrower to Broader Horizons'.

We have teased out the contributions by the UN in broadening the perspective of economic and social development, from early concerns with human rights and gender, to priorities and perspectives of national and international development to the management of global resources and the need to develop sustainable development strategies. The subtitles of the chapters also indicate that ideas are not static but change considerably over the UN's history. We have also noted more recently the UN's calls for action to combine continuing development with preserving the world's eco-systems from the consequences of greenhouse gases, global warming, and climate chaos.[36] Moreover, as mentioned already, the analysis necessarily goes beyond the economic, the social, and the environmental because development, human rights, and human security intersect and should be viewed together.

Our overall balance sheet maintains that the UN has often led the charge with pioneering ideas. Admittedly, the 'three UNs' enlarges what we count as the world organisation's specific contributions. However, that is the reality of the contemporary international system, of fledgling global governance.[37] Many key ideas are those that were often initially formulated or articulated by distinguished experts as members of UN panels or as work commissioned by UN staff or by governments. Examples are the first ideas about the construction of a global and consistent economic order that came out of the three committees that reported between 1949

---

[35] For a trenchant analysis, see Robert Wade, 'Japan, the World Bank and the Art of Paradigm Maintenance: The East Asian Miracle in Political Perspective', *New Left Review*, I/217 (1996). For a critique from a former insider, see Joseph Stiglitz, *Globalization and Its Discontents* (New York: Norton, 2003).

[36] Nico Schrijver, *From Destruction to Development: The UN and Global Resource Management* (Bloomington: Indiana University Press, 2010).

[37] See Thomas G. Weiss and Ramesh Thakur, *Global Governance and the UN: An Unfinished Journey* (Bloomington: Indiana University Press, 2010).

and 1951,[38] or more recently those on climate change presented by the IPCC,[39] or in between by Hans Singer on the terms of trade or UNCTAD staff on debt problems. In other cases, the UN's contributions have been less in providing the initial spark of creativity than in challenging the way a problem is framed – as with the ILO missions on basic needs in the 1970s.

Many times and on many occasions, UN contributions have been multiplied by using the system's capacity for disseminating and promoting ideas. The UNDP's annual *Human Development Report* and reports by UNICEF on the *State of the World's Children* or by the UN High Commissioner for Refugees (UNHCR) on *The State of the World's Refugees* achieved part of their global visibility and impact by being subsidised and disseminated widely – hundreds of thousands of copies in English, French, and Spanish and often other languages as well. There were also media launches in the 100 or so countries in which the UN system has country offices. Other than a few academic blockbusters written by such authors as Joseph Stiglitz, Jeffrey Sachs, or Paul Collier, few scholarly publications could have achieved such outreach. This global dissemination was increasingly reinforced by UNDP support for national and regional reports, taking the human development methodology and applying it to country problems and situations – another illustration of how ideas matter.

If the nature and impact of UN ideas are not clear enough, it is instructive to situate the overall balance sheet by asking two questions: Where would the world be without the UN and its ideas in the economic and social arena? Could the UN have done better, in follow-up or in crafting the ideas themselves? *UN Ideas That Changed the World* provides answers for the nine ideas and demonstrates the extent to which UN ideas have had influence. Here it is useful to think through two counterfactuals.

Counterfactual # 1: The world without the UN and its ideas?

One way of considering the impact of UN ideas is to imagine where the world might be without a world organisation or with one solely set up as a passive convener, with no capacity for generating or nurturing independent ideas. It would thus be a markedly different UN, with a minimum of staff, presumably only ex-diplomats to bring groups with differences together and help to resolve them but with few ideas of their own. It would be a strange and impotent international body although not totally different from the type that extreme critics, including such members of the flat-earth society as John Bolton and John Yoo, put forward as the sort of world organisation that they would prefer. Such a stripped-down UN would be more limited even than the League of Nations, which had staff members in a number of specialist areas, including some who did pioneering work on nutrition and food security as well as on economics, work that has almost always

---

[38] UN, *Measures for Full Employment* (New York: UN, 1949); *Measures for the Economic Development of Under-Developed Countries* (New York: UN, 1951); and *Measures for International Economic Stability* (New York: UN, 1951).
[39] See especially Intergovernmental Panel on Climate Change, *Summary for Policymakers of the Synthesis Report of the IPCC Fourth Assessment Report of the IPCC* (Geneva: IPCC, 2007).

been hailed as some of the best things that the League, weak in more political areas, achieved.[40]

In this counterfactual, what might have happened to the ideas that the UN has framed, massaged, and sometimes put into practice? In the economic arena, the need for rules and regulations to facilitate international trade and other economic transactions would have generated a more limited range of institutions, not so different from the Organisation for Economic Co-operation and Development, the EU, and other regional organisations. If the world organisation did not exist, it would have been invented, if not in 1945 then about 1960 with decolonisation, or in the 1970s with the floating of the dollar and the surge of oil prices. A series of *ad hoc* meetings to cope with wide-ranging issues of vital economic importance only for the wealthiest of industrialised countries would rapidly be seen as inadequate and something permanent with universal representation would have been created.

The evolution of the G-8 into the G-20 in September 2009 reflects the fact that wider, not narrower, membership is a necessary feature of world politics. Whatever the advantages of economic consultations among the upgraded G-20 that accounts for 90 per cent of the world's GDP, only the UN can formulate global norms, set global standards, make global law, and eventually enforce global treaties. The G-20 certainly is more representative and potentially effective than the Security Council for which there are endless proposals for reform that go nowhere. The new G-20 encompasses 4.2 billion people (instead of 900 million in the G-8), but another 2.6 mainly poor people are left out. And they and their governments are a prerequisite for solving most global problems. The G-192 has advantages that the upgraded G-20, *ad hoc* coalitions of the willing, and various proposals for 'leagues of democracies' do not. The policy preferences of the countries that count will need to be endorsed globally. The range of links between the G-20, on the one hand, and the universal UN, on the other hand, represents a potentially rich research vein.

Cynics might comment that a narrower focus would have been little different from the General Agreement on Tariffs and Trade (GATT) or its replacement, the World Trade Organization (WTO), which indeed have commanded the respect and support of industrialised countries. However, the WTO at present employs over 600 staff, just shy of the dimensions of the League of Nations in the 1930s. Most of the staff are economists and lawyers, many engaged in producing research and statistical reports in areas in which the UN over a much broader field is also engaged. The WTO takes the rules of the game as fixed and tries to interpret and enforce them while the UN tries to produce alternate policy ideas for new situations. The notion that international organisations engaged solely in facilitating interactions rather than contributing substantively – including questioning the fairness of the rules of the game and who sits at the gaming table as well as whether it is level – is not viable for an international institution that has universal membership.

But beyond the economic imperatives required for facilitating trade and the functioning of global markets, some of what the UN does in other areas would

---

[40] See Jolly, Emmerij, Ghai, and Lapeyre, *UN Contributions*, pp. 169–219.

also be required and need to be recreated. Two examples could illustrate this reality, namely the UN's work in international public goods as well as human rights and humanitarian concerns.

Providing public goods in the form of rule setting and regulation would be required in such areas as health, food, and agriculture, weather and meteorology, civil aviation, and maritime law. Economists describe them as such because they are needed for individual countries and for the international system.[41] At the same time, global public goods are beyond the capacity of the marketplace because individual countries lack the incentives and the capacity to provide them on the scale required – in part because of the classic 'free rider' problem. To ensure public goods, many specialised functional organisations would need to have been invented if they were not already part of the UN system. Indeed, many such institutions were created long before the current generation of post-war organisations. Examples include the Pan American Sanitary Bureau, which was founded in 1902 and transformed into the Latin American arm of the WHO in 1948 and renamed PAHO, the Pan American Health Organisation; and earlier international organisations like the Universal Postal Union (UPU) and International Telecommunications Union (ITU), whose origins are in the mid-nineteenth century.[42]

But beyond purely economic imperatives, some of what the UN does in areas with a values-orientation would certainly have had to be recreated. The human rights arena clearly illustrates how the world would be poorer without the UN.[43] Even a world focused solely on economic efficiency and free markets would be under public pressure to invent an organisation to embrace some rights. The UN, however, embraces the entire gamut not for reasons of economic efficiency or political necessity but as a reflection of the vision and humanity of its founders.

Such vision and idealism are also reflected in the mandates and work of the UN funds and specialised agencies – for instance, UNICEF and the UN Development Fund for Women (UNIFEM), the UNDP and the WFP as well as UNESCO, WHO, FAO, and the ILO. They are also at the core of the work of the offices of the UNHCR as well as of the High Commissioner for Human Rights (OHCHR), including activists' dealing with the rights of minorities and indigenous peoples as well as the prevention of torture and genocide. These are important and visible efforts in the forefront of the world organisation's work. And because their mandates put human values ahead of economic concerns and market efficiency, they often clash with the dominant interests of governments and market priorities, and they often call for more political and financial support than governments are prepared to provide.

UN institutions are obviously not without problems; and implementation lags far behind rhetoric. But the fact that human values are emphasised and sometimes are placed ahead of economic concerns and market efficiency is far from trivial.

---

[41] See, for example, Scott Barrett, *Why Cooperate? The Incentive to Supply Global Public Goods* (Oxford: Oxford University Press, 2007), and Inge Kaul, Isabelle Grunberg, and Marc A. Stern (eds), *Global Public Goods: International Cooperation in the 21st Century* (New York: Oxford University Press, 1999).

[42] See Craig Murphy, *International Organization and Industrial Change: Global Governance since 1850* (Cambridge: Polity Press, 1994).

[43] Roger Normand and Sarah Zaidi, *Human Rights at the UN: The Political History of Universal Justice* (Bloomington: Indiana University Press, 2008).

One undoubtedly can imagine a world without such concerns. But it would be much poorer and much less human than the one to which the UN aspires and, at its best, contributes to and achieves.

Counterfactual #2: A more creative UN?

Recalling the lofty vision and ideas of the UN offers no defence for its inefficiencies or a justification for its weaknesses. Nor is it a reason for suggesting that the world organisation could not have done far better in formulating ideas or in ensuring their follow-up. The project's volumes and oral history interviews of nearly eighty individuals contain specific suggestions for ways in which the UN could indeed have done much better.[44] Here, three substantive ones are highlighted that provide food for thought regarding the 'what if' of a more intellectually creative world organisation.

First, more creative work could have been done on political economy in areas in which the international system is failing. Economic weaknesses about how the global system limits opportunities for the poorest countries is one such crucial area that has become even more pressing as a result of the ongoing global economic and financial crisis. Inadequate progress toward the goals of sustainable development and environmental protection is another, which seems more acute as a result of evidence about climate change that appears almost daily. Biases in aid along with the lack of coherence in the global trade system and the failures of industrialised countries to make good on their public commitments to a free and open international economic system are issues that remain critical as does the lack of incentives for measures of disarmament and development. The fact that such ideas have little chance to be implemented in the immediate term is not a reason to give up the good fight for more solidarity and a better and less conflict-ridden world.

Across all these areas, more sustained attention could have been given to measures required to achieve a more egalitarian international system and to pursue national policies that combine redistribution with growth. It may sound hopelessly naïve even to utter the acronym 'NIEO' (New International Economic Order). Nonetheless, the sentiments that motivated the quest for framing an alternative to the global economic order in the 1970s and a fairer distribution of global wealth and the benefits of growth can hardly be ignored in today's world. Glaring inequalities are even worse than three decades ago; and the economic and financial meltdown of 2008 has hurt most of those on the bottom who already had too little.

Second, far more work could have been done on the conditions to create stability in weak and failing states – a crucial requirement, especially in Africa. Even if international inequities were reduced, far more fulsome efforts also are required to address glaring inequalities within countries. Since 2006, the effort to pull together UN inputs in the Peacebuilding Commission is an encouraging sign that preventing a return to war has emerged as a priority, but here too inequalities within fragile states continue to menace any return to stability.

---

[44] The complete transcripts of the oral history interviews are available on CD-ROM: UN Intellectual History Project, *The Complete Oral History Transcripts from 'UN Voices'* (New York: UNIHP, 2007).

Third, better promotion of UN ideas would have helped in *all* areas of its work. Production of new ideas is one task, but the distribution and dissemination of key UN reports to academics, policy analysts, and the media is also crucial. Outreach and distribution, including translation and subsidies, for high-visibility reports have sometimes been impressive, but too many quality analyses languish on bookshelves or in filing cabinets. Following UNDP's example of disseminating its annual *Human Development Report*, the world organisation as a whole should have ensured far greater outreach for the part of its work where it has originality and comparative advantage – work outside the box of neo-classical economic orthodoxy. The encouragement of wide discussions of multidisciplinary work is especially essential in areas in which economic issues interact with human rights, human security, and human development. The UN could and should have engaged in a broader debate over the weaknesses of Bretton Woods dogma and the Washington consensus. Even those convinced that such approaches are broadly correct now recognise that some of the UN's past work often led to crucial new insights into the weaknesses of mainstream thinking.

The UN could have been better and done more in all these areas. There is still time. How could this happen?

Improving UN intellectual output

Part of the reason for UN failures to fulfil mandates or achieve goals is that they are too visionary, or at least go far beyond where most governments are prepared to go. Meanwhile, the vast majority of analysts in international studies focus on one obvious explanation, the lack of political will among member states.

The concern here is not to throw up our hands in despair but rather to examine where change is possible, and an essential component of the preceding counter-factual consists of improving the intellectual quality of the Second UN.[45] Inefficiency and weak institutions and staff do less than they might, and governments provide less finance than required. We could have a more effective world organisation if there were more intellectual firepower and less interference from governments in the process of recruitment and promotion.[46]

The most visible champion of the Second UN was Dag Hammarskjöld whose speech at Oxford in May 1961, shortly before his calamitous death, spelled out the importance of an autonomous and first-rate staff. He asserted that any erosion or abandonment of 'the international civil service [...] might, if accepted by the Member nations, well prove to be the Munich of international cooperation'.[47] His clarion call did not ignore the reality that the international civil service exists to carry out decisions by member states. But Hammarskjöld fervently believed that

---

[45] See Thomas G. Weiss, Tapio Kanninen, and Michael K. Busch, *Creating Sustainable Global Governance for the 21st Century: The UN Confronts Economic and Environmental Crises Amidst Changing Geopolitics* (Berlin: Friedrich Ebert Stiftung, Occasional Paper No. 40, 2009).

[46] This argument is based on Thomas G. Weiss, 'Reinvigorating the International Civil Service', *Global Governance*, 16:1 (2010).

[47] Dag Hammarskjöld, 'The International Civil Servant in Law and in Fact', lecture delivered to Congregation at Oxford University (30 May 1961), reprinted by Clarendon Press, Oxford, quotes at p. 329 and p. 349. Available at: {www.un.org/depts/dhl/dag/docs/internationalcivilservant.pdf}.

UN officials could and should pledge allegiance to a larger collective good symbolised by the organisation's light-blue-covered *laissez-passer* rather than the narrowly perceived national interests of the countries that issue national passports in different colours.

The long-standing policy of setting aside UN staff positions for officials approved by their home countries belies integrity. Governments seek to ensure that their interests are defended inside secretariats, and many have even relied on officials for intelligence. The influx in the 1950s and 1960s of former colonies as new member states led them to clamour for 'their' quota or fair share of the patronage opportunities, following the bad example set by major powers and other member states. The result was downplaying competence and exaggerating national origins as the main criterion for recruitment and promotion. Over the years, efforts to improve gender balance have resulted in other types of claims, as has the age profile of secretariats. Virtually all positions above the director level, and often many below as well, are the object of campaigns by governments.

How many people are we speaking about? Professional and support staff number approximately 55,000 in the UN proper and in agencies created by the General Assembly, and another 20,000 in the specialised agencies. This number includes neither temporary staff in peace operations (about 125,000 in 2010) nor the staff of the IMF and the World Bank group (another 15,000). These figures represent substantial growth from the approximately 500 employees in the UN's first year at Lake Success and the peak total of 700 staff employed by the League of Nations.[48]

Neglected personnel issues are relevant because people, like ideas, matter – for good and for ill. In spite of its slavish image, international secretariats do more than simply carry out marching orders from governments. Thus, it is clear that this position differs with three analysts who dismiss 'the curious notion that the UN is an autonomous actor in world affairs that can and does take action independent of the will and wishes of the member governments'.[49] There is considerably more room for creativity and initiative than is commonly believed. UN officials can present ideas to tackle problems, debate them formally and informally with governments, take initiatives, advocate for change, turn general decisions into specific programmes, and implement them. They monitor progress and report to national officials and politicians gathering at intergovernmental conferences and in countries in which the UN is operating.

Thinking through the counterfactual of a more creative UN requires us to imagine what the world organisation would be if it aggressively maintained its ability to produce or nurture world-class public intellectuals, scholars, thinkers, planners, and practitioners who could aspire to Nobel and other prizes. Members of UN secretariats are typically considered second-class citizens in comparison with the researchers, thinkers, and practitioners from the World Bank and the IMF. This notion partially reflects vastly differing resources devoted to research as well as their respective cultures, media attention, dissemination outlets and the use of the research in decision-making.

[48] Thant Myint-U and Amy Scott, *The UN Secretariat: A Brief History (1945–2006)* (New York: International Peace Academy, 2007), pp. 126–8.
[49] Donald J. Puchala, Katie Verlin Laatikainen, and Roger A. Coate, *UN Politics: International Organization in a Divided World* (Upper Saddle River, NJ: Prentice Hall, 2007), p. x.

At the same time, reality is often different. Nine persons with substantial experience within the UN and its policy formulation processes have won the Nobel Prize in economic sciences – Jan Tinbergen, Wassily Leontief, Gunnar Myrdal, James Meade, W. Arthur Lewis, Theodore W. Schultz, Lawrence R. Klein, Richard Stone, and Amartya Sen – whereas only one from the World Bank, Joseph Stiglitz, has done so. But even he resigned in protest and is now deeply associated with the UN in New York. And this list is in addition to UN organisations and individual Nobel Peace Prize winners who worked for years as staff members of the UN: Ralph Bunche, Dag Hammarskjöld, Kofi Annan, Mohammed El Baradei, and Martti Ahtisaari.

In short, the UN requires ideas and the people who produce them to be taken more seriously. Improved research, analysis, and policy work would permit the Secretary-General and the system as a whole to play more important roles in world political, economic, social, and environmental decision-making. To this effect, the world organisation should implement three changes in human resources management.

First, human resources policy should do more to foster an environment that encourages creative thinking, penetrating analysis, and policy-focused research of the highest intellectual calibre. The quality of staff members is essential and will depend on improvements and better professional procedures in recruitment, appointment, promotion, and organisation of responsibilities. Some progress has been made, such as the establishment of a system of national competitive examinations for entry-level recruitment as well as internships and junior professional officer programmes – but even here competence is not the only criterion for those who have passed the exams or applied for the training efforts. But there could also be a continual infusion of young or senior scholars for fixed periods to the UN. This could be brought about through exchange procedures from universities and think tanks around the world, not just from the West. It would benefit not only the UN while these visitors were in residence but also the future research agendas of scholars thereafter.

Second, independent research and analysis requires space within the institution. Whenever the UN pursues a bold agenda, it is unable to please all 192 member states all of the time. Calling into question conventional or politically correct wisdom requires longer-term funding that sympathetic donors should provide. A less skewed allocation of international resources toward the IFIs is a place to start. The terms on which such finance is provided are of crucial importance, not only to ensure availability but sustained multi-year commitments without strings. Encouragement of freethinking and policy exploration is vital but not cheap.

Typically, messages are watered down to satisfy the lowest common intergovernmental denominator. The example of the *Human Development Report* suggests that independent teams could be liberated from the purported obligation to check analyses before publication with boards or donors.[50] Given the current 'culture' of the world body and the reluctance of its Secretary-General to ruffle any diplomatic feathers, this may well require 'safety zones' within UN organisations – where serious and independent analyses can take place, freed from daily urgent matters and where controversy is tolerated.

---

[50] See Craig Murphy, *The UN Development Programme: A Better Way?* (Cambridge: Cambridge University Press, 2006), pp. 232–62, and Khadiha Haq and Richard Ponzio (eds), *Pioneering the Human Development Revolution: An Intellectual Biography of Mahbub ul Haq* (New Delhi: Oxford University Press, 2008).

Third, the UN should seek as many alliances as possible as well as borrow personnel from centres of expertise and excellence – in academia, think tanks, government policy units, and corporate research centres. A prominent location for dialogue and for knitting together the international cooperative fabric, the UN also should be a place to network outstanding thinking. Independent international commissions beginning with the 1969 Pearson report on *Partners in Development* as well as the more recent High-level Panel on Threats, Challenges and Change have had research secretariats,[51] and this kind of independent staff borrowed from universities and think tanks but loosely affiliated with the UN should become a permanent feature of the organisation but with frequent and regular turn-over in personnel. Another possible route would be to replicate the experience with climate change by the IPCC and pool world-class expertise from a variety of disciplines for such global challenges as pandemics, finance, proliferation, and terrorism. Basic research is best done in universities, but many elements of applied research can and should be undertaken within the UN.

Conclusion

Even the harshest critic would admit that the UN's intellectual work could have been poorer. It could have been totally smothered by caution and controlled by Secretaries-General who allowed no scope for creativity by members of the Secretariat, lacked any vision, and were dogmatic. This could have happened so early in the world organisation's life that many non-state actors became definitively disillusioned and discouraged about the UN's potential for social change.

Instead, the world organisation has managed to attract participation and commitment from many people with outstanding intellectual or leadership capabilities to work for the Second UN as well as engage actively with relevant parts of the First and the Third UN. At each stage of its life, individuals and some governments have argued passionately for maintaining the original idealistic vision and for applying its inspirational values to the contemporary but ever-evolving international system. The United Nations could have gone the way of the League of Nations; it did not.

The UN's achievements have helped, including the impact of its ideas. Throughout its over six-and-a-half decades, many of the world organisation's core ideas have had remarkable impact; and even those that have been rejected, sidelined, or adopted only rhetorically after long periods of time have emerged, not unscathed but intact. Politically unacceptable to many powerful countries at first, they often later became part of mainstream international discourse. Readers should, for example, recall everything from climate change to gender equality; from concessional loans, debt relief, and other special measures for least developed countries to putting people at the centre of development; from the role of a high commissioner for human rights to human security and removing the license to kill from the attributes of sovereign states.

[51] See Commission on International Development, *Partners in Development* (New York: Praeger, 1969); and High-level Panel on Threats, Challenges and Change, *A More Secure World: Our Shared Responsibility* (New York: UN, 2004).

The UN's effectiveness cannot fairly be judged from a short-term perspective. The past record provides a benchmark on which future improvements could and should be made. Perhaps as much as any recent event, the ongoing global financial and economic meltdown, which the late John Kenneth Galbraith might well have dubbed 'the great crash 2008',[52] made even clearer what many previous crises had not – namely the risks, problems, and enormous costs of a global economy without adequate international institutions, regulation, democratic decision-making, and powers to bring order, spread risks, and enforce compliance.

The world body's role as an idea-monger provides some 'good news' that deserves to be better known and understood. Its contributions to economic and social thinking, policymaking, and action have been more successful than generally appreciated, or 'ahead of the curve' as the title of the UN Intellectual History Project's first volume puts it.[53] In short, the UN has distinctly influenced the ways that we as academics and, more importantly, states think and talk about issues, frame agendas for action, and constitute coalitions as well as the ways that both new and reformed public and private institutions deal with global problems.

That is how UN ideas have changed history.

[52] John Kenneth Galbraith, *The Great Crash, 1929* (Boston: Houghton Mifflin, 1954).
[53] Louis Emmerij, Richard Jolly, and Thomas G. Weiss, *Ahead of the Curve? UN Ideas and Global Challenges* (Bloomington: Indiana University Press, 2001).

Review of International Studies (2010), 36, 25–46   © *2010 British International Studies Association*
doi:10.1017/S0260210511000106

Responsibility and obligation in the 'Responsibility to Protect'

WILLIAM BAIN*

Abstract. This article takes up Louise Arbour's claim that the doctrine of the 'Responsibility to Protect' is grounded in existing obligations of international law, specifically those pertaining to the prevention and punishment of genocide. In doing so, it argues that the aspirations of the R2P project cannot be sustained by the idea of 'responsibility' alone. The article proceeds in arguing that the coherence of R2P depends on an unacknowledged and unarticulated theory of obligation that connects notions of culpability, blame, and accountability with the kind of preventive, punitive, and restorative action that Arbour and others advocate. Two theories of obligation are then offered, one natural the other conventional, which make this connection explicit. But the ensuing clarity comes at a cost: the naturalist account escapes the 'real' world to redeem the intrinsic dignity of all men and women, while the conventionalist account remains firmly tethered to the 'real' world in redeeming whatever dignity can be had by way of an agreement. The article concludes by arguing that the advocate of the responsibility to protect can have one or the other, but not both.

William Bain is Senior Lecturer in International Political Theory in the Department of International Politics, Aberystwyth University. He is the author of *Between Anarchy and Society: Trusteeship and the Obligations of Power* (Oxford University Press, 2003) as well as several articles that explore the politics and ethics of trusteeship, international administration, and post-conflict reconstruction. At present, he is working on a book that is provisionally entitled *The Political Theory of World Order: God, Man, and the Common Good.*

In her 2008 article in the *Review*, Louise Arbour has provided a fascinating defence of the responsibility to protect norm as being securely grounded in existing international law. From this specifically legal foundation she works-out an 'internationalised form of duty of care' that narrows the gulf between the demands of international legal obligations and the willingness of individual states and the international community to act with resolute purpose in preventing genocide, crimes against humanity, and ethnic cleansing. There is no doubt that Arbour's argument deserves to be read for what it says. More interesting, however, is what it does not say; and for that it deserves a response. The project Arbour wants to defend discloses a kind of incoherence which, contrary to her own assertion, clouds the 'intellectual clarity' of the responsibility to protect and, consequently, devalues

* The author would like to thank all who offered comments and questions at various stages of this work. In particular, I want to thank Kirsten Ainley, Chris Brown, Molly Cochran, Alexandra Gheciu, Ian Hall, Andrew Linklater, Nicholas Rengger, and Jennifer Welsh.

its 'political usefulness' as a guide to action. In short, the ostensible innovation of shifting the terms of debate from a *right* of intervention to a *responsibility* to prevent, protect, and rebuild, falls well short of the mark insofar as the idea of 'responsibility' does not of itself sustain the kind of action that the responsibility to protect norm demands. In other words, the idea of 'responsibility' tells us who might be held accountable for the commission of mass atrocities or the failure to prevent them; it does not, however, tell us who should act to remedy these actions or punish those who are to blame.

The principal argument of this article is that the coherence of the responsibility to protect depends on an unacknowledged and unarticulated theory of obligation that connects notions of culpability, blame, and accountability with the kind of preventive, punitive, and restorative action that Arbour and others advocate. Indeed, Arbour's frequent and perplexing shifts between the language of 'responsibility' and the language of 'obligation' highlights the limitations of what can be placed on the back of 'responsibility'; and it underscores the need to bring a degree of clarity to the responsibility to protect that it presently lacks. Therefore, I shall proceed by making three principal claims: (1) Arbour's argument and the larger project of which it is a part cannot be sustained by 'responsibility' alone; (2) a theory of obligation – natural or conventional – is required to connect the 'sovereign as responsibility' principle with the 'international responsibility to protect' principle; and (3) the ensuing clarity comes at a cost, as is illustrated in the context of the responsibility to rebuild, which is denominated in the metaphysical Truth of the naturalist account or the contingent truth of the conventionalist account. In other words, the naturalist account escapes the 'real' world to redeem the intrinsic dignity that is the birthright of all men and women, and the conventionalist account remains firmly tethered to the 'real' world to redeem whatever dignity that can be created and had in an agreement. The advocate of the responsibility to protect can have one or the other, but not both.

The imperative of action

The notion of a 'responsibility to protect' finds its origin in the peculiarities of the changing nature of conflict, particularly in post-colonial Africa. The incidence of conflict between states, the 'scourge' from which the UN system was founded to save 'succeeding generations', has steadily declined over the past several decades. But in its place a new kind of conflict, one that exacts a disproportionate toll on civilian populations, has emerged to challenge the cardinal principles upon which UN system was also founded: sovereign equality, non-interference, and territorial integrity. Indeed, the characteristic brutality of intra-state conflict has proved to be deeply corrosive of these principles, continued respect for which ends up sustaining what are otherwise unviable states.[1] It is against this backdrop that the 'sovereignty as responsibility' principle gained traction. No longer was it possible, so the argument goes, to act with impunity. Sovereignty issues no license. Instead,

---

[1] See Robert Jackson, *Quasi-States: Sovereignty, International Relations, and the Third World* (Cambridge: Cambridge University Press, 1990).

sovereignty is justified in terms effectiveness, understood as the provision of a system of law and order which attends to the provision of basic needs and to the development of human dignity. Where these core responsibilities are not fulfilled the legitimacy of a government is called into question, thereby inviting remedial action, including, in the worst cases, armed intervention carried out by the international community. Thus, any tension that might arise between state sovereignty and the imperative of action is resolved in favour of the international community, because 'living up to the responsibilities of sovereignty' implies the existence of a higher authority capable of holding the supposed sovereign accountable. Some form of international system has always existed to ensure that states conform to accepted norms or face consequences, in the form of unilateral, multilateral, or collective action.[2]

This line of argument is picked-up and extended in the report of the International Commission on Intervention and State Sovereignty (ICISS): *The Responsibility to Protect*. The report has been praised on a number counts, not the least of which is its measured tone, which has saved it from a long but undistinguished fate as an over-sized coffee cup coaster in many national capitols. It has been more successful than other reports of its kind, with the Secretary-General of the UN, Ban Ki Moon, taking special interest in the report's focus on protecting civilians from genocide and other atrocities. Members of the General Assembly endorsed the 'sovereignty as responsibility' principle in the 2005 World Summit outcome document, which declares: '[w]e accept that responsibility and will act in accordance with it.'[3] The Security Council too has given its approval, having recalled and reaffirmed this commitment on at least two occasions, including one which deals specifically with the situation in Darfur.[4] The report has also elicited a substantial scholarly response, focusing mainly on issues of institutional reform, capacity building, mobilising political will, and instances of failure to protect. Of course, some of these responses tack to a sober conclusion, arguing, for example, that the World Summit decision is likely to contribute 'very little' to ensuring that 'never again' really means 'never again'; others strike a more optimistic chord in seeing the responsibility to protect as a 'central conceptual reference point' in contemporary international relations.[5]

Louise Arbour, the UN High Commissioner for Human Rights, is the latest in a long succession of distinguished figures to advance the responsibility to protect framework as a way of redressing gross human rights abuses. Like others, she embraces the idea of responsibility to escape the problems of grounding 'intervention for human protection purposes' – to use the infelicitous phraseology of the report – in the language of rights. Rights are by definition discretionary in

---

[2] Francis Deng et al., *Sovereignty as Responsibility: Conflict Management in Africa* (Washington, DC: Brookings Institute, 1996), chap. 1.

[3] UN General Assembly, World Summit Outcome Document, 15 September 2005, A/60/L.1, paras 138–9.

[4] See Security Council Resolution 1674 (2006), Adopted by the Security Council as its 5430th Meetings, 28 April 2006, S/RES/1674 (2006); and Security Council Resolution 1706 (2006), Adopted by the Security Council as its 5519th Meetings, 31 August 2006, S/RES/1706 (2006).

[5] See Gareth Evans, 'The Responsibility to Protect: Meeting the Challenges', Lecture to the 10th Asia-Pacific Programme for Senior Military Officers, S. Rajaratnam School of International Studies, Singapore (5 August 2008), available at: {www.crisisgroup.org}; and Alex Bellamy, 'Whither the Responsibility to Protect? Humanitarian Intervention and the 2005 World Summit', *Ethics and International Affairs*, 20:2 (2006), pp. 143–69.

character; they inhere in a putative intervener. As such, rights prefigure a permissive mode of action, mediated by contingent motives and interests, which does not always make contact with victims who are in need of rescue. Rights are also susceptible to abuse; hence questions inevitably arise about 'purity of intent', especially in parts of the world where memories of colonial domination are still fresh.[6] This particular concern stems from a deep-rooted belief that honesty and interest do not always coincide, which is to say that too often the discourse of armed humanitarianism is invoked to disguise what are in fact less salubrious motives. Better, then, Arbour argues, to seek refuge in the idea of responsibility, which is anchored in the victim's point of view and interests as against a notoriously suspect axis of state motives and interests. Indeed, once stripped of a discretionary right of intervention states find themselves burdened with a responsibility to take action to prevent genocide, crimes against humanity, and war crimes, in what Arbour describes as a 'permanent duty to protect individuals against abusive behaviour'.[7]

There is thus far little to distinguish Arbour's position from other sympathetic accounts of the responsibility to protect. More interesting, however, is her suggestion that the intelligibility of the responsibility to protect begs no 'leap into wishful thinking' for the simple reason that the 'doctrine rests upon an undisputed obligation of international law: the prevention and punishment of genocide'.[8] An uncharitable response might interpret this claim as casting a long shadow over enthusiastic pronouncements heralding a new norm that marks a definite and long overdue break with the past. If taken seriously, a response of this sort ends up reducing the responsibility to protect to a cleverly thought-out marketing campaign aimed at getting states to fulfil already existing obligations, some of which are sixty years old. But there is something genuinely interesting in the argument from existing law, namely it holds potential interveners to a rather more exacting standard of accountability than if responsibility were construed as merely a political or moral consideration. For Arbour, the legal basis of the responsibility to protect imposes on would-be interveners a test of 'due diligence', the burden of which is evaluated in respect of influence, proximity, and knowledge, in what amounts to an 'internationalised form of duty of care'.[9] In elaborating this argument she pushes beyond the decision of International Court of Justice, which found Serbia in breach of its obligation to prevent genocide in Bosnia in Herzegovina, due to unusually close links with the perpetrators of genocide, to pose a rather more searching question: might logic of this 'duty of care' be applied to the wider international community?[10]

In attempting to answer this question Arbour lays out far-reaching consequences as to what this duty of care might entail for right conduct among states. For example, the doctrine of great power responsibility is taken in a new direction in the suggestion that the preponderant responsibility that falls on the permanent members of the Security Council extends, paradoxically, so far as to restrict the

[6] Louise Arbour, 'The responsibility to protect in international law', *Review of International Studies*, 34:3 (2008), p. 447.
[7] Arbour, 'The responsibility to protect', p. 448.
[8] Ibid., pp. 448, 450.
[9] Ibid., pp. 451–5.
[10] Ibid., p. 453.

threat or use of the veto in certain circumstances.[11] Arbour rehearses the standard doctrine in saying that, owing to their 'global reach', these powers bear a 'heavier responsibility' in matters of grave humanitarian concern. But the privilege that goes with preponderant power is immediately qualified by the duty of care, which asks veto-wielding great powers to 'cease inhibiting other States from discharging their duty to protect when those States are willing and able to discharge their obligations'.[12] The insulation afforded by great distance is also whittled away as the requirements of due diligence fall equally on all states, irrespective of location. Nor can inaction be excused on grounds of ignorance or the incredulity that often greets reports of heinous crimes. The question, Arbour contends, does not turn on the availability of information; it turns on the kind of action that available information prompts. The crucial point, then, is failure in respect of any of these elements of responsibility – influence, proximity, and knowledge – may incur legal as opposed to merely moral or political culpability for failing to prevent 'conscience shocking' crimes. It is then possible to argue, for example, that exercising the veto in a way that frustrates intervention for 'human protection purposes' may well 'constitute a violation of the vetoing States' obligations under the Genocide Convention'.[13]

The limits of responsibility

There is no doubt that 'the responsibility to protect' has left a definite imprint on the way in which human protection activities are conceived, and to that extent it offers a potent normative language with which to frame and to evaluate a broad range of issues that fall under the rubric of human security. And Arbour's intervention in the conversation is sure to bolster the currency of this language. But set aside a fondness for policy cheerleading, if only for a moment, to pull at the threads of the 'inherent soundness and justice'[14] of the responsibility to protect and we shall find a lack of conceptual clarity which leaves the entire project vulnerable to criticism, especially from those who would see the responsibility to protect as yet another manifestation of dominant power. In short, the shift from a *right* of intervention to a *responsibility* to protect does not sustain the kind of action envisioned by Arbour and other advocates of the cause. Consider the ICISS report's operative principles: (1) sovereignty entails responsibility for the security and well-being of a state's citizens; and (2) the international community assumes this responsibility when a state is either unable or unwilling to discharge is responsibilities.[15] The problem is that that principle (2) does not follow logically or morally from principle (1). In other words, sovereignty may well entail responsibility but saying so identifies only the person – natural or legal – to whom certain

---

[11] The 'capricious' threat or use of the veto was a central concern for the ICISS, which recommended the adoption of a code of conduct as to its use. Note, however, that Arbour's legal argument goes well beyond the political solution advocated by the Commission. See ICISS, *The Responsibility to Protect* (Ottawa: International Development Research Centre, 2001), pp. 51, 75.

[12] Arbour, 'The responsibility to protect', p. 453.

[13] Ibid., pp. 451–4.

[14] Ibid., p. 448.

[15] ICISS, *The Responsibility to Protect*, pp. 11–16.

actions of omission or commission are attributable; or, to push the concept further, it identifies the person who may be held accountable for these actions.[16]

It is this latter conception of responsibility, that is, responsibility understood in terms of accountability, which is particularly relevant to the responsibility to protect. The idea of responsibility is, of course, a central part of a shared normative vocabulary that is used to describe and to evaluate the character of human conduct. It is with reference to responsibility that expressions of praise and blame are communicated; and to that extent the idea of responsibility and the related concept of accountability are deeply entangled with judgements that interrogate conduct in light of expectations presupposed in shared normative standards.[17] Thus, the idea of responsibility discloses a forward-looking or 'prospective' face, which is to say, as Arbour suggests, that states are responsible prospectively for faithfully adhering to obligations laid out in the Genocide Convention. Crucially, prospective responsibility does not require the actual commission of harm for evaluative statements to make sense: the expectation that states *ought* to conduct themselves in this manner leaves them liable to blame when they fail to prevent harm. The idea of responsibility also discloses a backward-looking or 'retrospective' face, whereby praise or blame is apportioned in relation to an evaluation of specific actions and the consequences in which they result. Thus, a state is said to be retrospectively responsible for causing harm, resulting from conduct in breach of the Genocide Convention, which may merit blame and whatever punishment or reparations might be due.[18]

If the argument from responsibility is taken further we are able to describe the kind of agent to which it pertains as well as the conditions in which talk of responsibility is appropriate. The idea of responsibility conceived in terms of accountability is very closely connected to that of human freedom and the notion of voluntary action. For it makes little sense to blame a man for failing to prevent an earthquake or to praise a woman for desiring food for no other reason than to satiate her hunger. But considerations of blame and praise do arise when an earthquake results in the collapse of substandard construction, killing or injuring innocent persons as happened in China's Sichuan province; and they arise as well when a desire for food is motivated by a determination to deny it to others for political reasons, thereby threatening their well-being. Likewise, it is nonsensical to blame the government of Myanmar for the mere fact of cyclone Nargis and the destruction it wrought; but expressions of blame, imputing responsibility, do gain traction when projected against a backdrop of the government's tardy, if not negligent, response in assisting the victims of the disaster. In thinking through such questions it may matter that the person in question is mentally ill or below the age

---

[16] On the distinction between 'attributability' and 'accountability' see Gary Watson, 'Two Face of Responsibility', *Agency and Answerability* (Oxford: Oxford University Press, 2004), pp. 260–88. The ICISS report confirms this much in noting that agents of states 'are responsible for their actions; that is to say, they are accountable for their acts of commissions and omission'. See ICISS, *The Responsibility to Protect*, p. 13.

[17] See Lawrence Stern, 'Freedom, Blame, and the Moral Community', *The Journal of Philosophy*, 71:3 (1974), p. 84; and Peter Strawson, 'Freedom and Resentment', *Proceedings of the British Academy*, 48 (1962), pp. 1–25.

[18] On 'prospective' and 'retrospective' responsibility see Toni Erskine, 'Introduction: Making Sense of "Responsibility" in International Relations – Key Questions and Concepts', *Can Institutions Have Responsibilities?* (Basingstoke: Palgrave, 2003), p. 8.

of majority, in which case he or she may be absolved of responsibility altogether. These considerations might also diminish responsibility, as might extreme duress or genuine ignorance of cogent facts. Whichever the case, however, the idea of responsibility generally involves an agent who enjoys at least an element of freedom, discloses the capacity for deliberation and decision, possesses at least some knowledge of circumstances and foresight of likely consequences, and, therefore, may be held liable for the consequences of his or her actions.[19]

But we cannot glean what a third-party should do from the mere fact that someone is said to be responsible. In other words, the 'sovereignty as responsibility' principle does not of itself say anything about who should act to remedy atrocities or punish those who are to blame. The sanction for irresponsibility may be a feeling of inward distress, the torment of conscience, or alienation from one's self; it might also result in approbation that leads to social marginalisation or perhaps forfeiture of membership in a particular association. But Arbour and other advocates of the responsibility to protect have something more demanding in mind, namely a spectrum of action that includes a coercive sanction – including the use of force – which finds its imprimatur in international law. Thus, it might be argued, as does Arbour, that the responsibility to protect rests on already existing law, namely obligations pertaining to the prevention and punishment of genocide.[20] Unlike the idea of responsibility, which designates a locus of accountability, the idea of obligation does enjoin action; it is a way saying that something must be done independently of what considerations of interest or advantage might recommend. Indeed, the demand that states act to prevent genocide emanates from the fact that they have voluntarily assumed an obligation to do so. Only then does the language of responsibility become audible in any intelligible way. For it is in light this 'undisputed obligation' that states are (prospectively) responsible for conducting themselves in a manner that is consistent with the Genocide Convention; and it is in light of the same obligation that states are (retrospectively) responsible for harm caused by negligent or malicious conduct.

It is knowledge of this coordinated relation of obligation and responsibility that invests the responsibility to protect with the conceptual clarity which it presently lacks. Unfortunately, obtaining clear sight of this relation is frustrated by Arbour's frequent and bewildering oscillation between the language of obligation and the language of responsibility, obfuscating their different characters along the way. Indeed, it is 'obligation', rather than 'responsibility', which affords a 'comparative advantage' over a discretionary right of intervention. Arbour seems to concede that much as she shifts effortlessly from 'responsibility' to 'obligation' (and 'duty') to argue that it is the duty of all states to protect their citizens against abusive behaviour, to which she adds: '[a]bsent that State's ability or willingness to discharge such obligations, the onus of protection falls by default upon the broader international community.'[21] Similarly, the bedrock of her argument, the responsibility of third-parties to prevent genocide, is sustained by obligations enshrined in

---

[19] See generally Jonathan Glover, *Responsibility* (London: Routledge & Kegan Paul, 1970); Joel Feinberg, *Doing and Deserving: Essays in the Theory of Responsibility* (Princeton: Princeton University Press, 1970); and H. L. A. Hart, *Punishment and Responsibility: Essays in the Philosophy of Law* (Oxford: Clarendon Press, 1968).

[20] Arbour, 'The responsibility to protect', p. 450.

[21] Ibid., p. 449.

international law.[22] Thus, in making explicit what is now only implicit in Arbour's argument it is possible to make sense of the responsibility to protect as a doctrine founded on a coordinated relationship, whereby states are burdened with obligations for which they may be held responsible in instances of failure. It is also possible to give a coherent account of the ICISS report's operative principles without having to confront the vexed question of ascribing agency to an elusive and under-theorised international community. In other words, the residual responsibility that is said to reside in the international community as such is better understood in the context of an obligation, voluntarily assumed, which demands that (contracting) states act in a particular manner.

Curiously, Arbour and other advocates of the responsibility to protect have little, if anything, to say about the place or character of obligation in their thinking, although the language of obligation tends to run throughout their arguments, both explicitly and implicitly. Nevertheless, the 'sovereignty as responsibility' formula does provide a useful starting point for thinking about obligation insofar as it suggests the character that states should disclose and the kind of normative order of which they should be a part. It surely rules out the idea of the state as being nothing more than a coercive order – that is, an arrangement of force. This view of the state emphasises the ability to issue and enforce commands; it is a superior force that imposes itself on the individual will, the effectiveness of which provides evidence that the state does in fact exist.[23] However, reducing the relation of state and individual to one of force runs up against the objection that force ought not be arbitrary in a way that leaves the individual vulnerable to the capricious will of the magistrate. Making the state an order or laws, whereby power is subject to recognised rules, does provide a defence against the arbitrary exercise of power; unfortunately, it provides no defence against arbitrary laws, such as those which the Nazis enacted in the 1930s to strip Jews of their civil rights.[24] Thus, the ICISS report takes an additional step, thereby remedying this problem, in seeing the state as a superior force, subject to law, which is also legitimate – that is, a state in which power should be accepted and in which law should be obeyed.

This conception of the state immediately begs an age old question of political thought: why, after having identified an office of authority, should anyone be obliged to obey? It must be stressed that the capacity of the state to compel obedience has nothing to do with answering this question. To have power but not authority is to be a tyrant.[25] Moreover, it has nothing to do, contra to a common but nonetheless mistaken view among scholars of International Relations, with an assessment of what in fact a state does or does not do. Indeed, whatever answer might be furnished is firmly located in the domain of (objective) right, understood as the thing or state of affairs which is just, which, as Michael Oakeshott argues, is to leave behind the world of fact for an inquiry into its underlying justification.[26]

---

[22] Ibid., p. 450.
[23] A. P. d'Entreves, *The Notion of the State* (Oxford: Clarendon Press, 1967), pp. 1–3.
[24] d'Entreves, *The Notion of the State*, pp. 2–3.
[25] Michael Oakeshott, 'The Authority of Governments and the Obligations of Subjects (1)', in Terry Nardin and Luke O'Sullivan (eds) *Lecture in the History of Political Thought* (Exeter: Imprint Academic, 2006), pp. 428–9.
[26] See Oakeshott, 'The Authority of Governments', pp. 427–30. On the distinction between objective and subject right see Brian Tierney, *The Idea of Natural Rights: Studies in Natural Rights, Natural Law, and Church Law, 1150–1625* (Grand Rapids, MI: William B. Eerdmans Publishing, 1997); and

Of course, there are several possible answers that are intelligible historically, including wisdom, divine right, prescription, blood, and virtue; but in a world that tends to fetishise democracy as a universal elixir of whatever might ail the world, the answer from consent is surely the most powerful and recognisable. Hanna Pitkin explains consent as defining the limits of obligation as well as the person – again, natural or legal – to whom obedience is owed: '[l]egitimate authority is distinguished from mere coercive power precisely by the consent of those subject to it. And the justification for your obligation to obey is your own consent to it; because you have agreed, it is right for you to have an obligation.'[27] This answer, in turn, structures the direction of scholarly inquiry in a way that privileges certain fundamental (and familiar) subsidiary questions, such as 'whose consent is required?' and 'how is consent to be ascertained?'

But there are definite limits as to what consent can tell us, the most obvious being the reasons why any obligation underwritten by consent should be regarded as obligatory. H. L. A. Hart explains the significance of this problem when he says that the validity of obligations assumed in acts of consent depends on pre-existing rules that authoritatively establish that promises must be kept prior to entering into such an agreement. It follows, then, he continues, that 'such rules presupposed in the very notion of a self-imposed obligation obviously cannot derive *their* obligatory status from a self-imposed obligation to obey them'.[28] Some, such as Carol Pateman, dismiss this concern as a 'psuedo-problem', arising from an assumed nexus between the liberal state and abstract individualism, which 'dissolves' when self-imposed obligations are conceived as the product of inter-subjective 'social practice'.[29] But this rejoinder evades rather than dissolves the problem by substituting prescription for consent; it is a way of saying that self-imposed obligations are obligatory because that is the way it has been done for a long time. The limits of consent are also evident insofar as it tells us that (political) obligation is legitimate precisely because we have given our consent; it must remain silent, however, on the substantive content of obligation as well as the desirability, that is, the good, of any particular obligation or the political life to which it is ordered. In other words, argument from consent seeks 'to ground the obligation of the subject or citizen in the realm not of final but of efficient causes, not in the ends government exist to promote but in the source from which they derive their powers.'[30]

Even a cursory read of *The Responsibility to Protect* will confirm that the 'sovereignty as responsibility' principle is justified in terms of final causes – that is, the ultimate justification of state sovereignty is not found in the efficient cause of how it is legitimised, namely consent, but in the ends for the sake of which it is instituted. At the international level the same set of issues present themselves. The

---

Annabel Brett, *Liberty, Right and Nature: Individual Rights in Later Scholastic Thought* (Cambridge: Cambridge University Press, 2003).

[27] Hanna Pitkin, 'Obligation and Consent – I', *The American Political Science Review*, 59:4 (1965), p. 993.

[28] H. L. A. Hart, *The Concept of Law*, (Oxford: Clarendon Press, 1961), pp. 219–20.

[29] Carole Pateman, *The Problem of Political Obligation: A Critical Analysis of Liberal Theory* (New York: John Wiley & Sons, 1979), pp. 24–30.

[30] See Francis Oakley, 'Legitimation by Consent: The Question of the Medieval Roots', *Politics and Eternity* (Leiden: Brill, 1999), pp. 98–100. On the difference between 'final' and 'efficient' causes see R. W. Dyson, *Natural Law and Political Realism in the History of Political Thought*, vol. 1 (New York: Peter Lang, 2005), pp. 68–9; and Milja Kurki, *Causation in International Relations: Reclaiming Causal Analysis* (Cambridge: Cambridge University Press, 2008), pp. 218–22.

ICISS report notes that '[t]he Charter of the UN is itself an example of an international obligation voluntarily accepted by member states.'[31] However, the authority of this obligation depends, as is the case with domestic obligation, on a non-consensual rule found in extra-legal experience that grounds the binding force of consent; for in the absence of such a rule, the law, and the obligations that pertain thereto, are whatever states will them it to be at any given moment in time.[32] At this point we are left to confront anew the problem posed by medieval nominalism, whereby God can will that what is good today is evil tomorrow. To conceive the modern sovereign in similar terms is to reject the intelligibility of final causes and the 'sovereignty as responsibility' principle along with it.[33] Indeed, the justification of the obligations that ground Arbour's argument must at some point leave consent for the world of extra-legal experience, which is to say, as A. P. d'Entreves explains, that the ultimate 'validity of laws does not depend on their "positiveness", and that it is the duty of the individual to pass judgment on laws before he obeys them.'[34]

Nature

To admit this much is to open the door to a natural law approach to obligation. Of course, the mere mention of natural law is often all it takes to provoke sneers of derision. Nineteenth century legal theorists were particularly fond of dismissing natural law as little more than woolly aspiration: it could not be properly specified, it could not be adequately enforced, and therefore it did not deserve to be called law. But the high tide of legal positivism has since receded and with it natural law has experienced something of a revival, impelled in no small part by the crimes Holocaust and the ensuing trials at Nuremburg. For it was Nuremburg that restored the bridge between law and morality, hence acting in accordance with properly enacted and promulgated law was not enough to absolve persons charged with crimes against the peace and crimes against humanity. It is in this sense that some crimes, such as genocide, slavery, and apartheid, are widely regarded as being categorically wrong, irrespective of the fact that there is an instrument of (positive) international law that proscribes them. So in the event that a persistent objector enslaved a portion of his (or her) population, it would matter not a jot if the perpetrator were not a party to the relevant instruments of international law: the plea 'I am not bound because I have not consented' would be no plea at all. And it is in this context that James Leslie Brierly gets it right in pointing to both the difficulty and necessity of natural law: '[i]t may not always be easy to feel intellectually assured that such a belief is founded in reality, but it is a belief upon which even the most sceptical acts every minute of his life.'[35]

[31] ICISS, *The Responsibility to Protect*, p. 13.
[32] See Martii Koskenniemi, *From Apology to Utopia* (Cambridge: Cambridge University Press, 2005) pp. 309–12.
[33] Michael Allen Gillespie, *The Theological Origins of Modernity* (Chicago: University of Chicago Press 2008), pp. 22–9.
[34] A. P. d'Entreves, *Natural Law: An Introduction to Legal Philosophy* (London: Hutchinson University Library, 1952), p. 107.
[35] James Leslie Brierly, 'The Basis of Obligation in International Law', in Hersch Lauterpacht (ed.) *The Basis of Obligation in International Law and Other Papers* (Oxford: Clarendon Press, 1958) p. 67.

It is in view of this tension between intellectual uneasiness and practical necessity a puzzle arises: few people will declare themselves as fully signed-up advocates of natural law but the language of natural law is an omnipresent feature of contemporary political life, domestic and international. The justification of NATO's intervention in Kosovo, the event which in so many ways breathed life into the responsibility to protect, is a case in point. Vaclav Havel defended the intervention by appealing to a higher law, arguing that it 'acted out of respect for the law, for the law that ranks higher than the protection of the sovereignty of states. It has acted out of respect for the rights of humanity, as they are articulated by our conscience as well as by other instruments of international law.'[36] And it is this idea of a higher law articulated by our conscience, which, as Havel puts it, 'identifies justice with moral standards that are independent of the practices of actual communities', that grounds the common conclusion that intervention in Kosovo was illegal but morally justified.[37] The language of natural law is also intelligible in the Universal Declaration of Human Rights, Article 1 of which amounts to a classic statement of natural law: '[a]ll human beings are born free and equal in dignity and rights. They are endowed with reason and conscience and should act towards one another in a spirit of brotherhood.'[38] It should come as no surprise, then, that tucked away in the ICISS report is the admission that the responsibility to protect is supported by a wide array of legal sources, including 'fundamental natural law principles'.[39]

The character and content of these principles are not explained, nor is their origin, but a glimpse might be had in earlier explications of the 'sovereignty as responsibility' principle. Here again Nuremburg cast a long shadow as Francis Deng, the person credited with initially outlining the 'sovereignty as responsibility' principle, sees the trials as auguring a fundamental reinterpretation of state sovereignty. From then on the order of laws that is the state and the authority that enacts those laws are justified for the sake of a particular end, a final cause, namely the development of human dignity. Indeed, he suggests that '[i]n the search for normative principles it should be safe to reaffirm human dignity as an overarching goal to which all peoples and societies aspire and are committed, whatever the variations of their cultural perspectives on the details of the concept.'[40] The pre-eminence of this goal qualifies the relation of law and obligation in a crucial way: law that is inimical to the flourishing of human dignity exacts no obedience because it is not law properly so-called. Of course, argument of this sort has obvious appeal for advocates of the responsibility to protect, who proceed in the conviction that principles of sovereign equality and non-interference do not license abuse, just as they are not meant to shield tyrants from being held accountable internationally. They are quick to point to a growing consensus among states as tangible evidence of an emerging norm; but it is equally clear that the rightness of

---

[36] Vaclav Havel, Address of His Excellency Vaclav Havel, President of the Czech Republic to both Houses of Parliament in the House of Commons Chamber, Ottawa, on Thursday, 29 April 1999, Government of Canada, Department of Foreign Affairs and International Trade (11 August 1999), p. 4.

[37] Havel, *Address of His Excellency*, p. 5.

[38] Ian Brownlie, (ed.), 'Universal Declaration of Human Rights', *Basic Documents on Human Rights*, 3rd edition (Oxford: Oxford University Press, 1992), p. 22.

[39] ICISS, *The Responsibility to Protect*, p. 16.

[40] Deng, *Sovereignty as Responsibility*, p. 19.

this norm and the obligations it entails does not depend ultimately on any kind of consensus, no matter how broad it might be. Consensus plays a supporting role to the lead, that is, a determination of right, which is established in advance of whatever consensus might achieve.

But what is often asserted as self-evident fact, the value of human dignity as the goal of all societies, is unavoidably an evaluative concept that speaks to a specific conception of right relation among human beings. For the claim of human dignity, something which is not only independent of the will of the state but is the rule and measure of the whatever the state wills, is nothing less than the evaluative criterion of natural law, if not in name then at least in spirit and function. It is a mistake, however, to imagine a single tradition of natural law. Pre-modern theories of natural law are deeply tied-up in the idea of community, especially as it relates to human interdependence and perfection though social and political experience. Here, 'natural' names an end-point to be achieved; it is an ethical ideal or *telos* at which things should aim. This approach places special emphasis on the 'common good', although it never eclipses entirely the good of the individual.[41] In contrast, modern theories of natural law give priority to the individual as against the community in deference to the value of negative liberty: the freedom to act without interference. Thus, 'natural' is not an end to be achieved; it is a starting point from which to erect civil association and to work out a moral and legal order that stresses the importance of consent and the preservation of individual liberty.[42] Despite obvious differences, both approaches take as their point of departure a distinctive natural law problematic: human flourishing, however it might be conceived, cannot be achieved without the help of others. Natural law offers an answer to this problem while taking human beings as they are: self-aware, capable of moral discernment, free to act on those judgments, and manifestly flawed.

But difficulty arises to the extent which the answer to this problematic depends on the command of a superior in order to invest it with coherence, and in one way or another that superior has taken the form of God. Of course, the theologians and canonists of medieval Christendom made no attempt to separate natural law from God. Their disagreements concerned the difference between intellectualist and voluntarist approaches to natural law, which is expressed in the difference between the statement 'something is good, therefore God wills it' and the statement 'something is good because God wills it'.[43] When we look to the modern world we find that someone like Grotius too relies on God to give his theory of natural law coherence, although a persistent misreading of his words about God's existence – the infamous *etiamsi daremus* passage – is often said to be the watershed of a secular theory of natural law. But a Whiggish over-modernisation of Grotius' thought fails to comprehend that he was also addressing the intellectualist-voluntarist distinction in arguing against Ockhamist nominalism: hence God cannot make two and two equal five any more than he can make that which is intrinsically evil, good.[44]

[41] R. W. Dyson, *Natural Law and Political Realism in the History of Political Thought*, vol. 2 (New York: Peter Lang, 2007), pp. x–xi.

[42] Dyson, *Natural Law*, vol. 2, p. x.

[43] See J. B. Schneewind, *The Invention of Autonomy: A History of Modern Moral Philosophy* (Cambridge: Cambridge University Press, 1998), pp. 22–5.

[44] See D'Entreves, *Natural Law*, p. 56; Schneewind, *The Invention of Autonomy*, pp. 18–36, 69–76; and Oliver O'Donovan and Joan Lockwood O'Donovan (eds), *From Irenaeus to Grotius: A Sourcebook in Christian Political Thought* (Cambridge: William B. Eerdman's Publishing, 1999), pp. 787–92.

Moreover, the binding character of Grotian natural law also depends on God, so that the laws of nature are not obligatory, as his eighteenth century translator Jean Barbeyrac explains, until 'Reason has discovered the Author of the Existence and Nature of Things, whose Will gives those Maxims the Force of a Law.'[45]

That natural law accounts of obligation should rely on God is what Elizabeth Anscombe describes as the consequence of a distinctively Christian approach to ethics, whereby notions of licit and illicit and that of being bound follow from their correspondence with law. Thus, the idea of obligation specifies actions which in a moral sense must be done; and the good man (or the bad man) and good actions (or bad actions) are identified insofar as they correspond with relevant precepts of law. In other words, it is in respect of law instituted (for an intellectualist) or commanded (for a voluntarist) by God that the notion of 'ought' obtains its special moral sense, so that it is possible to say we ought to assist our fellow human beings in realising their goals as opposed to saying we ought to service the car regularly to ensure it is reliable through the winter. Unfortunately, the so-called 'new natural law', which seeks to escape the problem posed by God by taking refuge in underived, logically demonstrated self-evident values, provides little relief from this predicament because these values are pre-moral or outside the category of morality and, therefore, do not tell us very much about the man who faithfully subscribes to them. He is neither good nor bad.[46] There is, then, for Anscombe, little reason to retain the moral sense of 'ought' and the idea of moral obligation to which it is attached because, considered apart from a law-based conception of ethics, 'they are survivals, or derivatives of survivals, from an earlier conceptions of ethics which no longer generally survives, and are only harmful without it'.[47]

Convention

Difficulties with this approach to obligation lead us to a different mode of thought, one which sets history before reason and therefore convention before nature. It was David Hume's devastating assault on reason that did so much to destroy the foundations of natural law. Hume denied reason a necessary connection to morality as in naturalist thought: it tells us nothing about what is good and it cannot move us to action even if we know what is good. Reason is also shorn of its epistemological role in discovering and justifying moral claims on the back of the well known fallacy of deriving an *ought* from an *is*.[48] Instead, reason is limited to telling us what is available and how we might get what we want, which is to reduce reason to an instrumental faculty disconnected from considerations of morality.[49] In place of the rationalism of natural law theories Hume stressed the

---

[45] See Barbeyrac's commentary on Hugo Grotius, *The Rights of War and Peace*, vol. I, trans. Jean Barbeyrac, ed. Richard Tuck (Indianapolis: Liberty Fund, 2005), pp. 151–3.

[46] Dyson, *Natural Law*, vol. 2, p. 212. For a summary of the 'new natural law' and its critics see Howard Kainz, *Natural Law: An Introduction and Re-examination* (Chicago: Open Court, 2004).

[47] G. E. M. Anscombe, 'Modern Moral Philosophy', in Mary Geach and Luke Gormally (eds), *Human Life, Action and Ethics* (Exeter: Imprint, 2005), pp. 169–82.

[48] For an analysis of this distinction in the context of natural law see Dyson, *Natural Law*, vol. 2, pp. 200–3, 222–4.

[49] Schneewind, *The Invention of Autonomy*, pp. 357–9.

importance of virtue, natural and artificial, in explaining how human beings create principles of justice by their own effort. That we owe justice to our acquaintances and strangers alike, not to mention our enemies and those we might hate, leads Hume to deny that benevolence or love of humanity moves us to be just. On this point he is clear: 'there is no such passion in human minds as the love of mankind, merely as such, independent of personal qualities, of services, or of relation to ourself.'[50] Rather justice emerges slowly as individuals become aware that stability of possession – property being at the core of justice – would be beneficial to them all. Thus, justice arises as a matter of convention, the motive of which is self-interest rather than an imperative formulated as an obligation; and justice is said to be of moral value only when, through sympathy, we recognise these benefits accrue to all who participate in the convention. It is at this point that obligation comes into view, albeit not as a command tied to law, but as a motive that moves us to action.[51]

The importance of Hume's account of the artificial virtues has a crucial historical bearing on how we understand the notion of society. Artificial virtues like justice are those which are required for the existence of any complex society to exist, much less to function well. So whereas a society can exist in which a natural virtue like charity or benevolence is largely absent, it cannot exist without rules of justice, particularly those pertaining to man's peaceable enjoyment of his external goods. Indeed, Hume goes so far as to say that '[n]o one can doubt that the convention for the distinction of property, and for the stability of possession, is of all circumstances the most necessary to the establishment of human society.'[52] As it happens, it is precisely this notion of convention that informs Hedley Bull's notion of the elementary goals of international society: limitations on the use of force, the keeping of promises, and stability of possession.[53] Hume also showed how justice can arise and continue to exist without the help of a sovereign, for in arising spontaneously it is neither created nor maintained by the will of a sovereign, either in terms of command or law.[54] And because justice does not depend on a sovereign, matters such as the distribution of goods can be accomplished impersonally through the operation of the market. Indeed, the artificial origin of justice is an important part of what is perhaps the most influential alternative to natural law accounts of society and social change: the idea that societies undergo a process of historical development such as that exemplified by Adam Smith's 'four stage's theory', the pinnacle of which is commercial society.[55]

Argument from convention solves problem of securing obligation in God for the unbeliever and for the sceptic, but seeing the moral world as nothing but a human construction comes at a cost. A conventionalist approach such as Hume's reduces law to an inferior status, at least when compared to that which it enjoys

---

[50] See David Hume, in Stuart Warner and Donald Livingston (eds), *Political Writings* (Indianapolis: Hackett Publishing, 1994), pp. 4–7.

[51] Hume, *Political Writings*, pp. 11–12, Schneewind, *The Invention of Autonomy*, pp. 367–9.

[52] Hume, *Political Writings*, p. 12.

[53] Bull makes specific reference to Hume in elaborating this argument. See *The Anarchical Society* (New York: Columbia University Press, 1977), pp. 4–5.

[54] Schneewind, *The Invention of Autonomy*, pp. 370–1.

[55] See generally Christopher Berry, *Social Theory of the Scottish Enlightenment* (Edinburgh: Edinburgh University Press, 1997), chap. 6.

in natural law theory. Law is no longer the embodiment of justice; nor is it the first defence against odious custom such as female genital mutilation, honour killing, or the stoning to death of adulterers. Law is simply a codification, that is, an affirmation and clarification, of what convention is in a given state of society. Similarly, all societies might require certain arrangements of justice to secure the institution of property, stability of possession and promise keeping being the most obvious, but there is little scope for adjudicating these virtues as themselves just or unjust. To do so would require a moral point of reference that is external to the convention itself. For these virtues imply no more than society depends on the security of property and its orderly transfer; and whatever consideration of the value of these arrangements is related, not to the existence of these virtues, but to the results that come with exercising them. In other words, it is a sense of common interest, mutually expressed, which 'produces a suitable resolution and behaviour', and therefore determines the value of convention.[56] The consequence, then, is a world truly of our making, for it admits, as J. B. Schneewind puts it, 'Beyond that, all is local convention. And one convention is good as another, if both do the job.'[57]

It is at this point that convention shows its ugly face only to receive an ugly glare in return, for a world that begins and ends with convention leaves a precariously narrow ground on which to protest. All that is left to resolve disputes is argument by assertion or, failing that, the application of force, the latter being the preferred method of Charles Napier's attempt to suppress the practice of *sati* in 19th century British India:

This burning of widows is your custom. Prepare the funeral pile. But my nation has also a custom. When men burn women alive, we hang them and confiscate all their property. My carpenters shall therefore erect gibbets on which to hang all concerned when the widow is consumed. Let us all act according to national customs.[58]

Argument from convention also presents something of a conundrum for some widely held accounts of universal human rights. For example, the rights declared in the Universal Declaration of Human Rights (UDHR) depend on first principles that suppose the inherent dignity of the human person, the equal worth of all persons, and their membership in human family. One might look to something like a Rawlsian 'overlapping consensus' in order to vindicate these principles in a common community of value; look hard enough, however, and we shall find lurking in the background an unacknowledged *naturalis ratio* that argument from convention does not allow.[59] Indeed, the intrinsic human value presupposed by the UDHR would appear to founder on a tautological stipulation; for in lieu of an *a priori* and prescriptive account of human nature, reason cannot establish by itself the *moral* value of these first principles, which leaves us to wonder why human life should be regarded as intrinsically valuable at all. In other words, the intrinsic value that attaches to human life is not what follows from a human essence that

---

[56] Hume, *Political Writings*, p. 11.
[57] Schneewind, *The Invention of Autonomy*, pp. 366, 373.
[58] Quoted in A. P. Thornton, *Doctrines of Imperialism* (New York: John Wiley & Sons, 1965), p. 170.
[59] As Dyson argues, 'meaningful moral discourse depends not simply upon rationality, but upon the existence of shared values'. It is in respect of (unacknowledged) values or first premises that Rawls, like some modern natural law theorists, arrives at such a consensus. See *Natural Law*, vol. 2, pp. 100–6, 221.

transcends and therefore joins individual human beings in a universal moral relationship; it might be the case that '[w]e find ethical value in human nature in the way that the conjurer finds a rabbit in a top hat: only because we put it there ourselves.'[60]

The implications of obligation

Both the naturalist and conventionalist accounts of obligation connect the 'sovereignty entails responsibility' principle with the principle of an 'international responsibility to protect'; and in doing so they invest a degree of coherence in Arbour's argument – and the ICISS project generally – which it presently lacks. But the purchase of coherence comes at a cost as both accounts also give occasion to controversy which, from the academic's standpoint, invites further reflection, and from the practitioner's standpoint, may well frustrate the realisation of goals that justify the responsibility to protect project. Indeed, the stakes come into view in consideration of one aspect of the ICISS report: the responsibility to rebuild. Here again the limitations of responsibility are on full display. The report provides little insight as to what links the responsibility to rebuild to substantive action, apart from a seemingly unproblematic assertion that it follows as a logical consequence of the responsibility to protect. It does say that in the aftermath of military intervention there should a 'genuine commitment' on the part of the international community to help build a durable peace and to promote good governance and sustainable development, which involves, as any number of recent post-conflict missions attest, ensuring respect for human rights and the promotion of democratic institutions and free market economy.[61] But ask why any of these things should be done and the answer seems to be a prudential desire to avoid a return to conflict. In short, then, we are left with a calculation of contingent interest that counsels: '[t]here is no substitute for a clear and effective post-intervention strategy.'[62]

Missing in this counsel of prudence is an explication of the normative linkages which, elsewhere in the report, are said to run through the assistance, intervention and reconstruction spectrum. Indeed, a counsel of prudence will not do as a normative grounding of the responsibility to rebuild, not the least because it falls back on the same discretionary consideration of (contingent) state interest that the language of 'responsibility' is meant to circumvent. A theory of obligation does provide such a grounding, albeit in different ways and with different consequences. There should be no doubt that the pronounced and repeated emphasis that the ICISS report places on the dignity of the human person cleaves to natural law argument. It is to this kind of argument that Gareth Evans – a fervent champion of the ICISS project – appeals when he says 'the case for R2P rests simply on our

---

[60] Dyson, *Natural Law*, vol. 2, pp. 212–21.

[61] See ICISS, *The Responsibility to Protect*, p. 39; William Bain, *Between Anarchy and Society: Trusteeship and the Obligations of Power* (Oxford: Oxford University Press, 2003); and Dominik Zaum, *The Sovereignty Paradox: The Norms and Politics of International Statebuilding* (Oxford: Oxford University Press, 2007).

[62] ICISS, *The Responsibility to Protect*, pp. 17, 40.

common humanity'.[63] The notion of 'common humanity' usually refers to universal principles that are true for all men and woman for no other reason than they are human, which is to say they are neither willed nor enacted by any person or any legislature. And it is in virtue of these principles that all human beings are, by definition, subjects of equal moral concern. In other words, they provide a prescriptive benchmark in specifying how human beings should treat one another and they provide a standard against which to evaluate conventional arrangements, such as those relating to government, property, and positive law.[64]

Of course, the metaphysical vagaries of natural law are often all its takes to elicit fits of exasperation when it becomes apparent that these principles cannot be demonstrated in any empirical way. But insofar as their content is concerned we need not look any further than international human rights law and especially the UDHR, which after all is a pronouncement, indeed, a clarification, of principles that exist prior to their 'declaration'. Eleanor Roosevelt conveyed the underlying purpose of the UDHR, in an address before the General Assembly in 1948, as a 'common standard of achievement for all peoples of all nations', to which she added: '[t]his declaration is based upon the spiritual fact that man must have freedom in which to development [sic] his full stature and, through common effort, to raise the level of human dignity.'[65] The common standards to which she refers speak to conditions of life that are thought to be appropriate for all human beings; and because they are so appropriate there is a positive obligation to assist others in achieving them, which enhances respect for, and development of, the intrinsic worth and indestructible value of the human person. The natural law approach to obligation provides a way of saying that these things must be done irrespective of what the shifting sands of state interest might recommend.

When it comes to the responsibility to rebuild this approach to obligation does not disallow considerations of interest, nor does it discount the ways of power or the fact that interests, especially those of the great powers, are always at work. But it does require that rebuilding activities correspond with the demands of human dignity. Indeed, this requirement is hardly out of line with the declared aims of contemporary post-conflict reconstruction missions, which all converge on the view that the interests of states are as a matter of right leavened by the claims of individuals. Thus, the advantages of a natural law approach to obligation are obvious enough, for it makes not only sovereignty, but the state, the society of states, and international law, the servant of human flourishing, just as the ICISS report contemplates. It is an approach that requires rather than counsels a cooperative ethic of mutual assistance, according to which we should help our neighbours in realising their goals and protect them when they are in danger, even if they are distant strangers. Moreover, it is an approach that provides a standard against which to evaluate attempts at rebuilding war-torn territories, thereby linking human rights, democracy, and free market economy to the kind of life that is appropriate for all human beings; and it is for the sake of these things that states

---

[63] Gareth Evans, 'The Responsibility to Protect: An Idea Whose Time Has Come...and Gone?', Annual Lecture of the David Davies Memorial Institute, Aberystwyth University (23 April 2008), available at: {www.crisisgroup.org}.

[64] See Dyson, *Natural Law*, vol. 1, pp. xii.

[65] General Assembly, Third Session, Verbatim Record of the 180th Meeting, Held at the Palais de Chaillot, Paris (9 December 1948), A/PV 180, 62–3.

are required to act in respect of international legal obligations and for which they may be held responsible if they should fall short of the mark.

If we dig deep enough we shall find more than a faint residue of this kind of thinking in the ICISS report and in the writings of its most enthusiastic advocates. Indeed, the underlying rationale of the responsibility to protect, protecting people from war crimes, genocide, and crimes against humanity, is largely unintelligible without the help of natural law concepts and categories. The problem is that the appeal of natural law argument is not persuasive to a great many who hear it. Natural law has been criticised for a number of reasons, including a problematic relation between rationality and morality, doubts about the moral certainty of universal principles, and, for those who would set themselves up as the spokesmen for all humanity, an essentialist conception of human nature.[66] So if we dig deeper still we might find that that intrinsic value and inherent dignity of the human being is rather like an onion: 'peel away layer after layer and you are left, not with the "essential" or "natural" onion, but with nothing at all'.[67] It is at this point that we are left with little alternative than argument from convention, a version of which holds out the advantage of recognising the moral significance of difference while leaving open the possibility of agreement on moral action. The value of difference is preserved because there is no pre-existing moral law, expressing a common humanity, with which difference must conform in order to be valuable. In this way convention furnishes a response to the reality that we must cooperate with others to satisfy our wants and desires, albeit in a world that is home to many interests, some of which overlap while others conflict.

Unlike natural law, which is intelligible in terms of pre-existing or objective moral precepts, convention appeals to will and interest, which is to say it is created rather than discovered. In an important sense convention is arbitrary, although, as Leslie Green explains, the arbitrariness of convention should not be taken to mean that it is without purpose and, therefore, value.[68] That Americans drive on the right side of the road and Britons on the left is an arbitrary decision; but the purpose and the value of these arbitrary conventions is to promote the public interest of helping motorists arrive safely at their destinations. Thus, convention finds its footing in the world of common interest and its value is measured by the principle of utility – that is, the extent to which it is beneficial to the parties that participate in convention. In other words, the normative force of convention derives, not from its content, which is determined arbitrarily, but from satisfaction of relevant interests.[69] Of course, argument from convention holds out its own distinctive advantages, especially in a world that lacks a sovereign to enforce agreements. The authenticity of convention does not depend on effective enforce-ment, so that it is possible to speak of the declaratory (as opposed to legal) rights contained in the UDHR as part of a conventional (global) culture of human rights. Likewise, a convention might serve common interests but it does not (necessarily) entail an equal distribution of benefits, just as the institution of great power responsibility involves recognition of differences in power and differences in privilege so that all states might secure their (common) interest in peace and

---

[66] See Dyson, *Natural Law*, vol. 2, chap. 8.
[67] R. W. Dyson, 'Natural Law as a Problem in Moral Philosophy', Unpublished Paper (2005).
[68] Leslie Green, *The Authority of the State* (Oxford: Clarendon Press, 1988), pp. 89–90.
[69] Ibid., p. 93.

security. Indeed, convention provides an empirically ascertainable statement of common interest, rather than a metaphysical statement of universal right, which is both concrete social fact and concrete framework of action.[70]

Attractive though such an approach might appear, especially when scepticism undermines belief in a (metaphysical) universal moral law, argument from convention might not be strong enough to sustain the aspirations of the ICISS project. For the platform of interest and utility on which convention is founded also presupposes the fact that conformity with convention is fundamentally conditional.[71] Convention is a source of stability insofar as it cultivates regularity in expectation and action; and justice arises, not in compliance with law, but in recognition of the advantages that might be had by participating in convention. Thus, self-interest is the mother of justice, which is transformed into mutual interest once we realise that satisfaction of our interest entails satisfying the interests of others. And in recognition of this state of affairs a sense of obligation arises, albeit in a much weaker version than in natural law thinking, for the obligation to comply with rules of justice is tied to the satisfaction of these interests rather than the moral necessity of law.[72] Crucially, then, there is no existential good prior to convention because conforming with convention, such as keeping promises, produces whatever good might be had. Indeed, that good is the consequence of convention places emphasis on maintaining the convention before the exigencies of particular circumstances, hence Hume's suggestion that 'however single acts of justice may be contrary, either to public or private interest, it is certain that the whole plan or scheme is highly conducive, or indeed absolutely requisite, both to the support of society, and the well-being of every individual'.[73] There are times, then, to take his argument further, when injustice should be tolerated for the sake of the whole, such as injustice that arises in respect of sovereignty and non-intervention, because 'this momentary ill is amply compensated by the steady prosecution of the rule'.[74]

This voice too is plainly audible in contemporary world affairs, although it presents problems for the responsibility to rebuild that are no less daunting than those posed by a natural law approach. The emphasis on interests as the bedrock of convention, which, in turn, transform obligation into a motive of action, throws the door open to a kind of diversity that is at odds with the ICISS report. For once the notion of 'good' is relegated to a consequence of convention, and it is no longer something which activates or guides moral sentiment, there is no reason to privilege human rights, democracy, and free market economy as necessary goals of post-conflict reconstruction. There is no intrinsic human dignity to develop in respect of these goals. Indeed, there is little scope for evaluating the justice of convention, provided they offer a serviceable way of doing things, which is to admit decidedly illiberal customs and illiberal societies to the fold. And it is at this point that an ordinary Afghan's defence of the Taliban must be taken seriously: '[w]e have no TV. We can't listen to music. We don't have parties [...] But at least

---

[70] Ibid., pp. 93–4, 118.
[71] Ibid., p. 121.
[72] Hume, *Political Writings*, pp. 7–20.
[73] Hume, *Political Writings*, p. 17; and Schneewind, *The Invention of Autonomy*, pp. 368–73.
[74] Hume, *Political Writings*, p. 17.

we have security and justice.'[75] For the *modus vivendi* that is the achievement of convention begins to show its weakness once recognition of common interest begins to fray, perhaps to the delight of the persistent objector, at which point force assumes a place of especial importance in prolonging the life of convention. The problem, then, is that convention offers a kind of (contingent) truth, born of social fact, in place of metaphysical Truth, but its greatest advantage – facilitating cooperation in a condition of difference – is also its greatest weakness. For an agreement fashioned out of contingent interest is also vulnerable to the contingency of interest; and nowhere is this vulnerability more acute than when people require protection from egregious abuse. Convention offers a conditional answer when, more often than not, the seriousness of the situation demands one that is unconditional.

The wages of thought

An objection might be lodged at this point on grounds that the concerns raised in this article are those of an academic, and to that extent they have little relevance to real-life situations that call-out for urgent attention. Indeed, these concerns are likely to strike advocates of the responsibility to protect as trivial, even jejune, when placed alongside the immediacy of wanton massacre and ethnic cleansing. But responding in such a way is to indulge a version of the error committed by those who parry criticism of the responsibility to protect as *prima facie* evidence of bad faith or other less honourable motives. It is an error nonetheless. That the satisfaction of practical concerns should be made the test of worthwhile scholarship is a most unfortunate prejudice that misunderstands both the nature of theoretical reflection and the bearing that 'thinking' or 'thought' has on human conduct and how it is interpreted. It supposes that ideas, beliefs, and arguments are somehow separated from real-life experience, thereby severing any meaningful relation between abstract concepts and the goings-on of the 'real world'. For it fails to understand that after acknowledging the 'gap between thinking and experience', as J. G. A. Pocock describes it, the task of the theorist becomes one of inhabiting the gap with a view to understanding the immanent coherence of various ideas, beliefs, and arguments, and how they are employed in the context of action in particular situations. In other words, the gap between theoretical reflection and the desire to solve practical problems is not as great as it is sometimes thought: '[t]o solve a theoretical problem may have practical implications and, conversely, to state and solve a practical problem may raise new problems of wider generality.'[76]

It is a failure to appreciate the relation between 'thought' and 'experience' that leads Arbour (and others) to overstep the mark in confusing 'political usefulness' and 'intellectual clarity'.[77] Thus, in reflecting on 'the way forward' the authors of

---

[75] Anand Gopal, 'Some Afghans Live Under Taliban Rule – and Prefer It' (15 October 2008), available at: {www.csmonitor.com}.

[76] J. G. A. Pocock, 'The History of Political Thought: A Methodological Inquiry (1962)', *Political Thought and History: Essays on Theory and Method* (Cambridge: Cambridge University Press, 2009), pp. 5, 12–3, 17.

[77] Arbour, 'The responsibility to protect', pp. 457–8.

The Responsibility to Protect address the moral appeal of the argument, observing that '[g]etting the moral motive to bite means [...] being able to convey a sense of urgency and reality about the threat to human life in a particular situation.'[78] This is a most puzzling assessment of what is required to communicate the appeal of the argument, moral or otherwise. It is not a matter of effective marketing: publicising heart-wrenching images of rape camps, mass graves, and distended bellies of starving children. Nor is it matter of disseminating disclaimers as part of a public education programme, such as 'sovereignty may be hazardous to your health', in much the same way that cigarette packets carry warnings about the risks of smoking, often with the help of graphic images to drive home the point. The moral appeal of the responsibility to protect rests on the extent to which it is persuasive to those who hear it, which is to reduce the scope of the problem to a rather simple proposition, the satisfaction of which is infinitely demanding. The difficulty, then, is not found in the challenge of connecting the urgency and reality of particular situations with an appropriate (moral) motive; it is found in an over-emphasis on 'responsibility' which, for all its attractiveness, cannot bear the weight placed on it.

At this point experience must give way to thought. The burden of persuasion must shift from the invocation of symbols and images to an engagement that is the vocation of the theorist: an exploration of the rational coherence of ideas and arguments.[79] So we might all agree that the responsibility to protect finds support in existing international law, as Arbour argues; and we might also agree that this legal basis is buttressed by the declarations of the General Assembly and the decisions of the Security Council. But it is also true that legal realities are often confounded by philosophical problems. And if the responsibility to protect is to command widespread assent, as its authors hope, then these philosophical problems must be addressed in order to persuade those who hear but are not yet persuaded. For concern with practical problems, such as protecting civilians from state-sponsored slaughter, must at some point involve theoretical reflection on the ends of life as well as the prudential considerations that go with realising them. Otherwise we shall be left with an irresolvable shouting match between the 'righteous', who possess an all too sure sense of what morality requires, and the 'sceptical', who see morality as an charade or an inconvenience that stands before what they want.

In the end, the world must be made safe from both of these views by investing in the responsibility to protect a coherence that it presently lacks. I have attempted to interrogate two contrasting but pervasive accounts of obligation in order to clarify the 'sovereignty as responsibility' principle and how it might be connected to 'international responsibility to protect' principle. The argument from nature soars among the most ambitious aspirations of the ICISS project, an integral part of which is the development of human dignity by helping others build societies that respect human rights, adopt democratic values, and embrace free markets – all being parts of a life that is appropriate for all human beings. In contrast, the argument from convention remains securely tethered to the sensible world of social fact in seeking agreement in common, empirically ascertainable, subjective interests. Here, human rights, democracy and free market economy might be the ends

---

[78] ICISS, *The Responsibility to Protect*, p. 71.
[79] This thought is derived from Pocock, 'The History of Political Thought', p. 18.

for which societies aspire, but not necessarily so. The point of engaging these accounts of obligation should not be seen as the penultimate step before taking up a position in one camp or the other, thereby anointing a winner; it is, rather, to recognise that we are heirs to both approaches and to their peculiar advantages and disadvantages. For there is surely a compelling urge to seek security of belief in the demonstrable world of agreement, which provides proof of the world as it 'really' is; and yet what is often expressed in terms of interest and agreement finds its bearing from a presumed universal moral unity that is perhaps so obvious and so fundamental that most people do not think to call into question. In that, James Brierly was no doubt right; and yet we are still left to wonder if it is something in which we can really believe.

Review of International Studies (2010), 36, 47–54   © *2010 British International Studies Association*
doi:10.1017/S0260210511000088

A responsibility to reality: a reply to Louise Arbour

STEPHANIE CARVIN*

Abstract. Louise Arbour presents a pleasant picture of international society in her article on 'Responsibility to protect' (R2P) as a 'duty of care' – one where states not only have a moral responsibility but also a legal responsibility to intervene in some of the worst situations on the planet. However, this argument is misleading and based on faulty legal assumptions which pose significant problems for Arbour's case. This response will argue that upon examination, Arbour's legal case is not very strong or persuasive. Even more importantly, even if we accepted Arbour's legal arguments, it would not make much of a difference to how states respond to international crises. Arbour seems to misunderstand that the problems facing R2P have always been those of 'will' and not law – and this must be understood as a political rather than legal problem.

Stephanie Carvin is a Lecturer in International Relations at Royal Holloway, University of London. She holds a PhD from the London School of Economics and is the author of *Prisoners of America's Wars: From the Early Republic to Guantanamo* published by Columbia/Hurst in 2010. In 2009 she was a Visiting Scholar at George Washington University Law School during her sabbatical and has worked as a consultant to the US Department of Defense Law of War Working Group and the American Red Cross' Educating International Humanitarian Law Project. She currently researches in the areas of humanitarianism, international law, the war on terror and International Relations history.

It is with some trepidation that one challenges the understanding of both international law and politics of a former prosecutor of an international criminal tribunal, but the intention of this article is to do just that. Certainly, Arbour paints a nice picture in her article on 'The responsibility to protect' (R2P); a world where states not only recognise that the international community has a duty to protect their own citizens and the citizens of other countries from war crimes and genocide – but also that there may in fact be a legally enforceable duty to do so. In fact, no one is allowed to claim the status of 'impotent and powerless bystander'.[1] Yet, bursting this bubble of legal optimism is the fact that her arguments are based on legal assertions which are questionable or, at the very least, a problematic assessment of the politics of international law. Again, given Arbour's pedigree, I do not say this lightly. However, Arbour's contentions create a gap between

---

* I would like to thank Professor Chris Brown and two reviewers for their helpful comments on this response.
[1] Louise Arbour, 'The responsibility to protect as a duty of care in international law and practice', *Review of International Studies*, 34 (2008), pp. 445–58, 445.

understandings, expectations and capabilities (including willingness) so great as to cast a shadow over her legal thought-experiment.

This article will make three challenges to Arbour's assertion that states may have signed up for a legally-liable responsibility to protect. First, that legally there is no obligation and Arbour is incorrect to rely so heavily on the 1948 Genocide Convention and the recent International Court of Justice's (ICJ) 2007 decision in Bosnia-Herzegovinia vs. Serbia and Montenegro (*Bosnian Genocide Case*).[2] Second, even if such an obligation could be construed, it would not be a helpful or useful tool of international politics for R2P advocates because it does not help us answer the hard questions of R2P. Third, while there needs to be more research and academic commentary on R2P, this research is best done with a 'responsibility to reality' – that is R2P advocates must work within an imperfect world and UN system where this revolutionary idea remains an essentially contested concept. Attempts to create a legal entrapment for states out of a hodgepodge of international treaties and newly emerging norms do not actually advance the cause of R2P.

Legal liability?

Arbour predominantly rests her argument on Article 1 of the Convention on the Prevention and Punishment of the Crime of Genocide of 9 December 1948 (the Genocide Convention). This is the article which confirms 'that genocide, whether committed in time of peace or in time of war, is a crime under international law' and that signatories to the Convention will 'undertake to prevent and to punish'. Arbour's emphasis is on this last point, noting that this is 'an undisputed obligation of international law'.[3] This is combined with the decision in the *Bosnian Genocide Case* to provide an argument that there has emerged an international legal 'duty of care' when it comes to stopping the crimes outlined in R2P. For Arbour, the judgement which found that Serbia and Montenegro had failed in its obligation to prevent Genocide in neighbouring Bosnia, has strong implications for all states:

Might the judgement [...] also carry responsibilities not only for Serbia and its surrogates in Bosnia Herzegovina, but also to other States parties to the Convention, and indeed to the wider international community? Certainly the logic of the judgement would suggest such an assumption.[4]

She continues this line of reasoning regarding the responsibilities of the great powers of the Security Council:

If [the responsibility of the Permanent Five Members of the UN Security Council] were to be measured in accordance with the International Court of Justice's analysis, it would seem logical to assume that a failure to act could carry legal consequences and even more so

[2] International Court of Justice, *Case Concerning the Application of the Application of the Convention on the Prevention and Punishment of the Crime of Genocide (Bosnia and Herzegovina vs. Serbia and Montenegro)*, General List, no. 91 (26 February 2007), available at: {http://www.icj-cij.org/docket/files/91/13685.pdf}.
[3] Louise Arbour, 'The responsibility to protect', p. 450.
[4] Ibid., p. 451.

when the exercise or threat of a veto would block action that is deemed necessary by other members to avert genocide, or crimes against humanity.[5]

There are three problems with this line of reasoning. First, The International Court of Justice's decision in the *Bosnian Genocide Case* indicated that responsibility for the failure to prevent genocide only exists if genocide (or any of the activities outlined in Article III of the Convention) actually occurs.[6] This is relatively straightforward; it would be bizarre to prosecute a country for failure to prevent an action which never happens. But given the difficulty of actually recognising the occurrence of genocide as defined in international law, this also seems highly problematic. That ICJ judges recently rejected Prosecutor Luis Moreno Ocampo's argument to charge Sudanese President Omar al-Bashir with genocide because there was not enough evidence is a good example of this.[7] The crime of genocide requires proof of a special intent (*dolus specialis*) whereby the crimes committed must be done with the intent 'to destroy, in whole or in part, a national, ethnical, racial or religious group'. Without evidence of this special intent, genocide, by definition, cannot be said to be taking place. Bashir is, of course, accused of other international crimes, but, significantly, there seems to be a serious problem with Arbour's argument if the starting point for her obligation is frequently difficult and sometimes impossible to apply given its tricky definition.

To be clear, this is not to imply that the declaration of genocide must be *ex post facto*. The ICJ found that the plausible risk of genocide was sufficient to trigger a duty to prevent.[8] However, this does not take away from the fact that the risk must actually be 'real' (as far as risks can be). Yet the Court did not really indicate as to how such a determination was to be made or which criteria were to be used. The judgment does say that the Serbian government 'could hardly have been unaware of the serious risk' of genocide, and refers to facts that certain government officials likely knew that certain actions were going be taken as evidence.[9] Whether or not this constitutes a legal standard is not clear – or if it does, it remains a vague one. Therefore, the contention here is that the fundamental problem of determining the risk or existence of a genocide in order to trigger an international legal obligation to prevent largely remains.

Secondly, the ICJ recognised that the Genocide Convention is not the only legal instrument which creates a legal obligation for an activity for states to prevent. Rather, there are similar obligations for states to take measures against torture, harm against internationally protected persons and terrorism.[10] However, the

---

[5] Arbour, Ibid., p. 453.

[6] Judgement, para. 431.

[7] Although the judges argued that these charges could be reinstated with more evidence. On appeal genocide charges were issued against al-Bashir in a second warrant in July 2010. See the press release 'Pre-Trial Chamber I issues a second warrant of arrest against Omar al-Bashir for counts of genocide', International Criminal Court website (12 July 2010). Available at: {http://www.icc-cpi.int/NR/exeres/E9BD8B9F-4076-4F7C-9CAC-E489F1C127D9.htm}.

[8] Judgment, para. 430.

[9] Ibid., para. 436.

[10] Specifically, the Court acknowledged: the Convention against Torture and Other Cruel, Inhuman or Degrading Treatment or Punishment of 10 December 1984 (Article 2); the Convention on the Prevention and Punishment of Crimes against Internationally Protected Persons, Including Diplomatic Agents, of 14 December 1973 (Article 4); the Convention on the Safety of UN and Associated Personnel of 9 December 1994 (Article 11); the International Convention on the Suppression of Terrorist Bombings of 15 December 1997 (Article 15). Judgement, para. 429.

Court limited its judgement in an important ways that Arbour does not seem to acknowledge. The Court was clear that it did not 'purport to establish a general jurisprudence applicable to all cases where a treaty instrument, or other binding legal norm, includes an obligation for States to prevent certain acts.' Additionally, the Court refrained from finding that 'apart from the texts applicable to specific fields, there is a general obligation on States to prevent the commission by other persons or entities of acts contrary to certain norms of general international law.' Therefore, the Court confined itself to making its determination in the *Bosnian Genocide Case* to 'the specific scope of the duty to prevent in the Genocide Convention'. The application of the decision to create a legal principle of R2P seems contrary to the Court's pronouncement.[11]

Consequently, the level of precedent-setting for this decision, at least in the way that Arbour wants to use it, is very questionable. In fact, it is very strange that she relies on the judgement so heavily after such a warning by the Court was given. That international lawyers are often creative in their uses of the law or in their interpretations is one thing, but in this case, the Court seems rather clear about its intention and on the limitations of its judgement. While it is, perhaps, indicative of the kinds of findings the ICJ or other international criminal tribunals may produce in the future, Arbour should have been clearer about the Court's position on the uses of the judgement and her intention in invoking the decision as a basis of her claims.

Finally, and this is, perhaps, the most straightforward critique, is that while there can be little doubt that the Convention states that parties undertake to prevent genocide, the guidance as to what exactly 'prevent' means is not particularly useful. The Convention states that any contracting party may 'call upon the competent organs of the UN to take such action under the Charter of the UN as they consider appropriate.'[12] In other words, 'prevention' in the Convention is understood as bringing the matter back to the UN Security Council and General Assembly – the very problematic (or at least ineffective) forums which R2P advocates are seemingly trying to cajole into action. This is even more so in highly politicised cases which may divide the international community.

Additionally, there is no guidance as to who should make a determination that genocide is to take place, who should prevent it and what kind of international approval they would need. As Arbour points out, the Court did offer some guidance on these issues – but essentially this amounts to vague calculations of an obligation arising 'at the instant that the State learns of, or should normally have learned of, the existence of a serious risk that genocide will be committed.'[13] As for who should do the intervening, the Court in the *Bosnian Genocide Case* suggests a fuzzy combination of factors comprising a 'capacity to influence' made up of geographical proximity, political links, 'as well as links of all other kinds, between the authorities of that State and the main actors in the events'.[14] Despite Arbour's assertions, the reality is that this list is not very specific and not very helpful. Certainly none of this seems to constitute a clear, direct nor novel legal standard.

[11] Judgement, para. 429.
[12] 1948 Convention on the Prevention and Punishment of the Crime of Genocide, Article VIII.
[13] Judgement, para. 431.
[14] Judgement, para. 430.

The hard part

But this brings us to the second major critique of Arbour's argument – that even if a legal obligation could be established, the model that Arbour suggests is not helpful because such an obligation could not truly provide any guidance on the 'tough' questions about R2P. Just some of these questions include exactly who may intervene, under what kind of mandate, for how long and where – questions which have plagued debates over humanitarian intervention for decades. Can international law really help us answer them?

Two points may be raised here which suggest not. First, it is one thing to establish a law, principle or even a norm – it is quite another to change practices. As the saying has it, 'old habits die hard' – and this is also true for international bodies like the UN. As Alex J. Bellamy (a strong R2P advocate) writes, even when the international community is armed with criteria:

> [D]ecisions about intervention will continue to be made in an ad hoc fashion by political leaders balancing national interests, legal consideration, world opinion, perceived costs and humanitarian impulses – much as they were prior to the advent of R2P.[15]

If we have learned anything about international law in the last 20 years, if not the last century, it is that its existence rarely delivers consensus.

Yet, for the sake of argument (and the second point), let us assume that Arbour's case for the establishment of a 'duty of care' is broadly accepted by the international community. Other than establishing this liability, what else does Arbour's argument help us decide about R2P? The answer is not much. Of course establishing that states now have a burden to 'take action under the doctrine of responsibility to protect'[16] might be a small step forward, but other than this, it does not help international society answer the really difficult questions concerning the commitment required of states or over authorisation and participation.

Bellamy suggests that there are at least four major problems with prevention in terms of R2P: (1) it is difficult to discern measures which are directed specifically at preventing the international crimes listed by R2P (genocide, war crimes, crimes against humanity and ethnic cleansing) and those which relate more broadly to conflict prevention more generally; (2) there is an absence of limits on what exactly constitutes prevention (which may make states reluctant to commit themselves); (3) do preventative measures lead to additional encroachments on sovereignty; and (4) who should do the prevention work? As it stands the doctrine is unclear as to what sorts of agencies should take the lead.[17]

The establishment of a duty of care under a doctrine of R2P does not help establish answers to these questions. While the decision in the *Bosnian Genocide Case* does provide some rough guidance (as discussed above), this is of much less use and direction than Arbour implies. Bellamy suggests that part of the problem is that the understanding of 'prevention' in the 2001 R2P report issued by the International Commission on Intervention and State Sovereignty (ICISS) was concerned with internal wars more generally as well as other man-made crises

---

[15] Alex J. Bellamy, *Responsibility to Protect: The Global Effort to End Mass Attrocities* (Cambridge: Polity, 2009). p. 3.
[16] Arbour, 'The responsibility to protect', p. 449.
[17] Bellamy, *Responsibility to Protect*, pp. 99–100.

compared to the rather narrow international criminal focus in the 2005 World Summit outcome document.[18] The prevention requirements of the former understanding of R2P would, out of necessity, require a much wider focus, but whether this could be said for genocide, war crimes, ethnic cleansing, etc., is questionable.

This is not to say that the Court's judgment rendered the understanding of Article 1 of the Genocide Convention less clear or more confusing. Rather, it is to suggest that the Court's judgment may be significantly less novel and important that what Arbour is suggesting in her argument. If R2P is to become some sort of basis for international action or transformed into a legal principle, (based on Arbour's reading of the Judgment in *Bosnia vs. Serbia*) the questions outlined above are the ones that international lawyers will still have to wrangle with. In this way, Arbour's obligation seems to be little more than papering over a giant chasm of disagreements between R2P stakeholders. With all of the right intentions, it is still a roadmap to nowhere that gets us only a little past the first of many, many intersections.

Realistic R2P?

Answers, or compromise solutions, to these difficult questions will probably not be worked out in law so much as they will be determined through negotiations at various international organisations. This is something I am sure Arbour is aware of. Yet, a third line of critique which can be raised against her assertions is that Arbour is, at the very least, ignoring certain facts of world politics to the great detriment of her argument. At the end of the day the effective realisation of her legal thought-experiment entails a remaking of the world order. If nothing else, it would require a further revolution in the notion of state sovereignty – certainly beyond that which the Non-Aligned Movement and certain great powers like the US would be comfortable with.[19] There can be no question that R2P is a revolution in the notion of 'sovereignty', but translating this into a legally enforceable responsibility is, politically speaking, taking R2P to a whole new level. Whether such a revolution could be brought about in the present day and age by a group of lawyers and R2P advocates is highly suspect. Certainly a fairly small group of diplomats, politicians, international bureaucrats and activists were highly successful in getting the issue on the agenda at the 2005 World Summit. However, the long and arduous process of negotiation process required to get a very slimmed down version of R2P (derisively or depressingly referred to as 'R2P Lite') in the World Summit Outcome document as well as certain scepticism over the concept suggests that, at least for now, there are limits as to how far the doctrine can go. As Gareth Evans has written, by 2008 the Latin American, Arab and African delegates to the UN's budget committee flatly denied that R2P was even ever adopted by the General Assembly.[20]

---

[18] Bellamy, *Responsibility to Protect*, p. 100.
[19] In speaking off-record with government officials from the UK and US familiar with this issue and in a position to know, they all remarked that their governments would not have signed the World Summit Outcome Document if they felt it created a legal obligation for their state to intervene in a crisis. Interviews conducted by the author, London/Washington 2009.
[20] Gareth Evans, 'The Responsibility to Protect: An Idea Whose Time Has Come ... and Gone?', *International Relations*, 22:3 (2008), pp. 283–298, 288.

Is it then fair to speak of a 'responsibility to reality'? Reality is, of course, subjective and notoriously hard to judge. However, what does seem to be very clear is the fact that R2P advocates are going to have to work within a political system to achieve their goals rather than creating contrived legal obligations through stringing together vague and unenforceable laws and/or case law. It is very much a political system that allows for much scepticism, obstruction and provides for a lot of frustration. Yet, that some lawyers, like Arbour, often seem to want to leap over this international political system through asserting a supposedly neutral law is not, in the end, helping their cause. Additionally, it is not helping to solve the larger problems posed by the issues of sovereignty and intervention in the 21st Century. After its adoption by the World Summit in 2005 and the Security Council (Resolution 1674) in 2006, it is fair to say that R2P is an emerging principle in international society. Even better, it may yet work in creating a common language in which action may be debated and plans to help solve some of the world's worst problems may be asserted. R2P may actually work – but it is difficult to imagine that it will work in such a way as to effectively trap states into obligations into which they have not given their consent.

During the negotiation process leading up to the World Summit, the US consistently resisted the argument that the international obligation to protect was on the same level as the domestic duty of states. The notion that the Security Council could also be legally obliged to intervene was also criticised with then-US Ambassador to the UN John Bolton asserting that there needed to be the freedom to decide on courses of action on a case-by-case basis:

> The UN member states recognised their responsibility to protect their own citizens but *did not* recognise a responsibility to act beyond using peaceful means in cases of mass killing, genocide and ethnic cleansing. Instead, they simply reaffirmed their *preparedness* to use other measures if they saw fit – a significantly lower standard.[21]

If, as Bellamy suggests, the problem with humanitarian intervention is one of willingness rather than ability or even obligation to do so, asserting that a legal duty of care exists will accomplish little. The problem of 'will' should be understood as a problem of politics and not a problem of law.

Conclusion

Ultimately, the intention in this article is to not be defeatist but pragmatic. There can be little doubt that engagement with states on the brink of major catastrophe is good for all involved. The great hope of R2P is that it will provide a language for debate when it comes to addressing genocide and war crimes. Still, given these dilemmas that will inevitably arise, I do not think that sending in the lawyers is a good solution.

The difficulties of Arbour's argument go beyond a general concern as to what is the best approach for implementing R2P. It rests on particular interpretations of both the Genocide Convention and international criminal law that are far from unimpeachable. But even if we were to allow for Arbour's legal argument, it is

---

[21] Bellamy, *The Responsibility to Protect*, p. 90.

questionable as to how useful the founding of such an obligation would be for the international community.

It is not that establishing a legal obligation would hinder the implementation of R2P. Rather, the argument here is that Arbour's legal construction really does not bring anything new (that is practical) to the table. In truth, given its 2005 manifestation in the World Outcome Document, this may be a critique that could be levied at R2P in general – that, as indicated above, it does little else than provide a new vocabulary in which to discuss old issues.

However, keeping the focus on Arbour, it is clear that the supposed novelty of her argument is to suggest that states are under a legally enforceable 'duty of care' to which they may be held to account in cases of genocide and crimes against humanity. A summary of a response here is that such an obligation cannot really be said to legally exist. Additionally, such an obligation, even if it did exist, would not be particularly useful because other than establishing a 'duty', it does not really answer the 'hard questions' of R2P (such as who may or must intervene, where, when and under whose mandate). These are the giant obstacles that have thus far prevented meaningful action in cases where human security is threatened.

Of course, Arbour does not suggest that the judgment in *Bosnia vs. Serbia* and its implications will solve all political problems related to intervention and R2P. However, it is clear that she feels that such a legal obligation offers new norms, guidance and obligations in international society for states, particularly powerful states, faced with the possibility of a case of genocide. Arbour's contention that states are now under a legal 'duty of care' to prevent and punish genocide and crimes against humanity, can therefore be read as a radical theoretical challenge to notions of sovereignty and the understanding of the responsibility of states.

But practically speaking, her proposal does not add much in the way of clarity or usefulness in answering the tough questions of R2P. In addition, such an obligation would, without a doubt, be rejected by states who continue to be caught-up in the deficient practice of international politics and their own self-interest. This is particularly so when one considers that any fulfilment of her legal proposition is likely to bring the matter right back to the very institutions which have thus far proved inept and ineffective at preventing threats to human security, particularly the UN. In this sense, Arbour's argument actually becomes less novel and perhaps an almost tragic idea. The establishment of legal liability on neighbours or great powers will not get bickering states past the big challenges of R2P, such as what constitutes 'prevention'?, who is responsible?, and what may be done to effectively carry out 'prevention' while working within the framework of the UN Charter? Such challenges will likely be solved in an *ad hoc* manner, in times of urgency, by less-than-perfect international political forums. Advocates of a realistic responsibility would do well to keep this in mind.

Review of International Studies (2010), 36, 55–78 © *2010 British International Studies Association*
doi:10.1017/S0260210510000446

The responsibility to protect – much ado about nothing?

THERESA REINOLD

Abstract. Despite its newness, the concept of the responsibility to protect (R2P) looks back at a stellar career. It has been the subject of numerous conferences and academic publications and has been affirmed by the major UN bodies. Indeed, if one were to assess the development of an international norm by the amount of academic attention and general rhetorical support it enjoys, one could be inclined to believe that the responsibility to protect is rapidly evolving into a norm of customary international law.

This article subjects the R2P hype to critical scrutiny and asks probing questions about R2P's viability as a norm. Beneath the thin veneer of rhetorical acceptance of R2P lies a range of hotly disputed issues – in particular but not exclusively regarding the concept's implications for the use of force – which are unlikely to be resolved in the near future. In this article I examine R2P's potential to 'ripen' into an international norm. I argue that in the absence of an intersubjective consensus about what R2P actually *means*, the concept's chances to 'harden' into a norm of customary international law are remote. I posit that R2P cannot be considered a 'new norm' or an 'emerging norm' as it is frequently called, because the vast majority of states simply does not want to be legally bound to save strangers in remote regions of the world.

Theresa Reinold earned her PhD from Tuebingen University in 2009 and is currently a Postdoctoral Research fellow at Goethe University in Frankfurt, Germany. Previously, she worked as a research assistant at the German Institute for International and Security Affairs in Berlin. Her dissertation explored the development of the concept of sovereignty as responsibility into a norm of customary international law. In her postdoctoral research, Ms. Reinold analyses the interaction between regional and global constitutionalism, focusing in particular on the law-making contributions of subaltern actors such as the African Union to constitutionalisation processes at the global level.

Which landmark event did the international community commemorate on 9 December 2008? Anybody? Anybody? Few people would probably recollect that on 9 December 1948 the Genocide Convention[1] was adopted, which represented a (futile) attempt to save succeeding generations from the scourge of the most odious crime of all odious crimes. Six decades after the signing of the Genocide Convention we must ask ourselves how far the international community has come in preventing massive human rights violations since 1948. The responsibility to protect (R2P) is the modern variant of the duty to prevent which the Genocide Convention posited (somewhat vaguely) sixty years ago. Despite its newness, the

---

[1] Convention on the Prevention and Punishment of the Crime of Genocide, {http://www.unhchr.ch/html/menu3/b/p_genoci.htm}.

concept of R2P looks back at a stellar career. It has been the subject of numerous conferences and academic publications[2] and has been affirmed by the major UN bodies. Indeed, if one were to assess the development of an international norm by the amount of academic attention and general rhetorical support it enjoys, one could be inclined to believe that the responsibility to protect is rapidly evolving into a norm of customary international law.

This article subjects the R2P hype to critical scrutiny and asks probing questions about R2P's viability as a norm. The devil is in the details: beneath the thin veneer of rhetorical acceptance of R2P lies a range of hotly disputed issues – in particular but not exclusively[3] regarding the concept's implications for the use of force – which are unlikely to be resolved in the near future. While R2P encompasses three dimensions – the responsibility to prevent, to react, and to rebuild[4] – an examination of all of these dimensions would exceed the scope of this article, which focuses solely on the thorny issue of military intervention. At issue here is R2P's potential to ripen into an international norm – that is, an intersubjectively shared standard of appropriate behaviour. I argue that in the absence of an intersubjective consensus about what R2P actually *means*, the concept's chances to harden into a norm of customary international law are remote. The recent crisis in Burma following cyclone Nargis exposed the starkly diverging interpretations that states attach to the concept of R2P. The Burmese junta's deliberate obstruction of international relief efforts triggered a debate over whether this constitutes an R2P situation. To be sure, the Burmese junta is a despicable dictatorship, yet does its obstruction of relief efforts amount to crimes

---

[2] See, for example, Alicia L. Bannon, 'The Responsibility to Protect: The UN World Summit and the Question of Unilateralism', *Yale Law Journal*, 115:5 (March 2006), pp. 1157–65; Alex J. Bellamy, 'Whither the Responsibility to Protect? Humanitarian Intervention and the 2005 World Summit', *Ethics & International Affairs*, 20:2 (Summer 2006), pp. 143–69; Alex J. Bellamy and Paul D. Williams, 'The Responsibility to Protect and the Crisis in Darfur', *Security Dialogue*, 36:1 (2005), pp. 27–47; David Chandler, 'The Responsibility to Protect? Imposing the 'Liberal Peace', *International Peacekeeping*, 11:1 (Spring 2004), pp. 59–81; Graham Day and Christopher Freeman, 'Operationalizing the Responsibility to Protect – the Policekeeping Approach', *Global Governance*, 11:2 (April–June 2005), pp. 139–46; Amitai Etzioni, 'Sovereignty as Responsibility', *Orbis*, 50:1 (Winter 2006), pp. 71–85; Rebecca J. Hamilton, 'The Responsibility to Protect: From Document to Doctrine – But What of Implementation?', *Harvard Human Rights Journal*, 19 (Spring 2006), pp. 289–97; Victoria K. Holt and Tobias C. Berkman, *The Impossible Mandate? Military Preparedness, the Responsibility to Protect and Modern Peace Operations* (Washington, D.C.: The Henry L. Stimson Center, 2006); Jeremy L. Levitt, 'The Responsibility to Protect: A Beaver Without a Dam?', *Michigan Journal of International Law*, 25:1 (2003), pp. 153–77; William R. Pace and Nicole Deller, 'Preventing Future Genocides: An International Responsibility to Protect', *World Order*, 36:4 (2005), pp. 15–32; Carsten Stahn, 'Responsibility to Protect: Political Rhetoric or Emerging Legal Norm?', *American Journal of International Law*, 101:1 (2007), pp. 99–120; Ramesh Thakur, 'Outlook: Intervention, Sovereignty and the Responsibility to Protect: Experiences from ICISS', *Security Dialogue*, 33:3 (September 2002), pp. 323–40; Thomas G. Weiss, 'The Sunset of Humanitarian Intervention? The Responsibility to Protect in a Unipolar Era', *Security Dialogue*, 35:2 (June 2004), pp. 135–53; Nicholas J. Wheeler, 'The Humanitarian Responsibilities of Sovereignty: Explaining the Development of a New Norm of Military Intervention for Humanitarian Purposes in International Society', in Jennifer Welsh (ed.), *Humanitarian Intervention and International Relations* (Oxford: Oxford University Press, 2004), pp. 29–51.

[3] On the issue of legal liability and reparation, see Jose Alvarez, 'The Schizophrenias of R2P', panel presentation at the 2007 Hague Joint Conference on Contemporary Issues of International Law: Criminal Jurisdiction 100 Years After the 1907 Hague Peace Conference, The Hague (30 June 2007), pp. 11f, {http://www.asil.org/pdfs/r2pPanel.pdf}.

[4] International Commission on Intervention and State Sovereignty (ICISS), *The Responsibility to Protect* (Ottawa: International Development Research Centre, 2001), p. xi,{http://www.iciss.ca/pdf/Commission-Report.pdf}.

against humanity, which would then trigger the international community's responsibility to protect? French Foreign Minister Bernard Kouchner called for an activation of R2P and lobbied for a Security Council resolution forcing the Burmese government to accept outside aid.[5] Kouchner's rallying cry met with fierce opposition not only from China and other sovereigntist countries,[6] but also from NGO representatives, including some of the founders of the concept of R2P.[7] The criticism centered around questions of doctrine (is this really an R2P situation?) and feasibility (even if it is, would it be politically wise to enforce the delivery of aid against the will of the Burmese regime?).

The crisis in Burma has obviously thrown into sharp relief the lack of international consensus on the concept of R2P. In light of such dissent, I posit that R2P cannot be considered a 'new norm' or an 'emerging norm' as it is frequently called,[8] because the vast majority of states simply does not want to be legally bound to save strangers[9] in remote regions of the world. Despite the high-sounding rhetoric about R2P, sovereignty's constitutive norms – especially the non-use of force – have in fact not been replaced by a norm of responsibility (to be enforced militarily as a last resort) – therefore the international community has not moved 'beyond Westphalia'.[10]

Understanding institutional transformation – approaches from international relations and international law

Sovereignty is an institution which aggregates interrelated norms such as non-interference, domestic jurisdiction, diplomatic immunity, etc.[11] – norms which are produced, reproduced, and possibly transformed through the practices of states and other agents. Institutional change occurs when an institution's component norms are being transformed or replaced by new norms. The question that is at issue here is whether the rise of R2P has qualified the norms of non-interference and non-use of force, which in turn would signal a radical transformation of the institution of sovereignty. In order to conceptualise institutional transformation theoretically, we need to open the toolboxes of constructivist IR-theory and approaches to the formation of customary international law, which display striking similarities in their respective accounts of norm development.

---

[5] Jonathan Marcus, 'World Wrestles With Burma Aid Issue', *BBC News* (9 May 2008), {http://news.bbc.co.uk/2/hi/asia-pacific/7392662.stm}.

[6] Louis Charbonneau, 'China, Indonesia Reject France's Myanmar Push', Reuters.com (8 May 2008), {http://www.reuters.com/article/asiaCrisis/idUSN08518240}.

[7] See, for example, Ramesh Thakur, 'Should the UN Invoke the Responsibility to Protect?', *The Globe and Mail* (8 May 2008).

[8] See, for example, the report of the High-level Panel on Threats, Challenges, and Change, *A More Secure World: Our Shared Responsibility* (New York: UN, 2004), p. 57.

[9] Nicholas J. Wheeler, *Saving Strangers. Humanitarian Intervention in International Society* (Oxford: Oxford University Press, 2000).

[10] Gene M. Lyons and Michael Mastanduno (eds), *Beyond Westphalia? State Sovereignty and International Intervention* (Baltimore: Johns Hopkins University Press, 1995).

[11] Henning Boekle, Volker Rittberger, Wolfgang Wagner, *Norms and Foreign Policy: Constructivist Foreign Policy Theory* (Tübingen: Tübinger Arbeitspapiere zur Internationalen Politik und Friedensforschung, 1999), p. 21.

The agent-structure nexus provides the natural starting point for an analysis of international norm dynamics. Constructivists maintain that agents, through their discourses and practices, contribute to the production of international structure (international law being one element of this structure), while at the same time international structure shapes the identities and practices of agents.[12] The institution of sovereignty is therefore not a natural given but exists only in virtue of certain intersubjective understandings and in virtue of states acting in conformity with the rules it prescribes – sovereignty is an 'ongoing artifact of practice'.[13] Practices of (non-)recognition, of wars and interventions, as well as the language of justification contribute to the reproduction (and possibly, transformation) of sovereignty. In order to grasp institutional change, one must therefore not only study state practice, but also the discourses that form the conceptual universe in which state practice takes place. In discourses, actors debate how legitimate states should or should not act. States refer to particular norms or concepts to mobilise joint action, to explain unilateral action or to justify their abstention from or opposition to a certain course of action.[14]

The precise mechanism through which new international norms emerge from the practices and discourses of states and non-state actors is explored in Finnemore's and Sikkink's essay on 'International Norm Dynamics and Political Change'.[15] Finnemore and Sikkink model the 'life-cycle' of norms as a three-stage process. The first stage of norm emergence is characterised by the agenda-setting activities of norm entrepreneurs (NGOs, epistemic communities, states, etc.) who play a crucial role in raising the public profile of a particular grievance and in persuading a critical mass of states (norm leaders) that something needs to be done about it. When a critical mass of states has been convinced to embrace the norm candidate, a tipping point is reached, which triggers a 'norm cascade' (stage two). In many cases, transition from stage one to stage two is facilitated by the emergent norm's institutionalisation in specific sets of international rules or organisations. Upon successful completion of stage two, the norm acquires a taken-for-granted quality – 'norm internalization' occurs in the third and final stage of the process.[16]

Practices and discourses are crucial categories not only for constructivist researchers; they are equally indispensable for international legal scholars attempting to discern the formation of a rule of customary international law. In the Statute of the International Court of Justice, custom is defined as 'evidence of a general practice accepted as law'.[17] The formation of a customary norm thus requires two elements, state practice and a corresponding *opinio juris:* states must not only behave in a particular way, they must also believe that the practice is required by law. This definition of custom is problematic, however, because it implies that

[12] On the agent-structure nexus see David Dessler, 'What's at Stake in the Agent-Structure Debate?', *International Organization*, 43:3 (August 1989), pp. 441–73 (p. 452).
[13] Alexander Wendt, 'Anarchy is What States Make of It: the Social Construction of Power Politics', *International Organization*, 46:2 (April 1992), pp. 391–425 (p. 413).
[14] On the role of discourses see Albert S. Yee, 'The Causal Effects of Ideas on Policies', *International Organization*, 50:1 (February 1996), pp. 69–108 (pp. 95–8); and Jennifer Milliken, 'The Study of Discourse in International Relations: A Critique of Research and Methods', *European Journal of International Relations*, 5:2 (1999), pp. 225–54 (p. 229ff).
[15] Martha Finnemore and Kathryn Sikkink, 'International Norm Dynamics and Political Change', *International Organization*, 52:4 (November 1998), pp. 887–917.
[16] Ibid., pp. 895–904.
[17] Art. 38 of the ICJ-Statute, {http://www.icj-cij.org/documents/index.php?p1=4&p2=2&p3=0}.

states must believe that something already *is* law before it can become law. This formula in fact precludes normative change, because customary norms are transformed through *deviant* practice, that is, behaviour that is *not* in conformity with existing legal rules. D'Amato therefore defends a conception of customary law that allows for the transformation of *opinio juris* – or intersubjective understandings of proper behaviour, to use constructivist phraseology – triggered by states violating existing rules, which then eventually leads to a revision of existing normative beliefs: '[...] an "illegal" act by a state contains the seed of a new legality. When a state violates an existing rule of customary international law, it undoubtedly is "guilty" of an illegal act, but the illegal act itself becomes a disconfirmatory instance of the underlying rule. The next state will find it somewhat easier to disobey the rule, until eventually a new line of conduct will replace the original rule by a new rule.'[18]

This does not mean that the 'seed' sown by a law-violating state will always lead to the 'blossoming' of a new rule. If this were indeed the case, international law would cease to perform its stabilising function, that is, to guarantee a modicum of predictability in an otherwise very unpredictable world, which is the very basis of international law's compliance pull. Depending on the circumstances, rule-breaking may even ultimately lead to a strengthening of the rule in question, as the ICJ asserted in the *Nicaragua Case*, in which the customary rule of non-intervention was at issue. The Court held that whether states have successfully created a customary exception to the general norm of non-intervention depends partly on whether they 'justified their conduct by reference to a new right of intervention or a new exception to the principle of its prohibition'.[19] If the norm-violating states appeal to exceptions or justifications contained within the rule itself, the Court ruled, this will lead to a strengthening of this rule rather than to its erosion.[20] The ICJ Statute posits that state practice and its acceptance must be 'general'[21] – hence the reactions of other states (explicit support, tacit acquiescence, or outright condemnation) are an important determinant of whether law-breaking results in law-making: Only if an intersubjective consensus on the desirability of legal change exists will a new norm emerge. Methodologically speaking, the analysis of discourses which are constitutive of intersubjective meanings is therefore essential for the researcher wishing to understand how change in customary law occurs.[22]

Overall then, constructivism and theories of custom formation converge on a number of crucial points: Both accept that international legal rules are socially constructed, and both emphasise the significance of state practices and intersubjective beliefs, or *opinio juris*, respectively. Both IR and IL moreover share the assumption of a co-constitution of agents and structures: Whereas international legal scholars conceive of states as being simultaneously creators and subjects of

---

[18] Anthony D'Amato, *The Concept of Custom in International Law* (Ithaca: Cornell University Press, 1971), p. 97.
[19] International Court of Justice, *ICJ Reports 1986* ('s-Gravenhage: Sijthoff), p. 109.
[20] Ibid., p. 98.
[21] Supra note 17.
[22] On law as a 'linguistic affair' see Martti Koskenniemi, *From Apology to Utopia. The Structure of International Legal Argument*, re-issue with new epilogue (Cambridge: Cambridge University Press, 2005), p. 529.

the law,[23] this phenomenon has been discussed for quite some time under the heading of the agent-structure nexus in constructivist circles. Further, law is conceptualised as a dynamic social process, and not a static set of rules.[24] Finally, as explained above, both disciplines not only share fundamental premises but also employ similar research tools, that is, both delve into the study of discourses, in which the role of legal precedent and analogy – or normative fit, to use constructivist vocabulary – looms large.

The responsibility to protect – genesis of a concept

Although the International Commission on Intervention and State Sovereignty (ICISS) is usually credited for kicking off the debate over sovereignty as responsibility with the publication of its widely cited report *The Responsibility to Protect*,[25] it was in fact Francis Deng who introduced a broader audience to the notion of sovereignty as responsibility.[26] Deng *et al.* base their argument on the idea of a dual social contract – between each government and its citizens, and between nation states and the international community as a whole: 'The sovereign state's responsibility and accountability to both domestic and external constituencies must be affirmed as interconnected principles of the national and international order. Such a normative code is anchored in the assumption that in order to be legitimate, sovereignty must demonstrate responsibility.'[27] If a government manifestly fails to fulfil its part of the social contract, its claim to sovereign immunity becomes void. Consequently, discharging the responsibilities of sovereignty is in effect the best guarantee for sovereignty.[28] This notion of conditional sovereignty was reiterated in the ICISS report, which argued that 'state sovereignty implies responsibility, and the primary responsibility for the protection of its people lies with the state itself'.[29] However, if a state proves unwilling or unable to live up to its responsibilities, that is, if it violates basic human rights or does not prevent such violations, the international community has a residual responsibility to act. The principle of non-intervention thus yields to the international responsibility to protect.[30] This reflects a tendency in international law to view individuals, rather than states, as the primary beneficiaries of its protection, and to shift the focus of the debate from what the international community owes to sovereign states to the question of what nation-states owe to their own citizens.

---

[23] See Michael Byers, *Custom, Power, and the Power of Rules. International Relations and Customary International Law* (Cambridge: Cambridge University Press, 1999), p. 5.
[24] See, for example, Martha Finnemore's and Stephen Toope's interdisciplinary piece on 'Alternatives to "Legalization": Richer Views of Law and Politics', *International Organization*, 55:3 (August 2001), pp. 743–58 (p. 750), in which they describe international law as a dynamic social process.
[25] ICISS, supra note 4.
[26] Francis M. Deng, Sadikiel Kimaro, Terrence Lyons, Donald Rothchild and William I. Zartman, *Sovereignty as Responsibility. Conflict Management in Africa* (Washington D.C.: Brookings, 1996).
[27] Ibid., p. xvii.
[28] Ibid., pp. 1, 15.
[29] ICISS, supra note 4, p. xi.
[30] Ibid., p. xi.

Borrowing from just war theory,[31] the ICISS report listed a number of legitimacy criteria that should guide intervention on behalf of endangered civilians: just cause (gross violations of fundamental human rights), right intention (putting an end to these violations), last resort (military means as *ultima ratio*, after all non-military measures have been exhausted), proportional means (minimal duration and intensity of military strikes), and, lastly, reasonable prospects of success.[32] To its credit, the ICISS report did not duck the difficult issue of just authority. While emphasising the Security Council's primary responsibility for the maintenance of international peace and security, it tentatively suggested possibilities for action outside of the Security Council. The commissioners made the following propositions: first, states must in all cases seek Security Council authorisation prior to carrying out any military action; second, in cases of massive human rights violations, the Council's permanent members should agree not to use their veto power, unless vital national interests are at stake; and third, should the P-5 exercise their veto nonetheless, recourse may be made to the General Assembly under the Uniting for Peace procedure and to regional arrangements, subject to their seeking subsequent authorisation from the Security Council.[33] The Commission also reminded the P-5 that in the case of failure to discharge its primary responsibility for the maintenance of international peace and security, states may not rule out unilateral means to address 'conscience-shocking situations', which in turn would adversely affect the credibility of the Security Council.[34]

The concept of R2P was subsequently endorsed in the report of the High-level Panel on Threats, Challenges, and Change[35] and in Kofi Annan's report *In Larger Freedom*,[36] yet each of these documents introduced its own qualifications: Whereas the High-level Panel insisted on the Security Council's exclusive prerogative to authorise enforcement action – thus dodging the question of Security Council paralysis[37] – the Secretary-General avoided discussing R2P's consequences for the rules on the use of force altogether by thematically separating the normative aspects of R2P from the question of the use of force. Annan also urged UN member states to embrace this new concept.[38] As a result of his recommendation, the General Assembly debated the responsibility to protect for the first time during the 2005 World Summit deliberations. The inclusion of R2P language in the Outcome Document proved to be an arduous task but was ultimately hailed as one of the few successes of the Summit. That it happened was anything but inevitable, given the dogged resistance of many – especially developing – countries.[39] In the

---

[31] Theories of just war originated in Roman philosophy and typically comprise a set of criteria that determine the justness of a war, such as just cause, proper authority, right intention, etc. For a contemporary discussion of the concept of just war see Mark Evans (ed.), *Just War Theory: A Reappraisal* (Edinburgh: Edinburgh University Press, 2005).

[32] ICISS, supra note 4, p. xii.

[33] Ibid., pp. xii, xiii.

[34] Ibid., pp. xii, xiii.

[35] High-level Panel, supra note 8.

[36] Kofi Annan, *In Larger Freedom: Towards Development, Security and Human Rights for All* (New York: UN, 2005).

[37] High-level Panel, supra note 8, p. 57.

[38] Kofi Annan, supra note 36, pp. 35, 59.

[39] See Gareth Evans, 'The International Responsibility to Protect: The Tasks Ahead', presentation at the seminar on 'Africa's Responsibility to Protect', Centre for Conflict Resolution, Cape Town (23 April 2007), {http://www.crisisgroup.org/home/index.cfm?id=4801&l=1}.

end, a pragmatic rather than doctrinal reading of the concept prevailed: while stressing the international community's responsibility 'to use appropriate diplomatic, humanitarian and other peaceful means, in accordance with Chapters VI and VIII of the Charter, to help to protect populations from genocide, war crimes, ethnic cleansing and crimes against humanity' the General Assembly also implicitly rejected the idea of a generalised duty to intervene by emphasising that each case should be treated on its own merits: 'In this context, we are prepared to take collective action, in a timely and decisive manner, through the Security Council, in accordance with the Charter, including Chapter VII, on a case-by-case basis and in cooperation with relevant regional organizations as appropriate, should peaceful means be inadequate and national authorities are manifestly failing to protect their populations from genocide, war crimes, ethnic cleansing and crimes against humanity.'[40]

The Outcome Document obviously left critical elements of R2P unaddressed. The idea of a set of general legitimacy criteria did not survive the negotiations. While earlier drafts did call for the discussion of such criteria, this idea was dropped in the final version.[41] The omission was a concession to developing states that were uneasy about consenting to a set of criteria that would possibly legitimise hegemonic intervention into their internal affairs.[42] China and Russia also worried that the adoption of such guidelines would undermine the principle of non-intervention while the US did not want to include language in the Outcome Document that would limit its freedom of action in any way.[43] Unsurprisingly, another thorny aspect of R2P raised by the ICISS – the problem of just authority and Security Council deadlock – was not carried forward during the deliberations.

The Outcome Document was certainly helpful as an initial affirmation of R2P on the declaratory level, but the Security Council is the organ that matters when it comes to implementing rhetoric into action. It was therefore significant that in 2006 the Security Council adopted resolution 1674 on the protection of civilians in armed conflict.[44] In it, the Council emphasised its commitment to the sovereign equality and territorial integrity of all states, recalled the provisions in paragraphs 138 and 139 of the Outcome Document, highlighted the primary responsibility of the parties to an armed conflict for the protection of civilians, and reaffirmed its willingness to 'consider such situations' (of human rights violations against civilians in armed conflict), and 'where necessary, to adopt appropriate steps'. That same year the Security Council invoked R2P for the first time in a country-specific resolution where UN peacekeepers were to be deployed under Chapter VII: In resolution 1706 on Darfur the Council reaffirmed the responsibility to protect,

[40] A/RES/60/1 (24 October 2005).
[41] Draft Outcome Document, para. 47 (3 June 2005), {http://www.reformtheun.org/index.php/united_nations/991}.
[42] Nicholas Wheeler, 'A Victory for Common Humanity? The Responsibility to Protect After the 2005 World Summit', paper presented at the conference 'The UN at Sixty: Celebration or Wake?' University of Toronto (6–7 October 2005), {http://www.una.org.uk/humanrights/R2P%5B1%5D.pdf}, p. 3.
[43] Ibid., p. 7.
[44] S/RES/1674 (28 April 2006).

declared that the situation in Sudan constitutes a threat to international peace and security, and authorised the deployment of an international peacekeeping presence in Darfur with a mandate to use force for civilian protection purposes.[45]

The history of R2P, Stahn writes, 'sounds almost like a fairy tale'.[46] Rejecting the concept altogether has become politically untenable, and few governments would openly dispute the idea that sovereignty implies the obligation to govern responsibly. An intersubjective consensus on R2P seemed to have been achieved at the 2005 World Summit. In just four years, R2P came to be rhetorically endorsed by states around the world, including such strange bedfellows as the US, which has consistently sought to prevent the development of a general duty to intervene,[47] and the Non-Aligned Movement, which has vehemently opposed humanitarian intervention in the internal affairs of states.[48] Such unusual unanimity is suspicious – and indeed, the 'consensus' achieved at the 2005 World Summit proved shallow and has been undermined by America's interventions in Iraq and Afghanistan, which were partly justified in humanitarian terms.[49] The global War on Terror had a deleterious impact on the development of the responsibility to protect: Attention is a scarce resource in international politics, and US military engagement in Iraq and Afghanistan has diminished Washington's political will, military capability, but also diplomatic credibility to conduct humanitarian interventions,[50] and has reinforced developing states' suspicion of R2P.[51] The discussions over R2P following the World Summit revealed much need for conceptual clarification, as we shall see below. It has become fashionable to speak of R2P as a 'new norm'. However, we learned earlier that new norms emerge from a combination of consistent state practice and enunciated legal convictions. In the following I will show that neither the psychological (*opinio juris*) nor the material (state practice) criterion of custom formation is fulfilled, and that R2P thus does not possess the intersubjective qualities that would justify calling it a norm.

[45] S/RES/1706 (31 August 2006).

[46] Stahn, supra note 2, p. 99.

[47] In its interventions in Iraq 1991, Kosovo, and elsewhere the US – mindful of precedent – never expressly endorsed a right to humanitarian intervention. However, US officials have occasionally referred to humanitarian motives as a *policy* justification for the use of force, without, however, making a statement of general legal principle. See John F. Murphy, *The US and the Rule of Law in International Affairs* (Cambridge: Cambridge University Press, 2004), pp. 151f; see also Stewart Patrick of the US State Department's Policy Planning Staff, 'The Role of the US Government in Humanitarian Intervention', Remarks to the 43rd Annual International Affairs Symposium (5 April 2004), {http://www.state.gov/s/p/rem/31299.htm}.

[48] See, for example, paras. 15 and 16 of the Final Document of the XIII Conference of Heads of State or Government of the Non-Aligned Movement Kuala Lumpur (24/25 February 2003), {http://www.nam.gov.za/media/030227e.htm}.

[49] Jim Hoagland, 'Tony Blair, Reflecting', *Washington Post* (6 March 2005).

[50] Lee Feinstein, *Darfur and Beyond. What is Needed to Prevent Mass Atrocities* (Washington, D.C.: Council on Foreign Relations, 2007), {http://www.cfr.org/content/publications/attachments/DarfurCSR22.pdf}, p. 28.

[51] For an insightful discussion of this issue see Alex J. Bellamy, 'Responsibility to Protect or Trojan Horse? The Crisis in Darfur and Humanitarian Intervention After Iraq', *Ethics & International Affairs*, 19:2 (Summer 2005), pp. 31–53.

Is there a unified opinio juris *regarding the responsibility to protect?*

The short answer to this question is no. The long answer is that one must read the fine-print of the discourse over sovereignty as responsibility which reveals that good governance rhetoric notwithstanding, the large majority of states does not accept the substantial obligations that the concept of R2P – at least in its original version – would impose on states. R2P's conceptual history shows that all subsequent interpretations of the idea articulated by the ICISS – in the High-level Panel's report, Kofi Annan's report and finally, in the World Summit Outcome Document – put a different spin on it. While this vagueness obviously facilitated consensus-building at the World Summit, it raises considerable difficulties now that R2P's proponents seek to move beyond high-sounding rhetoric and push for its institutionalisation in the UN machinery, as NGO representatives involved in the deliberations over R2P told me. 'There is a general pattern of remorse', ICG's Donald Steinberg observed, with countries that acceded to the Outcome Document now beginning to wonder 'whether this is really what they intended to do, primarily regarding the military aspect'.[52] Sapna Chhatpar from the World Federalist Movement (WFM), which maintains a website that documents the positions of states on R2P[53] and regularly consults with government officials and civil society representatives on R2P issues agreed: 'Many governments viewed the language in the Outcome Document as a lofty phrase, they did not buy into the R2P principle as articulated in the ICISS report.'[54] Sudan expert William O'Neill put it even more bluntly: 'I get the feeling a lot of countries did not read the Outcome Document before they signed onto it.'[55] Despite the ICISS' attempt at changing the terms of the debate, R2P – just like the concept of humanitarian intervention – is obviously viewed as a hegemonic tool to legitimise aggressive intervention in the internal affairs of states.[56] Yet in the absence of a consensus on what the responsibility to protect actually means, no *opinio juris* can emerge. Currently unresolved issues include:

- Does the international community inherit the same responsibility that the host state has?
- Is R2P a legal duty or merely an option to intervene?
- Can states enforce R2P even in the absence of a Security Council mandate?

The positions of the major diplomatic players on these issues will be considered in turn.

Russia and China share the conviction that R2P should leave sovereignty's traditional principles such as non-interference and domestic jurisdiction unaltered.

[52] Interview (7 December 2007).
[53] {http://www.responsibilitytoprotect.org/}.
[54] Interview (27 November 2007).
[55] Interview (20 December 2007).
[56] At their Kuala Lumpur Summit NAM-governments highlighted the 'inherent dangers in the emerging trends toward a unipolar world', a world in which powerful states could trample upon the principles held dear by developing states such as non-interference and sovereign equality. NAM-governments reiterated their criticism of the 'so-called right to humanitarian intervention' and voiced suspicion that the concept of the responsibility to protect was merely the doctrine of humanitarian intervention in disguise. They therefore requested their Coordinating Bureau to carefully study the concept and its implications for the principle of non-interference. See supra note 48.

During the biannual debates on the protection of civilians in the Security Council, China has consistently stressed that the international community's responsibility to protect should be exercised without infringing upon the sovereignty and territorial integrity of member states, thus effectively denying the possibility of forcible measures that are not carried out with the consent of the host state.[57] China leads a group of countries who continue to stress that the responsibility to protect should be exercised in accord with traditional notions of non-interference and host state consent,[58] which of course would render the idea of R2P entirely meaningless.

R2P's normative development thus critically depends on the norm entrepreneurship of Western states. However, European governments have been wavering in their commitment to R2P. ICISS co-chair Gareth Evans notes that although Europeans were instrumental in the inclusion of the R2P paragraphs in the Outcome Document, they have not displayed much propensity to further the concept's institutionalisation at the regional level.[59] Evans observes that EU officials seem 'deeply reluctant' to invoke the concept in any relevant context, citing hollow statements made by the EU Commission such as 'While the Commission welcomes the development of this norm, it is for the UN member states to act upon it' or 'Where it can the Commission will seek to raise the importance of the Responsibility to Protect in its bilateral relations'.[60] The EU is obviously unwilling to adopt a principled approach and prefers to pass the buck of norm development on to the UN.

The UN in turn has become the primary forum for deliberations on the responsibility to protect, with the Security Council holding biannual open debates on the protection of civilians in armed conflict. These debates have helped to raise the public profile of civilian protection issues and provide states with a forum in which they can clarify their interpretations of R2P. Aside from these regular debates in the Security Council, further steps towards R2P's institutionalisation in the UN machinery have been taken by Secretary-General Ban Ki-moon, who appointed Prof. Edward Luck as his first Special Adviser for the Responsibility to Protect. Luck described his duties as threefold: First, to achieve conceptual clarity, that is, to work towards a coherent understanding of what the responsibility to protect means; second, to promote the concept's institutionalisation in the UN context; and third, to further dialogue about R2P with member states.[61] To promote R2P's translation into a programme of action, the Secretary-General moreover suggested the establishment of a Security Council expert-level working group on the protection of civilians tasked with facilitating 'the systematic and sustained consideration and analysis of protection concerns, and ensuring consistent application of the aide-memoire for the consideration of issues pertaining to the protection of civilians in Council deliberations on the mandates of UN peacekeeping and other relevant missions, draft resolutions and Presidential Statements, and

---

[57] S/PV.5781 (20 November 2007).
[58] Chu Shulong, 'China, Asia and Issues of Sovereignty and Intervention', *Pugwash Occasional Papers*, 2:1 (January 2001), {http://www.pugwash.org/reports/rc/como_china.htm}.
[59] Gareth Evans, 'The Unfinished Responsibility to Protect Agenda: Europe's Role", panel presentation at the EPC/IPPR/Oxfam Policy Dialogue on Europe's Responsibility to Protect: What Role for the EU?, Brussels (5 July 2007), {http://www.crisisgroup.org/home/index.cfm?id=4936&l=1}.
[60] Quoted in Ibid.
[61] Interview (27 November 2007).

in Council missions'.[62] The establishment of such a working group would aim at ensuring a systematic consideration of civilian protection issues and at mainstreaming R2P into the decision-making processes of the Security Council. Civilian protection, I was told by a research analyst familiar with Security Council dynamics, is currently the most difficult thematic debate in the Council.[63] The envisaged working group could increase the time the Council devotes to the issue of civilian protection and increase the quality of the analysis behind Council decisions. 'The subtext is to smooth out that allergy that some Council members have to the issue of civilian protection', the analyst explained to me. Reactions to the working group proposal were mixed. When the Secretary-General's report was discussed in the Security Council,[64] many smaller states such as Panama, Ghana, Slovakia, Peru, Switzerland, etc. welcomed the suggestion in principle (although many stressed the need for further consultation and clarification). Russia and China, by contrast, expressed strong reservations. The Russian representative spoke out against undertaking a 'very bureaucratized action' like the establishment of a formal working group. The Chinese delegate equally refuted the idea, emphasising that the country-specific consideration mechanism of the Council is functioning smoothly and that therefore there is no need to create a thematic working group.[65]

China's and Russia's lack of enthusiasm is mirrored by US attempts at downgrading R2P from an obligation to an *option* to intervene. This interpretation of R2P would in fact add nothing to the current state of affairs – the US has always reserved the right to intervene in the internal affairs of other states, unilaterally, if necessary.[66] The main rationale for US reluctance to accept a duty to intervene in cases of grave human rights abuses is the desire to maintain a free hand and not to be forced to save strangers when such a rescue action is not deemed in its national interest. Of course the US has never flatly rejected R2P. Rather, it has endorsed the concept in a very general and vague sense but has not shown any interest whatsoever in giving substance to its rhetoric. John Bolton, then-US Ambassador to the UN, repeatedly highlighted the *moral* (and thus non-legal) character of the responsibility to protect. In the run-up to the 2005 World Summit, information leaked that Bolton had voiced firm opposition to language in the Outcome Document that would constrain the US in using force and place new obligations on the international community to intervene in the case of serious human rights violations. In the now infamous 'Dear Colleague' letter, Bolton stated US principles relating to the R2P section in the draft Outcome Document. Bolton stressed that the UN Charter 'has never been interpreted as creating a legal obligation for Security Council members to support enforcement

[62] Ban Ki-moon, *Report of the Secretary-General on the Protection of Civilians in Armed Conflict*, S/2007/643 (28 October 2007, {http://documents-dds-ny.un.org/doc/UNDOC/GEN/N07/573/58/pdf/N0757358.pdf?OpenElement}, p. 19.
[63] Interview (27 November 2007).
[64] S/PV.5781 and S/PV.5781 (Resumption 1), (20 November 2007).
[65] Ibid.
[66] See Brad R. Roth, 'Bending the Law, Breaking It, or Developing It? The US and the Humanitarian Use of Force in the Post-Cold War Era', in Michael Byers and Georg Nolte (eds), *US Hegemony and the Foundations of International Law* (Cambridge: Cambridge University Press, 2003), pp. 232–63.

action in various cases involving serious breaches of international peace. Accordingly, we believe just as strongly that a determination as to what particular measures to adopt in specific cases cannot be predetermined in the abstract but should remain a decision within the purview of the Security Council'.[67] Regarding R2P specifically, the US rejected language indicating that the international community has a legal obligation to intervene to end massive human rights violations. Bolton wanted the Outcome Document to convey that the international community's responsibility is of a 'more general and moral' character: 'We do not accept that either the UN as a whole, or the Security Council, or individual states, have an obligation to intervene under international law.'[68] He therefore suggested to rephrase the section, to the effect that – instead of stipulating a duty to act – the international community would merely assert its 'preparedness' to take action, a formula that was ultimately accepted by other states. Carolyn Wilson of the US Mission to the UN confirmed that the US indeed intends to avoid the emergence of a customary law principle obligating states to intervene in cases of genocide, war crimes, and crimes against humanity: 'We have a rather conservative view of the responsibility to protect and consider it to be a moral rather than a legal obligation.'[69] This naturally begs the question of why we need R2P in the first place. We do not need the notion of the responsibility to protect to understand that it is *morally* objectionable to remain passive while scores of innocent civilians are being slaughtered. We also do not need R2P to understand that the host state has a duty to prevent genocide within its area of jurisdiction – this duty was accepted by states sixty years ago when they signed onto the Genocide Convention. What we do need is an international consensus that the international community's fallback duty to intervene is a *binding* obligation under international law that is applied in a more or less consistent fashion, and this is exactly what the US (and most other states) seek to obstruct. During last year's Security Council debate on the protection of civilians in armed conflict, for example, Ghana was alone in speaking out in favour of the idea that the international community has a *legal* duty to intervene.[70]

Considering Washington's desire to maintain a free hand, it comes as no surprise that the US rejects another element of the ICISS report, namely the proposal of establishing a code of conduct that would prevent the permanent Security Council members from using their veto in cases of grave human rights abuses where their vital national interests are not affected. When asked about the reasons for US opposition to a code of conduct, Wilson stressed the necessity of treating each case 'on its own merits' and avoiding any limitations on the use of the veto: 'We have consistently felt that the use of the veto is a very serious action that any of the permanent members can take. The Charter has given this right to

---

[67] John R. Bolton, Letter Sent to UN Member States Conveying US Amendments to the Section on the Responsibility to Protect of the Draft Outcome being Prepared for the September 2005 High Level Event (30 August 2005), {http://www.un.int/usa/reform-un-jrb-ltr-protect-8-05}.
[68] Ibid.
[69] Interview (21 November 2007).
[70] S/PV.5781 (20 November 2007).

the permanent members and we have consistently shied away from imposing restraints on the use of force. It is a responsibility that falls to each permanent member at the time to make a decision based on the specific situation.'[71]

Another leitmotif of US statements on the responsibility to protect is an emphasis on the qualitative difference between the responsibility of the host state on the one hand, and the fallback responsibility of the international community on the other hand. The US has repeatedly emphasised that the international community does not inherit the same responsibility that the host state has, as Bolton pointed out in his 'Dear Colleague' letter. During the biannual Security Council debates on the protection of civilians the US has regularly reiterated this position. In the debate on 9 December 2005, for example, the US representative emphasised that the international community should not assume responsibility for governmental failure to protect.[72] At the debate on 28 June 2006, the US delegate stressed that the effective protection of civilians depends largely not the actions of the international community, but on what governments do to protect their citizens.[73]

The foregoing analysis suggests that no intersubjective consensus on the meaning of R2P and its implications for the use of force exists. A handful of die-hard sovereigntists still refute the idea of limited sovereignty altogether. This in itself is not significant for the formation of *opinio juris*, because acquiescence to an emerging norm does not have to be universal, but merely nearly universal.[74] What is much more significant for the formation of *opinio juris* is the fact that states have been unwilling to adopt a principled approach to implementing R2P. They have expressed support for R2P in very vague terms, but refuse to make a principled commitment. Instead, UN member states stressed in the Outcome Document that they reserve the right to act on a 'case-by-case' basis. Second, the concept's implications for the use of force are far from consensual and the 2005 Outcome Document scrupulously avoids commenting on these. Very few states are ready to admit that the international community's responsibility to protect may be exercised unilaterally, if the Security Council does not live up to its responsibility.[75] The ICISS had suggested the drafting of general legitimacy criteria as a way out of this impasse.[76] However, most states oppose this idea, although for different reasons. Weaker states fear this would legitimise the unilateral use of force in the case of Security Council paralysis. The Non-Aligned Movement in particular views R2P as a potential revitalisation of the disfavoured doctrine of humanitarian intervention.[77] The US, by contrast, opposes the drafting of general guidelines because it

---

[71] Supra note 69.
[72] S/PV.5319 (Resumption 1), (9 December 2005).
[73] S/PV.5476 (28 June 2006).
[74] Michael Akehurst, 'Custom as a Source of International Law', *British Year Book of International Law 1974–1975* (Oxford: Clarendon Press, 1977), pp. 1–53 (p. 39).
[75] See Gareth Evans, 'The Responsibility to Protect: Rethinking Humanitarian Intervention', address to the American Society of International Law, Washington D.C., (1 April 2004), {http://www. crisisgroup.org/home/index.cfm/africa/rss/home/index.cfm?id=2561&l=1}. Evans noted that unilateral interventions 'do not – it would be an understatement to say – find wide favour. As a matter of political reality, it would simply be impossible to find consensus around any set of proposals for military intervention which acknowledged the validity of any intervention not authorized by the Security Council or General Assembly'.
[76] ICISS, supra note 4, p. xii.
[77] Supra note 48.

wants to retain its freedom of action.[78] This is not to deny that progress has been made in building an international consensus on the subject, but this process is still far from complete. The affirmation of the World Summit consensus in binding Security Council resolutions are encouraging developments, but words have yet to be matched by deeds. The real test for the formation of a customary norm is whether lofty ideals are translated into consistent state practice, which leads us directly to the problem of enforcing the Sudanese government's responsibility to protect in the province of Darfur.

R2P in state practice – the case of Darfur

'If Darfur is the first "test case" of the responsibility to protect', Lee Feinstein writes, 'there is not point in denying that the world has failed the entry exam'.[79] Unlike the humanitarian interventions conducted in the 1990s, the crisis in Darfur escalated *after* the publication of the ICISS report and hence provided the international community with a first opportunity to showcase its commitment to R2P. Darfur constitutes an obvious example of governmental failure to live up to its responsibility to protect and as such calls for the activation of the international community's fallback responsibility to protect. Yet the international community's response to the crisis has been painfully slow and ineffective. To be sure, there has been no shortage of public hand-wringing. However, governments around the world have shown little inclination to translate their noble ideals into practice and protect suffering civilians in Darfur. Without going into the details of the conflict,[80] it is patent that Western states and the international community at large have failed on several counts in Darfur: they chose not to strain relations with Khartoum by raising the crisis in Darfur at an early stage; they could not reach agreement in the Security Council on a Darfur resolution until July 2004; they failed to put coordinated pressure on Khartoum to allow for the timely delivery of humanitarian aid; they failed to convey a clear message to Khartoum that it would be held accountable for not meeting its responsibility to protect and rein in the *Janjaweed*; they failed to coerce the Sudanese regime into accepting the uncondi-tional and timely deployment of the hybrid peacekeeping force; they failed to equip UNAMID with the resources it needs to effectively carry out its civilian protection mandate, etc.

The crisis in Darfur began as a local conflict in the area of Jebel Marra between Arab nomadic herders – supported by the central government in Khartoum – and the Fur ethnic group over natural resources and access to land. The Fur in turn accused Khartoum of complicity in Arab raids against Fur villages and began to organise resistance not only against the nomads but also against nearby govern-ment garrisons. The government in Khartoum, rather than the Arab militiamen, quickly began to be perceived as the Fur's real enemy. Consequently, the Fur

---

[78] Supra note 71.
[79] Lee Feinstein, *Darfur and Beyond. What is Needed to Prevent Mass Atrocities* (Washington, D.C.: Council on Foreign Relations, 2007), p. 38.
[80] For a detailed analysis of the conflict in Darfur see for example Gerard Prunier, *Darfur. The Ambiguous Genocide* (Ithaca: Cornell University Press, 2007; rev. and upd. edition).

decided to package their grievances in more general terms and made the central government's marginalisation of the region of Darfur as a whole their rallying cry.[81] The Fur's demand for equitable wealth – and power sharing resonated with a broad audience and triggered the formation of two rebel movements – the Justice and Equality Movement (JEM) and the Sudan Liberation Movement/Army (SLM/A). Fighting escalated in 2003 when these movements declared an open rebellion against Khartoum. The central government was caught off guard by the intensity and initial success of the rebel campaign and resorted to the infamous *Janjaweed* militia to quell the insurgency. The *Janjaweed* has pursued a scorched-earth policy not only toward the rebels but also toward the civilian population. In concert with the Sudanese government, the *Janjaweed* had effectively turned Darfur into a killing field by the end of 2003.[82]

In the face of Khartoum's manifest failure to protect its citizens from gross human rights violations, the issue of international enforcement action became virulent. The international community initially decided to pass the buck on to the AU, advocating African solutions to African problems.[83] Yet this division of labour underestimated the scale of the humanitarian and security problems plaguing Darfur. The African Union Mission in Sudan (AMIS) suffered from inadequate resources and a limited mandate. As the situation worsened, the AU proposed a plan which envisaged the conversion of AMIS into a fully-fledged peacekeeping force with a robust mandate to effectively protect civilians and neutralise armed militias – a plan which failed, however, due to Khartoum's resistance.[84] After a prolonged period of haggling the Security Council in August 2006 finally agreed upon the replacement of AMIS by a more robust and larger UN force in Darfur. Resolution 1706[85] extended to Darfur the mandate of the existing UN mission in Sudan (UNMIS) which is currently charged with monitoring compliance with the North-South Comprehensive Peace Agreement (CPA).[86] In somewhat ambiguous language, resolution 1706 'invited' the consent of the government of Sudan to the deployment, which Khartoum refused, however. In November 2006, a compromise was struck which envisaged three phases of UN assistance to AMIS – a light support package, a heavy support package, and ultimately transition to a hybrid AU/UN force.[87] In June 2007, the government in Khartoum finally agreed to the deployment of the hybrid force and the Security Council adopted resolution 1769, which established the UN-African Union Mission in Darfur (UNAMID).[88] The hybrid force, which was supposed to take

---

[81] Adam Azzain Mohamed, 'The Comprehensive Peace Agreement and Darfur', in Alexander de Waal (ed.), *War in Darfur and the Search for Peace* (Cambridge: Global Equity Initiative, Harvard University, 2007), pp. 199–213 (p. 207f).

[82] M. W. Daly, *Darfur's Sorrow. A History of Destruction and Genocide* (Cambridge: Cambridge University Press, 2007), pp. 283f.

[83] Susan E. Rice, 'Why Darfur Can't Be Left to Africa', *Washington Post* (7 August 2005).

[84] Ruth Iyob and Gilbert M. Khadiagala, *Sudan. The Elusive Quest for Peace* (Boulder: Lynne Rienner, 2006), p. 154.

[85] S/RES/1706 (31 August 2006).

[86] The CPA was concluded in 2005 and ended Africa's longest-running civil war. It contains a schedule for political reform and a democratisation process, which is supposed to culminate in the holding of national elections in 2009.

[87] Sudan 'Backs' Darfur Force Plan', *BBC News* (17 November 2006), {http://news.bbc.co.uk/2/hi/africa/6153208.stm}.

[88] S/RES/1769 (31 July 2007).

over operations from AMIS by the end of 2007, acts under Chapter VII of the Charter to support the 'early and effective implementation' of the DPA as well as to protect civilians and aid workers. Critically important, however, is the change in mandate insisted upon by Khartoum and backed by China: unlike the mandate formulated in resolution 1706, resolution 1769 authorises neither the disarmament of combatants nor the confiscation of weapons introduced into Darfur in violation of resolution 1591, which imposed an arms embargo for the entire region. Moreover, language that would have threatened sanctions in the event of Khartoum's non-compliance was deleted from the draft, apparently at the insistence of China and others.[89]

At the time of writing (October 2008), little progress has been achieved in the deployment of UNAMID. The deployment is hampered by two factors: on the one hand, by the obstruction tactics employed by the government of Sudan, and secondly, by the international community's sluggishness in providing the requisite resources.[90] UNAMID currently lacks helicopters and critical heavy ground transport resources, which are indispensable if the peacekeepers are to carry out their civilian protection mandate effectively. When briefing the Security Council on the status of UNAMID's deployment in November 2007, UN Under Secretary General Jean-Marie Guehenno reported fundamental challenges in the area of force generation, noting a continuing lack of pledges for key mobility assets such as helicopters.[91] Secretary-General Ban Ki-Moon spent months soliciting contributions but has been unable to find countries willing to provide the two dozen helicopters which UNAMID desperately needs to patrol the vast countryside. 'Is there a world helicopter shortage that nobody told us about?' the *Los Angeles Times* asked in disbelief.[92] There is certainly no such shortage, considering that NATO-states alone have 18000 helicopters at their disposal. Apparently, European governments are reluctant to provide helicopters because they do not want to be associated with UNAMID's failure in Darfur, Roberta Cohen, a human rights expert at the Brookings Institution, explained to me after attending a conference with European government officials.[93] If this is true, one must ask: why send in UNAMID in the first place? Considering the shortage of critical capabilities as well as the bureaucratic hurdles to the deployment established by the government of Sudan, Guehenno warned that the international community would soon be faced with a tough choice: '[d]o we move ahead with the deployment of a force that will not make a difference, that will not have the capability to defend itself and that carries the risk of humiliation of the Security Council and the UN and tragic failure for the people of Darfur?'[94]

What does the international response to the crisis in Darfur tell us about R2P? In a caustic *New York Times* op-ed David Brooks observed that the international community's handling of the tragedy in Darfur follows an all-too-familiar pattern of inaction in the face of mass atrocities: the cycle begins with plenty of alarmist

---

[89] Human Rights Watch, *Darfur 2007: Chaos by Design. Peacekeeping Challenges for AMIS and UNAMID* (New York: Human Rights Watch, 2007), {http://hrw.org/reports/2007/sudan0907/}, p. 58.

[90] Amnesty International, 'Obstruction and Delay. Peacekeepers Needed in Darfur Now' (22 October 2007), {http://www.amnesty.org/en/library/asset/AFR54/006/2007/en/dom-AFR540062007en.pdf}.

[91] S/PV.5784 (27 November 2007).

[92] Los Angeles Times, 'Helicopters for Darfur' (13 December 2007).

[93] Interview (21 December 2007).

[94] S/PV.5784 (27 November 2007).

rhetoric. This is followed by the (vain) attempt to gather resolve and fruitless diplomatic haggling, which results in pathetic inaction, shame, and humiliation. Once the slaughtering is (conveniently) over, the international community fervently vows to never let this happen again – until the next crisis erupts and the cycle starts over: 'The "never again" always comes. But still, we have all agreed, this sad cycle is better than having some impromptu coalition of nations actually go in "unilaterally" and do something. That would lack legitimacy! Strain alliances! Menace international law! Threaten the multilateral ideal!'[95]

The US government has done more than most other governments to resolve the crisis, yet its efforts have been 'fitful in the extreme and responsive only to pressure'.[96] Washington has unilaterally imposed financial and economic sanctions,[97] it has generously provided aid to the people of Darfur, and, in a remarkable volte-face, decided to abstain from the Security Council vote that referred the situation in Darfur to the International Criminal Court[98] – an institution which the US has fiercely opposed from its very inception onwards. The Bush administration has also been the most outspoken advocate of the genocide-thesis. In a testimony before the Senate Foreign Relations Committee in September of 2004 then-Secretary of State Colin Powell claimed that genocide was taking place in Darfur.[99] To the surprise (and shock) of many, however, he declined any responsibility on the part of the US to take stronger action to end the killings: 'Mr. Chairman, some seem to have been waiting for this determination of genocide to take action. In fact, however, no new action is dictated by this determination. We have been doing everything we can to get the Sudanese Government to act responsibly. So let us not be too preoccupied with this designation of genocide.'[100]

Article 1 of the Genocide Convention reads as follows: 'The Contracting Parties confirm that genocide, whether committed in time of peace or in time of war, is a crime under international law which they undertake to prevent and to punish.'[101] The Convention thus imposes a (somewhat vague) duty to prevent genocide. Yet the genocide determination made by the Bush administration did not result in forceful action. Instead of keeping all options on the table, US officials effectively eliminated the military option: Assistant Secretary for African Affairs Jendayi Frazer stressed in a press briefing in 2006 that the US is not prepared to deploy international peacekeepers against the will of Khartoum: 'Clearly, we're not going to fight – the force is not going to fight its way in.'[102] The legacy of the Iraq war obviously still looms large: 'No way' was the answer a desk officer at the US State Department gave me when asked about the possibility of unilateral military action. 'I don't think the American people would encourage invading another Muslim

---

[95] David Brooks, 'Another Triumph for the UN', *New York Times* (25 September 2004).
[96] Daly, supra note 82, p. 293.
[97] 'Bush Toughens Sanctions on Sudan', *BBC News* (29 May 2007, {http://news.bbc.co.uk/2/hi/africa/6699479.stm}.
[98] S/RES/1593 (31 March 2005).
[99] Secretary of State Colin L. Powell, 'The Crisis in Darfur', written remarks, Senate Foreign Relations Committee (9 September 2004), {http://www.whitehouse.gov/interactive/sudan_gen.html}.
[100] Ibid.
[101] Supra note 1.
[102] Assistant Secretary for African Affairs Jendayi Frazer, 'Stopping Genocide in Darfur: Ongoing US Efforts and Working with the UN Security Council' (24 August 2006), {http://www.state.gov/p/af/rls/rm/2006/71515.htm}.

nation'.[103] A unilateral US intervention (even of a limited nature, for example in the form of targeted air strikes) is obviously not a realistic option at present – on this, all experts I interviewed agreed.

While it is understandable that US officials do not contemplate a full-scale invasion of the Sudan, it is much less obvious why the US and other Western countries have been so reluctant to enforce a no-fly-zone. The idea of a no-fly-zone, which would build on the ban on offensive military flights authorised in resolution 1591,[104] has surfaced repeatedly in the discussions over Darfur.[105] Despite Khartoum's defiance, no effective surveillance system was established, and aerial attacks have continued. In the spring of 2007, reports leaked that Sudan was brazenly violating the UN arms embargo, flying heavy military equipment into Darfur and painting Sudanese aircraft white to disguise them as UN planes.[106] Enforcing a no-fly-zone would be an expensive, asset-intensive operation in a logistically difficult environment. Any aircraft taking off in the zone would have to be shot down and Sudanese airfields in and around Darfur would have to be closed. Yet even if comprehensive patrolling is unrealistic, British and US officials supposedly weighed a more limited enforcement option: punitive air strikes against Sudanese airfields if Khartoum violated the non-fly-zone.[107] This option has not been implemented, however, and it seems rather unlikely that it will be realised in the future, because it seems that the US (and other militarily capable states) simply do not care enough to expend the requisite military resources: 'The US did not want to devote the forces, and the European states did not want to stand out by themselves', ICG's Donald Steinberg explained to me.[108] To be fair, calculations of military prudence, feasibility and prospects of success have also factored into the decision not to enforce a no-fly-zone. There is room for legitimate debate over whether the costs of enforcing a no-fly-zone would actually outweigh its benefits.[109] Yet leaving aside the question of enforcing a no-fly-zone, one could at least expect that the international community would do its utmost possible to enable UNAMID to carry out its civilian mandate effectively, which it has obviously failed to do.

When asked what the international community's response to the crisis in Darfur tells us about the responsibility to protect, Michael Matheson, former Legal Adviser at the US State Department, gave a simple but compelling answer: States, including the US 'obviously do not believe that they have a legal obligation to protect civilians'.[110] According to him, the US could always exert more of its economic and political power, but bilateral interests (relations with China and Russia) and other foreign policy concerns (counter-terrorism, military overstretch, fear of a backlash in the Muslim world) have prevented it from doing so. Matheson dashed hopes that the US would replicate the Kosovo experience in Darfur, pointing out that the US (and Europeans) had a much greater strategic interest in Kosovo than in Darfur. Anthony Lake, National Security Adviser to

---

[103] Interview (12 December 2007).
[104] S/RES/1591 (29 March 2005).
[105] Julie Flint, 'Darfur's Outdated Script', *International Herald Tribune* (9 July, 2007).
[106] Warren Hoge, 'Sudan Flying Arms to Darfur, Panel Reports', *New York Times* (18 April 2007).
[107] Julian Borger, 'Blair Wants No-Fly-Zone Enforced Over Darfur', *The Guardian*, (28 March 28 2007).
[108] Interview (12 December 2007).
[109] Flint, supra note 105.
[110] Interview (10 December 2007).

former President Clinton, underlined that the US does have an interest in pacifying Sudan, but also conceded that over the years, 'many people have learned to live with the thought that we haven't done enough in Darfur'.[111] The US has provided humanitarian aid to the people of Darfur, it has unilaterally imposed economic sanctions and it has worked hard to keep the Security Council unified, but that is simply not enough to give teeth to the promise that the responsibility to protect holds out for endangered civilians.

R2P – an emerging norm? Assessing the scope of institutional transformation

If one appraises the development of the responsibility to protect in terms of the norm life-cycle described by Finnemore and Sikkink, one would currently locate R2P in stage two. During the first stage, various non-governmental actors (such as the ICISS, the International Crisis Group, the World Federalist Movement, etc.) played a crucial role in putting R2P on the international agenda and in attempting to change the terms of the discourse over humanitarian intervention. These various actors in turn persuaded a critical mass of mostly Western, but also developing states ('norm leaders') to embrace the responsibility to protect and thus triggered a 'norm cascade' (stage two). At this stage, norm leaders sought to convince other states to become norm followers. As the 2005 World Summit Outcome Document and Security Council resolutions 1674 and 1706 show, these efforts were relatively successful, although the consensus achieved in 2005 proved shaky and there is a danger of backsliding. The transition from stage one to stage two is frequently facilitated by the emerging norm's institutionalisation in specific sets of rules or organisations. R2P's institutionalisation in the UN machinery is progressing, with the appointment of Edward Luck as the Secretary-General's Special Adviser for the Responsibility to Protect and the possible creation of a Security Council working group on civilian protection. Yet despite the progress made on the institutional level, it is very unlikely that stage three of the norm life-cycle ('internalization') will be reached any time soon. What is currently missing is: a) conceptual clarity, and thus an intersubjective consensus on the implications of R2P (in particular regarding the military aspect), and b) consistent application of R2P in state practice. In the absence of these two factors, norm internalisation cannot occur. Thus, from an IR-perspective, the responsibility to protect clearly has not evolved into a norm, that is, an *intersubjectively* shared standard of appropriate behaviour.

If one takes the IL-perspective, the result is even less encouraging. At present, neither the material, nor the psychological element of custom formation is fulfilled. Darfur and other recent cases of humanitarian (non-)intervention (Iraq 1991, Bosnia-Herzegovina, Somalia, Rwanda, Haiti, Liberia, Sierra Leone, East Timor, Kosovo) give rise to two interrelated questions: First, do states – through the Security Council – have an obligation to respond to mass atrocities in areas outside of their jurisdiction, possibly against the will of the host state? And second, if the Security Council fails to act, may states enforce R2P in the absence of a Security

---

[111] Interview (7 December 2007).

Council mandate? Whilst the ICISS answered both questions in the affirmative,[112] this certainly does not reflect the state of customary international law on the subject. The Kosovo war has thrown into sharp relief the lack of *opinio juris* on the subject of unilateral humanitarian intervention,[113] and subsequent discussions over R2P have shown that states' views on the difficult question of unilateral enforcement have not changed. This finding is corroborated by the international response to the Darfur crisis, which shows that states clearly do not believe that they have an obligation to use all means at their disposal to protect civilians in areas outside of their jurisdiction. There is thus no consistent practice of applying R2P, nor is there an intersubjective consensus on the obligation of the Security Council to react to mass atrocities (or, in the absence of Security Council action, on the right of states to take unilateral action). Hence no right to unilateral enforcement of R2P can be said to exist in customary international law.

If one adopts a historical perspective one will find it difficult to argue that such a right to unilateral action exists even in *statu nascendi*. A review of humanitarian interventions conducted in the post-Cold War world[114] suggests that the intervening states for the most part did not claim a right to (unilateral) humanitarian intervention but frequently couched their actions in terms of self-defence or simply declined to comment on the strict legality of their operations, hence implicitly affirming the traditional rules on the use of force.[115] With the notable exceptions of Belgium and maybe the UK,[116] Western states have consistently sought to prevent the emergence of a generalised right (let alone duty) of unilateral enforcement of the responsibility to protect. We learned from Professor D'Amato

---

[112] There may be room for debate over whether the ICISS indeed intended to legitimise unauthorised intervention. In the event of Security Council deadlock the ICISS suggested intervention by regional organisations subject to their *seeking* subsequent authorisation from the Security Council. 'Seeking' authorisation after the fact, however, does not mean that such authorisation is actually granted – a possibility which the ICISS must have been aware of. I therefore interpret the passage in the report to mean that the ICISS accepted the possibility of regional enforcement action which the Security Council refused to authorise *post hoc*.

[113] See Peter Hilpold, 'Humanitarian Intervention: Is There a Need for a Legal Reappraisal?', *European Journal of International Law*, 12:3 (2001), pp. 437–68 (p. 452).

[114] See, for example, Institut de Droit International – Session de Santiago, *10th Commission. Present Problems of the Use of Force in International Law. B. Sub-group on Humanitarian Intervention*, Rapporteur: W. Michael Reisman (Paris: Edition A. Pedone, 2007).

[115] When justifying the bombing of Serbia in 1999, NATO states – with the exceptions of Belgium and the UK – did not justify the war in legal terms. Instead of making statements of general (legal) principle, the intervening states mainly relied on moral and political arguments, as the case brought by Yugoslavia against NATO before the ICJ shows. Yugoslavia had instituted proceedings against NATO states after the start of the air campaign. Although the Court ultimately declined to exercise jurisdiction on the merits, a hearing on the preliminary measures application took place, in which the respondents had an opportunity to elaborate on the justifications for the bombardments. The vast majority of the intervening states did not seize this opportunity to clarify the legal basis of their action. During the hearings only Belgium justified the air strikes by invoking a legal right to humanitarian intervention. See International Court of Justice, *Legality of Use of Force Case (Provisional Measures)*, CR 1999/15 (10 May 1999), {http://www.icj-cij.org/docket/files/105/4513.pdf} and International Court of Justice, *Legality of Use of Force Case (Provisional Measures)*, CR 1999/24 (11 May 1999), {http://www.icj-cij.org/docket/files/114/4577.pdf}.

[116] Ibid. For the British position, see also Tony Blair's Sedgefield speech (5 March 2004), {http://www.guardian.co.uk/politics/2004/mar/05/iraq.iraq}: Declaring that 'we do not accept [. . .] that others have a right to oppress and brutalise their people', Blair went on to frame the war against Iraq as a logical extension of the R2P doctrine. This, however, was clearly not the intention of the founders of the concept and is one of the reasons why R2P continues to be viewed with suspicion by many developing nations.

that every illegal act contains the seeds of a new legality. Yet we also learned from the ICJ's *Nicaragua* judgement that if the intervening parties themselves do not justify their behaviour by reference to a new right of humanitarian intervention, law-breaking clearly does not lead to law-making. Isolated humanitarian interventions that are not even qualified as precedents by the intervening parties themselves and that are opposed by the majority of states are thus insufficient to give rise to a customary right to unilateral enforcement of R2P.

Non-acts are as important as acts for the formation of custom.[117] A consistent pattern of non-intervention on humanitarian grounds tells us as much about the status of R2P as humanitarian interventions that were actually conducted. The international reaction to the crisis in Darfur underlines the importance of hegemonic leadership for the translation of R2P into state practice. The US – by virtue of its preponderant resources – could contribute significantly to turning R2P into a programme of action and setting a precedent for R2P enforcement, yet has failed to do so in Darfur. If, by contrast, Washington decided to threaten non-consensual enforcement of Security Council resolutions, this would alter the Sudanese regime's strategic calculations significantly. So far, Khartoum's non-compliance has been largely cost-free. Yet in the absence of US leadership, a consistent practice of R2P enforcement is unlikely to develop. US opposition to R2P as a legal obligation has significant consequences for the further development of the concept. If the responsibility to protect is to ripen into a norm of customary international law, the US must be on board. Why? Washington is likely to shoulder the brunt of the burden when it comes to translating R2P in state practice, which makes it a 'specially affected state'. As the ICJ expounded in the *North Sea Continental Shelf Case*, for a rule of customary law to come into being, the state practice concerned must include that of states whose interests are specially affected.[118] Hence, the US can, by its abstention, prevent R2P from developing into a fully-fledged norm of customary international law. The desire to avoid the emergence of a generalised right to unilateral humanitarian intervention has been a consistent pattern of US foreign policy.[119] Washington's decisions not to act in the face of humanitarian emergencies, and its desire to limit the precedential impact of its interventions when it did act (by using moral and political instead of legal arguments and presenting each intervention as a case *sui generis*) had a significant impact on the development of the law in this area. Matheson put it bluntly: 'The US does not want the responsibility to protect to evolve into a binding legal obligation and that is why the responsibility to protect is not a norm of customary international law.'[120] Yet the US is not the only 'specially affected state'. This designation applies to the other P-5 as well, which are militarily capable actors with a stake in creating a practice of intervention and which are explicitly mentioned in the ICISS report as having a special role in enabling (or obstructing) a consistent practice of atrocity prevention.[121] However, neither Russia nor China has shown much appetite for civilian protection, and European states have declined to take the initiative in transforming R2P rhetoric into a programme of action. Europeans

[117] D'Amato, supra note 18, pp. 61f.
[118] International Court of Justice, *ICJ Reports 1969* ('s-Gravenhage: Sijthoff), p. 43.
[119] See Murphy, supra note 47.
[120] Interview (10 December 2007).
[121] ICISS, supra note 4, pp. 6, 49, 51, 75.

now have an independent rapid response capability at their disposal – the EU battlegroups reached full operational capacity in 2007 – that could be employed for the protection of civilians in humanitarian emergencies. Moreover, European states have proved their willingness to go ahead even against the opposition of the US when fundamental human rights issues are at stake – witness the negotiations over the International Criminal Court (ICC). If Europeans were thus to exercise determined leadership in pushing for a consistent application of R2P, US obstructionism would cease to be such a consequential factor in R2P's development. However, the problem is that the US is not the only country that wishes to prevent the emergence of a general legal duty to intervene: as I have argued throughout this article, the large majority of states has no interest in creating a binding obligation to save strangers.

Conclusion

Historical experience suggests that caution is in order when assessing R2P's long-term potential for effectuating political change. The duty to prevent enshrined in the Genocide Convention had sixty years to ripen into a strong norm but – considering decades of non-intervention on humanitarian grounds – has obviously not succeeded in compelling states to adopt a more or less consistent practice of atrocity prevention in areas outside of their jurisdiction. The responsibility to protect merely rephrases the wording of the Convention (and extends the duty to prevent to crimes against humanity and war crimes), but does not introduce substantial new obligations – at least as regards the military aspect. The historical perspective hence weakens the argument that R2P is still too young a concept and that using the crisis in Darfur as a yardstick for measuring the concept's effectiveness is unfair, because norm development in international relations is a slow process. Six decades of non-compliance with the Genocide Convention dictate a sober assessment of the future development of R2P.

Despite these obvious implementation deficits, it would be unfair to dismiss R2P out of hand entirely as an abstract academic exercise. What can be said in favour of the concept? First, the main UN bodies have affirmed R2P on several occasions. Moreover, the practice of the Security Council, which in a number of instances characterised intra-state humanitarian emergencies as threats to international peace (Somalia, Iraq 1991), provided *post hoc* endorsements of unauthorised humanitarian interventions (Liberia, Sierra Leone), or failed to condemn NATO's unilateral intervention in Kosovo, signals that indeed a qualitative shift in the understanding of sovereign responsibilities is about to occur. The AU, as the first regional organisation, has incorporated a right to humanitarian intervention in its Constitutive Act.[122] Beliefs about the moral purpose of the state are beginning to change as a result of the agenda-setting activities of non-state actors and the norm entrepreneurship of the US and other (mostly Western) states, who command the military resources – but not always the political will – to back R2P claims through concomitant actions. The discourse over R2P shows that patterns

---

[122] Art. 4h of the Constitutive Act of the African Union.

of accepted justifications in the field of human rights promotion have indeed changed, and that those states advocating an absolute right to non-interference clearly represent a minority. One of the great successes of the R2P debate is that nobody denies that the situation in Darfur constitutes a problem that the international community needs to deal with – civilian protection issues have effectively become internationalised, and the political and moral pressure on governments to address mass atrocities has clearly increased. The language of sovereign responsibility introduced by Deng and the ICISS has provided proponents of R2P with a powerful vocabulary to press for tough action against human rights violators. Because of the discussion over the responsibility to protect, the crisis in Darfur has received more attention than any other conflict on the war-torn continent of Africa – it was in fact the first civil war in which the US used the label genocide.[123] All of this indicates that – although a legal duty to intervene does not exist (yet) – a duty to *consider* intervention may be developing as a result of the R2P debate.[124]

Sovereignty's component norms – especially the norm of domestic jurisdiction – are thus being called into question, yet the extent of the transformation of sovereignty is still disputed, and the majority of scholars remain reluctant to make sweeping statements about the emergence of a customary right to unilateral enforcement of R2P, should the Security Council fail to act. Furthermore, even if the existence of a *right* to humanitarian intervention could be established, most states shy away from acknowledging the international community's *duty* to enforce a state's responsibility to protect.[125] Inconsistent practice as well as the lack of *opinio juris* thus pose significant obstacles to the emergence of the responsibility to protect norm. Hence, unless one conceives of R2P as some type of trans-empirical 'supercustom'[126] that does not require demonstration of state practice as proof of its validity one is forced to conclude that the responsibility to protect has not evolved into a binding legal obligation and is unlikely to do so in the near future.

---

[123] Supra note 99.
[124] I thank an anonymous reviewer for alerting me to this possibility.
[125] Supra note 70.
[126] W. Michael Reisman, 'Unilateral Action and the Transformation of the World Constitutive Process: The Special Problem of Humanitarian Intervention', *European Journal of International Law*, 11:1 (2000), pp. 3–18 (p. 15).

Review of International Studies (2010), 36, 79–96   © *2010 British International Studies Association*
doi:10.1017/S0260210511000076

Dangerous duties: power, paternalism and the 'responsibility to protect'

PHILIP CUNLIFFE

Abstract. This article provides a critique of Louise Arbour's article 'The responsibility to protect as a duty of care in international law and practice'. Proceeding through criticisms of Arbour's specific propositions, the thesis is advanced that the perverse effect of the 'duty of care' is to undermine political accountability and by extension, political responsibility. It is argued that this is an imperfect duty that no specific agent is obliged to fulfil. This poses insuperable problems of agency that are exposed in Arbour's efforts to actualise the doctrine. As there is no mechanism for enacting the 'duty of care', I argue that it will be powerful states that will determine the conditions under which the 'responsibility to protect' is discharged. This means that the 'duty' will remain tied to the prerogatives of states. In order to resolve this problem of agency, it will be shown how Arbour is forced to replace the idea of law with the principle of 'might makes right'. The 'duty of care' is also shown to have regressive effects on the domestic sphere: the demand that states be made accountable to the international community ends up making states responsible for their people rather than to their people.

Philip Cunliffe is a Lecturer in the School of Politics and International Relations at the University of Kent. He joined the School in September 2009.

Introduction

In recent years the idea of the 'responsibility to protect' has won widespread backing around the globe. The doctrine articulates a link between the management of violence by the international community and a vision of the fundamental elements of legitimate domestic rule. In her article 'The responsibility to protect as a duty of care in international law and practice' Louise Arbour argues that the 'vitality' of the doctrine 'flows from its inherent soundness and justice'.[1] I will argue here that the doctrine is neither sound nor just and that its vitality, such as it is, stems not from its capacity to protect the wretched of the earth but from the opportunity it offers states to extend the writ of their power both over their own peoples and over other (weaker) states. Arbour's article is a useful entry point into the debate. The rigour of Arbour's attempt to translate the 'responsibility to protect' into a legally actionable 'duty of care' allows us to pursue the problems with the doctrine to their logical conclusion. Criticisms of specific points in Arbour's argument establish a foundation for a more general critical discussion of the doctrine.

---

[1] Louise Arbour, 'The responsibility to protect as a duty of care in international law and practice', *Review of International Studies*, 34 (2008), p. 448.

In its most basic form, the doctrine holds that if a state is unable or unwilling to discharge its obligation to protect individuals against gross human rights violations then the 'onus of [such] protection falls by default upon the broader international community, which is then called upon to step in and help, or [. . .] even coerce States to put in place the requisite web of protection'.[2] According to Arbour, the appeal of the doctrine lies in its promise to privilege the suffering of ordinary people above the interests and scheming of states. The doctrine will strengthen the regime of international legal protection that is supposed to shield imperilled humanity against 'state-sponsored slaughter'.[3] I will argue that the 'responsibility to protect' threatens to repress popular sovereignty and in so doing, makes the exercise of power less rather than more responsible.

In her article Arbour identifies two types of opposition to the doctrine. The first is those who claim we are 'powerless' to halt 'gross violations of human rights' in far-off conflicts.[4] The second is those whom Arbour calls the 'custodians of the orthodoxy of non-interference', who worry that the 'responsibility to protect' will foster a 'moral imperialism' granting powerful states a license to interfere in the affairs of weaker states.[5] Although Arbour's dismissal of both these positions is unconvincing,[6] my argument here takes a different tack. I argue that the 'responsibility to protect' strengthens state power at the expense of popular power *within* states and that 'moral imperialism' between states is a corollary of this effect. Extending Arbour's 'web of protection' across the planet with no single identifiable authority responsible for keeping that web intact means that the 'duty of care' can only be 'imperfect'. 'Imperfect' because, in the words of Michael Walzer, it is 'a duty that doesn't belong to any particular agent'.[7] With only nebulous global principles at stake, inevitably it is power that will determine the conditions under

---

[2] Arbour, 'The responsibility to protect', p. 448.

[3] Ibid., p. 445.

[4] Ibid.

[5] Ibid., p. 448.

[6] Arbour criticises the claim that we are powerless in humanitarian crises by arguing that 'the global web of our interdependence' makes any such claims redundant. The result is a fortuitous symmetry between the needs of security and the demands of morality: 'indifference or inaction in the knowledge of violence, deprivation and abuse allow exclusion and resentment to fester [. . .] conditions that will ultimately affect everybody's rights, security and welfare' – Arbour, 'The responsibility to protect', p. 445. Here unspecified mechanisms of global integration function as a *deus ex machina* that obviates the need for argument. This allows Arbour to sidestep concrete analysis of actual conflicts. Yet the number of conflicts that have *not* seen intervention clearly demonstrates that intervention is not an automatic by-product of globalisation – a range of additional factors come into play before intervention actually occurs. In the second instance, Arbour contests the so-called 'orthodoxy of non-interference' by arguing later in her article that the 'responsibility to protect' is already embedded in the provisions of existing international law (Arbour, ibid., pp. 447–8). But this can only leave the reader wondering what precisely is 'orthodox' about the claims made by the 'custodians of non-interference'. Arbour's suggestion that the 'responsibility to protect' is part of the natural growth and progress of existing international law puts her in the position of claiming the mantle of legal orthodoxy.

[7] Michael Walzer, *Just and Unjust Wars: A moral argument with historical illustrations* (New York: Basic Books, 2000), p. xiii. Walzer is discussing humanitarian intervention rather than the 'responsibility to protect'. Kok-chor Tan considers the same problem in relation to the 'responsibility to protect' doctrine outlined in the 2001 report *The Responsibility to Protect*. Tan questions whether humanitarian intervention meets the strict definition of 'imperfect duty' as understood by Kantian scholars. Cf. Kok-chor Tan, 'The Duty to Protect', in Terry Nardin and Melissa S. Williams (eds), *Humanitarian Intervention* (New York and London: New York University Press, 2006), pp. 95–96. He nonetheless accepts the designation, and for the sake of consistency I will follow him in doing so.

which a duty is discharged. Insofar as this differs from humanitarian intervention, it will be for the worse. Invoking the 'responsibility to protect' will allow interloping states to claim a higher authority than the merely selfish claim to a 'right of intervention'.

In other words, the problem is not confined to international relations. The attempt to embed a 'duty of care' into the definition of legitimate statehood warps the principle of representative government. However noble the intent, if shielding individuals from the most degraded forms of barbarism is to become a fundament of legitimate statehood, this will have dangerous repercussions for the structure of political relations between peoples and their states. If states are seen less as emanating from their people's will but rather as one apparatus among others for the enforcement of disembodied global duties, this will dilute the relationship of representation between a people and state. If the sovereign people are no longer the sole legitimate arbiter of their state's behaviour, this can only mean that the state is *less* responsible to its people. Upholding a duty of care under the threat of external sanction pushes representative government into the realm of paternalism, wherein states have responsibilities *for* their people rather than *to* their people. In other words, the doctrine *fails on its own terms*. Whatever the alleged 'orthodoxy of non-interference' may be, it can be shown that the responsibility to protect renders the exercise of power less accountable, and unaccountable power is ultimately irresponsible power. Instead of disciplining states in favour of powerless victims, I will show how the doctrine will allow states to evade political responsibility.

Outline

The argument proceeds as follows. I begin by analysing Arbour's account of how the 'responsibility to protect' transforms a state's prerogative to intervene in other states into a duty to defend imperilled humanity. According to Arbour, making the defence of imperilled humanity an obligation transforms it from a selfish act by a single state into an altruistic function in line with the collective standards and interests of the international community. However, as this duty can only be an imperfect one, we shall see that there is an insurmountable problem of agency at the core of the doctrine.[8] I will argue that the enforcement of the 'responsibility to protect' can only be discretionary – and hence there is no means of preventing the selective and self-serving enforcement of the duty. Arbour struggles with the implications of this problem, striking out in a number of directions in her search to find a means by which she can ensure that the duty be realised.

I trace and criticise Arbour's various manoeuvres through international law and order, showing how the argument inexorably leads her to argue for expanding the remit of powerful states and her resignation to the principle of paternalism. I take issue with Arbour's suggestion that the 'responsibility to protect' should exact

---

[8] Note that this point is not restricted to questions of military or coercive intervention: the basic issue is the same across the spectrum of possibilities that Arbour outlines as falling under the responsibility to protect, ranging from help, through compellance to coercion. Arbour, 'The responsibility to protect', p. 448.

heavier duties from powerful states, as this proposition segues into the idea that might makes right – precisely the condition which law is supposed to curtail. Building on the issue of agency, I go on to say that this problem extends to the post-conflict engagement envisioned under the 'responsibility to protect', where the diffusion of duties leads to the dilution of concrete responsibilities in transitional administration. In the last third of the article, I put forward the case that a consistent reading of the doctrine of popular sovereignty, and its corollary of non-intervention, remains the best way to discipline states and ensure that they uphold their responsibilities.

From right to responsibility?

For Arbour, what lifts the 'responsibility to protect' over and above humanitarian intervention that preceded it is the embrace of 'the victims' point of view and interests'.[9] In doing this the doctrine ditches the 'questionable State-centred motivations' associated with the arguments regarding the so-called 'right' of intervention.[10] In place of a flexible 'right of intervention' that states can exercise as and when they please, the 'responsibility to protect' erects a global and 'permanent duty to protect individuals against abusive behaviour'.[11] Arbour's reasoning seems to be that if the decision to intervene is always left to the discretion of states, we can expect them to act against human rights abuses only when it suits them. As a result, we have no means of extricating the moral good of humanitarian intervention from the 'questionable motivations' that underpin state action.[12] If states are *obliged* to act however, whatever their underlying motivations may be will become less important.[13] This is one of the strong points of the doctrine. On the one hand, the prerogatives of interloping states are limited by the adoption of a more rigid policy that prevents them acting as and when they please. On the other, the potential 'recipients of international attention and action' are left none the worse (that is, always subject to potential predation by more powerful states).[14] What is more, as would-be interveners are now bearers of a duty, they can be held to account for their failure to act.[15]

There are two things immediately worth noting about Arbour's presentation of the doctrine. First, there is a sleight-of-hand in her treatment of humanitarian intervention. Arbour concedes that humanitarian intervention is problematic, but she locates the problem not where one might expect (that humanitarian intervention violates state sovereignty), but rather in the fact that the intervener's claim has to be framed in the selfish terms of a right belonging to that state. Casting the problem of humanitarian intervention in this way frees Arbour from having to account for the link between sovereignty and non-intervention. In other words, she

---

[9] Ibid.
[10] Ibid. Arbour also welcomes the way in which the 'responsibility to protect' systematises 'post-conflict engagement' by the international community – an issue we shall return to below.
[11] Ibid.
[12] Ibid., p. 447.
[13] 'No longer holders of a discretionary right to intervene, all States are no burdened with the responsibility to take action under the doctrine of the 'responsibility to protect.' Ibid., p. 449.
[14] Ibid., p. 449.
[15] Ibid., p. 450. As we see below, Arbour's faith in these mechanisms is misplaced.

has already tacitly privileged intervention. Second, this facilitates her presentation of the 'responsibility to protect' as embodying normative progress. If the problem with humanitarian intervention is its egotistical character, then a more communal version of the same practice will be sufficient to rectify the problem. This would indeed appear to be progress if we had correctly identified the problem with humanitarian intervention.

Arbour muddies the waters further in her one-sided account[16] of prior debates on intervention. The discussion is confused by the fact Arbour conflates intervention in general with the specific invocation of a 'right of humanitarian intervention'. Arbour claims that 'intervention is the prerogative of the intervener and has always been exercised as such, thereby creating a hierarchy among those who received protection and those whom the potential interveners could afford to ignore'.[17] Formulating the problem in such general terms means that Arbour is never forced to confront non-intervention as the corollary of sovereignty. But intervention has been proscribed between fully-fledged sovereign states since at least the mid-eighteenth century, as seen in 'the doctrine of the equal rights of states to sovereignty, and of their duty of non-intervention' propounded by Christian Wolff and Emmerich de Vattel.[18]

Humanitarian intervention, on the other hand, is more specific than a general right to intervention: the claim made by its advocates is that there exists a 'right' to intervene in other states in conditions of extreme human suffering and duress. Although proscribed by the very idea of sovereignty, intervention has remained the prerogative of states insofar as the rights of states cannot be *'actualised* [. . .] in a universal will with constitutional powers above [states], but [only] in their own particular wills', as G. W. F. Hegel put it.[19] What Hegel means is that in the anarchic conditions of the international realm, the clash of rights between states is also always a collision of political wills: the two are inextricably intertwined. As we shall see, the 'responsibility to protect' mystifies the inner link between the exercise of a state's right and a state's will.

By presenting the doctrine as an onerous imposition on would-be interveners Arbour glosses the fact that the status of the potential 'recipient' of international 'assistance' is ratcheted down a notch. For if the responsibility to protect could potentially force would-be interveners to account for their non-action in a particular context, it most certainly forces the state being intervened in to defend

---

[16] One-sided insofar as Arbour claims that 'neither the advocates nor the detractors of humanitarian intervention gained a definitive upper hand' in the debate (ibid., p. 447). If there is any truth to this claim, it is less to do with the fact that the legal arguments were equally robust on both sides as much as the fact that the doctrine of humanitarian intervention won the support of a minority of rich and powerful Western nations. To hold that a right of intervention has become an accepted part of international law is to discard a key principle of customary law: that it must be accepted evenly by a majority of its subjects, as pointed out by Jennifer Welsh: 'non-Western legal opinion opposes this interpretation of the customary law on intervention, since it seems to suggest that certain types of practice count more than others – that is, the actions of Western states versus the stated opposition from those such as China, Russia, and India.' Jennifer Welsh, 'Taking Consequences Seriously; Objections to Humanitarian Intervention', in Jennifer Welsh (ed.), *Humanitarian Intervention and International Relations* (Oxford: Oxford University Press, 2004), p. 55.

[17] Arbour, 'The responsibility to protect', p. 447.

[18] Hedley Bull, 'Introduction', in Hedley Bull (ed.), *Intervention in World Politics* (Oxford: Clarendon Press, 1986), p. 4.

[19] Georg Wilhelm Friedrich Hegel, *Elements of the Philosophy of Right*, ed. Allen W. Wood (Cambridge: Cambridge University Press, 2000), p. 368. Emphasis in original.

why it is entitled to be free from external interference.[20] The doctrine of humanitarian intervention at least recognises intervention as vice by paying homage to the virtue of non-intervention: the so-called 'right' to breach the sovereignty of another state is an exception that requires heavy justification.[21] By annulling the presumption of non-interference the doctrine of the responsibility to protect goes further. Taking away the right to non-intervention is like the erosion of civil liberties in domestic politics or revoking the presumption of innocence in criminal law.[22] To be sure, in the international realm eroding the presumption of non-intervention shifts the burden of justification on to a state rather than an individual. Nonetheless, it is no less invidious a principle.

For once states must justify their political authority to external powers, this means they are no longer solely legitimate by virtue of the people that they represent. A people's right to political representation is effectively made conditional on international license.[23] In the words of Amitai Etzioni, rendering sovereignty conditional in this manner blasts open 'a gaping hole' in the 'foundation of democratic theory': 'Sovereignty as responsibility [. . .] creates a democratic deficit that cannot be ignored'.[24] Second, this duty does not eliminate the problem of state prerogative (recall that Arbour singled this out as undermining the credible use of humanitarian force). Arbour's claim that the 'responsibility to protect' is a 'concurrent' burden that falls evenly on all states does not withstand scrutiny.[25] For a duty to be 'effectively claimable' there must be a specific agent to whom we can turn in circumstances where we wish the duty to be upheld.[26] This is what Kok-chor Tan calls the 'agency condition': a duty can only be actualised through a particular agent.[27] Of all the varied iterations of the 'responsibility to protect', not a single formulation of the doctrine to date is able succinctly to express and logically demonstrate that there is a single, identifiable agent *formally obligated* to act or intervene in a particular situation. There is no 'automaticity' in the doctrine – no governmental machinery or legislation that spontaneously comes into effect once the 'duty' is breached by a state.[28]

Imperfect duties and the problem of agency

Arbour is at least tacitly aware of this 'agency condition', as is shown by her speculation about 'States' lack of resistance regarding the responsibility to protect'.

---

[20] The argument here builds on that originally developed by David Chandler in '*The Responsibility to Protect?* Imposing the "Liberal Peace"', *International Peacekeeping*, 11:1 (2004), pp. 59–81.

[21] For an example of this type of argument, cf. Simon Chesterman, *Just War or Just Peace? Humanitarian Intervention and International Law* (Oxford: Oxford University Press, 2001) pp. 228–99.

[22] For a treatment of the dangers of this move in the domestic sphere, cf. Andrew Ashworth, 'Four Threats to the Presumption of Innocence', *International Journal of Evidence and Proof*, 10 (2006), p. 241.

[23] Peter Gowan, 'The New Liberal Cosmopolitanism', in Daniele Archibuigi (ed.), *Debating Cosmopolitics* (London and New York: Verso, 2003), p. 52.

[24] Amitai Etzioni, 'Sovereignty as Responsibility', *Orbis* (Winter 2006), p. 72.

[25] Arbour, 'The responsibility to protect', p. 454. Not least because, as we shall see, Arbour contradicts this claim later when she suggests that the doctrine exacts greater duties from powerful states.

[26] Tan, 'The Duty to Protect', p. 86.

[27] Ibid., p. 96.

[28] This problem is linked to the impossibility of articulating in advance the criteria to judge when the 'responsibility to protect' has been breached. See Alex J. Bellamy, 'The Responsibility to Protect and the problem of military intervention', *International Affairs*, 84:4 (2008), p. 148.

She muses whether the rapid uptake of the doctrine may be because states perceive it to be a 'merely moral or political' obligation; that is, the consequences resulting from 'a failure to discharge' the duty only being 'of limited' if not 'altogether negligible' concern to 'the [...] duty bearers' in question.[29] Arbour tries to get around this problem of agency in several ways. But, as we shall see, the contortions to which she submits her argument in order to render an imperfect duty obligatory show that her original instinct was the right one: the responsibility to protect can only be an imperfect duty offering plenty of advantages to states and exacting 'altogether negligible' political costs.

First, in keeping with other formulations of the doctrine, Arbour claims that this 'permanent duty' should be seen 'as a function of sovereignty': the first agent to whom we turn to claim the duty is the incumbent state ruling over the population and territory in question.[30] But this duty is not an absolute but a relative one, because the doctrine clearly holds that states bear responsibilities for 'human protection'[31] that diffuse and overlap across the planet's whole population. This is the only way to ensure that there exists the possibility of turning to other agents to uphold the 'responsibility to protect' should an incumbent state fail to do so. But, because it is everyone's duty it is also no one's duty.[32] Making the duty an imperfect one is, perversely, the only way of saving the duty from evaporating completely in the decentralised political system that is the international realm.

This has several further consequences. First, *pace* Arbour's earlier claims, in an international order where there is a widely accepted but nebulous responsibility to protect, we are still firmly in the realm of state prerogative. The 'permanent' but imperfect 'responsibility to protect' will only be actualised if states choose to do so. As Michael Walzer put it, 'There is no avoiding state action and therefore no avoiding state politics.'[33] What this means is that for all the talk of 'responsibility' the doctrine does not limit state prerogatives. Quite the opposite: the doctrine gives states enhanced flexibility and opportunity to interfere in other states' affairs. Indeed, insofar as the doctrine openly countenances coercion, it can be seen as a *de facto* extension of the right to wage war.

While the responsibility to protect does differ from discretionary intervention, it is not in the way that Arbour would have us believe. By tapping into an international consensus over the 'responsibility to protect', states can act on their own prerogative while claiming a legitimacy that goes beyond their rights as sovereign states. Specifically: invoking the 'responsibility to protect' allows states to claim they are acting on behalf of humanity itself. Humanitarian intervention has been attacked for its Manichean potential to normalise aggression and exacerbate conflict through the criminalisation of all political

---

[29] Arbour, 'The responsibility to protect', p. 450.

[30] Ibid., p. 448.

[31] This peculiarly cold and sterile phrase comes from the ICISS report. ICISS, *The Responsibility to Protect: Report of the International Commission on Intervention and State Sovereignty* (Ottawa: International Development Research Center, 2001), p. viii.

[32] In Kok-chor Tan's words, 'if the duty to protect is to be a perfect duty, there must be the additional condition that an agent capable of performing the duty be identified and assigned the responsibility to act' – Tan, 'The Duty to Protect', p. 86.

[33] Walzer, *Just and Unjust Wars*, p. xiv.

opposition.[34] Yet the 'responsibility to protect' goes further still. Even if justified in the most grandiloquent terms,[35] a 'right of humanitarian intervention' is still linked to the state(s) making the claim, with all the political costs and deterrents that come with claiming such a 'right' (such as arousing suspicion of self-serving motives). As the 'responsibility to protect' is elevated from a right that can be claimed by states to a disembodied duty that states can enforce at their own discretion, it offers all the potential for abuse as does a cosmopolitan 'right of intervention', but with fewer political costs.[36]

In terms of the potential beneficiaries of intervention, the fact that the 'responsibility to protect' is an imperfect duty means that it offers no guarantees to the wretched of the earth – the oppressed that the doctrine claims to defend against predatory or indifferent states. For in the end, all the doctrine can really offer is the vague assurance that remote foreign powers may involve themselves in a conflict if it happens to be convenient for them to do so. Worse, by virtue of being enshrined as a permanent duty the 'responsibility to protect' could cruelly raise expectations of outside support that have little hope of ever being fulfilled. Indeed, the danger also exists that the less specific the assurance of internationalised 'human protection', the greater the possibility that it may also prolong existing conflicts by encouraging belligerents to continue fighting in order to secure international intervention in their favour.[37] The doctrine may even encourage opportunistic secession and insurgency, generating the very conflicts that it purports to suppress.[38]

Arbour's second move to actualise the imperfect duty is to argue that the failure to discharge the duty has 'legal implications and consequences', which may even constitute 'a separate actionable harm'.[39] In other words, the imperfect duty can be actualised because states can be held to account through legal mechanisms if they fail to act to halt abusive behaviour. Arbour argues that 'the heart of the responsibility to protect doctrine' rests on an extant and undisputed obligation of international law – the prevention and punishment of genocide as codified in the Genocide Convention'.[40]

This is peculiar on the face of it, because if the doctrine adds no substantial value to the provisions of existing international law, why bother spending so much

---

[34] Cf. Mitchell Dean, 'Military Intervention as "Police" Action?', in Markus D. Dubber and Mariana Valverde (eds), *The New Police Science: The Police Power in Domestic and International Governance* (Stanford: Stanford University Press, 2006), pp. 196–200 and *passim*.

[35] Former British Prime Minister Tony Blair, for example, famously described the 1999 war over Kosovo as 'a battle between good and evil; between civilisation and barbarity; between democracy and dictatorship'. Blair, cited in Philip Hammond, 'The rise of the laptop bombardier', *Spiked Online* (24 March 2009).

[36] The idea that the 'responsibility to protect' imposes costs in terms of duties of post-conflict engagement and reconstruction is dealt with below.

[37] A danger that is even acknowledged in the ICISS report, though not by Arbour (cf. fn. 40 below). For the reality of this effect see Alan Kuperman 'Strategic Victimhood in Sudan', *The New York Times* (31 May 2006).

[38] This danger is recognised by the ICISS report (ICISS, *Responsibility to Protect*, p. 25).

[39] Arbour, 'The responsibility to protect', p. 450.

[40] Ibid. Arbour weakens her claim by expanding it to include the statutes of the international criminal tribunals for the former Yugoslavia and Rwanda – institutions notorious for their disastrous legal credentials and breach of 'every norm of impartiality'. Alberto Toscano, 'Sovereign Impunity', *New Left Review*, 50 (March–April 2008), p. 132. See more generally John Laughland, *Travesty: The Trial of Slobodan Milošević and the Corruption of International Justice* (London: Pluto Press, 2006). Unfortunately the problems with international criminal law are beyond the scope of this article.

time defending mere rhetoric? On the preventive side, Arbour turns to the findings of the International Court of Justice (ICJ) in the case of Bosnia-Herzegovina vs. Serbia. Arbour cites the Court's findings that Serbia failed in its legal obligation to prevent genocide given the manifold links it had with the 1992–1995 war in neighbouring Bosnia.[41] The various parameters used by the Court to assess the scope of Serbia's obligations range from geographic proximity to the strength of political links between the perpetrators of the crimes in Bosnia and the Serbian state. Arbour uses this judgement as the basis from which to extrapolate to the preventive duties of 'neighbouring and regional states' and those states who have 'pre-eminence, global reach and capabilities'.[42] Let us examine these two claims in turn.

In the first case, we have good grounds to query Arbour's conclusions about the responsibilities of neighbouring states. Even if we accept the Court's findings against Serbia, this could be turned against Arbour's conclusions. As is well known, the various relations on which the Court based its judgement relate to wars that arose from the disintegration of the Federal Socialist Republic of Yugoslavia in 1991. Indeed, the conflict itself was about the rights of secession of the various nations of Yugoslavia. Countries that previously formed a single larger country immediately prior to a conflict will obviously have far more links than countries that have no such history. For this reason, the highly exceptional circumstances surrounding the links between the ex-republics of former Yugoslavia seems a dubious basis on which to extrapolate to the appropriate behaviour and mutual relations of all neighbouring states throughout the world. Here again, Arbour is giving states greater leeway to involve themselves in their neighbours' affairs. Granting regional states the 'responsibility' not only to prevent genocide using 'all such tools as are at a State's disposal' but even to 'deter' potential perpetrators of such crimes (that is, to pre-empt genocide)[43] gives remarkable scope to regional states to intervene in their neighbours' affairs.[44]

This is quite apart from the larger questions of how international law or the findings of the ICJ can be upheld against powerful states, particularly given, as we shall see, the leeway that Arbour seems happy to grant to powerful states. Indeed, citing a ruling by which one of Europe's weakest, poorest and most isolated states was prosecuted by an international court is not a particularly convincing model to underpin a new era of equitable global law enforcement. In any case, Arbour clearly realises that calling for good neighbourly relations and drubbing small states into submission with international law is insufficient to make the 'responsibility to protect' genuinely actionable. This is apparent in the fact that Arbour is keen to prevent geographic distance being used as an excuse by remote countries to exonerate themselves from having to take action. Hence she broadens the links that could count as 'actionable' far beyond mere geographic proximity to

---

[41] We have no *prima facie* reason to join Arbour in accepting the Court's ruling as just, but the justice or otherwise of the Court's ruling is not directly relevant to the argument that I want to pursue here.

[42] Arbour, 'The responsibility to protect', p. 453.

[43] As David Chandler observes of such arguments in a different context: 'Armed with the ability to "to identify the early stages of genocide" [...] to judge "murderers before they kill", it would seem highly likely that the demand for military-led [...] interventions will rely more on prejudice than objective "justice".' David Chandler, *From Kosovo to Kabul and Beyond: Human Rights and International Intervention* (London and Ann Arbor: Pluto Press, 2006), p. 189.

[44] Arbour, 'The responsibility to protect', p. 453.

encompass 'relevant links of all kinds: historic, political, economic'.[45] Perhaps it is hoped that the more responsibility is shared around, the greater the likelihood that someone will take action. But the very need to promiscuously share the duty as much as possible speaks to the intractable character of the agency problem in the first place.

Sure enough, Arbour is forced to fall back on power to ensure that the responsibility to protect can be realised. Hence she makes 'pre-eminence' and 'global reach and capabilities' the basis for apportioning greater responsibilities in upholding the global duty. Indeed, Arbour is happy to go beyond even the vast powers invested in the permanent five members of the UN Security Council. She suggests that:

> being better positioned to avert and respond to atrocities may have as much to do with the capacity to project power and mobilise resources beyond national and regional borders as with physical proximity. In this respect [. . .] powerful States may be reasonably expected to play a leading role in bolstering appropriate measures of prevention, dissuasion and remedy across a geographic spectrum commensurate with their weight, reach and advanced capabilities.[46]

By this stage in her argument, Arbour's claim amounts to little more than the principle that undermines all law and justice – that 'might makes right'. She has granted powerful states the *de facto* right to police weaker states, up to and including the use of force. Here we have again returned to the discretionary 'rights' of states to interfere in other states' affairs – the very condition that the 'responsibility to protect' was supposed to move us beyond.

Despite Arbour clothing her argument in the language of 'duties' and 'burdens' the way in which she expressly singles out powerful states for a special role shows that this doctrine does not curb powerful states but actually augments their power. It can be said in Arbour's defence that she is at least consistent in following the logic of the 'responsibility to protect' to its conclusion. Relaxing the normative presumption against intervention always privileges powerful states, because it is precisely these states that are capable of projecting power across borders. The result is that the international hierarchy of power will subvert the already fragile and decaying edifice of formal international equality.[47]

As Arbour seems unconcerned about elevating powerful states over the rest, it is worth reminding ourselves of why formal standards of international equality are valuable. Once we use different (that is, unequal) standards to judge different groups of states and to accord greater rights to groups of powerful states, we adopt a self-referential account of political order. Without an antecedent conception of formal (legal) equality, inequality becomes its own explanation. The more that the structure of formal norms reflect real inequalities of wealth and power, the more entrenched these real inequalities become.The end-result is described by Benedict Kingsbury: 'The outcome seems likely to be the maintenance of a classificatory system which is itself both an explanation and a justification for those at the

---

[45] Ibid., p. 454.

[46] Ibid., p. 455.

[47] On the erosion of international equality in recent years throughout international law, cf. Benedict Kingsbury, 'Sovereignty and Inequality', in Andrew Hurrell and Ngaire Woods (eds), *Inequality, Globalisation and World Politics* (Oxford: Oxford University Press, 1999).

margins remaining there for generations.'[48] The distinctive features of the 'inferior', failing category of states is used to explain their very inferiority. Arbour's struggle with the implications of the 'agency condition' leads her from a half-heated invocation of international law to an embrace of power and the principle of 'might makes right'.

Arbour's blithe attitude towards international equality is complemented by an equally derisory treatment of what she calls 'the element of information'. After briefly genuflecting to the 'notion of presumption of innocence', Arbour pours scorn on the idea that information regarding atrocities may be uneven, suspect or contradictory.[49] She points out that 'perpetrators' will manipulate and poke holes in the information concerning atrocities in order to stave off an international response. She claims that the demand for 'unassailable evidence' is 'altogether preposterous in an age of high-speed communications and sophisticated fact-finding technologies'.[50] Given the record of media compromise witnessed in recent conflicts Arbour's faith in the existence of 'high-speed communications' seems naïve, to put it mildly. British journalist Maggie O'Kane famously describes how the media were manipulated by the British and American armed forces in the 1991 Gulf War: 'This is a tale of how to tell lies and win wars, and how we, the media, were harnessed like 2,000 beach donkeys and led through the sand to see what the British and US military wanted us to see in this nice clean war.'[51]

In any case, as is hopefully clear by now, the real problems with the 'responsibility to protect' do not lie with the issue of information or the lack thereof, or in the fact that information technology can be manipulated. The real problem is that the doctrine itself is regressive. The problem of agency does not just vitiate the 'responsibility to react', but also 'the commitment to rebuild'.[52] Much like the putative focus on victims is said to elevate the 'responsibility to protect' above humanitarian intervention, so too the emphasis on 'post-conflict engagement' – or the 'responsibility to rebuild' in the language of the ICISS report – is equally flagged up as a crucial new advance inaugurated by the doctrine. According to Arbour, the latter forms 'an integral part of protection rather than an afterthought'. In this way, the new norm is believed to bar 'both quick fixes and even quicker exit strategies'.[53]

But once the restraints imposed on interventionism are relaxed by emplacing the 'responsibility to protect' as a global and permanent duty, so it makes sense to diffuse the mechanisms for post-conflict governance. If intervention can be pursued for the collective purposes of the international community, it is only logical that no single state should bear the burden of transitional administration. As difficult as it is to specify an agent obliged to uphold the responsibility to protect, so it is just as difficult to identify a single agent responsible for overseeing post-conflict

[48] Kingsbury, 'Sovereignty and Inequality', p. 91.
[49] Arbour, 'The responsibility to protect', p. 455.
[50] Ibid. Whether this means that we have *more* unassailable evidence due to global telecommunications, or that we should relax our demand for firm evidence due to an overwhelming proliferation (of potentially contradictory) reports, is unclear.
[51] Maggie O'Kane, 'How to tell lies and win wars', *The Guardian* (16 December 1995). Cf. more generally on the issue of the media in humanitarian intervention, Philip Hammond (ed.), *Degraded Capability: The Media and the Kosovo Crisis*, (London: Pluto Press, 2000).
[52] Arbour, 'The responsibility to protect', p. 448.
[53] Ibid.

populations and territories. Instead in the 'new humanitarian empire'[54] there is 'no territorial center of power [...] fixed boundaries or barriers [...] The distinct national colours of the imperialist map of the world have merged and blended in the imperial global rainbow.'[55] In practice this means that direct political responsibility for transitional territories can be avoided. Roland Paris raises concerns about the 'networked' character of political authority in today's transitional administrations and peacebuilding operations. According to him, by virtue of being 'decentralized and lacking a single corporate identity' –

international governance structures lack clear lines of accountability, meaning that even if we [...] disapproved of the actions of the network of international agencies engaged in peacebuilding, there is no single mechanism through which we could demand a change of peacebuilding policy. Nor is there a single actor whom we could collectively hold responsible for the outcome of a particular operation.[56]

Sovereignty and responsible government

Having prised open the 'problem of agency' at the core of the doctrine, it is now incumbent on me to take my critique further by following the problem back to its source.[57] This problem of agency that vitiates the whole structure of the responsibility to protect can be traced back to its founding assumption – its erosion of the authority of the sovereign state. In Arbour's words, 'sovereignty is not absolute in an interdependent world'.[58]

The problem here is the misconception engendered by the term 'absolute sovereignty' – a rhetorical construct that blurs the issues more than it clarifies them. The ICISS report sagely observed that talk of humanitarian intervention tends to 'prejudge the issue in question' by assuming that the intervention in question must be humanitarian and any opposition inhumane by default.[59] The

---

[54] Michael Ignatieff, *Empire Lite: Nation-Building in Bosnia, Kosovo and Afghanistan* (London; Vintage, 2003), p. 17.

[55] Michael Hardt and Antonio Negri, *Empire* (Cambridge, MA and London: Harvard University Press, 2000), pp. xii–xiii. Hardt and Negri's description is evocative even if their explanatory power is limited. Cf. Scott McLemee, 'Empire Burlesque', *Book Forum* (Dec/Jan 2009).

[56] Roland Paris, 'Broadening the Study of Peace Operations', *International Studies Review*, 2:3 (2000), p. 43.

[57] One frequently mooted solution to the 'agency condition' is a standing cosmopolitan or humanitarian defence force independent of state interests. While such proposals are beyond the scope of the article, one observation can be made, apart from questions of their improbability. It is far from clear that proposals for standing cosmopolitan forces of whatever variety would go much further in resolving the 'ageny condition'. On the contrary, such a force could exacerbate the agency problem, as is suggested by John T. O'Neill and Nicholas Rees:

    A [standing] force of this kind would very likely be regarded as a mercenary body willing to, and capable of, performing any kind of military task. Since no [...] state would bear direct political responsibility for it, everyone would opt out of obligations and frivolously call for its deployment in any small conflict around the world. Far from the answer to global concerns, a UN Foreign Legion would be another excuse for [...] states to do nothing. (*UN Peacekeeping in the Post-Cold War Era*, (London: Routledge, 2005), p. 205).

Although O'Neill and Rees are surveying proposals for a standing UN peacekeeping force, the issue would be the same for a standing humanitarian defence force (in any case, there are now significant humanitarian expectations placed upon UN peacekeepers – cf. Alex J. Bellamy, *Responsibility to Protect: The Global Effort to End Mass Atrocities* (Cambridge: Polity, 2009), pp. 159–60).

[58] Arbour, 'The responsibility to protect', p. 448.

[59] ICISS, *Responsibility to Protect*, p. 9.

same could be said of 'absolute sovereignty':[60] it prejudges the issue in question by suggesting that the absolute monopoly of power is at once untenable in an era of globalisation and morally dubious as a quasi-totalitarian concentration of power. But the idea of 'absoluteness', as far as it is related to sovereignty, is nothing to do with totalitarianism. This is emphasised by Martin Loughlin:

> The absolutist aspect of sovereignty lies in danger of being misunderstood; it can properly be understood only from the perspective of law. Since sovereign authority is expressed through those established institutional forms which enable the general will to be articulated, that general will, although absolute, has nothing in common with the exercise of an arbitrary power. *Sovereign will is the antithesis of subjective [individual] will.*[61]

The 'absoluteness' of sovereign power is 'absolute' insofar as it is related to the binding force of law, which emerges from the relationship between the institutional framework of the state and the people of the state, the latter being the 'constituent power' that generates the 'constituted power' of the state.[62] Sovereignty is not about the *form* of government (democracy, dictatorship, monarchy) nor about the institutions which exercise power (bureaucracy, parliament) but about 'the relationship of political power to other forms of authority'.[63] The fact that sovereign power is supreme, with no higher constituted power above it, asserts the pre-eminence of public authority, and with it the autonomy of the political sphere.[64] The 'absoluteness' or 'impunity' of sovereignty is often tendentiously described as if it existed merely to allow states to perpetrate genocide against their people.[65] But if to be sovereign is to act as one pleases, then sovereignty enshrines the freedom of the people that the state represents, to structure their collective affairs as they see fit.

Sovereignty preserves the freedom of a people to be self-determining, not the impunity of the state apparatus. To erode or call into question 'absolute sovereignty' is to erode or call into question the idea of representative government and the self-determination of nations. As sovereignty inheres in the relationship between people and state, once it is properly understood then the idea of sovereignty already answers the question of who should alleviate human suffering or stamp out gross abuses of human rights: it is the people themselves who must impose their will on the state. If the 'absoluteness' of sovereignty alienates a potentially awesome power of oppression to the state, the dialectic of sovereignty contains within itself the potential to check and overthrow tyranny. It is a concept that relates people to state and subdues the latter to the former. 'People power' is a meaningless slogan in the absence of sovereignty. Without effort it is possible to

---

[60] Another variant on this theme is 'traditional' or 'Westphalian' sovereignty. Though the epithets may vary, they function in essentially the same way.

[61] Martin Loughlin, 'Ten Tenets of Sovereignty', in Neil Hart (ed.), *Sovereignty in Transition* (Oxford: Hart Publishing, 2003), p. 73. Emphasis added.

[62] On the relational character of political power, Loughlin notes 'The relational aspect of the political conception of sovereignty is mainly concerned with elaborating the ways in which constitutional arrangements serve state-building purposes. This feature of political sovereignty is the product of the peculiarly communal character of political power, which requires that individuals act in concert.' Ibid., p. 71.

[63] James Sheehan, 'Presidential Address: The Problem of Sovereignty in European History', *The American Historical Review*, 111:1 (2006), p. 1. Cf. also Loughlin, 'Ten Tenets of Sovereignty', p. 68.

[64] On the autonomy of the political, see Loughlin, 'Ten Tenets of Sovereignty', p. 56.

[65] Louis Henkin, for example, criticises this caricatured portrayal of sovereignty: 'Kosovo and the Law of "Humanitarian Intervention"', *American Journal of International Law*, 93:4 (1999), pp. 824–48.

bring to mind historical examples of when people have risen up against even the most fearsome and unjust of tyrannies. Indeed, the Franco-American revolutions of the eighteenth century that advanced universal human rights as a political force were precisely examples of such struggles for popular self-determination.

The real issue then is not whether states are responsible to their citizens – this is after all given in the very idea of modern political representation. What becomes clear is that under the banal talk of 'state responsibilities' the responsibility to protect doctrine is calling into question people's capacity for and rights of self-determination. Small wonder that 'victims' occupy such an important place in the doctrine. As we saw previously, the emphasis on the victims of international politics is celebrated as the strong point of the doctrine.[66] No more of the unseemly squabbling and shenanigans of states, the doctrine's supporters say, and instead let us focus on the practical problem of alleviating human suffering. But we have no reason to accept the 'ideology of victimization' at face value.[67] Quite the opposite: we would be naïve not to be at least initially sceptical when we hear the powerful, the great and the good declaiming for the rights of the powerless.

Indeed, it is revealing that the intended beneficiaries and constituents of the doctrine have to be assumed to be politically passive. Victims by their very nature are weak and pliable, offering exceptional political advantage to those who would seek to represent them. After all, the weak and powerless have difficulty holding their putative benefactors to account. To paraphrase Marx, what is appealing about victims as a political constituency is that 'They cannot represent themselves, they must be represented. Their representative must at the same time appear as their master, as an authority over them, [...] that protects them [...] and sends them rain and sunshine from above.'[68] What is true in general is even truer of the international sphere, where there exists no machinery of cross-border government that would enable the victims of a particular conflict to hold the government of another intervening country to account in any meaningful way. Indeed, in certain cases international interveners have not only assumed the political passivity of their intended beneficiaries, they have actively imposed it. NATO's support for the human rights of Kosovars during the war of 1999 came at the expense of the self-determination for which the Kosovo Liberation Army was fighting (Kosovo was administered as a UN-NATO protectorate from 1999 to 2008, and remains a ward of the international community to this day).[69] It would seem that the victims of conflict are good enough to be flattered by august international conventions and UN resolutions, but not it seems, good enough to be granted self-government.

While Arbour openly recognises that the doctrine gives powerful states greater leeway to coerce smaller powers, what she does not recognise is that it also gives states greater freedom from accountability to their own peoples. This returns to the 'gaping hole' that the doctrine tears open in the structure of democratic politics. For once the principle is established that states must uphold a certain standard to

---

[66] Arbour, 'The responsibility to protect', p. 448.

[67] The phrase is taken from Slavoj Žižek, 'NATO: the Left Hand of God?', *Nettime* (29 June 1999).

[68] Karl Marx, *The Eighteenth Brumaire of Louis Bonaparte* (London: Lawrence and Wishart, 1934), p. 109. Marx is here relating the form of Louis Napoleon's mid-nineteenth century dictatorship to the socio-political fragmentation and weakness of the French peasantry that supported him.

[69] Even today, nominally independent Kosovo is an international protectorate. Cf. Philip Cunliffe, 'Kosovo: the obedient child of Europe', *Spiked Online* (18 February 2008).

which they may be held to account by outside institutions and other states, this cannot but have the effect of making the people less central to a state's political choices. Perversely, being forced to take greater account of the international community does not strengthen a state's commitment to its own people so much as granting states the opportunity to distance themselves from their people's demands and interests, by citing the pressures and responsibilities owed to the international community. In short, the doctrine of the responsibility to protect establishes the insidious principle that states hold responsibilities *for* their people more than *to* their peoples. For a doctrine that invites us to be suspicious of state power, it is peculiar on the face of it that it offers such clear opportunities for states to entrench their powers at the expense of popular accountability. But this is the logic of a doctrine that expands responsibilities without accountability: paternalism.

Lest it be thought that these concerns only apply to those states 'which may assume that they could be targets of intervention', Arbour's internationalised duty of care also has consequences for domestic politics in those 'countries that would most likely be the potential interveners'.[70] The 'responsibility to protect' not only lowers the justification necessary for any state to mount an intervention in the international realm, but also in the domestic sphere. Embedding the possibility of intervention as a duty of generalised 'human protection' provides governments with a ready means of quashing domestic opposition to foreign crusades – doubtless a prospect that would appeal to the likes of former British Prime Minister Tony Blair, who infamously insisted that the invasion of Iraq was the 'right thing to do' regardless of the expressed will of his people.[71] The more that states bear diffuse and abstract duties to all people, the more they are able to evade responsibility to a concrete people.

Sovereignty and intervention reconsidered

Where does all this leave the issue of offering people an additional bulwark of (international) protection from 'state-sponsored slaughter'? What of circumstances when self-help is not possible, where there is no popular domestic movement or organised political opposition of sufficient strength to overthrow an oppressive regime or halt systematic atrocities? Is it possible to take cross-border action to halt 'gross violations of human rights' without compromising the imperative of popular sovereignty and self-determination? What is certain is that it is always possible to concoct hypothetical scenarios in the abstract, in which the case for intervention is unarguable. Concrete crises are always more complex and contra-dictory than those dreamt up in 'what if?' scenarios.[72] Nonetheless, as Martin

---

[70] Arbour, 'The responsibility to protect', p. 450.

[71] Philip Webster, 'Tony Blair: "I wanted war – it was the right thing to do"', *The Times* (17 November 2007).

[72] Indeed, the formation of institutions and policy around the precautionary principles of preparing for extreme scenarios is a problem in itself – the problem of political exceptionalism that vitiates the whole debate around intervention and the responsibility to protect. It is incumbent on us to think through not only how we should respond to exceptional scenarios, but also in the words of Jef Huysmans, reflect on how 'claims of exceptionality' function politically. How do such claims

Wight justly observed, 'adherents of every political belief will regard intervention as justified under certain circumstances'.[73] Equally it would be dishonest and remiss not to acknowledge that even those interventions which we may believe to have been justified under the circumstances are still deeply problematic.[74] There is no avoiding issues of 'the utmost moral complexity' in intervention[75] – something which is obliterated in the Manichean vision promulgated by humanitarianism, which sees only oppressors and victims, good and evil.[76]

What should be apparent by now is that it is not possible innocuously to insert this internationalised 'duty of care' without distorting the normative edifice of the international order and warping the structure of representative government. It is not possible to loosen the normative restraints on intervention – whether conceived of as the use of military force or 'milder' forms of coercion – without impinging on self-determination and boosting paternalistic forms of political authority. Intervention should always be proscribed and sovereignty upheld. If these are the keystones of international order, then even specific instances of intervention or violations of sovereignty will leave intact the normative value and content of self-determination as a principle. Recognising that intervention will take place and may even be necessary in some circumstances is crucially different from making the case that intervention should be encouraged or facilitated.[77]

It is possible, without being inconsistent, to uphold non-intervention as a precondition of sovereignty while also admitting that particular interventions may be necessary. At the very least, this would have the benefit of honesty: acknowledging that intervention involves the violation of sovereignty would not require tortuous and unconvincing arguments about 'responsibilities'. It would impose political penalties, preventing states from grandiloquently claiming that they were acting on behalf of humanity itself. The principle of self-determination would remain as one from which criticism could be mounted and interveners held to account.[78] It would also by default clarify the responsibilities incumbent on interveners in any post-conflict period, preventing the flight from political responsibility witnessed in the networked authorities of today's transitional administrations.

This begs the question of course, of whether we live in 'special times' – in a period where human suffering is so dramatic, grave and shocking that we must discard principled attachments to norms of self-determination, international

'structure [the] stakes and positions in international struggles for legitimacy and authority?' – Jef Huysmans, 'International Politics of Insecurity: Normativity, Inwardness and the Exception', *Security Dialogue*, 37:1, (2006), p. 12. Alas, for reasons of space, this is a problem that I tackle elsewhere: Philip Cunliffe, 'The Responsibility to Protect as a Practice of Political Exceptionalism'. Paper presented to LSE Forum in Legal and Political Theory (17 March 2010).
[73] Martin Wight, *Power Politics* (Harmondsworth: Penguin, 1979), p. 191.
[74] For example, see Joshua Kurlantzick's account of the vagaries of the international criminal tribunals in contemporary Cambodia, and of the legacy of political authoritarianism inherited from the Vietnamese occupation of that country. Joshua Kurlantzick, 'In Pol Pot Time', *London Review of Books* (6 August 2009).
[75] Wight, *Power Politics*, p. 191.
[76] For a critique of this reflexive depiction of a conflict in Manichean terms, cf. Mahmood Mamdani, 'The Politics of Naming: Genocide, Civil War, Insurgency', *London Review of Books* (8 March 2007).
[77] The way in which one proposition segues into the other is usually through claims for political exceptionalism. Cf. fn. 66 above.
[78] This is the argument advocated by Simon Chesterman. Cf. f n. 21 above.

equality and anti-imperialism and simply accept the routine violation of sovereignty.[79] This belief, in many variants, is the corollary assumption that shadows all discussion of humanitarian intervention and the responsibility to protect. As David Chandler observes, 'Most human rights books start with stories of genocide, mass rape, ethnic cleansing, and torture, to emphasise the urgency of their cause.'[80] Arbour herself begins her article by citing 'a proliferation of devastating internal wars' that unfolded across the 1990s.[81] Are these justifiable depictions of today's international order? The claims of the 'neo-barbarism' school – the idea that conflicts in the developing world today are disproportionately violent and brutal – have now been subjected to extensive and penetrating criticisms, so there is no need to recapitulate such criticisms here.[82] In any case, there is always the point that the focus of humanitarian concern is notoriously partial: some cases of human rights violations receive international attention while others do not.

The point is not to draw attention to the hypocrisy that may underlie any particular humanitarian claim. Rather the inconsistency should alert us to the fact that there is something else that intercedes between identifying a focus for humanitarian compassion and maintaining the international duty of care which Arbour enjoins us to do. As Slavoj Žižek observes,

> The death of a West Bank Palestinian child, not to mention an Israeli or an American, is mediatically worth thousands of times more than the death of a nameless Congolese. Do we need further proof that the humanitarian sense of urgency is mediated, indeed overdetermined, by clear political considerations?[83]

Despite the hysteria surrounding the threats posed by failed states and 'new wars', as the 2005 *Human Security Report* has shown, levels of global violence have been declining from the early 1990s, including both inter – and intra-state conflict.[84] All of this suggests that the rise of the 'responsibility to protect' cannot be straightforwardly justified or mechanically attributed to a rise in the levels of conflict, violence or human suffering, as this rise has simply not happened. As Jon Holbrook noted long before the *Human Security Report* was published, 'The point is not that there are no humanitarian crises: there are. But [. . .] the existence of human suffering cannot explain the phenomenon of humanitarian intervention.'[85] Nor is the argument about globalisation or interdependence any more straightforward: 'Pressures on Western governments to respond to humanitarian crises existed before the 1991 relief operation in northern Iraq. What needs to be explained is why Western governments did not, until 1991, translate these pressures into coercive action'.[86]

---

[79] The question of *whether* or not we accept a particular claim made for political exceptionalism is not necessarily the same as providing an account of *why* claims are systematically advanced in the form of political exceptionalism. The latter is beyond the scope of this article. Cf. fn. 66 above.

[80] Chandler, *Kosovo to Kabul*, p. 232.

[81] Arbour, 'The responsibility to protect', p. 446.

[82] See Chapter 5 in Mark Duffield, *Global Governance and the New Wars: The Merging of Development and Security* (London and New York: Zed Books, 2001).

[83] Slavoj Žižek, *Violence: Six Sideways Reflections* (London: Profile Books, 2008), p. 3.

[84] *Human Security Report*. Available: {http://www.humansecurityreport.info} accessed 9 August 2009.

[85] Jon Holbrook, 'Humanitarian Intervention and the Recasting of International Law', in David Chandler (ed.), *Rethinking Human Rights: Critical Approaches to International Politics* (Basingstoke: Palgrave Macmillan, 2002), p. 139.

[86] Ibid.

The argument that we have increasing recourse to intervention as a result of enhanced levels of international violence does not hold up. If anything, recent international history is remarkable for its relative calm and stability more than anything else.[87] This gives us no reason of historic exceptionality to jettison sovereignty and self-determination. Instead these facts should prompt us to reconsider the context for the rise of humanitarian intervention and the 'responsibility to protect'. If we cannot attribute these norms to greater levels of international violence, then we must root it in the changing political order – Western victory in the Cold War, economic globalisation and the subsequent struggles between the developing and developed worlds.[88] Locating this as the context for the responsibility to protect sheds a very different light on how we understand and approach the doctrine.

Conclusion

Arbour celebrates the responsibility to protect as a means of bolstering the international legal defences available to the wretched of the earth. She presents the doctrine as offering important normative advances on the problems posed by humanitarian intervention. But Arbour misdiagnoses the problems of humanitarian intervention, and in so doing, simply reproduces the real problems of interventionism in her defence of the responsibility to protect. The problem remains that of the violation of state sovereignty involved in intervention, and the concomitant violation of self-determination. The responsibility to protect remains as discretionary a prerogative as humanitarian intervention. At the most, the doctrine can only offer vague assurances to the victims of world politics, who in any case are assumed to be politically passive and apathetic, prostrate before the mercy of both their oppressors and their benefactors.

Where the responsibility to protect does differ from humanitarian intervention, it is for the worse. The responsibility to protect does not merely ensconce coercion in relations *between* states; it also has the potential to distort the structure of representative government *within* states. It further erodes the presumption of non-intervention in the internal affairs of states, thereby calling into question the very foundation of representative government, by making such government conditional on international license. At the international level, the promotion of the responsibility to protect yields all the advantages of intervention to the powerful states that are likely to wield it, with fewer political costs. Invoking a 'permanent' duty allows states to claim a higher legitimacy than their own political will in pursuit of their aims. As the doctrine enhances power with no countervailing check, we can only reach the conclusion that the doctrine will have the effect of making the exercise of power less responsible. The doctrine fosters the paternalism of strong states over weak states and of states over their peoples. Perversely, instead of disciplining states in favour of the wretched of the earth, states are given further justification to slip out of the grasp of popular accountability.

---

[87] For example, cf. Raimo Väyrynen, *The Waning of Major War: Theories and Debates* (Oxford, New York: Routledge, 2006).
[88] See the 'Foreword' in the ICISS' *Responsibility to Protect*.

Review of International Studies (2010), 37, 97–112 © *2011 British International Studies Association*
doi:10.1017/S0260210511000118

Global justice, national responsibility and transnational power

DAVID OWEN*

Abstract. This article focuses on David Miller's recent and influential study *National Responsibility and Global Justice* (2007). After outlining Miller's methodological commitments in the book, the article offers an interpretation of the major aspects of Miller's case against 'Cosmopolitan egalitarianism' before focusing especially on the issue of migration and refugees. Here the article argues that while membership of a nation is (under certain conditions) of intrinsic value, it is not the only thing that is of intrinsic value – friendship, family and other practices can also be sources of intrinsic value – nor is it necessarily the most important. It is therefore not clear, the article argues, why an account of global justice that seeks to take seriously the existence of national communities on the grounds of their intrinsic value, should propose rules of justice concerning freedom of movement that entail the *de jure* privileging of the value of national community over other sources of intrinsic value. The article concludes by assessing how Miller's arguments can support the movement from mere 'distributivism' towards political justice, towards an account that more adequately integrates agency, responsibility and power into our account of global justice.

David Owen is Professor of Social and Political Philosophy and Deputy Director of the Centre for Philosophy and Value at the University of Southampton. His research focuses on problems of political community; contemporary democratic theory; the ethics and politics of migration, theories of power and freedom, post-Kantian moral and political philosophy and the philosophies of Nietzsche, Wittgenstein and Foucault. He is currently working on two books, *Nietzsche's Contest: Freedom, Perfectionism and Realism in Political Theory* (Rowman and Littlefield) and *Migration and Political Theory* (Routledge).

In the context of contemporary debates on justice, a new work by David Miller is always an event – and this is perhaps particularly the case with his latest study *National Responsibility and Global Justice.*[1] As the most articulate critic of a global egalitarianism that has become the dominant liberal paradigm in debates on global justice, Miller plays a dual role: on the one hand, he offers a richly elaborated alternative view of the requirements and responsibilities of global justice and, on the other hand, he forces the advocates of global equalitarianism to raise their game. However, a particularly important feature of this new work is that it also

---

* I am grateful to Chris Armstrong, Bert van Brink, Peter Niesen, Nick Rengger and Jonathan Seglow for their helpful comments on a draft of this article. I owe particular thanks to Andy Mason for discussing many of the issues raised herein and for his comments on two earlier versions.
[1] David Miller, *National Responsibility and Global Justice* (Oxford: Oxford University Press, 2007). All references to Miller in the main text will be to this book unless otherwise specified.

helps to move discussions of global justice away from what Iris Young referred to as 'the distributivist paradigm'.[2] The salient issue has been nicely glossed by Rainer Forst:

> To put it in a (simplistic) nutshell, since the ancient formula of justice to *each his own* was coined, philosophical thinking about justice has developed along two very broad lines. One line focuses on the goods persons receive in a distributive scheme, comparing their share either with what relevant others have or with what persons need or deserve by some ethical standards, or both; the other line focuses on the relationship between the persons involved and their relative standing within a scheme of exercising power. One could call the first a focus on distributive justice, the latter one on political justice.[3]

In contrast to, say, Simon Caney,[4] Miller's arguments in this book mark a significant shift from distributive justice towards political justice (though he does not adopt these terms and might well resist this description) and it is in part against the background of this contrast that I will be concerned to address his account of global justice.

However, I should also acknowledge that this article be attempting to cover all of the issues raised in Miller's book, despite the fact that this work has a complex architecture of argument which means that leaving some issues aside raises the worry of misrepresenting Miller's position as less subtle and supple than it is. In the space available, though, this is a risk that will have to be run and my strategy will be to attend to what I take to be Miller's core argument before focusing in specifically on his account of migration.

An outline of Miller's approach

Miller's carefully crafted account is framed by three methodological commitments. First, *a dual aspect* approach to human beings as subjects of justice which present us not simply as 'needy and vulnerable creatures who cannot live decent, let alone flourishing, lives unless they are *given* at least a minimal bundle of freedoms, opportunities, and resources' (emphasis added) but also as 'choosing agents who must take responsibility for their own lives' (pp. 5–6). This insistence on viewing others under *both* aspects is an expression of respect: 'Our relationship [to others] becomes a more equal one to the extent that we consider not only their needs but also their capacities for choice and responsibility.' (p. 7). Second, a *contextualist* approach to principles of justice: 'the principles that tell us what counts as a just distribution of some good are specific to the context in which the distribution is taking place [...] the relevant principle will depend on what is being distributed, by whom and among whom: especially on the kind of relationship that exists between the people among whom the distribution is occurring.' (pp. 13–4). Note that it is perfectly possible for an egalitarian theorist to endorse this kind of contextualist stance concerning distributive justice and Simon Caney does so when

[2] Iris Marion Young, *Justice and the Politics of Difference* (Princeton: Princeton University Press, 1990).

[3] Rainer Forst, *Das Recht auf Rechtfertigung. Elemente einer konstruktivistischen Theorie der Gerechtigkeit* (Frankfurt/Main, Germany: Suhrkamp Verlag, 2007), p. 260.

[4] Simon Caney, *Justice Beyond Borders: Towards A Global Political Theory* (Oxford: Oxford University Press, 2005).

he accepts that the existence of a sense of nationality of the kind Miller defends *could* function as establishing a relevant *disanalogy* between domestic and global realms as far as principles of justice are concerned.[5] Thus, the methodological contextualism at work in Miller's argument is compatible with both egalitarian and non-egalitarian positions; it simply specifies a set of terms on which this substantive argument about distributive principles is to be played out. The third and final of Miller's methodological principles is his adoption of the late Rawlsian notion of *realistic utopianism* as specifying the level or kind of theorising with which he is engaged. This does, as Miller recognises, open the theorist to attack from two directions in that their normative claims can be criticised as either too weak (bound by too limited an account of what is practically possible) or too strong (not limited enough by its account of what is practically possible). Interestingly, Miller only considers (to set aside) such responses as global responses (for example, by IR realists) and does not draw attention to the more interesting case of a global endorsement of this approach combined with local rejections of some parts (perhaps all) of Miller's normative arguments as reliant on, for example, economic and/or sociological assumptions that can't be substantiated.

Against this methodological backdrop, the structure of Miller's substantive argumentation falls into two parts: first, a core anti-egalitarian argument and, second, two elaborations of the implications of this anti-egalitarian view for global justice with respect to migration and global poverty respectively. The core argument is offered through four steps: (1) establishing the distinction between weak (equal moral concern) and *strong* (equal treatment in some substantive sense) forms of moral cosmopolitanism; (2) making plausible the claim that membership of a nation can be a source of special obligations; (3) offering a critique of global egalitarianism; and (4) showing that members can be liable in respect of the actions of their nations. Granting (1) for the sake of argument, I will focus on (2), (3) and (4).

Nationality and special obligations

Isn't one's nationality simply a morally arbitrary feature that should be discounted for purposes of justice? Such is the position of Joseph Carens', for instance, in his classic moral cosmopolitanism argument for open borders.[6] To defuse the force of this intuition, Miller offers a conceptual argument and a substantive argument. The

[5] See Caney, *Justice Beyond Borders*, p. 277. Notice also that if one adopts a distinction between *fundamental* and *regulative* principles of distributive justice, then while it clear that Miller is a contextualist about regulative principles of distributive justice, it is less clear that he is so about fundamental principles. Thus, on one reading, the distinction between *weak* and *strong* forms of cosmopolitanism that plays a crucial role in Miller's argument (see section II below) may be construed as a distinction between an invariant fundamental principle (roughly, 'every human being is equally an object of moral concern') and contextually variable regulative principles derived from it; although, on another plausible reading, Miller may simply be situating the principle of equal moral concern as a fundamental constraint on substantive theorising rather than as a fundamental principle from which substantive principles are contextually derived.

[6] See Joseph Carens, 'Aliens and Citizens: The Case for Open Borders', *review of Politics*, 49 (1987), pp. 251–73 and 'Migration and Morality: A Liberal Egalitarian Perspective', in B. Barry and R. Goodin (eds), *Free Movement: Ethical Issues in the Transnational Migration of People and Money* (Hemel Hempstead: Harvester Wheatsheaf, 1992).

former distinguishes two senses of 'morally arbitrary', the descriptive sense that some feature is a product of unchosen luck and the normative sense that a feature should not count in determining distributions. Miller argues the second does not track the first by noting disabilities are products of unchosen luck yet most people would acknowledge that they should effect distributions (pp. 32–3). The latter argues that in the same way that family relationship may give rise to special obligations that should be recognised in any account of justice, so too may relationships between co-nationals. On what grounds? Miller's argument runs thus: Nations can (at least in principle) meet three conditions that are jointly sufficient for this claim: (a) that nationality (like friendship) is an intrinsically valuable relationship that gives rise to special obligations; (b) that these special obligations are internally related to the good of the relationship; and (c) that this relationship does not entail injustice with respect to those excluded from it (what Samuel Scheffler calls 'the distributive objection',[7] although distributive injustice is hardly the only form of injustice that exclusion might involve). Of course, even if true, this argument only shows that nations *can be* a legitimate source of special obligations to co-nationals, not that any existing nations meet this standard and thus Miller asserts that we 'have obligations to our compatriots *to the extent* that our nation meets the [specified] conditions' (p. 37, fn. 21). This argument raises three significant issues for the plausibility of Miller's account and, given their importance, it is worth attending to each in a little detail.

The first issue involves drawing attention to the point that at various points Miller's account mobilises two distinct senses of nationality: nationality as membership of a national community and nationality as the external legal face of citizenship. Although Miller's 'official' position is that he is addressing nations and not states, this position seems to slip on more than one occasion. Thus, for example, in initially framing his argument Miller writes in relation to the circumstances of global justice that 'if we consider how people relate to one another at that level, one very important mode is as citizens of independent national communities' (p. 17) and again 'I have drawn attention to particularly to citizenship in nation-states as a key factor that differentiates people's relationships within political communities from their relationships at [a] global level.' (p. 17) and again: 'The particular question we are examining is whether the circumstances of global justice should be taken to include the existence of separate states whose members belong to different national cultures, and who therefore value their capacity to be politically self-determining.' (p. 19). While it is true that Miller's discussion of national responsibility in chapters five and six does restrict itself to a focus on the nation, the discussion of immigration in chapter 8 is more or less entirely state-focused. In general, his default position seems to be one of addressing nation-states rather than nations as such. This matters since, as Miller acknowledges,[8] one can construct accounts of the intrinsic value of citizenship and of special obligations to compatriots that makes no appeal whatsoever to the notion of national belonging. Both Jurgen Habermas' conception of *constitutional patriotism* and Andrew Mason's conception of *belonging to a polity* denote clear

---

[7] Samuel Scheffler, *Boundaries and Allegiances: Problems of Justice and Responsibility in Liberal Thought* (Oxford: Oxford University Press, 2001).

[8] See, for example, 'Immigrants, Nations, and Citizenship', *Journal of Political Philosophy*, 16 (2008), pp. 371–90.

(and distinct) theoretical alternatives to Miller's favoured liberal nationalist account.[9] Moreover, whether or not we have reasons *in justice* to prefer these civic models, if they are feasible practical alternatives, we certainly have *moral* reasons to prefer them since they impose lesser costs and burdens on culturally diverse citizens as well as being less restrictive with respect to resident aliens seeking to become members of the polity. Miller must, then, be committed to the claim that the models proposed by Habermas and Mason are not feasible practical alternatives to the liberal nationalist model – yet, as far as I can tell, Miller offers no compelling empirical evidence for this claim either in *On Nationality*,[10] where the empirical evidence considered would apply equally to all three models[11] nor in this latest work. This is not entirely Miller's fault since direct evidence is hard to come by and, in a more recent article, Miller has tried to support his position through the use of indirect evidence; however, it remains the case, given the centrality of the claim concerning national belonging to Miller's whole account, that what grounds this account – as well as the accounts of his rivals – is currently a wager on what the empirical conditions of maintaining social democratic states turn out to be.

The second topic concerns Miller's claim that we 'have obligations to our compatriots *to the extent* that our nation meets the [specified] conditions' (p. 37 fn. 21). Two problems arise here. First, it is not exactly clear what this claim means. Does this mean, for example, that as the degree of injustice that arises as a by-product of our valuing national community increases or declines, then so, as a matter of inverse proportionality, do our obligations to compatriots? It is unclear why we should think this and Miller's own account of human rights addressed to generic basic needs would appear to cut against such a view. Second, there are further problems concerning the determination of the scope and extent of co-nationals' special obligations to each other. On the one hand, a problem arises concerning scope since the class of persons enjoying the formal legal status of nationality need not coincide with the class of persons who appropriately recognise each other as having special obligations to each other as co-nationals. On the other hand, since, in contrast to the case of friendship, certain requirements of mutual recognition of special obligations to co-nationals are given coercive institutional expression through law, the fact that our co-nationals act *as if* they recognise the value of national community does not entail that they do so (unless we have good reason to believe that institutional recognition reliably tracks interpersonal recognition).[12] In terms of Miller's own analogies of friendship and family, we may ask if I owe special obligations to individuals who act *as if* friends or family but for reasons (prudential or moral) not based in an acknowledgment of the intrinsic value of friendship or family. If the answer is 'no', then this finding stands in real tension with Miller's implicit strategy of treating the legal status of nationality and the performance of the

---

[9] See Jurgen Habermas, *The Inclusion of the Other* (Oxford: Polity Press, 2002) and Andrew Mason *Community, Solidarity and Belonging* (Cambridge: Cambridge University Press, 2000).

[10] David Miller, *On Nationality* (Oxford, Oxford University, 1995).

[11] Miller, *On Nationality*, pp 161–5.

[12] Moreover if, as seems likely, many (perhaps most) of our co-nationals do endorse the value of nationality but endorse it as a result of institutional recognition of special obligations to co-nationals (legal, educational and otherwise), we can at the very least legitimately raise the question of whether or not such endorsement is *ideological* in the critical sense of this term. The logical gap between 'intrinsically valued' and 'intrinsically valuable' facilitates this question and the identity-forming powers of institutional modes of recognition encourage it.

duties of citizenship as proxies for these issues of scope and extent precisely because this strategy puts rather too much emphasis on the institutional rather than the interpersonal, where the latter (and not the former) is the key justificatory ground for special obligations between co-nationals. If the answer is 'yes', then it is not clear why we should be focusing on national identity rather than simply on citizenship. (None of which is to say that one cannot specify special obligations in terms of institutional structures that are both coercive and cooperative structures with respect to citizens, simply that Miller does not take this route.)

The third of the three conditions that Miller specifies – that the special obligations between co-nationals should not entail injustice to outsiders – leads directly to the third issue I wish to consider. Miller's key move in relation to the distributive objection to special obligations is to point out that answering the question of whether special obligations entail injustice hangs on how one specifies the general obligations that obtain between the persons or groups in question. If these general obligations are understood in egalitarian fashion, special obligations are likely to be judged unjust unless they serve as effective delivery mechanisms for general obligations specified; by contrast, if the general obligations are construed in a non-egalitarian fashion, say, as a basic needs account, then there is likely to be more scope for viewing special obligations that do not serve the delivery of general obligations as not unjust. Thus, the distributive objection cannot be used to ground commitment to global egalitarianism (or, for that matter, Miller's global non-egalitarianism), rather independent arguments concerning the nature of the general obligations we owe to each other are required. Notice though that implicit in this view – or at least Miller's elaboration of it – is the claim that the only general obligations at stake are those that we owe to each other as human beings *qua* human being; but this claim should, I think, be rejected since we may also reasonably view each other as individuals and groups (including nations) who are all subject to a regime of global governance comprised in significant degree by the international society of states as well as the regional and transnational institutions of governance which have emerged within and from it – and, consequently, as owing each other general and reciprocal justification of the political structures and power dynamics of inclusion and exclusion currently characteristic of this regime of global governance. Thus, to take an issue that one would think of direct relevance to Miller's nationalist concerns, we might think that such general and reciprocal justification is required for the fact that the capacities of 'nations' as agents in the global political arena and their vulnerabilities to other actors are significantly shaped by, for example, their recognition or non-recognition within international law: the comparison between the non-recognition of 'First Nations' (indigenous peoples) as persons in international law and the contrasting recognition of nations that have the political form of a sovereign state is an obvious and poignant example. In this context, I incline to Rainer Forst's view that the most basic principle of justice – at any level – is a right to justification.[13] The main point here is that, despite Miller's welcome emphasis on issues of agency, he pays relatively little attention to the political question of how particular forms of individual and collective agency are constituted through power relations (nor, more

---

[13] Though I differ from Forst in wishing to ground this right in a political rather than a moral standpoint.

specifically, in how the actions of powerful agents can shape the landscape of international law).[14] As we will see, this issue returns in respect of his discussion of national responsibility.

Against global egalitarianism

Miller's argument against global egalitarianism involves specifying two problems with this position: the *metric* problem (global distributive egalitarians cannot specify what substantive equality of treatment would mean) and the *dynamic* problem (the problem posed for global equality by the existence of self-governing political communities whose decisions structure the current and future availability of resources and opportunities). I shall leave aside the first issue in order to focus on the second. This is in part because the argument offered in relation to the *dynamic* problem helps itself to the assumption – for the purposes of argument – that there is some metric in terms of which a principle of global equality can be couched and thus we can reasonably take Miller to be offering the *dynamic* problem to be the fundamental issue at stake in that it persists regardless of the validity of argument concerning the metric problem (it is also in part because Miller's consideration of metrics is limited to equality of resources and equality of opportunity which hardly exhausts the range of metrics available).

Miller imagines two pairs of nation-states each starting from an equal resource base: (a) Affluenza which decides to use up its resource base rapidly to sustain high consumption and Ecologia which chooses to conserve resources by engaging in sustainable development; and (b) Procreatia which encourages large families and population growth, and Condominium which adopts a strictly enforced family planning policy to ensure a stable population. Miller then assumes that level of advantage are determined solely by domestic policy and, other things being equal, *per capita* resource levels will become greater in Ecologia than in Affluenza and greater in Condominium than in Procreatia (pp. 68–90).[15] The point of these examples is to undermine the attractiveness of an egalitarian policy by showing that it is *either* too weak if limited to the notion of equal starting points *or* creates perverse incentives if recast as preserving equal access to advantage over time and unfairly penalises the citizens of Ecologia and Condominium (pp. 70–2). Miller acknowledges that a possibility 'would be to deny nations rights to self-determination in all those areas of policy that have an impact of levels of advantage' but insists that 'this is tantamount to doing away with self-determination altogether'. He further claims this position cannot be saved by requiring each generation to have an equal starting point since generations are fictions in the relevant sense so allowing nations to decide autonomously for a generation and then applying an international tax-and-transfer regime would not solve the problem (p. 73).

[14] Relevant considerations of which have been acutely addressed in Michael Byers, *Custom, Power and the Power of Rules: International Relations and Customary International Law* (Cambridge, Cambridge University Press, 1999); 2001), his edited collection *The Role of Law in International Politics* (Oxford, Oxford University Press, 2001) and his edited collection with Geog Nolte, *US Hegemony and the Foundations of International Law* (Cambridge, Cambridge University Press, 2003).

[15] Neither of these assumptions is very realistic but let that pass.

This argument does not strike me as overly convincing since it constructs too stark a contrast between autonomous decision-making and lack of self-determination. Autonomous decision-making does not mean being able to choose anything, it means being able to choose within a structure of just rules. *If* it is a rule of justice that we have obligations to future generations to try to ensure that they are no worse off in terms of access to advantage than we are, it would be perfectly reasonable to have an international tax regime that applied to all nations and that taxed activities on the basis of our best current knowledge of their probable implications, other things being equal, for the access to advantage of the future generations. Such a tax regime would no more undermine the right of nations to determine their own policies than a just tax regime within a state undermines the capacity of its members to engage in autonomous decision-making; in both cases, all that has happened is that the costs of various choices are regulated by more general concerns of justice (consider how the example of a global carbon tax in conjunction with the possibility of trading carbon tax credits allows states to pursue different paths). Moreover, as in the state context, such a tax regime could apply continuously as could transfers in the form of a resource allocation at birth to each individual. There is not, I think, anything particularly difficult in principle about this scenario.

On the basis of Miller's argument, I can find two objections to such a proposal. The first is that, under the scenario he envisages, the resource-poorer children of Affluenza and Procreatia should direct their complaints towards their predecessors and don't have a claim on the citizens of Ecologia and Condominium (p. 72). But this objection is addressed by the fact that, under my proposal, it is their predecessors who are more highly taxed for their profligate ways and by the further point that, in the absence of such tax revenue, these children do have a claim against the international society of states (and, hence, against Ecologia and Condominium as members of this international community) for not ensuring that such resources are available. The second objection is Miller's rejection of the principle of ensuring that future generations have an equal resource entitlement as a principle of justice; he comments thus:

Assume that the resource level have not fallen to the point where the rising generation are unable to secure minimally decent lives. The charge, then, is that their access to advantage is lower than it might be if the previous generation had pursued more prudent policies, of the kind prevailing in Ecologia and Condominium. But this is not a very weighty complaint: it does not seem to be a matter of justice that our predecessors should leave us with any particular level of *per capita* resources, so long as the level does not fall below that required to sustain the institutions that make a decent life possible. (p. 72)

But this objection presupposes the validity of the non-egalitarian principle of justice that Miller is proposing in the course of presenting the very arguments that are meant to lead us to it. Since, on my view, a consistent global egalitarianism will hold the principle of ensuring that future generations are not worse off in terms of access to advantage than the current generation, Miller can't simply assume away this fact in order to facilitate his objections to egalitarianism.

Even if these responses by Miller are unconvincing, however, he does have two further fallback positions available to him. The first would be to argue that any such international tax-and-transfer regime would require a global state on the grounds that people would only comply with such a system given the global equivalent of a shared sense of national belonging. While this response is not at all compelling in the context of the stylised example constructed by Miller, it would be foolish to underestimate its force in real world circumstances in which nation-states of inherited privilege confront nation-states of inherited deprivation on the scale of privilege and deprivation that currently prevails in our world. The second fallback position is the argument concerning the metric problem. Miller may not wish to fallback onto this position since presumptively it does less work for his argument than would be accomplished than the substantive critique of global egalitarianism and because it is unclear that this argument would itself hold up under pressure. Arguably, Miller makes the argument plausible by demanding more fine-grained comparative judgments than may be possible, but it is not an objection to the possibility of measurement that our available instruments of measurement can only yield more coarse-grained judgments than we would ideally like; one should be a realistic utopian about measurement as well as principles.

National responsibility

Bracketing off the fact that Miller's critique of global egalitarianism does not strike me as fully persuasive, what of his final move – that of establishing that members can be liable for the responsibilities of their nation? There are three elements to Miller's argument. First, he offers an account of collective responsibility in general that shows how individual members of such collectives can be held liable for the outcomes of collective actions. Second, he tries to show that this analysis covers nations as contemporaneous groups of people. Third, he attempts to extend this argument to cover liability for the past actions of nations (pp. 113–4).

Miller offers two ideal-typical models of collective responsibility: the like-mindedness model and the cooperative practice model. In the first model, exemplified by the figure of the mob, the focus is on that fact that the collective brings about some outcome (even if the individual members do not intend to do so) that is a product of their collective behaviour where this behaviour is characterised by common-mindedness. In the second model, exemplified by the figure of the employee-controlled firm, the focus is on the responsibility of members of a cooperative practice for the damage caused by that practice, where the presumption is that the costs of repairing the damage be borne by all members (including those who dissent with respect to continuing the damaging aspects of the practice but benefit from its continuance). The distinction between the two models is, first, that the former requires the notion of a common identity, whereas the latter does not and, second, that the latter imposes fairness requirements that the former need not (pp. 114–9). What, then, do members have to do to avoid acquiring liability for the actions of the collective? Miller writes: 'Unfortunately, it is difficult to say anything more precise than that he or she must take all reasonable steps to prevent the outcome occurring [that are compatible with not incurring greater costs than people in general could be reasonably expected to bear].' (p. 121, my insertion – cf. p. 122). In the case of the like-minded model, this seems reasonable but in the case of the cooperative practice model, we can say more. Thus, Miller himself notes that if we change 'our example in such a way that decisions [...] are taken by a small clique who keep the rest of the workforce in the dark about the whole issue, or skew the distribution of rewards in such a way that one section of the workforce could reasonably claim to be working on exploitative terms, and collective responsibility no longer extends to all members but at most to the decision-makers or the leading beneficiaries of the practice.' (p. 119). We might also add that, even on the unadjusted example, an individual who dissented, contributed the additional benefit that he or she received through the persistence of the damage-generating element of the practice towards repairing the damage incurred, and encouraged others to do likewise would seem to be relieved of responsibility.

Miller then proceeds to argue that both models can be applied to nations since (i) they are characterised by like-mindedness expressed in and through the shared national culture and (ii) they are engaged in a cooperative practice, not least insofar as they are concerned to reproduce their shared national culture. The key issue that I want to draw attention to here concerns the relationship between nation and the political self-determination to which it aspires; this matters on Miller's account because, roughly, the greater the degree of collective self-determination, the more applicable the claim that individual members are liable for the outcomes produced by national actions.

Miller picks out three possibilities that he takes as particularly important: a nation subject to external imperial rule that, consequently, lacks self-determination at all; a nation which possesses its own state but is subject to authoritarian rule; and a democratic nation-state. Now these are certainly real possibilities and working through them does reveal much about the conditions under which ascriptions of responsibility to the members of the nation or some subset of members can be justified; however, it seems strange not to have considered a fourth case, the nation within a multinational federal democratic state that possesses real but limited self-determination rights. Of course Miller may have good reason to avoid this case since it would seem to lend support to the view expressed in my criticism of his argument against global egalitarianism that self-determination can be real even when significantly constrained by wider principles of justice – and, in this case, on Miller's own view, principles of social justice that are egalitarian in character. Be that as it may, the interesting point about this case in the present context is that while it may make sense to hold members of nations liable for their actions, the issue of responsibility for acts that are articulated through the apparatus of the state no longer seems to be tied to the sub-state national communities. One could address this by construing the acts of the state as products of a cooperative practice between either its constituent nations or its citizens or some differentiated combination of the two – but which of these options would be pertinent would depend on the specific political structure of the state, that is, the arrangements that specify and formally constitute the agents who participate (directly or indirectly via representatives) in decision-making. The upshot of this observation is twofold. First, it points out that states can be construed as collective agents on the cooperative practice model and, more importantly, second, it highlights the point that in addressing issues of responsibility, one also needs to attend to relations of power involved in the constitution of forms of agency and the justifiability of those power relations.

This point returns once more in Miller's discussion of national responsibility for the past in which he offers a thoroughly sane and sensible discussion of the principles that should guide reflection on four kinds of issues:

First, we have claims for restitution, for example the handing back of land, art treasures, or sacred objects [...] Second, we have claims based on the idea of unjust enrichment, for instance those made by descendants of victims of exploitation such as slaves or colonial peoples [...] Third we have claims based on the idea of a compensable historic wrong – for instance the internment of Japanese-Americans by the US government during the Second World War [...] Fourth, we have demands which involve simply asking perpetrators to set the record straight and acknowledge their responsibility for historical injustice [...] (pp. 138–9)

What is conspicuously missing from this list, however, is the kind of issue that concerns many 'First Nations', namely, the historic wrong of being deprived of their status as agents who are recognised as nations in international law and can engage in activities such a treaty-making, foreign relations, etc.[16] The nature of this wrong is, we may think, more fundamental (which need not always mean more serious) than the kinds of wrong to which Miller draws attention since it pertains to the character of the agency of a people itself.

Migration and refugees

At this stage, I want to turn to address a more specific thematic focus of Miller's argument, namely, his reflections on immigration. To do so, however, we need to note that whereas our focus thus far has been on outcome responsibility (that is on responsibility for the causal outcomes of one's acts and omissions), Miller offers a needs-based account of human rights (as the anti-egalitarian view of the general obligations owed to human beings) as triggering remedial responsibility (that is responsibility considered from the standpoint of capacity to relieve the harm). Such human rights are understood as related to basic generic human needs and are intended to secure the minimal conditions of a decent life. As we'll see this account plays a central role in his reflections on migration. We should also recall a point that I made earlier here, namely, that in his discussion of migration, Miller gives up talk of nations in favour of talk of states. In one way, this is perfectly understandable since, in our current world, states have (only slightly qualified) sovereign authority over their borders. However, it is a pity since it entails that Miller's discussion leaves aside complexities of the issue of free movement within states that might be raised by multinational states and bear on the topics that he is engaging. Consequently, it may be worth beginning with some reflections on this issue.

Rather strangely Miller starts by considering the right to freedom of movement as the right to move in physical space (pp. 205–6) rather than the right to move within and across public jurisdictions which is the issue actually at stake (pointing

---

[16] See, for example, James Tully, 'The Struggles of Indigenous People for and of Freedom', in Duncan Ivison et al. (eds), *Political Theory and the Rights of Indigenous Peoples* (Cambridge, Cambridge University Press, 2000), pp. 36–59 and, for relevant background, S. James Anaya, *Indigenous Peoples in International Law* (Oxford: Oxford University Press, 1996).

out that we can't invade someone's private property, except under special conditions, and that our movement in relations to public spaces is regulated in various ways is rather besides the point in this context except as a rhetorical device). But setting this aside, we may reasonably raise the question of why a sub-state nation should not have the right to restrict movement of non-national citizens into its territory? Given Miller's concerns with the preservation of national cultures, the assimilation of incomers into the nation, etc., would it not seem reasonable that sub-state nations could restrict entry on the same kind of grounds that allow nations that are also states to restrict entry? It seems likely that Miller will resist this suggestion on the grounds that states (even when not nation-states?) are appropriate sites of social justice and, hence, that it would be unjust to restrict the freedom of one's fellow citizens to move within and across sub-state public jurisdictions in pursuing their interests. If this is Miller's response, then his argument for restricting entry ends up hanging entirely on his independent critique of global egalitarianism. However, if Miller accepts that *in principle* it is acceptable that within a multinational state with no overarching (supra-)national identity, there could be restrictions on freedom of movement that are grounded the interests of the discrete national communities, then one of the fundamental tenets of liberal political thought is undermined. Neither prospect looks especially inviting.

In practice, Miller's strategy is to argue that a right of freedom of movement across state jurisdictions is not required to provide the (basic) human rights that comprise our general obligations to one another except in circumstances where one's own state does not protect one's human rights. So let us consider this argument.

Miller's position with respect to so-called 'voluntary' migration is this:

One reason a person may wish to migrate is in order to participate in a culture that does not exist in his native land – for instance, he wants to work at an occupation for which there is no demand at home, or to join a religious community which again is not represented in the country from which he comes. These might be central components in his plan of life, so he will find it very frustrating if he is not able to move. But does this ground a right to free movement across borders? It seems to me that it does not. What a person can legitimately claim as a human right is access to an *adequate* range of options to choose between – a reasonable choice of occupation, religion, cultural activities, marriage partners, and so forth. Adequacy here is defined in terms of generic human needs rather than in terms of the interests of any one person in particular – so, for example, a would-be opera singer living in a society that provides for various forms of musical expression but not for opera can have an adequate range of options in this area even though the option she most prefers is not available. (p. 207)

We may perhaps agree with Miller that such cases don't ground an unlimited human right of freedom of movement, but it is not clear *contra* Miller that they can't ground a circumscribed human right to move to another state. Let us then consider the case of Fred who is engaged to his fellow-citizen Annabel but on a final short bachelor holiday in another state meets Claire and falls head over heels in love; consequently, Fred breaks off his engagement with Annabel and he and Claire decide to marry. The questions that arise for Miller's view are whether Fred or Claire have: (i) a *right* to marry; (ii) a *right* to live in the same state; and (iii) a *right* to determine which state to live in? I raise the first question because Miller's argument appears to be that insofar as your own state provides you with an adequate range of marriage partners, then you don't have a right to travel to other states to find other potential marriage partners. Fair enough, but given that you have found one either by tourist travel (which I assume Miller would allow) or, if you prefer, on the internet, what then? I think that we can reasonably assume that being able to live with the person that you love (and one may generalise this to family members among who on Miller's view, and mine, there are agent-specific special obligations of care) is a generic human need insofar as that person is a *singular* non-substitutable source of value for you and, hence, you would not be 'frustrated' but 'devastated' to be denied the right to live together – perhaps no longer seeing any compelling reason to go on with life. Moreover, there seems to me to be no compelling reason why the (let us assume) happily married couple should not be allowed to choose in which of the two states of which one is national to reside.

If one grants this case, however, it is no longer clear whether one's interest in joining a religious community not represented in one's home state should not also ground a right to move to another state, at least insofar as practising that religion requires that you participate in such a religious community in a way that rules out remote participation. (To confess, one requires a confessor.) For the religious believer, it is just a mistake to characterise her relationship to her faith as the option 'she most prefers' because her faith is not a preference within a range of options, it is a necessity governing the fate of her soul. In this case, the Christian believer would object that not only is Miller undermining her chance of a minimally decent life in this world but also in the next! We can extend this line of argument (albeit without the additional issue of immortality) to question whether access to the practice of opera is so easily denied to Miller's would-be opera singer since it is also a feature of human beings that they can come to love certain practices – say, opera – where, as in the case of marriage and religion, this means simply that the practice becomes a singular non-substitutable source of value for them. Thus, if the opera lover is in state A and across the border in state B, there is a widespread practice of opera. I see little reason to deny a right to cross the border for opera-training.

In relation to all of these cases, we can recall here a point that Miller admits early in this work, namely, that while membership of a nation is (under certain conditions) of intrinsic value, it is not the only thing that is of intrinsic value – friendship, family and other practices can also be sources of intrinsic value – nor is it necessarily the most important. This being so (and it is!), I find it hard to see why an account of global justice that seeks to take seriously the existence of national communities on the grounds of their intrinsic value, should propose rules of justice concerning freedom of movement that entail the *de jure* privileging of the value of national community over other sources of intrinsic value. Appealing to *adequacy* defined in terms of generic human needs is not an adequate answer here since while it may be that for George what is of intrinsic value is music and so an adequate range is fine, for Caroline it may be opera, opera, and only opera. To push this point home, note that if we don't run legal and identity senses of nationality together (as Miller does throughout this argument), we can envisage cases such as Gareth whose national identity is Welsh but whose legal nationality is Argentinean and ask: 'should Gareth have a human right to move to Wales?' Given how important and valuable Miller takes national identity to be, one rather suspects that he will want to say 'yes' to this question. But on his own account of basic human rights, the answer looks like being 'no'. Moreover, if Miller does answer 'yes' to this question, then it is unclear why the admission would not presumptively apply to other sources of intrinsic value (after all, rights to family re-union migration are well-established in law and political practice – and rightly so).

Finally, let me turn to the case of refugees. We should note two initial points. First, Miller's account of human rights would entail a widening of the current 1951 UN Convention definition of refugees in line with the more expansive definitions adopted by the OAU and the Cartegena Declaration in Latin America – and cogently advanced in intellectual terms in Andrew Schacknove's classic essay 'Who is a Refugee?' to which Miller refers (p. 225, fn. 29). Second, Miller argues that: 'Refugees, then, have a very strong, but not absolute, right to be admitted to place of safety, a right now widely recognized in both law and political practice.' (p. 227). Why not an absolute right? Miller's argument runs thus:

> Realistically [. . .] states have to be given considerable autonomy to decide how best to respond to particular asylum applications: beside the refugee's own choice, they are entitled to consider the overall number of applications they face, the demands that temporary or long-term accommodation of refugees will place on existing citizens, and whether there exists any special link between the refugee and the host community [. . .] The best hope is that over time conventions will emerge that distribute responsibilities in such a way that refugees from particular places become the special responsibility of one state in particular (or a coalition of states). There can be no guarantee, however, that every bona fide refugee will find a state willing to take her in. *The final judgment must rest with the members of the receiving state, who may decide that they have already done their fair share of refugee resettlement. Recall [. . .]: the duty we are considering is a duty either to prevent rights violations being inflicted by third parties [. . .] or to secure the rights of people where others have failed in their responsibility. Such duties are weaker than the negative duty not to violate human rights oneself, and arguably weaker than the positive duty to secure the rights of those we may be specifically responsible for protecting.* At the limit, therefore, we may face tragic cases where the human rights of the refugees clash with a legitimate claim by the receiving state that its obligations to admit refugees has already been exhausted. (pp. 226–7, emphasis added)

I confess to finding this passage perplexing on two levels. First, it focuses on whether a given receiving state may legitimately refuse entry to bona fide refugees. But the right of refugees to sanctuary is a claim against the international society of states, not against a particular state, since it is the normative structure of this global governmental order (most particularly the Janus-faced *grundnorm* of state sovereignty/non-intervention) that grounds the necessity of a right to refuge from one's own state when it breaches the minimal legitimacy requirements of the state-citizen relation. Another way of putting this point is to say that if we adopt Miller's own standard of universal basic human rights, then this standard serves to specify the legitimation criteria for the current regime of global governance (also known as, for the most part, the international society of states) and, consequently, a failure to ensure that bona fide refugees receive the protection of a state which is not their own weakens the claim to legitimacy of this global political order. This suggests, *contra* Miller, that the refugee's right to sanctuary is an absolute right but that this right does not entail a right to residence in a state of their choice, rather it simply designates a right to sanctuary in some state which is not their own. This argument does, of course, entail the possibility of a mechanism for distributing refugees fairly – that is, as far as possible, both taking into account the wishes, language skills, and suchlike attributes of refugees and the different capacities of states to receive them. What may motivate Miller's confusion is that the current international refugee regime has no effective mechanism for the equitable distribution of refugees – which is why weak states in the proximity of the major refugee producing states tend to bear the brunt of the burden.

This issue bears directly on the second dimension of my perplexity in relation to this passage, namely, Miller's claim that the 'final judgment must rest with the members of the receiving state, who may decide that they have already done their fair share of refugee resettlement'. *Why on earth would anyone think this?* One would have thought that to be justified, it would have to be the case not simply that members of the receiving state *decide* that they have done their fair share but that they actually have done their fair share – and making that judgment requires reference to some internationally endorsable standard of equitable distribution for refugees of the kind that we could reasonably hope that a *realistic utopian* account might aim to supply. What Miller's discussion fails to acknowledge is that the obligations of any state to refugees are not simply a matter of: (i) not acting in a way such as to produce refugees; and (ii) accepting one's fair share of refugees but also; (iii) acting with other states to ensure the operation of an international refugee regime that (a) provides effective protection to the global refugee population; and (b) distributes the burdens of refugee protection equitably across receiving states; and (iv) supporting the development of international political mechanisms that (a) encourage states to comply with the requirements of human rights; and (b) provide the resources needed for states to fulfil this role. This matters because, for example, to the extent that a state fails to engage in working for – or even obstructs – the development of such a fair scheme of refugee protection, so too its claim to legitimately refuse admission on the basis of 'having done its fair share' is weakened. Moreover, as experience painfully attests, without some international norms concerning the equitable distribution of the burdens of refugee protection, 'doing one's fair share' tends to collapse into whatever a given state perceives as doing one's fair share – which isn't satisfactory on any grounds. What is most frustrating in this dimension of Miller's account is that his own immensely helpful and subtle discussion of outcome and remedial responsibility would provide much of the intellectual apparatus needed for an adequate treatment of this issue.

Conclusion

While I don't think Miller has fully established the case against global egalitarianism, he has at least made the anti-egalitarian position into a serious rival to that liberal orthodoxy. More important than this, though, are the very many conceptual refinements and innovations that Miller introduces in the course of constructing his argument – as my somewhat frustrated reflections on his discussion of refugees illustrates. Particularly welcome is the way that Miller's arguments can support the movement from mere 'distributivism' towards political justice, towards an account that more adequately integrates agency, responsibility and power into our account of global justice. While it will be clear that I don't think that Miller's argument goes far enough in the direction of attending to the extent to which the modes of agency available to individuals and groups facilitate their vulnerability to injustice and misfortune, on the one hand, and their capacities for the effective exercise of power (not least in distributing resources and opportunities as well as threats and harms), on the other hand – and, hence, does not adequately address the issue of the justification in relation to the production and transformation of such modes of agency, he offers central conceptual resources for pursuing this goal.

Review of International Studies (2010), 36, 113–135   © *2010 British International Studies Association*
doi:10.1017/S0260210510000793   *First published online 31 Aug 2010*

Non-state authority and global governance

DIMITRIOS KATSIKAS

Abstract. Non-state actors are increasingly assuming an active part in the design and construction of the institutional framework of global governance. The introduction of the concept of private authority in the literature has provided us with an insightful analytical tool for a deeper understanding of the role of private actors in the context of global governance. However, in order to achieve this objective the concept of private authority needs to be defined accurately and applied consistently in the examination of non-state governance schemes. This article aims to delineate the concept of private authority in the context of global governance first, by outlining the main characteristics of authority and identifying instances of inconsistent and loose application of these characteristics in the private authority literature and secondly, by offering a starting point for an analytically consistent typology of non-state authority. Following this analysis, a more thoroughly defined and analytically consistent concept of transnational *in* authority is presented. This new conceptualisation locates non-state *in* authority in the amalgamation of public authority and private power in the context of complex transnational governance structures, and can hopefully helps us gain a deeper understanding of the increasing institutionalisation and legitimation of transnational non-state governance.

Dimitrios Katsikas received his PhD from the Department of International Relations at the London School of Economics. He has been recently elected Lecturer of International and European Political Economy at the University of Athens. His research interests include non-state actors, global governance, challenges to political authority and democracy in the context of multilevel global governance, transnational business regulation, and the politics of international finance.

Introduction

The involvement of non-state actors (NSAs) in global governance initiatives both in the context of inter-state regimes and organisations and through the development of non-state governance schemes is increasingly taking on an institutionally acknowledged and legitimate standing. This development has resulted in an increasing array of governance functions taking place away from the territorial cradle of political authority, the nation-state. In recent years new research has examined the role of NSAs in the design and creation of the institutional and regulatory framework of global governance.[1] In the context of this literature, a

---

[1] Richard Higgott, Geoffrey R. D. Underhill and Andreas Bieler (eds), *Non-State Actors and authority in the Global System* (London: Routledge, 2000); Daphne Josselin and William Wallace (eds), *Non-State Actors in World Politics* (Basingstoke: Palgrave, 2001); Jean-Christophe Graz and Andreas Nölke (eds), *Transnational Private Governance and Its Limits* (Abingdon and New York: Routledge, 2008).

particularly interesting approach to examining the governance role increasingly assumed by non-state actors has been the introduction of the concept of private authority.[2] The concept of private authority refers to a situation where 'an individual or organization has decision-making power over a particular issue area and is regarded as exercising that power legitimately'.[3] Moreover, 'such authority does not necessarily have to be associated with government institutions'.[4]

This addition to the global governance vocabulary has been a positive development, because authority embodies both a political and a normative dimension. Using the concept of authority may help us to identify and analyse with greater accuracy and consistency the political/institutional aspects of the shift of authoritative governance from the public and the national, to the private and transnational arenas, while allowing us to also address the normative implications of this shift. However, it should be said that the literature on private authority is still in its initial stages and significant work remains to be done, especially when one takes into account the inherent analytical problems associated with the concept of authority.

More specifically, I believe that the first wave of the literature on private authority exhibits an analytical inconsistency that has not been adequately addressed, and as a result, a variety of non-state governance arrangements are treated as authoritative even when they lack the particular attributes of authoritative governance. Consequently, we often observe a failure to distinguish adequately between cases of private authority, power, or influence, as well as between cases of authority limited to a private setting, of authoritative knowledge and expertise, and of authoritative non-state governance of areas of public life and activity. This tendency confuses rather than clarifies the institutional and political characteristics of various non-state governance arrangements and obscures the clarity of the concept of private authority. To address this problem, an analytically consistent typology of non-state authoritative governance schemes is needed, based on criteria soundly anchored to the concept and analytical attributes of authority.

This article aims to contribute to this objective. This is done first, by outlining the main characteristics of authority and identifying instances of inconsistent and loose application of these characteristics in the private authority literature. Secondly, the article aims to offer a starting point for an analytically consistent typology of non-state authority. More specifically, I try to identify and describe the strongest manifestation of non-state authority, that of authoritative governance of issue-areas at a global level, which is arguably the most novel and consequential aspect of non-state authority. As we saw above, this is also the phenomenon that the literature on private authority has been aiming to examine as well.

Contrary to the literature however, I define this authority in a more specific way by identifying it as *in* authority. *In* authority derives from rules and offices created by rules, and is different from either expertise (*an* authority) or simply power to change or influence the behaviour of others. It is only those *in* authority that issue

---

[2] Claire A. Cutler, Virginia Haufler and Tony Porter (eds), *Private authority and International Affairs* (Albany: State University of New York Press, 1999); Rodney B. Hall and Biersteker J. Thomas (eds), *The Emergence of Private authority in Global Governance* (Cambridge: Cambridge University Press, 2002).

[3] Cutler, Haufler and Porter, *Private Authority*, p. 5.

[4] Ibid.

and apply rules and commands which entail obligations to act. Following from this definition I locate non-state *in* authority in the amalgamation of public political authority with private power in the context of non-state governance structures. In this sense, this article offers a conceptualisation of non-state authority that is quite different from that found in most of the private authority literature, by positing as a pre-requisite for the emergence of non-state authority, the explicit delegation of, or endorsement by public (state or inter-state) authority.

This approach admittedly places significant limitations on the concept of non-state authority, and excludes instances of non-state governance that many would be willing to categorise as authoritative. Nonetheless, I believe that this approach moves the analysis in the right direction as the delineation and demarcation of the concept of private authority is what is needed before our understanding of this phenomenon can progress. It should be noted that this approach is not in any way meant to diminish the importance of other types of non-state governance. By linking *in* authority with the state, I do not intend to somehow reassert the dominance of the state as the only significant actor, or to dispense with private actors. On the contrary, the engagement with private authority begins with the acknowledgment that the international and transnational structures and mechanisms that have emerged in recent years in response to a growing demand for governance are increasingly characterised by processes of pluralisation and privatisation.[5] This does not mean however, that all instances of non-state governance are equally important or that they have the same political and normative implications. The failure to adequately distinguish between different types of non-state governance can actually hinder the research objective of identifying and illuminating the role of NSAs in global governance, as consequential non-state structures are effectively treated in the same way as less important and innovative non-state governance arrangements. By focusing on a specific type of governance which involves both state and non-state actors we can identify more readily non-state organisations that play a significant role in global governance, because the presence of state authority usually means that the work of these governance arrangements has acknowledged legal implications (with varying degrees of obligation). Prominent cases of such governance schemes are for example the work of the International Accounting Standards Board (IASB) or that of the Internet Corporation for Assigned Names and Numbers (ICANN).[6] This focus on legal consequences does not mean that other types of voluntary or soft law arrangements are unimportant or necessarily less effective;[7] however I do believe that an analytical distinction is necessary between non-state governance

---

[5] Claire A. Cutler, *Private Power and Global Authority* (Cambridge: Cambridge University Press, 2003).

[6] While both the IASB and the ICANN are private institutions, their operation and their regulatory outcome is heavily dependent upon, and interlinked with national and regional public regulatory authorities. For a review on the origins and politics of the IASB see David Cairns, with Brian Creighton, and Anne Daniels, *Applying International Accounting Standards* (Tolley LexisNexis, 3rd ed., 2003). For ICANN see Hans Klein, 'ICANN and the Internet Governance: Leveraging Technical Coordination to Realize Global Public Policy', *The Information Society*, 18 (2002), pp. 193–207.

[7] For works that show how compliance can be achieved without formal hard law instruments see Oran R. Young, 'Is enforcement the Achilles' Heel of International Regimes?', in *Governance in World Affairs* (Ithaca and London: Cornell University Press, 1999); Dinah Shelton (ed.), *Commitment and Compliance*, Oxford: Oxford University Press, 2000).

schemes that generate formal legal results and those that do not, since the former are clearly associated with institutional, political, and symbolic transformations that the latter do not necessarily invoke.

Authority

The identification and analysis of instances of non-state authority has to begin with a clarification of the concept of authority. Authority is a very complex concept and different approaches have been competing to establish their own definition of authority.[8] Despite the differences however, there are some characteristics which are commonly accepted as essential constitutive features of authority by most scholars.

First, we should distinguish between authority and power. Authority is usually called legitimate power, the main difference being that authority has to be viewed as legitimate by the people that are subject to it. Authority therefore entails the obligation of its subject to conform to its rules and commands, while the acceptance of power does not result in a comparable obligation to yield to it. This sense of obligation also distinguishes authority from persuasion. This is because authority is not founded on the exercise of rational calculation and the exchange of argument, but rests on the fact that the person or organisation that issue a pronouncement or a command warrant acceptance solely on the basis of their authoritative status. Authority is not obeyed because people consider its individual commands and pronouncements to be in their individual interest but due to a sense of obligation and an acknowledgement of the legitimate right of authority to issue commands and pronouncements.

By differentiating authority from both persuasion and coercion and therefore the rational calculation of both interests and threats, we are left with what has been characterised as a central element of authority, the 'surrender of private judgment'. While the surrender of private judgment is considered central to the concept of authority, there is no general agreement on exactly how much judgment people are supposed to surrender. At a minimum, the subjects of authority have to exercise their judgement in order to decide whether a command is indeed authoritative and therefore warrants their obedience as such.[9] To do this, they use certain criteria, usually referred to as the 'mark of authority'. These criteria can be specific procedures, uniforms, insignia or even social attributes such as wealth. These criteria offer a public verification of the authoritativeness of the source that makes a pronouncement.

---

[8] For a number of different approaches to the concept of authority see Max Weber, *The Theory of Social and Economic Organization* (New York: Oxford University Press, 1947); Friedrich, C. J. (ed.), *NOMOS I: Authority* (Cambridge: Harvard University Press, 1958); Ronald Pennock and John W. Chapman (eds), *NOMOS XXIX: Authority Revisited* (New York and London: New York University Press, 1987); Richard. E. Flathman, *The Practice of Political Authority: authority and the Authoritative* (Chicago and London: The University of Chicago Press, 1980); Joseph Raz (ed.), *The authority of Law: Essays on Law and Morality* (Oxford: Clarendon Press, 1979) and Joseph Raz (ed.), authority (Oxford: Basil Blackwell, 1990).

[9] Flathman, *The Practice of Political Authority*.

Moreover, the subjects of authority have to exercise their judgement to identify the type of authority being employed. A basic distinction is commonly made between 'an' and 'in' authority. *An* authority 'is based on, is possessed by virtue of, demonstrated knowledge, skill, or expertise concerning a subject matter or activity', while *in* authority 'is a property of rules and offices created by rules. Individuals possess it by virtue of holding an office in an organization, such as a state, a corporation, a university or a trade union that is (partially) governed by more or less formalized or codified rules'.[10] This distinction is crucial because the surrender of private judgment is not equally important for both *in* and *an* authority. Indeed, in the case of *an* authority often there needs to be no surrender of individual judgment at all. This is ironic given that *an* authority is founded on the fact that some individuals know more about certain issues than others. This inequality is the source of *an* authority; it is antecedent to the authority relation, since *an* authority is based on the fact that 'it is *because* of the superior insight of some person that he should be acknowledged as "an authority" by others: the deference relation is thus supposed to reflect the antecedent concrete "personal" differences between the parties'.[11] Therefore, someone who is *an* authority can make a statement that carries his or her authority as an expert and for that reason people can give such a statement added weight compared to other statements or factors in order to make a judgment. By doing so however, people do not necessarily surrender their judgment for that of the expert (although often they do so) but can actually exercise their individual judgment to both weigh the expert view against other views, and after considering all views, to reach a judgment of their own.

Things are quite different with *in* authority however. Contrary to *an* authority, *in* authority is based on a premise of equality, not inequality; it is a subtle type of equality: 'the assumption is not that nobody actually knows more than anyone else, that no one is wiser, better or superior; but rather that no one can "persuade" the others that his judgment is superior, such as to justify deference'.[12] It is because of the difficulty to reach collectively agreed decisions therefore that *in* authority is established as the remedy to collective action problems. The authority relationship then appears as an agreement at the procedural level in the face of disagreement at the substantive level, by defining whose judgment is to count as authoritative and whose not.[13] The substantive content of commands or pronouncements issued

---

[10] Ibid., p. 16–7.
[11] R. B. Friedman, 'On the Concept of Authority in Political Philosophy', in Raz, *Authority*, p. 82.
[12] Friedman, 'On the Concept of Authority', p. 82.
[13] It is obvious that here *in* authority is defined strictly as the result of a procedural agreement embodied in a set of rules. Obviously, in practice things are not always that clear-cut, and other types of authority, for example, traditional, charismatic or even *an* authority can at times lead a person to occupy a position of *in* authority. I would argue however that this does not negate the overall validity of this conceptualisation of *in* authority because, in modern societies at least, the bureaucratisation and formal institutionalisation of most instances of *in* authority means that the everyday operation of *in* authority and therefore eventually even its recognition rely on a set of procedural rules, whatever the initial origins of the authoritative relation. Weber's discussion of the routinisation of charismatic authority illustrates the point well: 'in its pure form charismatic authority may be said to exist only in the process of originating. It cannot remain stable, but becomes either traditionalized or rationalized, or a combination of both'(Weber, *The Theory*, p. 364). This can be seen for example in the case of religious authority where the initial charisma of the founder of the religion is conceptualised and passed on as if it were an entity, a '[...] charisma of office. In this case the belief in legitimacy is no longer directed to the individual, but to the acquired qualities and to the effectiveness

by authority is irrelevant because people obey a command solely on the basis that it is authoritative.[14] Nonetheless, the surrender of private judgment even in this extreme sense, does not entail surrendering judgment altogether. People may judge and disagree with the content of a specific pronouncement or command but they will obey it nonetheless; in this sense 'what is suspended is not judgment but choice: the subject desists from acting on his own judgment, even though he may "privately" dissent from the authoritative utterance'.[15]

The distinction between *an* and *in* authority has important implications for our purposes. As we saw, *in* authority requires the surrender of private judgment because it is created to design and enforce rules necessary for the community that perhaps would not otherwise exist given the problematic nature of collective action. If people acted on their own judgments about substantive issues, even if that meant disobeying the rules of the established authority, then there would be no point in having such an authority. Individuals have to obey the utterances of *in* authority; it has to be *obligatory* to be meaningful. This is why *in* authority is usually accompanied by the ability to use sanctions to enforce its rules. It follows therefore that obligation is a feature associated with *in* authority. *An* authority on the other hand, does not require the surrender of private judgment; while people take seriously an expert opinion its pronouncements need not be obligatory. Having said this, a note of caution is in order. The fact that *an* authority does not entail an obligation to submit to its pronouncements does not negate its significance in conditioning human or institutional behaviour. A basic tenet of constructivist thought is that ideas can shape the interests and even the identities of actors, including states.[16] Therefore, it is possible that based on its expert knowledge, *an* authority, can redefine the interests of actors in a way that they may view its pronouncements as obligatory. Indeed, it has been argued that expert knowledge can even claim a type of moral authority over its subjects.[17] The distinction between *an* and *in* authority advocated here, is not intended to deny the validity of this claim. However, I do believe that there is an analytical distinction between the two types of authority that is consequential, namely that *in* authority is based on specific rules and procedures, and it derives from a procedural agreement.

This conceptualisation of *in* authority in a polity means that, at least in liberal democratic states, public *in* authority resides with a democratically elected government which operates according to certain prescribed and agreed upon constitutional rules. It follows therefore, that in such states, without this public procedural agreement, this public mandate, neither expert knowledge alone, nor brute force or charisma, are adequate for an actor or institution to legitimately assume a governance role that entails an unequivocal obligation to obey.[18] This

---

of the ritual acts. The most important example is the transmission of priestly charisma by anointing, consecration, or the laying on of hands' (Weber, *The Theory*, p. 366).

[14] As we later see this strong condition can be somewhat relaxed for instances of *in* authority limited to a strictly private setting, for example within a private firm or organisation.

[15] Ibid., p. 72.

[16] Alexander E. Wendt, 'Anarchy is What States Make of It: The Social Construction of Power Politics' *International Organization*, 46 (1992), pp. 391–425.

[17] Michael Barnett and Martha Finnemore, *Rules for the World* (Ithaca and London: Cornell University Press, 2004).

[18] This does not mean that political authority is possible only under a democratic regime. However, it means that other types of authoritative rule (for example, monarchy or theocracy) rest on different

does not mean that public authority always takes into account the opinions of all the subjects of its authority, neither that all these subjects are in a position to voice their views, however it does mean that public authority is both bound to act in the public interest and authorised to do so by society at large. The public mandate of *in* authority creates the overarching authority of government that will decide on the substantive aspects of the regulation of the various issue-areas and activities. Given the dominance of the state as the political structure for the organisation of human life (today), this overarching authority is embodied in the state mechanism. That means that private actors cannot just assume the governance of an issue-area on their own initiative, at least not in an authoritative way, without the participation or at least consent of the state, because even when they claim to be *an* authorities acting in the public interest, they do not possess a comparable public mandate.

Private authority in global governance

Having identified the central elements of authority, we can now move on to the concept of private authority as used in the literature on global economic governance. According to Cutler, Haufler and Porter authority exists when an individual or organisation has decision-making power over a particular issue-area and is regarded as exercising that power legitimately. Such power need not be associated exclusively with government institutions; however, it needs to be binding to be considered authoritative.

While capturing much of the essence of non-state authority, these characteristics do not adequately distinguish between *in* and *an* authority. By failing to distinguish analytically between the two aspects of authority, the authors attribute to private *an* authority characteristics that are not necessarily associated with it. Thus while the authors note that obligation is an essential element of authority and link this obligation, rightly so, with the 'right to rule',[19] they then go on to ascribe this right to rule to both *in* and *an* authority. As noted earlier however, this right to rule is a feature associated primarily with *in* authority, not *an* authority.

The omission to adequately distinguish between private *an* and *in* authority leads to an exaggeration of private authority's novelty and significance for global governance and obscures analytical work. Thus, while the involvement of both civil society Non-Governmental Organisations (NGOs) and private sector actors in most international organisations has increased dramatically in recent years, this development *by itself* does not constitute a qualitatively new phenomenon in the area of international governance, to the degree that these actors still perform the traditional consultative and lobbying roles of non-state actors. A distinction should be made between these traditional roles that constitute the bulk of NSAs' involvement in international organisations, and instances of institutionalised and

---

sources, for example tradition or charisma, rather than collectively agreed procedures enshrined in some form of constitutional rules. As argued in note 13, eventually they will also come to rely on *in* authority; however, this procedural set of rules will not necessarily be based on democratic or equalitarian principles. Obviously, the scope of the argument presented here, is limited to modern liberal democratic states, and does not refer to all possible and historical types of political authority.

[19] Claire A. Cutler, Virginia Haufler and Tony Porter Cutler, 'The Contours and Significance of Private authority in International Affairs', in Cutler, Haufler and Porter, *Private Authority*, pp. 363–64.

acknowledged delegation of specific governance functions to NSAs in the context of their involvement with international organisations' work. I would argue that in the context of this delegation, NSAs may have the right to perform certain functions that invoke an obligation of obedience. However, this delegated authority has to be *in* authority since it has to flow and operate according to rules that spell out its purpose, its scope and its mode of operation.

This kind of ambiguity is encountered in other aspects of the analytical work underpinning the concept of private authority as well. To illustrate the point let us look at the way Cutler, Haufler and Porter try to address the conceptual and theoretical obstacles inherent to the notion of private authority.[20] The authors identify at least two obstacles to theorising about private authority: a) conceptualising international authority in conditions of anarchy, and b) conceptualising private action as authoritative. Here, we will concentrate on the second obstacle since it is that which deals directly with the concept of private authority, while the first obstacle will be addressed later. The authors admit that the common understanding of public governance is associated with the concept of *in* authority, which in turn depends on rules and procedures according to constitutions that guarantee the representativeness and accountability of government.[21] Under this view, private judgement in contrast is non-authoritative: it is not accountable to democratic institutions.

However, they argue that this obstacle of the established conceptualisation of authority is only convincing if one accepts that the normative argument, that private power 'ought' not be regarded as legitimate and binding, and is enough to validate the empirical statement that in fact private power is non-authoritative and legitimate. The public dimension of authority is only an obstacle if one accepts that private power does not *in fact* operate in an obligatory and legitimate way. The authors thus argue that it is only a normative statement that prevents us from conceptualising private authority. Moreover, the authors argue that this conceptual obstacle is only convincing if one limits rules to commands and directives. They acknowledge that private actors lack the authority to enforce and prescribe domestic laws of general application unless such authority is delegated to them by governments and that the rules most relevant to private authority are those called 'soft law', characterised as mutually consensual.[22] They assert however, that the instruments of 'soft law', while not law proper, do in effect govern relations among a variety of actors and therefore the obstacle of conceptualising private authority can be overcome.

I would argue that this thesis is somewhat ambiguous. First, it is not only a hypothetical normative argument that stands in the way of acknowledging private authority. The fact is that in many of the cases that the authors have in mind, the private organisations that attempt to regulate an issue-area do not have an explicit or implicit mandate from the parties that are affected by their rules, that is, there

---

[20] Ibid., pp. 365–9. The reason for selecting Cutler, Haufler and Porter as the main target for criticism is not only that they introduced the concept of private authority, but also because their work represents the most comprehensive attempt to conceptualise private authority in global governance to-date.

[21] Obviously they also assume a democratic form of government.

[22] Friedrich Kratochwil, *Rules, Norms, and Decisions: On the Conditions of Practical and Legal Reasoning in International Relations and Domestic Affairs* (Cambridge: Cambridge University Press, 1989).

exists no procedural agreement that establishes the authority of these organisations. These organisations represent only the parties that are involved in their work
and not the totality of the people and institutions that would be affected by their
rules. As noted previously, public authority does not guarantee the effective
representation of all interested or affected parties either. However, it has a
legitimate public mandate to engage in governance functions in the service of the
public interest. Therefore, the argument that private rules 'ought' not to be
considered authoritative is not only a normative argument, but derives from an
empirical fact, their unaccountability, that is, their failure to satisfy the conditions
of public *in* authority. Interestingly, many of the analysts of private authority 'raise
explicit concerns about the limited degree (or virtual absence) of accountability of
private authority'.[23] Secondly, the identification and acknowledgement of authority
is itself a normative process; it depends on the inter-subjective values and norms
shared among the subjects of authority. Shared beliefs and values are necessary not
just for the practical operation and identification of authority, but for its very
existence. The common acknowledgement of these beliefs and values '[...] posits
acceptance of some set of propositions according to which it is right or proper that
there be authority at all and that such authority be established, lodged, distributed,
exercised and so on in this or that manner'.[24] The question of whether a rule is
authoritative or not, cannot be considered apart from the question of whether it
is legitimate or 'ought' to be considered as legitimate. If people see private power
as unaccountable and undemocratic then by definition they do not consider it
legitimate and thus authoritative. The very nature of authority, the necessity of a
sense of obligation and legitimacy, makes the issue of identifying and acknowledging authority an inescapably normative one.

The argument concerning the obligatory nature of private rules also deserves
detailed examination. The authors' agreement with Kratochwil on the character-
isation of soft law' as mutually consensual and their acknowledgement of the
uncertainty of the exact nature of these instruments which are not 'strictly binding
norms of law',[25] underlines the fact that the essence of these instruments is their
mutual, voluntary adoption by the participating actors. The voluntary nature of
soft law instruments is not by itself a reason for disqualifying them as authoritative. Indeed, all authority is ultimately voluntary for if it was not, then we would
be talking about coercion not authority. As we saw however, and as the authors
themselves note, *in* authority explicitly involves obligation.

This obligation can take two forms:[26] a) legal obligation, defined strictly as an
obligation to conform to certain rules. Failure to do so can result in the use of
(legitimate) force to bring about obedience with the rules, and b) 'moral'
obligation, defined as the voluntary acceptance of authority as legitimate which
produces a voluntary decision to consider the commands of authority as binding
on one's self. The former cannot exist without the latter. Moral obligation is

---

[23] Rodney B. Hall and Thomas Biersteker, 'Private authority As Global Governance', in Hall and
Biersteker, *The Emergence of Private Authority*, p. 211.

[24] Flathman, *The Practice of Political Authority*, p. 20.

[25] Michael Akehurst (ed.), *A Modern Introduction to International Law* (London and New York:
Routledge, 1997, 6th ed.), p. 54.

[26] Friedman, 'On the Concept of Authority', makes a similar distinction for legitimacy in relation to
authority: a) legitimate reasons to obey an authority, and b) legitimate use of force to exact
obedience to authority.

necessary to maintain obedience to authority even when the content of its commands is not popular. Without it, authority would not be effective. While, initially this might not be a problem, eventually the continuous use of force to impose the rules of authority would lead to its discredit and collapse, since people would judge that it is not anymore serving the objectives of its creation and that the use of force has become abusive and eventually coercive.

Non-state soft law instruments do not invoke legal obligation and there are no legal sanctions that usually emanate from disobeying or ignoring them. What is more, I would argue that soft law arrangements in the private sector do not exhibit signs of moral obligation necessary for public *in* authority. The reason is that the organisations that produce such rules are explicitly instrumental. This means that they address specific regulatory needs of the participating parties. In that sense they represent one of the strongest manifestations of an 'enterprise association'.[27] The crucial element that distinguishes such an association is its purpose. The members of these associations may have some rules that can be considered authoritative in the sense of *in* authority, which establish the association and determine its procedural mode of operation. However, 'these rules are not to be confused with the managerial decisions, agreements, etc., which constitute the pursuit of the purpose'.[28] These managerial decisions are the most important distinctive element of the association, not the procedural rules that establish it, because it is the former that are decisive for the pursuit of the common objective. It follows then that 'even a denial of the authority of these rules would not itself be an act of dissociation, as it would be if the terms of association were the rules themselves'.[29]

Therefore, the procedural agreement to establish a private 'regulatory' organisation does not define the organisation, but acts only as a facilitating factor. The reason behind the creation of such an organisation is not to have an authority which can then decide which rules are appropriate. The procedural rules that establish and define the structure and operation of the organisation do not create an authority that can claim surrender of the judgement of the participating actors irrespective of the content of its proposals. In contrast, in the case of public *in* authority the procedural rules which establish it are the very source of authority.[30]

---

[27] Michael Oakeshott, *On Human Conduct* (Oxford: Clarendon Press, 1991). Oakeshott defines an enterprise association as a 'relationship in terms of the pursuit of some common purpose, some substantive condition of things to be jointly procured, or some common interest to be continuously satisfied', p. 114.

[28] Ibid., p. 116.

[29] Ibid., p. 117.

[30] Oakeshott introduced the concept of enterprise association in contrast to the 'civil association' which describes the relation between the *cives* (citizens) of a polity. The civil association enjoys 'self-sufficiency', a characteristic that Oakeshott describes as 'being always self-complete in the sense of having no extrinsic substantive purpose' (Oakeshott, *On Human Conduct*, p. 110). In this sense the civil association 'begins and ends with the recognition of rules' (Oakeshott, *On Human Conduct*, p. 128). This conceptualisation of civil association is often hard to distinguish in the practice of everyday politics from the pursuit of substantive purposes, which is the characteristic of enterprise associations, and Oakeshott has been criticised for being too formalistic in his definition of civil association (Flathman, *The practice of Political Authority*; Ben Minoque, 'Oakeshott and the Idea of Freedom', *Quadrant*, October (1975), pp. 77–83). Nonetheless, in terms of describing the nature of the modern nation-state, even Oakeshott admits that some kind of combination of the two ideas is needed. Still, while an occasional mix of these two elements in the everyday operation of the state occurs, I do believe that there is a valid qualitative difference in emphasis in the significance of the rules, and consequently the resulting moral obligation, between a civil or more widely construed political association (state), and a private enterprise association.

It is exactly because of the legitimacy of the procedural rules that parties believe the substantive rules to be authoritative. It is therefore the authority of the procedure that creates the moral obligation on the subjects of authority to abide by its rules even when they disagree with it. In non-state regulatory organisations, the participating parties do not feel this kind of moral obligation towards the rules that establish the organisation and its decision-making body.[31]

This becomes more evident when we consider that in such organisations the parties subject to the 'authority' of the organisation are not adequately separate from it. They are the ones that really create the rules through a continuous process of bargaining and negotiation that represents their conflicting interests. Such organisations resemble more a meeting place, an agreed procedural and institutional context within which the interested parties meet to deliberate and decide upon mutually agreed norms, rules and standards, through processes of negotiation, bargaining and power politics. The operation of such organisations does not reflect a mutual deference of authoritative decision making over the activities of interested parties to an organisation that enjoys some degree of autonomy from its foundational members.[32] Compliance with the rules is dependent upon the continuous rational calculation of interests by the participating parties, which may very well decide to depart from the informal agreement to uphold these norms and rules if they deem that these no longer serve their interests.[33]

These analytical problems can lead to a deceptive diagnosis of reality. It is not surprising therefore, that we often see in the literature cases of private authority that at best refer only to *an* authority and at worst exhibit no features of authority at all. It is thus inaccurate to characterise the endorsement and adoption of the Trade Related Intellectual Property Rights (TRIPS) agreement as an instance of private authority because of the influential role of the Intellectual Property Committee (IPC), a private organisation representing the interests of the American industry.[34]

---

[31] According to Hall and Biesteker, NGOs enjoy a moral authority associated with their emancipatory and progressive agendas ('The Emergence of Private authority in the International System', in *The Emergence of Private Authority*, pp. 14–6). This point does not change the core of the argument presented here. First, this is again a different type of moral authority than the one associated with *in* authority, since it refers to a substantive 'morally valued' goal not the moral duty to obey to a set of agreed procedural rules, and secondly, it is doubtful that the private companies that NGOs' work usually targets are convinced of this moral authority or see it as obligatory. Obviously other types of non-state moral authority exist as well. Religious authority for example is at least partially founded on moral authority. Religion may enjoy moral authority in terms of its pronouncements as statements of high moral value that may induce obedience by believers in how they conduct their private life, again however, at least in liberal democratic states such pronouncements do not create a moral obligation to obey them as *political pronouncements*, deemed obligatory, for the members of a polity.

[32] This as we shall see later, is a significant difference between non-state regulatory organisations and inter-state organisations and one of the reasons that the latter can claim to exercise authority in international affairs.

[33] An example involving the International Accounting Standards Committee (IASC), the predecessor of the IASB, is a case in point. During the 1980s over one hundred Canadian companies referred to the standards produced by the IASC in their statements; by 1998 only five companies referred to IASs in their statements. The explanation for this decline is that during the 1990s, and under the pressure of the US Securities and Exchange Commission (SEC), the numerous alternative accounting treatments allowed in IASC's standards, and used by Canadian companies, were eliminated. See David Cairns, *International Accounting Standards Survey 2000* (Henley-on-Thames: International Financial Reporting, 2001).

[34] See Susan Sell, 'Multinational Corporations as Agents of Change: The Globalization of Intellectual Property Rights', in Cutler, Haufler and Porter, *Private Authority*, pp. 169–98, and Susan Sell, *Private Power, Public Law* (Cambridge: Cambridge University Press, 2003).

The TRIPS agreement was an intergovernmental agreement in the context of the WTO, an intergovernmental organisation. The significant, even decisive influence of private sector lobbying, is not a case of private authority, it is a case of private power and influence that was able to persuade the US government to adopt its cause in this international negotiation.

Similarly, knowledge-based network oligopolies do not govern authoritatively their industries.[35] Such networks may be able to extend beyond territorial boundaries, redefine the structure of particular industries, generate new knowledge or even control the generation of new knowledge.[36] They may even be able to use their control over knowledge to erect barriers to entry.[37] These activities however are not a testament to authority but rather to private power: the ability to use financial and other corporate assets to gain control over valued resources, such as knowledge, in order to manipulate the market structure and rip abnormal profits. Changing the way business is done in an industry, may affect the regulatory framework that governs that industry, but does not in itself constitute an assumption of authoritative regulatory powers. At best it confers a competitive advantage to the pioneering firms and potentially, a temporary loosening of regulatory control due to the emergence of new, previously unanticipated consequences of economic activity.

Finally, perhaps the most telling example of overstretching and therefore misapplying the concept of private authority can be found in Hall and Biersteker's proposed typology, which includes, along with market authority, private moral authority and even illicit authority.[38] In the first type of market authority, the authors include a form of normative market authority which 'refers to the general acceptance of the more abstract idea that markets should determine decision-making over important issues'.[39] However, such abstract ideas about the role of the market in the governance of economic activity do not automatically create the authority of the market. Such ideas are very important for the emergence of non-state authority; however, they operate primarily by changing the set of inter-subjective values and norms upon which authority rests. They may be changing the normative criteria for judging the legitimacy of authority and thus contribute to the emergence of a new type of non-state authority, but they do not constitute by themselves an authoritative mechanism in the sense of *in* authority. Even more confusing are the examples of private moral authority which includes the authority of transnational religious terrorist networks,[40] and of illicit authority which includes transnational organised crime.[41] The application of the concept of private authority to describe religious terrorist groups or mafias, is very difficult to be justified not only as a form of *in* authority, but rather as authority more

---

[35] Lynn K. Mytelka and Michel Delapierre, 'Strategic Partnerships, Knowledge-Based Networked Oligopolies, and the State', in Cutler, Haufler and Porter, *Private Authority*, pp. 129–49; Stephen J. Kobrin, 'Economic Governance in an Electronically Networked Global Economy', in Hall and Biersteker, *The Emergence of Private Authority*, pp. 43–75.

[36] Kobrin, 'Economic Governance'.

[37] Mytelka and Delapierre, 'Strategic Partnerships'.

[38] Hall and Biersteker, 'The Emergence of Private Authority'.

[39] Hall and Biersteker, 'Private Authority', p. 214.

[40] Mark Juergensmeyer, 'The Global Dimensions of Religious Terrorism', in Hall and Biesteker, *The Emergence of Private Authority*, pp. 141–57.

[41] Phil Williams, 'Transnational Organized Crime and the State', in Hall and Biersteker, *The Emergence of Private Authority*, pp. 161–82.

generally, since it ignores or confuses basic elements of authority, such as legitimacy, moral obligation and surrender of judgement. Indeed, even some of the authors themselves doubt whether these cases can be viewed as private authority.[42] Such an application of the concept, by effectively substituting for concepts better suited to such cases, such as coercion, domination, power and ideology, stretches its analytical foundation to such lengths that eventually renders it ineffective as an analytical concept, turning it into a blanket-concept that can be used to describe everything and anything.

Non-state *in* authority

From the previous discussion it is evident that we need a more precise and analytically consistent conceptualisation of private authority. The aim here is not simply to identify instances of private *in* authority.[43] The type of private *in* authority that we seek needs to be able to provide governance for a whole industry, issue-area or sphere of economic activity; in other words it needs to be public. However, as we have seen, public *in* authority needs to be based on rules and constitutions that are founded on a mandate by society and non-state actors lacking such a mandate, cannot just assume the governance of an issue-area on their own initiative, at least not in an authoritative way, without the participation or at least consent of the state.

To illustrate this point, we can turn to the literature on regulation in domestic economies and societies. Regulation scholars have long acknowledged the dominance of the state in the domain of regulation; one of the most common definitions of regulation is 'all state initiatives to intervene in the economy'.[44] However, the centrality of the state for the conceptualisation of regulation does not mean that the state has to regulate itself all aspects of public life. It does not preclude the possibility of non-state regulation. It does mean however that non-state regulation needs the explicit or implicit acknowledgement of state authority in order to be considered legitimate and therefore authoritative. A good illustration of how this can actually happen is provided by the concept of self-regulation. Contrary to the widely-held notion that self-regulation is an instance of regulation without the

---

[42] Williams, 'Transnational Organized Crime', pp. 178–9.

[43] As mentioned in the definition of *in* authority at the beginning of this article, *in* authority can be found at a corporation, a university or a trade union. This does not contradict the previous analysis on enterprise associations, where as was mentioned, *in* authority can also be found. Indeed, corporations, universities, trade unions, organised religions, etc., are also examples of enterprise associations. However, as mentioned previously, the difference between *in* authority in such associations, and public *in* authority, is that the former performs a facilitating function, towards the pursuit of a specific substantive purpose and does not define the association in the way the latter does, and therefore does not invoke the same kind of moral obligation. While this difference may not create problems for a private corporation pursuing a private goal, as it can change or abandon easily the procedural rules of association depending on the pursuit of its objective, and where arguably moral obligation is much less significant than legal obligation for its operation, it is a significant problem for private governance organisations which aim to perform a public governance function, without however enjoying the necessary public *in* authority. Besides, such public authority, as already argued, requires a public mandate which private governance organisations also lack.

[44] Robert Baldwin, Scott Colin and Christopher Hood (eds), *A Reader on Regulation* (Oxford: Oxford University Press, 1998), pp. 2–4.

state, the fact is that self-regulatory schemes are never entirely independent and free of public scrutiny and state involvement. Indeed, regulation analysts see the relation between self-regulation and state regulation as an important, mutually constitutive element of both these mechanisms. Public regulation and self-regulation are always interconnected and interpenetrated.[45] More specifically there are four different types of relation between self-regulation and the state: a) mandated self-regulation; b) sanctioned self-regulation; c) coerced self-regulation, and d) voluntary self-regulation.[46] It becomes obvious from this typology that while self-regulation is a pervasive and significant feature of public regulation, the consent of the state is needed for the *legitimate* existence of self-regulatory schemes. The state either promotes actively self-regulation (enforced, sanctioned, mandated) or at least allows it to exist (voluntary), usually under some form of indirect supervision or monitoring.[47]

It is in this same sense that private *in* authority can acquire a public dimension. This type of authority is neither entirely private nor entirely state, yet it is backed by formal state authority and therefore is able to govern public social and economic space. This is why it would be more appropriate to call it *non-state in authority* rather than private *in* authority. Therefore, we could define non-state *in* authority, as the type of *in* authority that resides with a governance mechanism in a sphere of activity, which functions not only effectively, but also authoritatively, due to the partial participation or endorsement of the state which lends it formal authority, but which due to the participation of non-state actors cannot be considered as part of government.

Transnational inauthority

We can now address the question of whether non-state *in* authority can be reproduced at the transnational level. The task of conceptualising non-state *in* authority at the transnational level presents even more complications. As we saw earlier, Cutler, Haufler and Porter identified the lack of international government as one of two main obstacles that stand in the way of conceptualising private authority. The difficulty here is not limited to the issue of trying to combine private power and public authority, but extends to the difficulty of identifying instances of

---

[45] Alan C. Page, 'Self-Regulation: The Constitutional Dimension', *The Modern Law Review*, 49:2 (1986), pp. 141–67.

[46] Julia Black, 'Constitutionalising Self-Regulation', *The Modern Law Review*, 59 (January 1996), pp. 24–55.

[47] This also applies for the widely used example of the independence and self-regulation of various professions. For example, the accounting profession's significant autonomy in the UK, has been granted through explicit state actions, such as legislation, and always exists under the broad supervision of the state, which in times of crisis may decide that self-regulation has failed and step in and assume regulatory control. For detailed accounts of the status and operation of the accounting profession in the UK see, Mary Canning and Brendan O'Dwyer, 'Professional Accounting Bodies' Disciplinary Procedures: Accountable, Transparent and in the Public Interest?', *The European Accounting Review*, 10:4 (2001), pp. 725–49; Prem Sikka and Hugh Willmott, 'The Power of "Independence": Defending and Extending the Jurisdiction of Accounting in the United Kingdom', *Accounting, Organizations and Society*, 20:6 (1995), pp. 547–81.

any type of *in* authority, in an international system comprised of nominally equal and sovereign states.

Obviously this difficulty does not extent to *an* authority. Both international and transnational (non-state) *an* authority are not difficult to find. *An* authority is a feature of individuals and organisations. Therefore, we could say that *an* authority is essentially a non-state type of authority. Hence, there is no *a priori* reason why international or transnational organisations or individuals acting in a transnational or transgovernmental capacity should not be able to hold considerable authority as experts.

However, things are more complicated for *in* authority. In the previous section we saw that non-state *in* authority presupposes the presence of state authority (or more precisely political authority). This presents an obstacle for conceptualising non-state *in* authority at the transnational level because there is no overarching international government that exercises political authority at that level. Part of the problem lies with the now entrenched notion that political authority is synonymous with the state. Although we previously acknowledged the primacy of the state as the dominant political structure today, and accepted that in most countries political authority (public *in* authority) resides with the state, we also noted earlier that this does not mean that political authority and the state are the same thing, nor does it mean that there can be no political authority without a state. Indeed, as analysts have observed while the nation-state is currently the dominant form of political organisation, it is not the only possibility.[48] Monarchy, feudalism, theocracy and classical democracy have been some of the dominant forms of political organisation in different places at different times. While they all had an administrative mechanism, unlike the modern nation-state, this mechanism was not always organised along the principles of territoriality and hierarchical centralisation as is evident from the examples of feudalism and classical democracy where personal or lineage allegiance and polyarchy replaced territoriality and hierarchy respectively. It follows therefore, that the existence of an overarching hierarchical or territorial state is necessary neither for the existence nor for the exercise of political authority. There should be no *a priori* reason therefore, why decentralised *loci* of political authority cannot arise to provide governance for specific issue-areas and spheres of activity in the realm of international relations, where no procedural agreement among states for a single overarching authority exists.

The question arises then, whether there are any institutions that exhibit the features of *in* authority in the international system. One example is the institution of sovereignty which enjoys almost universal acceptance as an authoritative institution among states.[49] Sovereignty is an overarching principle that manifests itself in more concrete rules and norms such as non-intervention and mutual recognition among states. Sovereignty, and the rules of conduct that follow from it are authoritative because they are seen by states as legitimate and obligatory; states feel obliged to abide by these rules even when their interests seem to run against them or rather because '[. . .] their *interests* [. . .] have been conditioned by a community standard that delimits the acceptable [territorial] reach of state

---

[48] See for example, John Gerard Ruggie, 'Territoriality and Beyond: Problematizing Modernity in International Relations', *International Organization*, 47:1 (1993), pp. 139–74.

[49] Ian Hurd, 'Legitimacy and authority in International Relations', *International Organization*, 53:2 (1999), pp. 379–408.

sovereignty'.[50] Such authority is not to be found only in fundamental rules and principles like sovereignty that could perhaps be dismissed as exceptional since they lay the basic framework for any type of communication among states. Many countries for example, even those considered dominant economic powers, routinely abide by the rulings of the World Trade Organization (WTO) on trade-related issues, even if that means having to reverse or cancel policies agreed at the national level.[51] Indeed, many similar examples can be found in other issue-areas, where the rules of international organisations are considered authoritative and are obeyed as such by states.

Despite these examples of international authority, sceptics could still dispute them as a definite proof of authority. A traditional realist argument could be levelled against them: such governance mechanisms are not really authoritative because states can ultimately exit agreements and leave international organisations. Consequently, they are not obliged to follow the international rules they have adhered to. In principle, the argument that states can ultimately exit these organisations and agreements is correct, but is this enough to dismiss the authoritative status of these institutions? It is inaccurate to characterise such arrangements as non-authoritative because of this possibility. As was argued previously, authority is voluntary by definition: people choose to consider it obligatory. It follows therefore, that just as people are free to choose to acknowledge and obey authority they are equally free to abandon it. Indeed, even in a domestic society individuals may place themselves outside the rule of authority and refuse to recognise its power over them. Such an action however should not be considered as proof that authority does not exist in that society. As we have seen, authority presupposes the existence of inter-subjective values and norms that establish, among other things, the necessity of authority itself. Obviously no human society can exhibit a complete consensus of values, norms and principles. As long as the authority that stems out of this inter-subjective framework is accepted by the majority of the people in a society, then the concept of authority should not be rejected when a few individuals choose to place themselves outside its sphere of influence. Indeed, depending on their behaviour, these individuals are often treated as abnormal and potentially dangerous by the rest of society. The same applies for the international society of states. Hurd makes a similar observation about states that decide to reject the institution of sovereignty:

> Those states that do question such fundamentals [the institution of sovereignty] are regarded with horror by the other actors in the system. The fact that these states are so few, and thus so notable, is what allows the rest to define them as 'rogues' in contrast to the bulk of the population of states, who take the institution for granted.[52]

As long as a significant number of states consider the power of these institutions legitimate and obligatory, and abide by their decisions and rules even when they do not agree with them, then these institutions should be considered authoritative.

---

[50] Ibid., p. 397.
[51] For example, following a series of WTO decisions, the EU was obliged to remove in 2001 its discriminatory import policy for banana imports, while in December 2003, following a ruling by the WTO, the US was forced to scrap the steel tariff it had unilaterally imposed the previous year.
[52] Hurd, 'Legitimacy and Authority', p. 397.

Still, the examples that were given above refer only to inter-state and inter-governmental institutions. What about non-state *in* authority? First of all we should acknowledge that there exists a significant variety of non-state governance schemes. Many of them do not aspire to provide governance and regulation but rather guidance and assistance. However, there are organisations at the transnational level that explicitly aim to provide governance for a whole industry, sphere of activity or issue-area. These organisations obviously aspire to achieving authoritative status as 'regulators'. Despite their ambition however I do not believe that their governance can be considered authoritative in the sense of *in* authority. First of all, these organisations are subject to the same criticism that was developed previously with regard to the potential for private *in* authority. Like voluntary associations at the domestic level, non-state transnational organisations cannot just assume governance of an area of public life even if it is dominated by activities of a transnational nature. The reason is that every economic actor whose behaviour these organisations aim to regulate is legally anchored in one (or many) national, legal jurisdictions.[53] Moreover, those actors' overseas economic activities also have to take place within the boundaries of a national legal jurisdiction. Within these jurisdictions, the regulation of the issue-areas that these economic actors engage in is already undertaken by local regulatory authorities. Issues pertaining to individuals or private organisations in a transnational capacity are addressed by private international law, which usually treats them as issues between different national legal jurisdictions, a conflict of laws, since private organisations or individuals always operate under the rules of a national jurisdiction.[54] Therefore, in the absence of transnational legal space, in order to characterise any rules as binding, they need to be applied in some national jurisdiction and be incorporated in its legal or regulatory structure. Non-state transnational organisations cannot do that; states are needed for the incorporation of transnational non-state rules in the body of domestic law or regulation.

The example of the IASB, which is one of the most celebrated cases of successful non-state governance, can illustrate the point. The International Accounting Standards Committee (IASC), the IASB's predecessor, has existed since the early 1970s. For the first two decades of its existence and despite its success in producing a significant number of accounting standards the actual impact of the IASC on national accounting regulatory frameworks was quite limited.[55] It was only the 1995 agreement with the International Organization of Securities Commissions (IOSCO) to develop a set of core standards for cross-border listing purposes[56] that produced some limited voluntary adoption by a few large European companies, and most significantly, the EU's decision to adopt IASC's standards as legally binding[57] that

---

[53] For example, every company has to be legally incorporated somewhere.
[54] Cutler, *Private Power*.
[55] For empirical studies see T. G. Evans and M. E. Taylor, 'Bottom Line Compliance with the IASC: A Comparative Analysis', *International Journal of Accounting*, (Autumn 1982), pp. 115–28; S. M. McKinnon and P. Jannell, 'The International Accounting Standards Committee: A Performance Evaluation', *International Journal of Accounting*, (Spring 1984), pp. 19–34; Christopher W. Nobes, 'Compliance by US Corporations with IASC Standards', *British Accounting Review*, 22 (1990), pp. 41–9.
[56] See *IASC Insight* (July 1995).
[57] Commission of the European Communities, *EU Financial Reporting Strategy: the Way Forward*, (COM 2000) 359, 13.06.00.

changed the status of the IASC/IASB and catalysed the subsequent changes in policies and cooperation between the IASB and other significant national regulators and standard-setters. Without the endorsement of such regulatory authorities the IASB standards would still have a very limited (if any) impact on accounting practices around the world.

Moreover, as was argued previously, members of private governance organisations also lack the sense of moral obligation that would make them regard the rules of the association as obligatory and therefore surrender their private judgement to its authority. One could argue that international organisations could similarly be conceived as instrumental organisations, where likewise, negotiation and bargaining are taking place and therefore they should not be considered authoritative. I believe that this is not the case. It is possible to argue that international organisations are primarily self-sufficient associations. That is, like political authority at the domestic arena, they do not have an explicit substantive purpose. Obviously, they are created to provide governance for a sphere of activity. However, they are created to provide governance according to some procedural rules that establish the authoritative nature of their substantive decisions, and this authority also grants them a degree of autonomy from their state-members.[58] When the organisation is established fierce negotiations and bargaining will ensue, but once an agreement has been reached and a decision has been made the authority of the organisation will make this agreement obligatory on its members and they will see it as such. Indeed, the most common criticism of international organisations is that they are not productive enough; they do not produce an adequate number of sufficiently detailed and up-to-date rules to provide much needed governance at the international and transnational levels. This happens because states negotiate fiercely at the preparatory stage exactly because they know that once they have signed an international agreement its authority makes it very difficult to renege on their obligations.

Finally, transnational organisations also face a considerable problem of external legitimacy. They often represent only a small part of the actors, national or transnational, that would be affected by their rules if these were obligatory. To a greater extent than domestic non-state associations, these organisations cannot be said to be truly representative of, and accountable to the actors active in their industries or sphere of activity. This impression is made worse by the fact that the power differential among their participants is much greater than in the case of domestic organisations. Indeed, the very participation in these organisations often entails costs that cannot be afforded by many small actors who could nevertheless be affected by their rules. Moreover, the absence of an international overarching authority means that these organisations are not endorsed or supervised by a public authority according to a minimum set of rules regarding participation, transparency and accountability, as is usually the case with mandated or sanctioned domestic self-regulatory organisations, which makes their accountability deficit even more serious.

The rules of transnational non-state organisations should not therefore be considered authoritative in the strict sense of *in* authority. Lack of legitimacy, legal

---

[58] See Barnett and Finnemore, *Rules for the World*, for an elaboration of the argument that international organisations' authority grants them a degree of autonomy, and related evidence.

and moral obligation, and the ultimately state-based legal character of the activities they aim to regulate, make the governance of such organisations non-authoritative. Non-state *in* authority at the transnational level needs political authority to infuse it with obligation and legitimacy. As we saw however, political authority at the international level is fragmented and decentralised. Therefore, this political authority can come from two different sources: a) from international organisations that already enjoy such authority in an issue-area, and b) from the consent of a sufficient number of states, or at least of a number of sufficiently significant states in an issue-area or activity, to make the rules of these organisations authoritative at the international level.

The anatomy of transnational *in* authority

There can be a variety of ways that non-state actors can come together in an authoritative structure with public authorities. To identify these different modes of blending private power with state authority we need to take a step back and examine the variety of functions that *in* authority performs in any structure of governance and therefore government as well: creating rules, implementing them and adjudicating the disputes that arise from them. Non-state *in* authority emerges when one or more of these functions are undertaken by non-state actors while the remaining functions are performed by state authorities. Table 1 exhibits all the possible modes of combining state and non-state actors in the performance of these governance functions. We see that there are eight possible combinations of non-state and state actors that produce different governance structures. Evidently, group one represents pure state governance, in other words government at the domestic level, or inter-state governance at the international level. At the opposite end we have group eight, which represents what Rosenau calls governance without government.[59] Here we find the majority of transnational non-state governance schemes, where various types of regulatory mechanisms operate on a voluntary basis among participating parties. Between these two extremes we can find a number of possible combinations of state and non-state actors which render the resulting governance structure into an authoritative mechanism.

To review the simplest cases where non-state actors assume only one of these functions, we could have a state agency deciding the rules for an issue-area and referring any disputes about them to public courts, while the actual implementation of the rules is taking place through the actions and procedures of a non-state organisation such as a self-regulatory agency. At the transnational level, a comparable situation has been encountered increasingly in recent years, when inter-state organisations delegate the implementation of policies decided at the international level to non-state actors and organisations. This is a very interesting development in the context of global governance and undoubtedly this delegation confers, to some degree, public *in* authority to the specified non-state organisations.[60] These

---

[59] James M. Rosenau and Ernst-Otto Czempiel (eds), *Governance without Government: Order and Change in World Politics* (Cambridge: Cambridge University Press, 1992).

[60] An example of this process is the participation of NGOs in the implementation of the national Poverty Reduction Strategies (PRS) in less developed countries in the context of the World Bank's Heavily Indebted Poor Countries Initiative (HIPC).

Authority Functions	Type of Actors	
Rule-Making Implementation Adjudication	1. State State State	2. Non-State State State
Rule-Making Implementation Adjudication	3. State Non-State State	4. State State Non-State
Rule-Making Implementation Adjudication	5. Non-State Non-State State	6. State Non-State Non-State
Rule-Making Implementation Adjudication	7. Non-State State Non-State	8. Non-State Non-State Non-State

Table 1. *Variations of non-state in authority*

organisations have the authority to implement on the ground the decisions agreed at the international level; they are the embodiment of inter-state authority at the local level where the implementation of policies takes place. Alternatively, we can have a situation where non-state actors have undertaken not the implementation but the adjudication of disputes relating to a specific set of rules which have been drawn by state authorities or the legislature. This is an increasingly recurrent phenomenon in commercial disputes, especially in transnational disputes, and it is known as private commercial arbitration.[61] The rules to be used are usually drawn from a specific national, legal jurisdiction, commonly agreed by the parties as most relevant for the dispute at hand. Likewise, the implementation of the decisions of such tribunals takes place through the public courts and authorities of the jurisdiction in question.[62] Finally, there can be a situation where the rules regulating an issue-area, sphere of activity or industry are designed by non-state actors but implemented by state authorities and adjudicated by public courts.

However, these are not the only modes of governance that can result from the cooperation of state and non-state actors. It may be the case that state and non-state actors share not only different functions in the governance structure of an issue-area but that they also share different parts or stages of the same function. Figure 1 demonstrates how each function can be jointly performed by both state and non-state actors. In this case, all different modes of governance collapse to the same basic format which can exhibit a high degree of variation depending on the balance between state and non-state actors within any single function. The exact configuration of non-state *in* authority becomes a matter of degree, as the balance between state and non-state actors often shifts along a continuum rather than taking discrete positions. This depends to a large extent on the nature of the issue-area which may allow or even require that different parts or stages of the same function are performed by different actors.

---

[61] Cutler, *Private Power*.
[62] The UN Convention on the Recognition and Enforcement of Foreign Arbitral Awards (New York Convention) obliges the signatory states to acknowledge and enforce such arbitration awards.

Figure 1. Same function variations of non-state in authority

Therefore, considering again the examples we reviewed above, we may have NGOs implementing only part of a particular project authorised by an inter-state organisation, while the remainder is carried out by the executive organs of that inter-state organisation or perhaps by local governmental agencies. Similarly, in the case of adjudication, private commercial arbitration forms only the initial part of the adjudication process, since the decision reached through the arbitration process has to be implemented in a specific national, legal jurisdiction, and therefore requires ratification by the local, public courts (see Figure 2). Finally, state and non-state actors could assume different parts of the legislative process. It is thus common, state supervisory agencies or ministries to set the general guidelines or principles that form the foundation of governance in an issue-area, while the day-to-day, detailed regulation and governance of that issue-area is assigned to a non-state organisation.[63]

Conclusion

The purpose of this article has been to delineate the concept of non-state authority in the context of global governance. In the course of this process the somewhat loose and inconsistent use of the term in the literature on private authority in global governance was criticised, and a more thoroughly defined and analytically consistent concept of transnational *in* authority was presented. This concept represents a type of governing authority where non-state transnational governance schemes are endorsed by states or inter-state organisations, thus bestowing on them public *in* authority, and allowing them to exercise not only effective but also authoritative governance of an issue-area. The concept of transnational *in* authority can hopefully help us distinguish between cases of authority limited to the private sector, authoritative knowledge and expertise, and authoritative non-state governance of areas of public life and activity. This distinction is

---

[63] A characteristic example is the dual regulatory structure of the European internet domains system, where the European Commission provides rules and principles, while a private organisation, Eurid, is responsible for operating the system and creating detailed rules and procedures. See George Christou and Seamus Simpson, 'Limitations to transnational governance of the Internet' in Graz and Nölke, *Transnational Private Governance*.

Rule-Making	Implementation	Adjudication			Implementation
		Stage 1	Stage 2	Stage 3	
State Legislates/ Regulates or Mandates/ Sanctions Self-Regulation	Law/Regulation Implemented Nationally - Private Contracts Drawn According to National Legislation/ Regulation	Dispute Arises Transnationally	Dispute Resolved through Transnational Private Arbitration	National Public Courts Ratify Private Arbitration Decision	Decisions Implemented Nationally

Time Line ———————▶

Figure 2. An example of same function variation: fragmented adjudication in private transnational commercial arbitration

significant because it is the latter case of non-state authority that is the most novel and consequential development in the context of global governance.

Focusing on non-state governance schemes endowed with public *in* authority promotes the research agenda of non-state authority in a number of ways. First, it allows us to differentiate among the increasing array of non-state governance organisations, and bring to light NSAs that can have a significant impact on global governance, and which produce regulatory instruments enjoying formal legality. As noted earlier, the aim is not to favour the compliance or enforcement capacity of hard law over soft law instruments, but to illuminate the political and institutional transformations needed for the emergence of transnational *in* authority. Thus, this focus on formal authority and legal results provides us with an opportunity to trace and analyse the increasing institutionalisation and legitimisation of non-state actors in the context of the domestic political authority's apparatus. In this context it is possible to examine transnational *in* authority as a potent example of the process of denationalisation,[64] and thus explore more systematically the changes of domestic regulatory/governance institutions that have to take place in order to accommodate transnational governance structures which produce legal results intended to be implemented nationally. In addition and related to this, the focus on transnational *in* authority brings the state's role in non-state governance much more sharply and clearly into focus. Analysts have often tended to treat states as unwilling or unable to provide adequate governance in a continuously globalising world; in view of this governance deficit, NSAs are increasingly stepping in and assuming this role.[65] This 'inability/unwillingness of the state' thesis attributes to state actors a passive role. Contrary to this tendency and without denying the

[64] For a detailed presentation and analysis of the concept of denationalisation see Saskia Sassen, *Territory, Authority, Rights* (Princeton and Oxford: Princeton University Press, 2006).
[65] See for example Phipil G. Cerny, 'Globalization and the Changing Logic of Collective Action', *International Organization*, 49:4 (1995), pp. 595–625; Ann M. Florini, 'Who Does What? Collective

constraints that globalisation poses on state autonomy, transnational *in* authority offers a way into the exploration of state's role in multi-level global governance, since its emergence begs the question: why and under what conditions have states attributed legal obligation to regulation produced by transnational non-state institutions? Finally, this conceptualisation of non-state authority offers an insight into the nature and workings of political authority itself. Given that the research literature on private authority falls within the wider research agenda of the transformation of such basic concepts as the state, authority, and sovereignty in an era of globalising forces, an analytical construct that explicitly links non-state and state authority into a complex transnational structure, has potentially a lot to offer to our understanding of such transformations.

These concerns become more significant when we consider that transnational non-state governance and consequently transnational *in* authority are not likely to be ephemeral phenomena. There is a web of institutions and interactions being developed, whereby governance functions performed by some organisations are increasingly dependent on the work done by other organisations. This makes a reversal of the transnationalisation of global governance unlikely. To the degree that transnational *in* authority embeds transnational non-state structures in domestic political economies through institutionalisation and legalisation, it makes such a reversal even less probable.

Action and the Changing Nature of Authority', in Higgott, Underhill and Bieler, *Non-State Actors*; Kobrin, 'Economic Governance'.

Review of International Studies (2010), 36, 137–155   © 2010 British International Studies Association
doi:10.1017/S0260210510000823   First published online 26 Aug 2010

The uncritical critique of 'liberal peace'

DAVID CHANDLER*

Abstract. For many commentators the lack of success in international statebuilding efforts has been explained through the critical discourse of 'liberal peace', where it is assumed that 'liberal' Western interests and assumptions have influenced policymaking leading to counterproductive results. At the core of the critique is the assumption that the liberal peace approach has sought to reproduce and impose Western models: the reconstruction of 'Westphalian' frameworks of state sovereignty; the liberal framework of individual rights and winner-takes-all elections; and neo-liberal free market economic programmes. This article challenges this view of Western policymaking and suggests that post-Cold War post-conflict intervention and statebuilding can be better understood as a critique of classical liberal assumptions about the autonomous subject – framed in terms of sovereignty, law, democracy and the market. The conflating of discursive forms with their former liberal content creates the danger that critiques of liberal peace can rewrite post-Cold War intervention in ways that exaggerate the liberal nature of the policy frameworks and act as apologia, excusing policy failure on the basis of the self-flattering view of Western policy elites: that non-Western subjects were not ready for 'Western' freedoms.

David Chandler is Professor of International Relations, Department of Politics and International Relations, University of Westminster, London. He is the founding editor of the Journal of Intervention and Statebuilding. His recent books include: *International Statebuilding: The Rise of Post-Liberal Governance* (Routledge, 2010); *Hollow Hegemony: Rethinking Global Politics, Power and Resistance* (Pluto, 2009); and *Empire in Denial: The Politics of Statebuilding* (Pluto, 2006).

Introduction

Since the late 1990s, commentators have developed critical frameworks of the 'liberal peace' to understand the new, more interventionist, approaches to the problems of post-conflict rebuilding and the threat of state failure.[1] In essence, the 'liberal peace' is held to go beyond traditional approaches of conflict prevention, or 'negative peace'; towards the external engineering of post-conflict

---

* The author would like to thank Aidan Hehir, Nik Hynek, Oliver Richmond, Julian Reid and David Roberts for their suggestions and support in engaging with this theme and the RIS reviewers for their insightful and helpful comments.
[1] See, for example, Mark Duffield, *Global Governance and the New Wars: The Merging of Development and Security* (London: Zed Books, 2001); Roland Paris, 'International Peacebuilding and the "Mission Civilisatrice"', *Review of International Studies*, 28:4 (2002), pp. 637–56; Michael Pugh, 'The Political Economy of Peacebuilding: A Critical Theory Perspective', *International Journal of Peace Studies*, 10:2 (2005), pp. 23–42; Oliver P. Richmond, *The Transformation of Peace* (Basingstoke: MacMillan, 2005); Richmond and Roger MacGinty, Special Issue, 'The Liberal Peace and Post-War Reconstruction', *Global Society*, 21:4 (2007).

societies through the export of liberal frameworks of 'good governance', democratic elections, human rights, the rule of law and market relations.[2] As Alex Bellamy summarises: 'The principle aim of peace operations thus becomes not so much about creating spaces for negotiated conflict resolution between states but about actively contributing to the construction of liberal polities, economies and societies.'[3] The critical discourse of the liberal peace flags up the problem that – under the guise of universalising Western liberal frameworks of democracy and the market – the needs and interests of those subject to intervention are often ignored, resulting in the maintenance of inequalities and conflicts and undermining the asserted goals of external interveners. The critique of international intervention and statebuilding, framed by the construction of the liberal peace, has been highly effective in challenging assumptions of easy fixes to post-conflict situations.[4]

This article seeks to forward an alternative framework and to question the use of the 'liberal peace' rubric to describe and analyse post-conflict and international statebuilding interventions in the post-Cold War period. It will be argued that the critique of liberal peace bears much less relation to policy practice than might be assumed by the critical (radical and policy) discourses and, in fact, appears to inverse the relationship between the critique of the liberal peace and the dominant policy assumptions. The shared desire to critique the liberal peace leads to a set of assumptions and one-sided representations that portray Western policy interventions as too *liberal:* too fixated on Western models and too keen to allow democratic freedoms and market autonomy. It will be explained here that this view of 'liberal' interventions transforming post-conflict societies through 'immediate' liberalisation and 'rapid democratization and marketization' is a self-serving and fictional policy narrative.[5] This narrative fiction is then used, in the frameworks of policy orientated critiques, as the basis upon which to reflect upon Western policy and to limit policy expectations (while often extending regulatory controls) on the basis that the aspirations of external interveners were too ambitious, too interventionist, and too 'liberal' for the states and societies which were the subject of intervention.

It is unfortunate that this policy narrative can appear to be given support by more radical critiques of post-Cold War intervention, similarly framed through the critique of liberal peace. For example, Oliver Richmond is not exceptional in re-reading the catastrophe of the invasion and occupation of Iraq in terms of an 'attempt to mimic the liberal state', which has 'done much to discredit the universal claims of the transferability of the liberal peace in political terms'.[6] Michael Barnett argues that 'liberal values' clearly guide peacebuilding activities and that their

---

[2] For an overview, see Richmond, *Peace in International Relations* (London: Routledge, 2008).

[3] Alex Bellamy, 'The "Next Stage" in Peace Operations Theory', in Bellamy and Paul Williams (eds), *Peace Operations and Global Order* (London: Routledge, 2008), pp. 17–38, 4–5.

[4] This is in part reflected in the much more limited goals set for external intervention in the policy literature, see, for example, Simon Chesterman, Michael Ignatieff and Ramesh Thakur, *Making States Work: State Failure and the Crisis of Governance* (New York: UN University Press, 2005); James Dobbins et al., *The Beginners' Guide to Nation-Building* (Santa Monica, CA.: RAND Corporation, 2007); Paris and Timothy Sisk (eds), *The Dilemmas of Statebuilding: Confronting the Contradictions of Postwar Peace Operations* (London: Routledge, 2009).

[5] Roland Paris, *At War's End: Building Peace after Civil Conflict* (Cambridge: Cambridge University Press, 2004), p. 235.

[6] Oliver Richmond, 'Reclaiming Peace in International Relations', *Millennium: Journal of International Studies*, 36:3 (2008), pp. 439–70, 458.

'explicit goal' is 'to create a state defined by the rule of law, markets and democracy'.[7] Beate Jahn has argued that 'the tragedy of liberal diplomacy' lies in the ideological drive of liberalism, in which intervention is intensified despite the counterproductive results.[8] Foucaultian-inspired theorists, Michael Dillon and Julian Reid, similarly reinforce the claims that the key problematic of intervention is its liberal nature in their assertion that we are witnessing a liberal drive to control and to regulate the post-colonial world on the behalf of neo-liberal or biopolitical power, seeking 'to globalize the domesticating power of civil society mechanisms in a war against all other modes of cultural forms'.[9]

This view of a transformative drive to regulate and control the post-colonial world on the basis of the liberal framings of power and knowledge stands in stark contrast to the policy world, in which, by the end of the Cold War, leading policy institutions were already highly pessimistic of the capacities of non-liberal subjects to cope with liberal political, economic and social forms and suspicious of even East and Central European states coping with democracy and the market, let alone those of sub-Saharan Africa. Bringing the critique back in relation with the policy practices seems to suggest that the policy critics of the liberal peace offer succour and consolation to the policymakers rather than critique. This leads to the concern of this article that more radical critiques of the liberal peace may need to ensure that they are not drawn into a framework in which their critical intentions may be blunted.

There are many different approaches taken to the critique of liberal peace approaches and often authors do not clearly stake out their methodological frameworks or develop a 'scattergun approach' using a range of different critiques.[10] Nevertheless, for heuristic purposes, it will be useful to frame these diverse critiques within two broad, distinctive, but often interconnected, approaches; which are here categorised as the radical, 'power-based', and the more policy orientated, 'ideas-based', critiques. The former approach tends to see the discourse of liberal peace as an ideological and instrumental one, arguing that the rhetoric of freedom, markets and democracy is merely a representation of Western self-interest, which has little genuine concern for the security and freedoms of those societies intervened in. The latter approach suggests that rather than the concepts being misused, in the discursive frameworks of the projection of Western power, the problem lies less with power relations than with the universal conceptualising of the liberal peace itself.

The 'power-based' critique

In this framework, the liberal peace is critiqued on the basis that it reflects the hegemonic values and the political, economic and geo-strategic needs of Western

---

[7] Michael Barnett, 'Building a Republican Peace: Stabilizing States after War', *International Security*, 30:4 (2006), pp. 87–112, 88.

[8] Beate Jahn, 'The Tragedy of Liberal Diplomacy', *Journal of Intervention and Statebuilding*, 1:1 (2007), pp. 87–106; 1:2 (2007), pp. 211–29.

[9] Michael Dillon and Julian Reid, *The Liberal Way of War: Killing to Make Life Live* (London: Routledge, 2009), p. 20.

[10] See the range of understandings of liberal peace itself in Richmond, *The Transformation of Peace*.

states. This critique focuses on the role played by the interests of Western powers in shaping policy and the impact of the economic and structural inequalities of the world economy. It also pays attention to the naturalising of policy assumptions based upon this perspective. There are three main versions of this power-based perspective.

Firstly, there is a critical approach which tends to engage with a Left or neo-Marxist structural critique of liberal peace approaches. This framing suggests that Western intervention is inevitably reproducing hierarchies of power due to the structural constraints of neo-liberal market relations – opening up societies and economies through the demands for democratisation and the free market.[11] This approach focuses on the problems of neo-liberal economic policies for the reconstruction of post-conflict societies and suggests that, in serving the interests of dominant Western powers and the international financial institutions, the policies of the liberal peace inevitably reproduce the conditions and possibilities for conflict.[12]

This approach often draws upon Robert Cox's critical theory to suggest that the narrow problem-solving approach taken by Western policymakers is problematic as it takes for granted the interests of these actors and treats market-based economic solutions as merely technical 'problem-solving' approaches to address problems of post-conflict development.[13] These critical approaches to the liberal peace suggest that it is necessary to reflect on these assumptions to reveal the power interests that lie behind them and to question the presentation of these policies in policy neutral technical terms.[14] Michael Pugh, for example, has consistently highlighted how neo-liberal economic practices are naturalised as technical solutions to development and reconstruction, marginalising or preventing political discussions of economic alternatives better suited to post-conflict societies.[15]

Secondly, there is a more Foucaultian structuralist approach, which critiques the 'liberal peace' not so much on the liberal basis of its interventionary policies *per se* as on the interests behind these policies: understood as perpetuating the needs and interests of liberal, neo-liberal or biopolitical capitalism in the West. Mark Duffield has pioneered this approach in his 2001 book, *Global Governance and the New Wars*.[16] Here the focus is less on the opening up of non-Western economies to the world market and more on the reshaping and transformation of these societies in order to prevent instability. In his 2001 work, Duffield argued that the project of 'liberal peace reflects a radical development agenda of social

---

[11] This critique is probably most associated with the work of Michael Pugh, see, for example, 'The Political Economy of Peacebuilding'; see also Pugh, Neil Cooper and Mandy Turner (eds), *Whose Peace? Critical Perspectives on the Political Economy of Peacebuilding* (Basingstoke: MacMillan, 2008).

[12] See also, Rita Abrahamsen, *Disciplining Democracy: Development Discourse and Good Governance in Africa* (London: Zed Books, 2000); Julien Barbara, 'Rethinking Neo-liberal State Building: Building Post-Conflict Development States', *Development in Practice*, 18:3 (2008), pp. 307–18; Christopher Cramer, *Why Civil War is Not a Stupid Thing: Accounting for Violence in Developing Countries* (London: Hurst & Co., 2006); Tim Jacoby, 'Hegemony, Modernisation and Post-War Reconstruction', *Global Society*, 21:4 (2007), pp. 521–37.

[13] See Robert W. Cox, 'Social Forces, States and World Orders', *Millennium: Journal of International Studies*, 10:2 (1981), pp. 126–55.

[14] See, for example, Bellamy, 'The "Next Stage" in Peace Operations Theory'.

[15] See note 7.

[16] Duffield, *Global Governance*.

transformation' with the aim 'to transform the dysfunctional and war-affected societies that it encounters on its borders into cooperative, representative and, especially, stable entities'.[17]

This transformative liberal intervention has necessitated the radicalisation of both development and security discourses, giving the external institutions of global governance new mandates to: 'shift the balance of power between groups and even to change attitudes and beliefs'.[18] In his later work, Duffield expands on this framework of the projection of liberal interests in stabilising 'zones of conflict' through the use of the Foucaultian conception of biopolitics, where intervention is understood as saving, developing, or securing the Other, at the same time legitimising and extending external regulatory control.[19] Duffield argues that in the interests of stabilising the neo-liberal economic order, the divisions between the 'developed' and the 'undeveloped' world are reproduced through policies of containment such as 'sustainable' or 'community-based' development.[20]

The third approach engages from the approach of critical theory and human security. Like the first approach, it highlights that 'liberal peace' policies should be seen as political and power-based, rather than as purely technical solutions.[21] However, the focus is less on the assumptions about market relations or securing the needs of global neo-liberal or biopolitical power and more on the assumptions made about the political and institutional framework and positivist and rationalist forms of Western knowledge. For writers, such as Alex Bellamy, a central concern is the problematic focus on the rebuilding of Westphalian state forms,[22] for Oliver Richmond, the focus is on the liberal assumptions of political community assumed in the approach of 'liberal peace', which tends to ignore vital local concerns of identity and culture.[23]

The power-based approaches in this third category clearly take on board the concerns over universalising Western liberal assumptions which will be dealt with in the following section, sketching the 'ideas-based' critiques. However, they are classed within the first category as the conception of Western 'power' still plays a vital role. Unlike the first two approaches, these more subjective or constructivist

---

[17] Duffield, *Global Governance*, p. 11.
[18] Ibid., p. 15.
[19] Duffield, *Development, Security and Unending War: Governing the World of Peoples* (Cambridge: Polity, 2007). See also, Michael Dillon and Julian Reid, *The Liberal Way of War: Killing to Make Life Live* (London: Routledge, 2009), who argue (p. 20) that:
> [...] the liberal way of rule is therefore biopolitical [...] The same goes for the liberal way of war, which waging war on the human in the name of the biohuman, systematically also now demonizes human being, from the individual to the collective, as the locus of the infinite threat posed...by the diverse undecidability of the human as such.
[20] See also, Vivienne Jabri, *War and the Transformation of Global Politics* (Basingstoke: MacMillan, 2007), applying a Foucaultian framework to the divisive politics of neo-liberal intervention, she states (p. 124):
> The discourse, from Bosnia to Kosovo to Iraq is one that aims to reconstruct societies and their government in accordance with a distinctly western liberal model the formative elements of which centre on open markets, human rights and the rule of law, and of democratic elections as the basis of legitimacy. The aim is no less than to reconstitute polities through the transformation of political cultures into modern, self-disciplining, and ultimately self-governing entities that, through such transformation, could transcend ethnic or religious fragmentation and violence. The trajectory is punishment, pacification, discipline, and ultimately 'liberal democratic self-mastery'.
[21] See, for example, Bellamy, 'The "Next Stage" in Peace Operations Theory'.
[22] Ibid.
[23] Richmond, *Peace in International Relations*.

frameworks of critique suggest that frameworks of liberal peace, projected through Western power, can be successfully challenged by other more reflective, emancipatory, or 'bottom-up' approaches to liberal peace; suggesting that there is not necessarily a clash of interests between those intervening and those intervened upon.[24] Some commentators from within this perspective would argue that elected Western politicians could pursue alternative polices by constructing their interests in a more enlightened way, for example, through pursuing more human security orientated policies, which could be conceived as in Western self-interest, in a globalised and interconnected world, or that non-state actors may be able to intervene in ways which engage more equally and empathetically with those on the ground.[25]

The 'ideas-based' critique

The 'ideas-based' critique of liberal peace presents itself as a critique of the grounding universalising assumptions of the liberal policy discourse itself, rather than merely as a critique of the forms of its implementation. These critics of liberal peace advocate less liberal frameworks of intervention, with less attention to the reconstruction of sovereign states, democracy and the free market. While upholding the values of democracy and the free market aspirationally, these critics argue against the liberal peace approach on the basis that it is unsuitable in the context of post-conflict states and situations of state failure.

This approach tends to focus on the problem of Western interventionist 'ideas' or 'values' rather than on interests or power relations. While their critique of the liberal peace thesis therefore may appear to be more radical, their intentions can also be understood as more conservative or policy orientated.[26] Rather than problematising relations of power or the interests behind policymaking, there is a tendency to view the liberal peace approach as a projection of Western ideals in a context where they can be counterproductive. This critique has been developed by Jack Snyder, Fareed Zakharia, Stephen Krasner, Robert Keohane, and Roland Paris, amongst others, who argue that liberal peace assumptions have undermined the effectiveness of international statebuilding.[27]

[24] As Richmond states:
    Interdisciplinary and cross-cutting coalitions of scholars, policy makers, individuals – indigenous, local, transnational – and civil society actors can develop discursive understandings of peace and its construction [facilitating] a negotiation of a discursive practice of peace in which hegemony, domination, and oppression can be identified and resolved. (Richmond, 'Reclaiming Peace in International Relations', p. 462).
[25] See, for example, Shahrbanou Tadjbakhsh and Anuradha M. Chenoy, *Human Security: Concepts and Implications* (London: Routledge, 2007); Sandra M. Maclean, David R. Black and Timothy M. Shaw (eds), *A Decade of Human Security: Global Governance and New Multilateralisms* (Aldershot: Ashgate, 2006).
[26] Nevertheless, authors such as Roland Paris have been happy to defend their rejection of critiques based merely on the interests of power, asserting, perhaps not unreasonably, that: 'Peacebuilding missions have taken place in some of the poorest and most economically stagnant parts of the world [...] countries that, to put it bluntly, have little to offer international capitalists [...] The balance sheet of peacebuilding simply does not sustain the economic exploitation thesis.' Paris, 'International Peacebuilding and the 'Mission Civilisatrice', p. 653.
[27] See, for example, Jack Snyder, *From Voting to Violence: Democratization and Nationalist Conflict* (New York: W. W. Norton, 2000); Fareed Zakharia, *The Future of Freedom; Illiberal Democracy at*

One of the core liberal assumptions problematised in this approach is that of sovereign statehood. These critics argue that focusing on (re)constructing sovereign states is unlikely to solve the problems of post-conflict societies, merely to reproduce them. Krasner argues that sovereignty is problematic for many states because they lack the capacity for good governance and require an external regulatory framework in order to guarantee human rights and the rule of law.[28] Robert Keohane forwards a similar perspective with differing levels of statehood applicable to different levels of governance capacity: 'We somehow have to reconceptualise the state as a political unit that can maintain internal order while being able to engage in international cooperation, without claiming exclusive rights [. . .] traditionally associated with sovereignty.'[29]

Pursuing a similar approach, Paris argues that the assumptions of the liberal peace – that democracy and the free market will ensure social progress and stability – neglects to consider the problematic nature of transition. Questioning the assumption that 'liberalization fosters peace', Paris advocates less emphasis on interventionist policies which promote democracy and the market, both of which can encourage competition and conflict without adequate institutional frameworks.[30] Instead, Paris advocates a policy of 'Institutionalization before Liberalization' in order to establish the regulatory frameworks necessary to ensure that post-conflict societies can gradually (and safely) move towards liberal models of market democracy.[31]

These critics of liberal peace do not argue that they are anti-liberal; merely that liberalism, as projected in liberal peace frameworks, has to take into account the non-liberal context in which intervention takes place. Fareed Zakharia, for example, argues that, while in the West, we have historically associated liberalism and democracy, in much of the non-Western world we have to make a choice between liberalism and democracy as, without the institutional framework of limited government, 'elections provide a cover for authoritarianism' and are 'merely legitimized power grabs'; in this context, therefore, 'what Africa needs more than urgently than democracy is good governance'.[32]

This critique of the liberal peace is that, rather than being based on the needs and interests of Western hegemonic powers and international financial institutions, the problem is one of projecting an idealised understanding of the West's own historical development; one which tends to naturalise the smooth working of the market and understand liberal political frameworks as an organic product of

Home and Abroad (New York: W. W. Norton, 2003), pp. 98–9; Stephen Krasner, 'sharing Sovereignty: New Institutions for Collapsing and Failing States', *International Security*, 29:2 (2004), pp. 5–43; Krasner, 'The Case for Shared Sovereignty', *Journal of Democracy*, 16:1 (2005), pp. 69–83; Robert Keohane, 'Ironies of Sovereignty: The EU and the US', *Journal of Common Market Studies*, 40:4 (2002), pp. 743–65; Paris, *At War's End*.

[28] Krasner, 'Sharing Sovereignty', p. 89. See also, James D. Fearon and David D. Laitin, 'Neo-trusteeship and the Problem of Weak States', *International Security*, 28:4 (2004), pp. 5–43.

[29] Robert O. Keohane, 'Political Authority after Intervention: Gradations in Sovereignty', in J. L. Holzgrefe and Keohane (eds), *Humanitarian Intervention: Ethical, Legal and Political Dilemmas* (Cambridge: Cambridge University Press, 2003), p. 277. See also, Keohane, 'Ironies of Sovereignty'.

[30] Paris, *At War's End*, pp. 40–51.

[31] Ibid., pp. 179–211. This critique of the export of liberal models to non-liberal societies echoes that made in the 1960s by Samuel Huntington, *Political Order in Changing Societies* (New Haven: Yale University Press). See also David Chandler, 'Back to the Future? The Limits of Neo-Wilsonian Ideals of Exporting Democracy', *Review of International Studies*, 32:3 (2006), pp. 475–94.

[32] Fareed Zakharia, *The Future of Freedom*, pp. 98–9. See also, Jack Snyder, *From Voting to Violence*.

democratic processes such as free elections. For these critics, the founding assumptions of the liberal peace are the problem: attempts to universalise Western models in non-liberal contexts, will merely reproduce, and maybe even exacerbate, the problems of conflict and instability.

A 'critical' consensus?

This article seeks to argue that the radical intent of the critics of interventionist Western policies has been blunted by their articulation within the problematic of a 'liberal peace', enabling their critique to be assimilated into the policy discourse of how policy might be reformed and legitimated in the wake of the discrediting of the claims of Western policymaking after the debacles of Iraq and Afghanistan. The two fairly distinct critical framings of the 'liberal peace' stem from very different methodological perspectives and political and policy intents. While the 'ideas-based' critics tend to seek to defend and legitimate regulatory external intervention, the 'power-based' critics tend to challenge and oppose these frameworks as the projection of Western power and interests. Nevertheless, in critiquing Western policy interventions, developed since the end of the Cold War, within the problematic of 'liberal peace' it seems that there is often much less distance between the radical approaches and the policy approaches than might be assumed on the basis of political intent and occasionally there is a surprisingly large area of confluence.

It seems that both sides of the divide, regarding the dynamics driving frameworks of liberal peace, start from the basis that the liberal peace (in its various framings) is actually an adequate description of the policy framework being devised and implemented in international intervention and external statebuilding approaches since the end of the Cold War. This would, of course, appear to make intuitive sense if we understood the post-Cold War period as one in which there was a new confidence in the power of liberal frameworks, with assumptions that the collapse of non-market alternatives meant the 'End of History' and the end of any political or ideological challenge to the ascendency of liberal perspectives and discursive judgements on the economic, political and social frameworks of states and societies. This article seeks to make the counterintuitive point that the rise of critiques of liberal peace is, in fact, indicative of a lack of confidence in classical liberal assumptions about human behaviour and the political and socio-economic institutions needed for human flourishing.

In the critiques of the liberal peace, this growing consensus on the problematic nature of liberalism appears to cross the political and policy spectrum. The fundamental and shared claim of the critics is that the lack of success of external interventions, designed not only to halt conflict but to help reconstruct the peace, is down to the liberalism of the interveners. If only they were not, in various ways, so *liberal*, then it is alleged external intervention or assistance may potentially be much less problematic. It can appear that the main academic and political matter of dispute is whether the liberal peace discourse is amenable to policy change. Here the divide seems to roughly approximate to the division highlighted above, in terms of the heuristic categories of 'power-' and 'ideas-based' liberal peace critics.

The more radical, 'power-based', critics, with a more economically deterministic approach to the structural dynamics or the needs of 'neo-liberalism' are less likely to be optimistic of reform. On the 'ideas-based' side, those critics of liberal peace frameworks who tend to be more engaged in policy related work are more optimistic with regard to a shift away from the policy emphasis of liberal peace.

In a recent article, Endre Begby and Peter Burgess argue that the majority of the critics of the liberal peace seem to share two key assumptions about external intervention: firstly, that external Western intervention (of some kind) is necessary, and secondly, that the goal of this intervention should be the liberal one of human freedom and flourishing.[33] They state that, in which case, the problem is not so much with the aspirations or goals of 'liberal peace' but with the practices of intervention itself. They have a valid point regarding the limited nature of much of this 'critical' discourse, but do not reflect adequately on the diminished content of the 'liberalism' of the policy interventions themselves nor the 'liberal' aspirations of those who advocate for the reform of practices of external intervention. It seems that the common ground in the broad and disparate critiques of the liberal peace, is not the critique of the external practices of intervention as much as the classical assumptions of liberalism itself.

The critique of liberalism as a set of assumptions and practices seems to be driving the approach to the study of post-Cold War interventions in ways which have tended to produce a fairly one-sided framework of analysis in which the concept of liberalism is ill-equipped to bear the analytical weight placed upon it and appears increasingly emptied of theoretical or empirical content. Liberalism appears to be used promiscuously to explain a broad range of often contradictory policy perspectives and practices across very differing circumstances and with very differing outcomes. In this sense, it appears that liberalism operates as a 'field of adversity'[34] through which a coherent narrative of post-Cold War intervention has been articulated both by critical and policy orientated theorists. The promiscuous use of liberalism to explain very different policy approaches is, of course, facilitated by the ambiguous nature of the concept itself.

It is this ambiguity which enables liberalism to be critiqued from opposing directions, sometimes by the same author at the same time. Good examples of this are Roland Paris and Timothy Sisk who criticise 'liberal' peacebuilding for being both too *laissez-faire* and too interventionist in its approach to the regulation and management of conflict. In the peacebuilding literature today, the experience of the early and mid-1990s and the 'quick exit' policies of the 'first generation' peacebuilding operations in Namibia, Nicaragua, Angola, Cambodia, El Salvador, Mozambique, Liberia, Rwanda, Bosnia, Croatia and Guatemala has been repackaged as evidence that Western interveners had too much faith in the liberal subject.[35] Similarly, the *ad hoc* responses to the problems of the early 1990s in the development of 'second generation' peacebuilding with protectorate powers in

---

[33] Endre Begby and Peter Burgess, 'Human Security and Liberal Peace', *Public Reason*, 1:1 (2009), pp. 91–104.

[34] See, Michel Foucault, *The Birth of Biopolitics: Lectures at the Collège de France 1978–1979* (Basingstoke: Palgrave-MacMillan, 2008), p. 106.

[35] See, for example, Paris and Sisk, 'Introduction: Understanding the Contradiction of Postwar Statebuilding', in Paris and Sisk (eds), *The Dilemmas of Statebuilding*, pp. 1–20.

Bosnia, Kosovo and East Timor, has been criticised as liberal hubris, on the assumption that international overlords could bring democracy, development and security to others. It seems that, rather than adding clarity, the critique of the 'liberalism' of intervention tells us very little.

The mechanism through which these liberal framings have been facilitated and critiqued is that of the discursive centring of the non-liberal Other; on whose behalf the policy critics assert the need for different policy practices. In this way, the policy critics of past policy approaches evade a direct critique of liberal assumptions about equality, autonomy, and transformative capacity, instead, arguing that the non-liberal Other (in various ways) invalidates, challenges or resists (passively as well as actively) policy practices which may otherwise have been less problematic.

Rather than a critique of liberalism for its inability to overcome social, economic and cultural inequalities, both the policy, 'ideas-based', critique of the liberal peace and the more radical, 'power-based', critiques argue that social, economic and cultural inequalities and differences have to be central to policy practices and invalidate universalising liberal attempts to reconstruct and rebuild post-conflict societies. In this context – in which the dichotomy between a liberal policymaking sphere and a non-liberal sphere of policy intervention comes to the fore – there is an inevitable tendency towards a consensual framing of the problematic of statebuilding or peacebuilding intervention as a problem of the relationship between the liberal West and the non-liberal Other.

The rock on which the liberal peace expectations are held to crash is that of the non-liberal Other. The non-liberal Other increasingly becomes portrayed as the barrier to Western liberal aspirations of social peace and progress; either as it lacks the institutional, social, economic and cultural capacities that are alleged to be necessary to overcome the problems of liberal peace or as a subaltern or resisting subject, for whom liberal peacebuilding frameworks threaten their economic or social existence or fundamental values or identities. The 'critique' becomes apology in that this discursive focus upon the non-Western or non-liberal Other is often held to explain the lack of policy success and, through this, suggest that democracy or development are somehow not 'appropriate' aspirations or that expectations need to be substantially lowered or changed to account for difference.

International statebuilding and the critique of liberalism

It would appear that the assumptions held to be driving liberal peace approaches are very much in the eye of their critical beholders. The most obvious empirical difficulty is that international policy regarding intervention and statebuilding seems to have little transformative aspiration: far from assumptions of liberal universalism, it would appear that, with the failure of post-colonial development, especially from the 1970s onwards, international policymakers have developed historically low expectations about what can be achieved through external intervention and assistance. The lack of transformative belief is highlighted by one of the key concerns of the policy critics of the liberal peace – the focus on capacity-building state institutions and intervening to construct 'civil' societies. The focus on institutional solutions (at both the formal and informal levels) to the problems of conflict and transition is indicative of the narrowing down of aspirations from transforming society to merely regulating or managing it – often understood critically as the 'securitising' of policymaking. This is a long way from the promise of liberal transformation and the discourse of 'liberating' societies economically and politically.

In fact, it is the consensus of opinion on the dangers of democracy, which has informed the focus on human rights and good governance. For the policy and radical critics of liberal peace, liberal rights frameworks are often considered problematic in terms of the dangers of exclusion and extremism. Today's 'illiberal' peace approaches do not argue for the export of democracy – the freeing up of the political sphere on the basis of support for popular autonomy. The language of illiberal institutionalist approaches is that of democratisation: the problematisation of the liberal subject, held to be incapable of moral, rational choices at the ballot box, unless tutored by international experts concerned to promote civil society and pluralist values. In these frameworks, the holding of elections serves as an examination of the population and the behaviour of electoral candidates, rather than as a process for the judgement or construction of policy (which it is assumed needs external or international frameworks for its production).

The focus on institutionalism does not stem from a critique of liberal peace programmes; institutionalist approaches developed from the 1970s onwards and were rapidly mainstreamed with the end of the Cold War.[36] From 1989 onwards, Western governments and donors have stressed that policy interventions cannot just rely on promoting the freedoms of the market and democracy, but need to put institutional reform and 'good governance' at the core.[37] Even in relation to Central and Eastern Europe it was regularly stressed that the people and elected representatives were not ready for freedom and that it would take a number of generations before it could be said that democracy was 'consolidated'.[38] The transitology literature was based on the critique of liberal assumptions – this was why a transitional period was necessary. Transition implied that markets and democracy could not work without external institutional intervention to prevent instability. While markets needed to be carefully managed through government

---

[36] These policy frameworks originated, in part, as a response to criticism of US-led development policies and sought to explain why the introduction of market-orientated policies did not lead to the equalisation of development possibilities but instead appeared to perpetuate inequalities. For institutionalist approaches, the problem is not the market but the formal and informal institutions of the societies concerned, which are held to prevent or block the market from working optimally. See the theoretical framing developed in Douglass C. North and Robert P. Thomas, *The Rise of the Western World: A New Economic History* (Cambridge: Cambridge University Press, 1973); North, *Structure and Change in Economic History* (New York: Norton, 1981); and in North, *Institutions, Institutional Change and Economic Performance* (Cambridge: Cambridge University Press, 1990).

[37] See, for example, the seminal World Bank papers highlighting the shift towards institutionalist approaches: *Sub-Saharan Africa: From Crisis to Sustainable Growth: A Long-Term Perspective Study* (Washington, D.C.: World Bank, 1989); *Governance and Development* (Washington, D.C.: World Bank, 1992); *The State in a Changing World: World Development Report, 1997* (New York: Oxford University Press, 1997); *Assessing Aid: What Works, What Doesn't, and Why. A World Bank Policy Research Report* (New York: Oxford University Press, 1998).

[38] See, for example, Ralph Dahrendorf, *Reflections on the Revolution in Europe: In a Letter Intended to Have Been Sent to a Gentleman in Warsaw, 1990* (London: Chatto & Windus, 1990).

policymaking it was held that civil society was necessary to ensure that the population learnt civic values to make democracy viable.[39]

It was through the engagement with 'transition' and the problematic negotiation of EU enlargement that the discursive framework of liberal institutionalism – where human rights, the 'rule of law', civil society, and anti-corruption are privileged over democracy – was programmatically cohered. It was also through the discussion of 'transition' that the concept of sovereign autonomy was increasingly problematised, initially in relation to the protections for minority rights and then increasingly expanded to cover other areas of domestic policymaking.[40] It would appear that the key concepts and values of the 'liberal peace' held to have been promoted with vigour with the 'victory of liberalism' at the end of the Cold War were never as dominant a framing as their radical and policy critics have claimed.[41]

Rather than attempting to transform non-Western societies into the liberal self-image of the West, it would appear that external interveners have had much more *status quo* aspirations, concerned with regulatory stability and regional and domestic security, rather than transformation. Rather than imposing or 'exporting' alleged liberal Western models, international policy making has revolved around the promotion of regulatory and administrative measures which suggest the problems are not the lack of markets or democracy but rather the culture of society or the mechanisms of governance. Rather than promoting democracy and liberal freedoms, the discussion has been how to keep the lid on or to manage the 'complexity' of non-Western societies, usually perceived in terms of fixed ethnic and regional divisions. The solution to the complexity of the non-liberal state and society has been the internationalisation of the mechanisms of governance, removing substantive autonomy rather than promoting it.

While it is true that the reconstruction or rebuilding of states is at the centre of external projects of intervention, it would be wrong to see the project of statebuilding as one which aimed at the construction of a liberal international order.[42] This is not just because external statebuilding would be understood as a

---

[39] See, for example, Francis Fukuyama, 'The Primacy of Culture', *Journal of Democracy*, 6:1 (1995), pp. 7–14; Philippe C. Schmitter and Terry Lynn Karl, 'What Democracy is...and is Not', *Journal of Democracy*, 2:3 (1991), pp. 4–17; Guillermo O'Donnell, 'Illusions about Consolidation', *Journal of Democracy*, 7:2 (1996), pp. 34–51; Richard Gunther et al., 'Debate: Democratic Consolidation: O'Donnell's "Illusions": a Rejoinder', *Journal of Democracy*, 7:4 (1996), pp. 151–9.

[40] See, for example, Karl Cordell (ed.), *Ethnicity and Democratisation in the New Europe* (London: Routledge, 1998).

[41] Where there has been the rhetorical use of liberal claims of promoting democracy and the market this has often been a *post hoc* response to policy failure, used for public relations rather than as a driver of policymaking; see Aidan Hehir, *Humanitarian Intervention after Kosovo: Iraq, Darfur and the Record of Global Civil Society* (Basingstoke: MacMillan, 2008).

[42] A liberal international order would be one which excluded interventionist projects exporting universal models, such as those described under the rubric of the 'liberal peace'. For liberal political theory there can be no liberal order outside the borders of sovereign states, where there are frameworks of legal and political equality. As long as we live in a world of sovereign states the international sphere is of necessity pre-liberal; only the creation of a global state would create the institutional framework of a liberal global order. In the narrow terms of IR theory this is confused and what is often described as 'Realism' – an ontological framing of the international sphere as one made up of states ascribed the formal status of legal equality and treated as autonomous rational actors – is a classical liberal conception of the international realm, explaining why liberal assumptions cannot apply. See, for example, Justin Rosenberg, *The Empire of Civil Society: A Critique of the Realist Theory of International Relations* (London: Verso, 1994). Faisal Devji makes

contradiction in liberal terms but, more importantly, because the states being constructed in these projects of post-conflict and failed state intervention are not liberal states in the sense of having self-determination and political autonomy. The state at the centre of statebuilding is not the 'Westphalian state' of classical International Relations (IR) theorising. Under the internationalised regulatory mechanisms of intervention and statebuilding the state is increasingly reduced to an administrative level, in which sovereignty no longer marks a clear boundary line between the 'inside' and the 'outside'.[43] Whether we consider European Union (EU) statebuilding, explicitly based on a sharing of sovereignty, or consider other statebuilding interventions, such as those by the international financial institutions in sub-Saharan Africa, it is clear that the state is central as a mechanism for external coordination and regulation rather than as a self-standing actor in so-called 'Westphalian' terms.[44]

Too liberal?

There is little evidence here of the assertions of the critics of the liberal peace, that external interveners imagine that they have the power to reshape state institutions and societies in accordance with Western norms.[45] The limited results would appear to demonstrate that the process of internationalising the governance of non-Western states, through the process of 'state institution-building' has increasingly resulted in states which have little in connection with their societies, and where the formal political process is increasingly marginalised. Empirically, the radical critics of liberal peace may be correct to argue that external policies of intervention – which operate at the formal level of exporting human rights frameworks, the rule of law and mechanisms of 'good governance' – marginalise the people of these societies. This, however, is not the same as arguing that this is because the frameworks of intervention are too *liberal*.

It is quite possible to argue that external mechanisms of international engagement ignore the economic and social context of these societies and are satisfied with non-Western states paying lip-service to external donor and institutional requirements without asserting that these external actors are attempting to transform these states into Westphalian liberal democracies. At the empirical level it is unproblematic to argue that the result of these external programmes of

---

the point that the emergence of global framings of the political demonstrates the implosion of liberal theory and liberalism as a political form, *The Terrorist in Search of Humanity: Militant Islam and Global Politics* (London: Hurst, 2008), p. 173.

[43] See, R. B. J. Walker, *Inside/Outside: International Relations as Political Theory* (Cambridge: Cambridge University Press, 1992).

[44] See, Ashraf Ghani and Clare Lockhart, *Fixing Failed States: A Framework for Rebuilding a Fractured World* (Oxford: Oxford University Press, 2008); I use the term 'phantom states' in describing the impact of internationalising state structures in EU approaches to Eastern Europe and the Balkans; see, for example, Chandler, *Empire in Denial: The Politics of State-Building* (London: Pluto Press, 2006); in relation to sub-Saharan Africa, this process of internationalising state institutions is described by Graham Harrison through the concept of the 'governance state', see, for example, *The World Bank and Africa: The Construction of Governance State* (London: Routledge, 2004).

[45] The focus on institutional capacity, rather than on development and democracy, is, in fact, recognition of the limits to transforming these societies upon Western lines.

intervention might be seen as 'façade democracy' or as 'reproducing state failure'[46] or to highlight that Western policy aspirations have little purchase on very different realities and often therefore result in 'hybrid polities' where the state formally accords to Western norms but informally still operates on the basis of traditional hierarchies and exclusions.[47]

Where this critical discourse becomes problematic is in the confidence with which its proponents assert that the reasons for these policy failings can be located in the liberalism of the interveners or the illiberalism of the subjects of intervention. Roland Paris, for example, argues that 'there is no logical requirement for international agencies to resurrect failed states *as states*, rather than [as] some other type of polity', and argues that this is the 'latest chapter in the globalisation of the Westphalian state', where this state form is being propped up despite its failings.[48] Paris argues that just as the non-liberal Other cannot deal with the liberal state form, they are similarly ill-suited to handle electoral democracy, warning particularly against the holding of elections in post-conflict situations. It is asserted that holding elections when societies are still divided or segmented will be counterproductive, often giving enhanced legitimacy to warring parties and bolstering the legitimacy of the forces successful in conflict. Often the solutions advocated by the policy critics are along similar lines with regard to both sovereignty and democracy: the need for greater international engagement in the state institutions, under the guise of guaranteeing that no voices are 'excluded' and the need to constrict the autonomy of elected authorities. Under the rubric of the critique of the liberal peace, these critics of the liberal peace often advocate the reform of policy interventions away from the focus on liberal rights frameworks and electoral democracy.

Dominik Zaum, for example, through a series of case studies, argues that the aspirations of the technocratic approach of international statebuilding fails to appreciate that the liberal discourse of self-government undermines the authority of external interveners and enables local elites to assert pressure and influence.[49] These liberal normative commitments mean that international interventions are limited both in time and scope and therefore find it difficult to resist compromising their initial goals through giving greater authority to local actors.[50] Other authors have a similar perspective, explaining the failures of international intervention as a product of external actors assuming that liberal models can merely be exported, rather than understanding the contradictions involved in bringing liberalism to non-liberal societies. Michael Barnett and Christopher Zürcher, for example, have

[46] Christopher J. Bickerton, 'State-building: Exporting State Failure', in Bickerton, Philip Cunliffe and Alex Gourevitch (eds), *Politics without Sovereignty* (London: University College Press, 2007), pp. 93–111; Jarat Chopra, 'Building State Failure in East Timor', in Jennifer Milliken (ed.), *State Failure, Collapse and Reconstruction* (Oxford: Blackwell, 2003), pp. 223–43.

[47] See, for example, David Roberts, 'Hybrid Polities and Indigenous Pluralities: Advanced Lessons in Statebuilding from Cambodia', *Journal of Intervention and Statebuilding*, 2:1 (2008), pp. 63–86; Roberts, 'The Superficiality of Statebuilding in Cambodia; Patronage and Clientelism as Enduring Forms of Politics', in Paris and Sisk (eds), *The Dilemmas of Statebuilding*, pp. 149–69.

[48] Paris, 'International Peacebuilding and the "Mission Civilisatrice"', p. 654.

[49] Dominik Zaum, *The Sovereignty Paradox: The Norms and Politics of International Statebuilding* (Oxford: Oxford University Press, 2007).

[50] See also, Ignatieff (ed.), *Empire Lite: Nation-Building in Bosnia, Kosovo and Afghanistan* (London: Vintage, 2003).

sought to analyse why liberal interventions tend to be no more than surface, on the basis that elites at both national and subnational levels can 'capture' and 'compromise' peacebuilding leading to the reproduction of state-society relations and patrimonial politics.[51]

Some of the policy critics argue not merely that these Western models are perverted by the power of the non-liberal Other but that the attempt to export Western models to non-liberal societies is inevitably going to fail to bridge the gulf between liberal and non-liberal state-society forms. Noah Feldman, for example, suggests that these non-Western states and societies are so alien to Western liberal interveners that 'the high failure rate strongly supports the basic intuition that we do not know what we are doing'.[52] Feldman suggests that we need to continue to provide external assistance but should reject the idea that 'our comparative advantages of wealth and power [give] us any special ability to identify the institutional structures that will succeed in promoting democracy'.[53] Michael Ignatieff similarly argues that 'we do not actually know how to make states work in non-liberal societies that are poor, divided on religious or ethnic lines or lacked a substantial state tradition in the first place'.[54] The work of Roland Paris and Timothy Sisk, supports this view, suggesting that, in dealing with the non-liberal Other, the issues are so complex and dilemma-laden that pragmatic 'muddling through' is the only solution.[55]

Discursively, the alleged 'voice' of the non-liberal Other has also been central to the shifting discourse of development. While some commentators suggest that little substantive has changed in the shift from the modernising frameworks of the liberal 'Washington Consensus' to the post-liberal, post-conditionality, 'New York Consensus' focus on pro-poor policy making, sustainable development and poverty reduction strategy papers,[56] there is little doubt that the aspirations for social and economic transformation have been scaled back.[57] It is quite clear that broad

---

[51] Michael Barnett and Christopher Zürcher, 'The Peacebuilder's Contract: How External Statebuilding Reinforces Weak Statehood', in Paris and Sisk (eds), *The Dilemmas of Statebuilding*, pp. 23–52. See also, Miles Kahler, 'Statebuilding after Afghanistan and Iraq', in Paris and Sisk (eds), *The Dilemmas of Statebuilding*, pp. 287–303, who argue that this thesis of 'policy capture' by local elites is the key to solving the 'recurring puzzle' of 'The absence of a clear relationship between an apparent asymmetry in bargaining power between the international coalition and local political agents on the one hand, and statebuilding outcomes on the other', p. 296.

[52] Noah Feldman, *What We Owe Iraq: War and the Ethics of Nation Building* (Princeton, NJ.: Princeton University Press), p. 69.

[53] Feldman, p. 71.

[54] Ignatieff, 'Human Rights, Power and the State', in Chesterman, Ignatieff and Thakur (eds), *Making States Work*, pp. 59–75, 73.

[55] Paris and Sisk, 'Conclusion: Confronting the Contradiction', in Paris and Sisk (eds), *The Dilemmas of Statebuilding*, pp. 304–15.

[56] For example, Pugh, 'The Political Economy of Peacebuilding'; Paul Cammack, 'Global Governance, State Agency and Competitiveness: the Political Economy of the Commission for Africa', *British Journal of Politics and International Relations*, 8:3 (2006), pp. 331–50; Cammack, 'What the World Bank Means by Poverty Reduction and Why It Matters', *New Political Economy*, 9:2 (2004), pp. 189–211; Harrison, 'Post-Conditionality Politics and Administrative Reform: Reflections on the Cases of Uganda and Tanzania', *Development and Change*, 32:4 (2001), pp. 634–65.

[57] Gordon Crawford, 'The World Bank and Good Governance: Rethinking the State or Consolidating Neo-Liberalism?', in Alberto Paloni and Maurizio Zanardi (eds), *The IMF, the World Bank and Policy Reform* (London: Routledge, 2006), pp. 115–41. See also William Easterly, *The White Man's Burden: Why the West's Efforts to Aid the Rest Have Done so Much Ill and so Little Good* (Oxford: Oxford University Press, 2006).

frameworks of development intervention have much lower horizons than during the Cold War period;[58] for example, the replacement of Cold War desires for modernisation with the Millennium Development Goals (MDGs). The MDGs focus not on social and economic transformation but on the situation of the poorest in society with the aspiration that, by 2015, people will be able to live on $1 a day.[59] The view that there is a universalising transformative liberal agenda is a peculiar way to understand the focus on sustainable development, small and medium enterprises and the shift away from large development projects.[60] With regard to the critique of universal liberal aspirations for progress, it is often difficult to tell the policy perspectives apart from the viewpoints of some of the more radical critics of the liberal peace. There is a danger that liberalism is criticised not for its inability to universalise economic growth and overcome the problems of combined and uneven development, but for the aspirations of development itself. For example, Michael Pugh asserts that rather than the 'economic rationalism of (capitalistic) entrepreneurship', other, 'non-liberal', values need to be taken into account. Following the work of those critical of liberal development models, such as Amartya Sen,[61] he argues that in non-liberal societies:

> Inequalities and non-physiological needs are considered more significant than either absolute poverty or, beyond a survival point, physiological needs. This means that provided people are not destitute [...] they may choose to live humbly in order to be fulfilled. Such an approach recognises that the paths to modernisation may not be convergent at all, and the marginalised peoples of the world are entitled to choose the extent to which, and how, they integrate in the global economy.[62]

It would seem that at the core of the policy and radical critiques of the liberal peace is a critique of liberal aspirations rather than a critique of international interventionist policies and practices. The critique reflects the ease with which liberalism has become a 'field of adversity', through which both policy reform and critical claims for theoretical advance can both be made. The construction of a liberal 'field of adversity' seems to have little relation to policy realities. This is reflected in the fact that, while there is a consensus on the view that Western policies are problematic in that they are too liberal, there is much less attention to how the problems of the post-colonial world might be alternatively addressed. Here, as discussed below, the discursive critique of the liberal peace unfortunately has very little to offer in ways that go beyond present policy perspectives.

---

[58] See, for example, Colin Leys, *The Rise and Fall of Development Theory* (Oxford: Indiana University Press, 1996); John Pender, 'From "Structural Adjustment" to "Comprehensive Development Framework": Conditionality Transformed?', *Third World Quarterly*, 22:3 (2001), pp. 397–411.

[59] See Jeffrey Sachs, *The End of Poverty: How We Can Make It Happen In Our Lifetime* (London: Penguin, 2005).

[60] Mark Duffield's work on the divisive effects of post-Cold War development policies draws out well what could, perhaps more critically, be called the 'illiberal' nature of the shifting discourses on development and security, see *Development, Security and Unending War*.

[61] See, for example, Amartya Sen, *Development as Freedom* (Oxford: Oxford University Press, 1999).

[62] Pugh, 'The Political Economy of Peacebuilding', p. 34.

Beyond the critique of the liberal peace?

It would appear that the ostensibly more radical critics, those who draw out the problematic nature of power relations – the 'power-based' critiques above – in fact, have very little to offer as a critical alternative to the current policies of intervention and statebuilding, other than a scaling back of the possibilities of social change. The leading critics of the liberal peace, like Mark Duffield, Michael Pugh and Oliver Richmond – working through critical theoretical frameworks which problematise power relations and highlight the importance of difference – suggest that the difference between the liberal West and the non-liberal Other cannot be bridged through Western policymaking. For Pugh, as we have seen above, taking critical theory to its logical conclusion, capitalist rationality is itself to be condemned for its universalising and destabilising impulses. Similarly, for Duffield, it seems that the problem of hegemonic relations of power and knowledge cannot be overcome, making any projection of the ideals of development or democracy potentially oppressive.[63] Oliver Richmond, has systematised this perspective, highlighting the problems of the disciplinary forms of knowledge of 'liberal peace' approaches and suggesting that while it may be possible to go beyond them through the use of post-positivist and ethnographic approaches – enabling external interveners to have a greater access to the knowledge of 'everyday life' in non-liberal societies being intervened in – any attempt to know, rather than merely to express 'empathy', is open to hegemonic abuse.[64]

It would appear that, without a political agent of emancipatory social change, the radical 'power-based' critics of liberal peace who draw upon the perspectives of critical theory, cannot go beyond the bind which they have set themselves, of overcoming hegemonic frameworks of knowledge and power. In fact, it could be argued that these critical approaches, lacking the basis of a political subject to give content to critical theorising, ultimately take an uncritical approach to power. Power is assumed rather than theorised, making the limits to power appear merely as external to it. It is assumed that there is an attempt to transform the world in liberal terms and that the failure to do so can therefore be used to argue that liberal forms of knowledge are inadequate ones. The critique is not essentially of power or of intervention but of the limited knowledge of liberal interveners. The alternative is not that of emancipatory social transformation but of the speculative and passive search for different, non-liberal, forms of knowledge or of knowing. This comes across clearly in the conclusions reached by Duffield, Richmond and others, and highlights the lack of a critical alternative embedded in these approaches.

The more ostensibly conservative critics of the liberal peace, drawn largely to the policymaking sphere, have much clearer political aims in their critique of the liberal peace. This is manifest in their focus on institutional reform, understood as

---

[63] Duffield, *Development, Security and Unending War*, pp. 215–34.

[64] See Richmond's 'Conclusion', in *Peace in International Relations*. See also his 'Whose War? Whose Peace?' presentation at the Committee for Conflict Transformation Support seminar (5 June 2008); in this piece, Richmond goes further to state that the problem of relating to the 'non-Liberal other' needs to be resolved, not through greater knowledge but the development of empathy, where intervention aims not at social engineering but at 'allowing unscripted conversations [...] which give voice to the local'. Available at: {http://www.c-r.org/ccts/ccts38/index.htm} last accessed on 19 May 2009.

a way of reconciling non-liberal states and societies both to the market and to democratic forms. This, like the transitology discourse before it, is a radical critique of classical liberal assumptions. In their advocacy of these frameworks, discursively framed as a critique of the 'liberal peace', they have a clear point of reference. Although, as highlighted above, this point of reference is a fictional one: a constructed narrative of post-Cold War intervention, which enables them to ground the scaling-back of policy expectations against a framework of allegedly unrealistic liberal aspirations.

This critique of liberalism is not a critique of interventionist policymaking but rather a defence of current practices on the basis that they have not been properly applied or understood. Institutionalist approaches, which have informed the interventionist frameworks of international institutions and donors since the early 1990s, are explicit in their denunciation of the basic assumptions of classical liberalism. This critique of liberalism is however an indirect one, inevitably so, as the institutionalist critique developed at the height of the Cold War.[65] This is why, while the classical concepts of the liberal rights framework remain – 'sovereignty', 'democracy', 'rule of law', 'civil society' – they have been given a new content, transforming the universal discourse of the autonomous liberal rights-holder from that of the subject of rights to the object of regulation.[66] This new content has unfortunately been of little interest to the more radical 'power-based' critics of the 'liberal peace'. But, in understanding the content of institutionalist approaches, it is possible to tie together the superficial nature of external engagement with the fact that it has a non-liberal content rather than one which is too liberal.

The institutionalist discourse of intervention and regulation is not one of liberal universalism and transformation but one of restricted possibilities, where democracy and development are hollowed out and, rather than embodying the possibilities of the autonomous human subject, become mechanisms of control and ordering. Institutionalisation reduces law to an administrative code, politics to technocratic decision-making, democratic and civil rights to those of the supplicant rather than the citizen, replaces the citizenry with civil society, and the promise of capitalist modernity with pro-poor poverty reduction.[67] To conceptualise this inversion of basic liberal assumptions and ontologies as 'liberalism' would be to make the word meaningless at the same time as claiming to stake everything on the assumed meaning and stakes involved in the critique of the 'liberal' peace.[68]

---

[65] See, for example, Leys, *The Rise and Fall of Development Theory*.

[66] This is the key point being made in Foucault's study of the transformation of liberal discourse in *The Birth of Biopolitics*.

[67] Critiques of institutionalist approaches are provided in Chandler, *Empire in Denial*; Foucault, *The Birth of Biopolitics*; and with regard to their depoliticising effect, see, for example, Colin Hay, *Why We Hate Politics* (Cambridge: Polity, 2007); Robert Williams, 'Democracy, Development and Anti-Corruption Strategies: Learning from the Australian Experience', in Alan Doig and Robin Theobald (eds), *Corruption and Democratisation* (London: Frank Cass, 2000), pp. 135–48; Ivan Krastev, *Shifting Obsessions: Three Essays on the Politics of Anticorruption* (Budapest: CEU Press, 2004).

[68] A similar process of conflating liberalism with Nazism and Stalinism, and reducing rights to regulatory control, can be seen in the work of Giorgio Agamben, see, for example, *Homo Sacer: Sovereign Power and Bare Life* (Stanford: Stanford University Press, 1998); *State of Exception* (Chicago: University of Chicago Press, 2005). For a critique, see Chandler, 'Critiquing Liberal Cosmopolitanism?: The Limits of the Biopolitical Approach', *International Political Sociology*, 3:1 (2009), pp. 53–70.

Conclusion

The critique of the liberal peace is based upon the assumption that Western intervention is too 'liberal'. The fact that it is too liberal is alleged to be revealed in its lack of success on the ground; in its failure to achieve liberal outcomes. For the policy critics, the sources of this failure are held to be located in the non-liberal nature of the societies intervened upon. In the dominant policy framing of interventionist agendas, this failing is because of the lack of capacity of domestic societies and political elites; for more radical readings, the problematic impact of external policymaking is often re-read as the resistance of indigenous ways of life and knowledges, which should instead be understood and empathised with.

If the critique of intervention is for its liberalism, then it suggests that the self-image of the West is being projected where it cannot work. The critique can easily flatter the self-understanding of liberal interveners that if they are incapable of transforming the post-conflict societies and failing states, that they are engaged with, it is merely because they cannot easily be anything other than liberal and that the societies being intervened in are not ready for liberal frameworks of governance. This critique, can, in fact, result in the reproduction of the ideological binary of the civilisational divide between the interveners and the intervened in, which is seen to be confirmed the more interventionist approaches appear to have little impact and to have to be scaled back.

There are a number of problems with the critical construction of 'liberal peace'. These stem not merely from the fact that the interventionist policies being critiqued seem to be far from 'liberal'. Of greater concern is the way that the term 'liberal' appears to have become an easy and unproblematic assertion of critical intent. The critique of the 'liberal peace' – and its ability to encompass both policy advocates and radical critics of intervention – appears to reveal much more about the problematic state of radical and liberal thought than it does about the policies and practices of intervention and statebuilding. The ostensible framework of the 'liberal peace' – of the transformative dynamic ontology of the universal rational subject – had already long since been critiqued and displaced by the framework of governance and regulatory power. It is peculiar, in these circumstances, that the dominant policy discussion and the radical discursive framing of post-Cold War intervention should both therefore take this form.

While apologetic intent can perhaps be reasonably applied to some critics working within policymaking circles and attempting to justify the continuation and revamping of current policy framings, this charge cannot so easily be placed at the feet of those articulating more 'power-based' critiques of the liberal peace. That the radical critique of the 'liberal peace' should reproduce similar framings to that of the policy orientated institutionalist critique of liberal peace, highlights the use of the liberal paradigm as a 'field of adversity' to give coherence to radical frameworks of critique. However, in focusing on the target of liberalism rather than on the policy practices and discourses themselves, there is a danger that radical criticism can be enlisted in support of the institutionalist project, which seeks to rewrite the failures of post-Cold War intervention as a product of the universalising tendencies of a liberal approach and suggests that we should give up on the liberal aspirations of the past on the basis of an appreciation of the irreconcilable 'difference' of the non-liberal subject.

Review of International Studies (2010), 36, 157–180   © 2010 British International Studies Association
doi:10.1017/S0260210510000975   First published online 13 Sep 2010

What is a (global) polity?

OLAF CORRY*

Abstract. Despite sustained theoretical and empirical criticism of 'statism', a recognisable *model* of political structure other of hierarchy and anarchy (the models that underpin the state system-model) has long been lacking. Even many proponents of radical transformation of the international system often remain 'post-international', describing world politics essentially in terms of complications to the international system. This article agrees that a new point of departure is needed but offers a different model of political structure by redefining the term 'polity' – a term which is increasingly used to capture non-territorial political entities neither constituted by hierarchy nor by the lack of it. With the new definition building on Waltz's theory of theory as a 'picture, mentally formed' in order to simplify a domain, a polity is deemed to exist when a set of subjects are oriented towards a common 'governance-object'. The new polity model is applied illustratively to the idea of a global polity and a new polity research agenda of international relations is suggested.

Olaf Corry is an Affiliated Lecturer at the Department of Politics and International Studies at the University of Cambridge where he teaches International Relations theory. He is also currently a research associate at the Judge Business School, University of Cambridge. He is the author of articles on the third sector in global politics and is working on a book on theories of global politics and global social movements.

The term 'post-international' has been closely associated with the work of James Rosenau[1] but can be used more generally for perspectives that begin from the model of the international system and then add complications or modifications. For such approaches to world politics 'statism' – involving the assumption that world politics is ultimately reducible to the model of the inter-state system – is untenable and needs to be transcended. Two leading authors argue that 'the task of remapping political space is a critical one, precisely because the 'Westphalian moment' is passing'.[2] Citing the rise of non-state actors in world politics, the decline of the superpower blocs, the (re)emergence of novel political entities that straddle conventional boundaries, the sheer velocity of global flows of information

---

* Thanks to Jens Bartelson, Vibeke Tjalve, Mikkel Vedby Rasmussen, Barry Buzan, Martin Albrow, Lasse Thomassen, Ole Jakob Sending, Kimberley Hutchings, Trine Villumsen and several anonymous reviewers for their helpful comments on this or earlier versions of the argument. The usual caveats apply of responsibility resting with the author.
1 James N Rosenau, *Turbulence in World Politics: A Theory of Change and Continuity* (Princeton: Princeton University Press, 1990); James N Rosenau, *Along the Domestic-Foreign Frontier: Exploring Governance in a Turbulent World* (Cambridge: Cambridge University Press, 1997); Heidi H Hobbs. (ed.), *Pondering Post-Internationalism. A Paradigm for the 21st Century*, (Albany: State University of New York Press, 2000).
2 Yale H. Ferguson & Richard Mansbach, *Polities. Authority, Identities and Change* (Colombia: University of South Carolina Press, 1996), p. 1.

and objects and the rise of 'global consciousness' and non-territorial communities, post-internationalists have called for a 'conceptual jailbreak' from the theories and concepts of International Relations (IR)[3] that 'seem hopelessly obsolete' or even 'obfuscate the main features of present-day global politics'.[4] Moreover, post-internationalism is just one example of a wider search of for approaches that enable us to identify 'alternative ways in which the world is politically partitioned'.[5] However, all too often such efforts lead to descriptions of complexity that rely on the old models and discourse for coherence. 'Plus non-state-views'[6] of international relations, though focussed on all things below and beyond the state, suffer from an underlying reliance on statist categories which generates hyphenated terminology such as 'trans-border', 'transnational', 'de-centred' and 'non-state' that reassert the significance of borders, nations, centres, states, etc. and the models of hierarchy and anarchy that underly those categories. Post-internationalism's persistent claims about change thus end up sitting uncomfortably astride concepts and terminology soaked in what Rob Walker has called the 'discursive horizons that express the spatiotemporal configurations of another era'.[7]

This article aims to provide a new option for getting beyond this post-international condition, namely by appropriating and redefining the term 'polity'. Interestingly, though seldom defined or theorised, the term is typically used in contemporary efforts to describe how hierarchies are disintegrating or being 'unbundled'[8] or in situations where anarchy is clearly also not appropriate because new 'assemblages' of authority, rights and territory[9] such as the EU[10] are congealing. In public discourse too, the polity concept has taken on a similar function. The British broadsheet *The Daily Telegraph* speculated that 'Tony Blair, the new Middle East envoy, will be hard put to reconcile an Israeli government that continues to limp along and a dramatically split Palestinian polity'.[11] On the

[3] James N. Rosenau, *The Study of World Politics*. (London: Routledge, 2006), p. 16.
[4] Yale Ferguson & Richard Mansbach, *Remapping Global Politics. History's Revenge and Future Shock* (Cambridge: Cambridge University Press, 2006), p. 1.
[5] Michael Shapiro, 'Michael Shapiro' *Theory Talk #36*, available at: {http://www.theory-talks.org/2010/02/theory-talk-36.html}.
[6] Alan Chong, 'The Post-International Challenge to Foreign Policy: Signposting "plus non-state politics"', *Review of International Studies*, 28 (2002), pp. 783–95, 794.
[7] R. B. J Walker *Inside/Outside. International Relations as Political Theory*. (Cambridge: Cambridge University Press, 1993), p. x.
[8] John Ruggie, *Constructing a World Polity*. Thus, Algeria was termed a 'broken polity'. See, Hugh Roberts, *The Battlefield Algeria 1988–2002. Studies in a Broken Polity* (London: Verso, 2003). Israel an 'overburdened polity'. See, Dan Horowitz and Moshe Lissak, *Trouble in Utopia. The Overburdened Polity of Israel* (Albany: State University of New York Press, 1989); pre-Maoist China a weak polity, see, Julia C Strauss, *Strong Institutions in Weak Polities: State Building in Republican China, 1927–1940* (Oxford: Oxford University Press, 1998); and Canada 'a polity on the edge', see Harold D Clarke, Allan Kornberg, Peter Wearing, *A Polity on the Edge: Canada and the Politics of Fragmentation* (Peterborough, Ontario: Broadview Press, 2000).
[9] Saskia Sassen, *Territory, Authority, Rights. From Medieval to Global Assemblages* (Princeton: Princeton University Press, 2006).
[10] See, for example, Chris Ansell, 'The Networked Polity: Regional Development in Western Europe', *Governance*, 13 (2000), pp. 303–33; Joschka Fischer, Christian Joerges,Yves Mény, J. H. H. Weiler (eds), *What kind of constitution for what kind of polity?* (Cambridge Mass.: Robert Schumann Centre for Advanced Studies, 2000); Douglass Imig and Sydney Tarrow, *Contentious Europeans: Protest and Politics in an emerging Polity* (Lanham: Rowman & Littlefield, 2001); Gary Marks and Marco Steenbergen, 'Understanding political contestation in Europe', *Comparative Political Studies*, 35:8 (2002), pp. 879–92.
[11] *Daily Telegraph* (5 July 2007).

same day another newspaper referred to Belgium as 'an already much devolved polity'.[12] When existing models of political space are under strain 'polity', it seems, comes to the rescue, including where there is talk of a 'global polity'.

Despite this – and despite a whole academic discipline being named after it (politi-cal science) – a generic definition of what a polity is, for example stipulating what constitutes the boundaries and characteristics of such an entity, has been attempted surprisingly little. Existing accounts of a global polity, for example describe it a post-international way in terms of a 'nascent' or 'incomplete' global state[13] or in terms of how it differs from an idealised version of the international system of states (anarchy), emphasising 'complications' to that model such as the growth of international institutions, proliferation of non-state actors and a weakening of the nation-state.[14] How would such conceptions of a global polity help us to understand other putative instances of polity-formation like the Palestinian polity the EU-polity or the Christian Polity, for example? They would not because they amount more to a list of features of globalisation (interconnect-edness, weakening states, thin community, etc.) than to a theoretical model of polity which is then applied to 'the global'.

With a generic notion of polity, conceiving of a global polity would no longer automatically involve reliance on either of the two classical models of hierarchy or anarchy. To pre-empt the argument it is suggested in this article that a polity-structure exists when a group of units become oriented towards the governance of a common 'governance-object'. The latter can be defined as an object that is constructed as real, distinct, malleable and subject to political action, for example, constructs such as 'France' or 'the climate'. By extension, a global polity will hence have emerged to the extent that actors of whatever kind have become oriented towards the governance of specifically global governance-objects (that is, objects considered real and malleable that are constituted in terms of an understanding of the 'world as one place' – see discussion of globality below). Thus, if for example 'global poverty' or in wider terms a 'global society' comes to be considered real and meaningful as an object that can and should be operated upon politically – and a set of actors become oriented towards governing this object, then a global polity will have come into existence.

Though simple, this definition of polity can be used to provide criteria for when a polity exists, where its boundaries lie, what its basic logics are and how one might vary while still remaining 'a polity'. Rather than being a vague term for any set of political institutions, polities thus conceived would be a distinct analytical category picking out a specific kind of entity.

What is more, with a theory of polity, we have at least the option of going beyond the usual post-international notions of the international system of states and complications. Those wary of complexity should not be compelled to stick with the state model and its domestic-international distinction simply because they are in favour of analytical simplifying. It should, for example, become clear that

---

[12] *The Guardian* (5 July 2007).

[13] Martin Shaw, *Theory of a Global State* (Cambridge: Cambridge University Press, 2000); Morten Ougaard *Political Globalization. State, Power and Social Forces* (Basingstoke: Palgrave Macmillan, 2004).

[14] Richard Higgott and Morten Ougaard, *Towards a Global Polity* (London: Routledge, 2002).

an 'American polity' will not be the same entity as the US state. A global polity will not be the same object as a global state or a global society, or a modified international anarchy. It is suggested below that 'polity' defined anew could become a useful analytical construct in a world of increasingly deterritorialised politics where networks of governance, construction of new objects of governance and a multitude of different types of actors play a significant role and cannot be captured satisfactorily within the hierarchy-anarchy dichotomy (or the continuum between them) that so much IR theory remains wedded to.

The emphasis in this article will be presentation of the theory and the difference in research agenda that it implies. In particular, to date, governance-objects, their origins and significance and their changing natures have received far less attention than the subjects doing the governing. While there has been much debate about state-centric perspectives, it has seemingly gone unnoticed that almost all IR conceives of identity (implicitly or explicitly) in terms of relations between *subjects*[15] (both hierarchy and anarchy are defined according to whether *subjects* stand in relations of super and subordination). States gain their distinctive identities in relation to 'Others'[16] or through inward-looking self-reflection – or by a mixture of the two.[17] The polity model, in contrast, draws attention to relations between subjects and *objects*. Perhaps because 'domestic society' within sovereign states have been the dominant governance object during the Westphalian moment, the idea of identifying and analysing governance-objects has not seemed necessary and polities have been roughly considered coterminous with hierarchies. The on-going search for tools to identify other kinds of political units indicates that this is no longer sustainable.

The rest of this article explores these ideas in the following stages. First the post-international problem of trying to describe change including a 'global polity' in terms of old models of political space and the discourses they created is set out further. And although they remain locked within the models they aim to move beyond post-international approaches are shown to have worthwhile aims. Second, existing alternative notions of political structure beyond hierarchy and anarchy such as 'heterarchy' are reviewed and found wanting, as are common existing definitions of 'polity'. Third, the new definition of polity is expanded upon providing analytical building blocks for what a polity consists of, how it is ordered, how membership is decided upon and how polities may vary. Fourth, in order to illustrate, this definition of polity is briefly applied to the idea of a global polity contrasting it to two existing accounts of the global polity. The conclusion evaluates the new definition on offer and points to the research questions opened up by the new hierarchy-anarchy-polity triad of models.

[15] Hansen is an exception pointing out that Otherness can be articulated in relation to geographical as well as political representations. The examples she lists are however group identities such as "'nations', 'tribes', 'terrorists', 'women'" (Lene Hansen *Security as Practice* (Abingdon: Routledge, 2006) p. 7) which again implies that identity is assumed to be forged in relation to other subjectivities rather than objects.

[16] See, for example, Iver Neumann, *Uses of the Other. 'The East' in European Identity Formation* (Minneapolis: University of Minnesota Press 1998).

[17] See, for example, Alexander Wendt who includes both (pre-social) corporate and (relationally acquired) social identity. See, Alexander Wendt, *Social Theory of International Politics* (Cambridge: Cambridge University Press, 1999), p. 182.

The post-international problem

In the search for new ways of making sense of political space in a globalising world, post-international writers have provided a host of innovative terms and metaphors for analysing political processes that cut across, complicate or evade the familiar structures of the international system of anarchically arranged hierarchies: 'multi-level governance',[18] 'complex multilateralism',[19] 'the attrition of established patterns, the lessening of order', the Frontier, or the two-way process of 'frag-megration',[20] 'complex multilateralism',[21] 'fuzzy' borders,[22] even the *nébuleuse*[23] to name but a few. While such concepts capture significant trends and undoubtedly reflect a genuinely complex globalised reality, none of them rely on their own models of political space, often depending for coherence – paradoxically – on the ones they seek to move beyond, namely hierarchy and anarchy. For instance, complex multilateralism is characterised as 'a movement away from a multilateralism based primarily on the activity of states'.[24] Multilevel governance is used to describe how overarching policy networks are 'unraveling the central state'.[25] Rosenau describes a new Domestic-foreign Frontier 'not so much as a single frontier but as a host of diverse frontiers [. . .] in which background often becomes foreground, time becomes disjointed, nonlinear patterns predominate, organizations bifurcate, societies implode, regions unify, markets overlap and politics swirl about issues of identity, territoriality, and the interface between long-established patterns and emergent orientations'.[26] Irrespective of whether these are reasonable descriptions or not, the main alternative leitmotif suggested is complexity cast *in relation to* the orthodox IR models. The basic terminology and categories of the old era are used to declare the end (or illusory nature) of that era.

While useful for pointing out the deficiencies of the state model of sovereign states in anarchy, if we only have the old distinction and models to compare a fluid new reality to, the latter will tend to be framed in terms of 'not being', trans-this, post-that, etc. The resulting picture may focus on anomalies to the old model but as Thomas Kuhn suggested, anomalies without an alternative theory rarely seriously challenge a paradigm.[27] If those critical of the selective vision of the

---

[18] Gary Marks, 'Structural policy and Multi-level governance in the EC', in A. Cafurny and G. Rosenthal (eds), *The State of the European Community: The Maastricht Debate and Beyond* (Boulder: Lynne Rienner, 1993), pp. 391–411.

[19] Robert O' Brien, Anne Marie Goetz, Jan Aart Scholte and Marc Williams, *Contesting Global Governance: Multilateral Economic Institutions and Global Social Movements* (Cambridge: Cambridge University Press, 2000).

[20] Rosenau, *Along the Domestic-Foreign Frontier*; James N. Rosenau, *Distant Proximities. Dynamics Beyond Globalization* (Princeton: Princeton University Press, 2003).

[21] O'Brien et al., *Contesting Global Governance*.

[22] Thomas Christiansen, Fabio Petito, and Ben Tonra. 'Fuzzy politics around fuzzy borders: The EU's "near abroad"',*Cooperation and Conflict*, 35 (2000), pp. 389–415.

[23] Robert Cox, 'Democracy in Hard Times', in Anthony McGrew (ed.), *The Transformation of Democracy*, (Cambridge: Polity Press, 1997), pp. 49–72, 60. According to the *Encyclopedia Britannica* this term was 'formerly applied to any object outside the solar system that had a diffuse appearance and could not be resolved telescopically into a point-like image'. (EB Online).

[24] O'Brien et al., *Contesting Global Governance*.

[25] Lisbeth Hooghe and Gary Marks, 'Unravelling the Central State, But How? Types of Multilevel Governance', *American Political Science Review*, 97 (2003), pp. 233–43.

[26] Rosenau, *Along the Domestic-Foreign Frontier*, p. 4.

[27] Thomas Kuhn, *The Structure of Scientific Revolutions* (Chicago: University of Chicago Press, 1962), p. 77.

statist model only offer essentially notions of complexity, fuzziness and disorder, then discarding statism carries the extortionate analytical price tag of falling back on complexity as the prime analytical category. This is the essence of what can be called 'the post-international problem'.

According to many – even constructivists – this condition is virtually unavoidable:

'the distinction between domestic and international has broken down, we hear. But the only way to talk about this is to say that – the distinction between domestic and international has broken down. So we can get to the current complex situation from the distinction by adding complexity, but not from the complex situation and build the reality of the play around that (broken?) distinction?'.[28]

The choice, we are told, is between going via the state or unwieldy complexity. Is there no other distinction to begin from? Barry Buzan, in defending a statist point of departure, warns against 'the severe loss of analytical leverage that results from bundling huge complexities into a single concept, whether it be globalization or god'.[29] But this is more an argument against having *no* distinctions than a justification of the state/non-state distinction.

While simply beginning from the idea of complexity appears an increasingly popular strategy,[30] beginning from a new model or simplification of political space has been mooted by several approaches and for good reasons. Most explicitly, the global polity approach[31] recommends a 'reversal of strategy for theory-building'.[32] Instead of always beginning from the model of the international system and then adding a number of complications, this urges us to begin with 'a conception of one world political system, or an aspect of world politics, and then add the complications arising from the persistent reality that this system lacks a unified authority structure and has formally sovereign states among its fundamental building blocks'.[33] They see this as a necessary methodological move to avoid framing global politics in terms of modified anarchy or in terms of a nascent global hierarchy, rather than because they are claiming the wholesale disappearance of the state system.[34]

Getting beyond post-internationalism makes sense if one shares post-internationalism's own legitimate worries about the blind spots of statist discourse.[35] Without a new idea of political space, statism's 'impoverished picture of

[28] Ole Wæver, 'isms, paradigms, traditions and theories – but why also "schools" in IR?', Paper presented at Standing Group on International Relations (ECPR), *5th Pan-European International Relations Conference*, The Hague (9–11 September 2004).

[29] Barry Buzan, *From International to World Society? English School Theory and the Social Structure of Globalisation* (Cambridge: Cambridge University Press, 2004), p. 229.

[30] Nigel Thrift, 'The Place of Complexity', *Theory, Culture and Society*, 16 (1999), pp. 31–69; John Urry *Global Complexity* (Cambridge: Polity Press, 2003); Robert Axelrod & Michael D Cohen, *Harnessing Complexity. Organizational Implications of a Scientific Frontier* (New York: The Free Press, 1999).

[31] Higgott and Ougaard, *Towards a Global Polity*. Global polity writers are not alone in trying to move beyond the state system-model but their idea is explored here as the most theoretically conscious attempt to go beyond the post-international perspective.

[32] Ougaard and Higgott *Towards*, p. 30.

[33] Ibid.

[34] See, for example, Yale H Ferguson. and Richard Mansbach, *Polities. Authority, Identities and Change* (Colombia: University of South Carolina University Press, 1996). p. 12; Ronnie Lipschutz, *After Authority* (Albany: State University of New York Press, 2000).

[35] Martin Coward, 'International Relations in a Post-Globalisation Era', in *Politics*, 26 (2006), pp. 54–61.

morphology' remains in place perpetuating a sterile state-versus-global debate that pits the new as the inverse of the old.[36] Reliant on the old models, IR 'has found it difficult to conceive of globality except as the negation of statehood and politics'.[37] This has polarised the debate unhelpfully and, paradoxically, kept the future of the state as the central question in the globalisation debate even in 'third way' transformationist literature.[38] The idea of a global polity has thus been discarded on the grounds that the state remains the main actor.[39] Moreover, going beyond post-internationalism and searching for 'alternative ways in which the world is politically partitioned'[40] can be justified even if one is quite sanguine about the blind spots that statism has or happen to believe that it remains prudent to prioritise the state system for whatever reason. Even for those sceptical of the globalisation and radical change-thesis, the availability of an alternative lens for analysing political space can be considered important in terms of methodological pluralism. We may be over-estimating the importance of hierarchy and anarchy simply because we always begin with them. Finally, the utility of an alternative way of delimiting political entities could be of potential use beyond IR in other disciplines exploring political entities outside the settled framework of the nation-state. Other disciplines such as anthropology have a long history of studying non-state constellations,[41] policy studies increasingly explores policy-making across borders and sectors,[42] political geographers also focus on the unruly, complex and chaotic reconfigurations of globalised space,[43] political theorists rework classical problems of democracy, authority and legitimacy outside the hierarchic state setting,[44] and legal studies have shown an interest in rule-setting practices beyond traditional law or treaty-making.[45] Essentially they all operate with groups of actors oriented towards governance objects. However, the argument here is developed in relation to the field of IR and specifically the idea of a 'global polity'.

While the aims of post-international perspectives are thus laudable, they have not had much success in providing a new analytical point of departure. Higgott & Ougaard see the 'global polity approach' as a collection of attempts to 'transcend the state-centred perspective in a conscious theoretical fashion'[46] and they and others have deployed the term 'polity' attempting to break the mould of the

---

[36] Morphology refers to 'the shape of constituent parts and their arrangement into a whole', p. 56. Coward, 'Post-Globalisation Era'.

[37] Shaw, *Theory of a Global State*, p. 81.

[38] David Held, Anthony McGrew, David Goldblatt and Jonathan Perraton (eds), *Global Transformations* (Cambridge: Polity Press, 1999).

[39] Paul Hirst, 'Book review of Martin Shaw, *Theory of the Global State in International Affairs*, 77 (2001), pp. 407–76.

[40] Michael Shapiro, 'Michael Shapiro' *Theory Talk #36*, available at: {http://www.theory-talks.org/2010/02/theory-talk-36.html}.

[41] See, for example, Claudio Cioffi-Revilla, and Todd Landman, 'Evolution of Maya Polities in the Ancient Mesoamerican System', *International Studies Quarterly*, 43 (1999), pp. 559–98.

[42] See, for example, Morten Hajer, 'Policy without Polity', *Policy Sciences*, 36 (2003), pp. 175–95.

[43] See, Gearoid O Touthail, Andrew Herod and Susan Roberts, 'Negotiating Unruly Problematics', in Andrew Herod, Gearoid O Touthail, Susan M Roberts. (eds), *An Unruly World. Globalization, Governance and Geography* (London: Routledge, 1998).

[44] See, for example, David Held, *Democracy and the Global Order: From the Modern State to Cosmopolitan Governance*, or James Bohman, 'From *Demos* to *Demoi*: Democracy across Borders', *Ratio Juris*, 18 (1995), pp. 293–314.

[45] See, for example, Christian Brütsch and Dirk Lehmkuhl (eds), *Law and Legalization in Transnational Relations* (London and New York: Routledge, 2007).

[46] Ougaard and Higgott, *Towards a Global Polity*, pp. 9–10.

state-centric frameworks.[47] But there has been no root and branch consideration of what a polity is. Higgott and Ouggaard thus define a global polity as 'that totality of political structures, agents and processes, with transnational properties, that in the current historical context have developed a high level of interconnectedness and an element of thin community that transcends the territorial state'.[48] Such definitions of a global polity remain, it seems, post-international. 'Transnational' invokes the (crossing of) the national border as a defining feature of a global polity. The 'element of thin community' points towards a society 'transcending' the nation-state. Going via the story of the state system – again – is quite legitimate in itself, but affects no real methodological reversal. World politics is still compared to the model of international anarchy or alternatively as an approximation to global hierarchy when concepts developed in the context of a domestic state framework are transferred to the global. Elsewhere Ougaard makes the case for using concepts developed for analysis of domestic politics to understand a global polity in terms of a global state superstructure.[49]

The root of this persistent post-internationalism even in global polity approaches may be found the lack of an analytical definition of polity or another 'notion of totality' that defines in positive terms what a polity is and how it is delimited.

Models of political structure

If polity is to be recast as a kind of political structure, it makes sense to look at what models we already have. Kenneth Waltz famously had some success in suggesting that only two models are necessary: hierarchy, where the units are ordered in relations of super – and subordination and therefore functionally differentiated (X, Y, Z), and anarchy, where the ordering principle is coordination among formally undifferentiated units that differ in strength (X, x, etc. – see Figure 1). Waltz warned that 'a new concept should be introduced only to cover matters

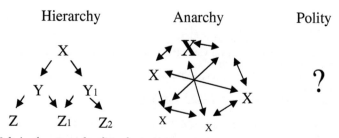

Hierarchy   Anarchy   Polity

Figure 1. *Waltz's theories of political structure.*

[47] Ferguson and Mansbach, *Polities*; John Gerrard Ruggie, *Constructing a World Polity. Essays on International Institutionalization* (London: Routledge 1998); Hajer, *Policy without Polities*; Seyom Brown, *International Relations in a Changing Global System. Toward a Theory of the World Polity* (Oxford: Westview Press, 1996).
[48] Ougaard and Higgott, *Towards a Global Polity*, p. 12.
[49] Ougaard, *Political Globalisation*, p. 4.

that existing concepts do not reach'.[50] Mixtures and borderline cases do not represent a third type: 'To say that we have borderline cases is not to say that at the border a third type of system appears'.[51] By assuming that ordering principles are solely to do with one-dimensional power relations of super – and subordination, Waltz created a neat tautology: structure is hierarchy or the lack of it.

Volumes of criticism (beyond the remit of this article) have been directed towards this dichotomy, especially in terms of it being unrealistically simplifying and structurally deterministic, unable to account for change.[52] The whole post-international approach is of course dedicated to – even defined by – showing how the model of the international system falls short because the system is changing and becoming more complex, post sovereign or interconnected. However, the question of an alternative *model* of political structure for grouping units and understanding their dynamics has been attempted surprisingly little.[53] In rejecting the twin models of anarchy and hierarchy, the very idea of models as ways of simplifying complex reality have often implicitly been rejected too, leaving little in the way of simplifying tools for heterodox scholars to reach for when describing world politics (hence the penchant for complexity and metaphors).

That critics of neo-realism have left this flank open is perhaps why, as Ole Wæver points out,[54] Waltz has of late defended his theory not so much in terms of what the world looks like but in terms of what he argues a theory is or should be, namely a 'picture, mentally formed, of a bounded realm or domain of activity. A theory is a depiction of the organization of a domain and the connections among its parts'.[55] It is a simplification, invented by the analyst ('mentally formed') to make sense of a certain field and it is, in an important way 'a picture': 'A theory [...] is not a collection of variables' it is, literally, a *depiction* that also simplifies: 'to criticize a theory for its omissions is odd, because theories are mostly omission'.[56] This is different from the medium-range idea of a theory as a set of propositions about causes and effects, something Waltz considers to be a specification of a theory, rather than the theory itself. While many would disagree with this definition and concentrate on how a theory such as anarchy should be specified, perhaps including more variables or opening up the units to scrutiny, it is fair to say that a relatively small amount energy has gone into alternative 'theories' in the sense of pictures, mentally formed that make sense of the structure of a field. Therefore, a defense of this idea of theory can parade as a defence for

---

[50] Kenneth Waltz, *Theory of International Politics* (Boston, Mass.: McGraw-Hill, 1979), p. 116.

[51] Waltz *Theory*, p. 116.

[52] John G. Ruggie, *Constructing the World Polity*; Heikko Patomäki, *After International Relations: Critical Realism and the (Re)Construction of World Politics* (London: Routledge, 2002); Barry Buzan, Charles Jones and Richard Little, *The Logic of Anarchy: Neoralism to Structural Realism* (New York: Columbia University Press, 1993).

[53] Hall (2004) argues with some justification that the core-periphery model makes up another basic morphology or picture of political structure, but this is ultimately a version of hierarchy, based on the relative autonomy or dependence of one set of actors in relation to another only with other units than states. See, Martin Hall, 'On the morphology of international systems', CFS Working paper, University of Lund (2004).

[54] Ole Wæver, 'Waltz's Theory of Theory'. Paper presented at the conference 'The King of Thought: Theory, The Subject and Waltz', Aberystwyth (15–17 September 2008).

[55] Waltz *Theory*, p. 8.

[56] Kenneth Waltz, 'Neorealism: Confusions and Criticisms', in *Journal of Politics & Society*, XV (2004), pp. 2–6.

one particular theory, namely Waltzian neo-realism. If pictures are crucial this would explain some of Waltz's success and resilience.

None the less intimations of alternative models of political structure exist within IR. Beyond hierarchy and anarchy, some like Ruggie have employed the concept of 'heteronomy' to denote interwoven and overlapping jurisdictions.[57] 'Heterarchy' has likewise been defined as a structure in which each element is either unranked relative to other elements, or possesses the potential for being ranked in a number of different ways[58] such concepts typically applied to structures such as the EU[59] or Medieval Christendom.[60] In heterarchy we learn that 'political authority is neither centralized (as under conditions of hierarchy) nor decentralized (as under conditions of anarchy) but shared'.[61] The network metaphor used typically to capture political alternative structures particularly in a globalised world is another possible example of an alternative theory of political structure.[62] Organisation theory has posited 'networks' as the third organisational structure after hierarchy and the market (roughly equivalent to anarchy which Waltz of course moulded on economic theory).[63]

However, although doubtless of value in themselves, such concepts remain generally difficult to *picture*, and typically rely on complexity (often explicitly in relation to hierarchy or anarchy) for their analytical power and are therefore not suited to the task we have set ourselves here of, in the interests of theoretical pluralism, facilitating a 'reversal of strategy for theory-building'[64] starting from an alternatively delimited entity (in this case a global one – the global polity).[65] 'Heteronomy' remains essentially a complication of hierarchy (many overlapping ones) while 'heterarchy' is defined as 'neither hierarchy nor anarchy' leaving unspecified when a heterarchy is positively constituted and when not and how the limits of one might be decided upon (not to mention what the 'logic' of a heterarchy might be). Picturing a heterarchy is not easily done from this description. Networks, on the other hand, are sometimes defined simply as a set of units (or nodes) with connections between them.[66] Unlike hierarchies these

[57] Ruggie, *Constructing*, pp. 23–4. See also Nicholas Onuf & Frank F Klink, 'Anarchy, Authority, Rule', *International Studies Quarterly*, 33 (1989), pp. 149–73.

[58] C. Crumley, 'Heterarchy and the analysis of complex societies', pp. 1–6 in R. M. Ehrenreich, C. L Crumley and J. E. Levy (eds), *Heterarchy and the Analysis of Complex Societies'* (Washington, DC: American Anthropological Association, 1995).

[59] Jurgen Neyer, 'Discourse and Order in the EU', *Journal of Common Market Studies*. 41 (2003), pp. 687–706, 689.

[60] Ruggie, *Constructing*, p. 149.

[61] Neyer, *Discourse and Order*, p. 689.

[62] Manuel Castells, *The Rise of the Network Society* (Oxford: Blackwell, 1996); Margaret E. Keck. & Kathryn Sikkink, *Activists Beyond Borders* (Ithaca: Cornell University Press, 1998); Anne-Marie Slaughter, *A New World Order* (Princeton, NJ: Princeton University Press, 2004); Mette Eilstrup-Sangiovanni and Calvert Jones 'Assessing the Dangers of Illicit Networks. Why *Al-Qaeda* May be Less Threatening Than Many Think', *International Security*, 33 (2008), pp. 7–44; Fritz W Scharpf, 'Coordination in Hierarchies and Networks', in Scharpf (ed.), *Games in Hierarchies and Networks: Analytical and Empirical Approaches to the Study of Governance Institutions* (Boulder, Colorado: Westview, 1993), pp. 125–65.

[63] Walter Powell, 'Neither Market nor Hierarchy: Network Forms of Organization', *Research in Organizational Behaviour*, 12 (1990), pp. 295–96.

[64] Higgott and Ougaard, *Towards a Global Polity*, p. 30.

[65] Olaf Corry, 'Theories of Global Politics', Unpublished paper presented at the Staff and PhD Colloquium, Department of Politics and International Studies, University of Cambridge.

[66] Castells, *Network Society*, p. 501.

nodes-with-connections-constellations are not fixed or constituted by a dominant node or sovereign. Unlike anarchies the nodes in a network are not necessarily functionally equivalent or in competition. Beyond those negatives, however, networks can be structured in any number of ways. That something is 'a network' tells us little of the nature of the relations between units except that they are not fixed or hierarchical (since we would then call them 'structures' or 'hierarchies', respectively). Keck and Sikkink specify in more detail defining networks as essentially cooperative organisations 'characterized by voluntary, reciprocal, and horizontal patterns of communication and exchange'[67] although it remains unclear why a network could not coerce or contain vertical patterns of communication and exchange. For the purposes of this argument it suffices to point out that a network can assume any number of basic morphologies and cannot thus be likened to a pictorial model of political structure or perform the function of effectuating a methodological reversal. Applied to the case of the global polity: describing a 'global network' may be worthwhile but is not equivalent to claiming a global polity, unless 'polity' is defined as simply connected actors (I argue that 'system' is the appropriate label for sets of connected actors of which hierarchy, anarchy also are types).

Saskia Sassens use of the term 'global assemblages' is promising too, concerning new constellations of key elements of the nation state (territory, authority and rights) but is expressly left un-theorised.[68] Nigel Thrift works creatively with new forms of social space and also makes use of 'assemblage', defining it in terms of old elements put together in a novel way that 'breathes life into the elements that compose it and induces a novel perception of reality'.[69] Polities are of course assemblages in the sense of being entities that come into being through constellations that at some point are novel, but to be a pictorial theory of political structure polity must suggest how they are put together. Not all assemblages are polities, in other words, and so this concept is also of a different order. Finally, the idea of global or world *society* is also something different and broader than a global polity, denoting an integrated global social body with some form of community of shared norms or a more abstract world system of connected parts which again equates 'polityness' with interconnectedness.[70] Social theories of globality will be crucial for our understanding of global politics but do not equate to a pictorial theory of political structure.

This brings us to existing definitions of polity. Using the term as the label for a new model puts aside older definitions and focuses instead on the way the term currently functions. Some define 'polity' as a broad label roughly for any agent capable of commanding resources with some degree of common internal identity and institutions like empires, states or clans.[71] This relies at base on the model of hierarchy although it denotes a wider and more generic entity than a state and approximates Rosenau's idea of 'spheres of authority'.[72] Most famously, Ferguson and Mansbach define a polity as something constituted by: (i) a distinct identity or

[67] Keck and Sikkink, *Activists Beyond Borders*, p. 8.
[68] Sassen, *Territory, Authority, Rights*, p. 3.
[69] Thrift Nigel, "'It's the romance, not the finance, that makes the business worth pursuing": disclosing a new market culture', in *Economy and Society*, 30 (2001), pp. 412–32, 421.
[70] See, Mathias Albert, 'Globalization Theory. Yesterday's fad or more lively than ever?', in *International Political Sociology* (2007), p. 171.
[71] Waltz, *Theory* (1979), p. 81; Ferguson and Mansbach, *Polities*, p. 34; Meyer, 'The World Polity'.
[72] Rosenau, *Along the Domesti-foreign Frontier*, p. 171.

'we-ness'; (ii) a capacity to mobilise resources and, (iii) 'a degree of institutional-ization and hierarchy'.[73] In comparison many current uses of 'polity' are intended precisely to capture broken or dispersed hierarchies (for example, 'the Palestinian polity', the 'EU polity' or 'global polity'). Thus defined polity brings a more accommodating and historically sensitive idea of hierarchy than the usual narrow state-sovereignty conception, but it does not provide a new morphology or theory of political structure that transcends the hierarchy-anarchy continuum.

Polity is also at times defined in a more generic way, one modern encyclopaedia defining a polity as 'a society's system for governance'.[74] This casts polity as an overarching term, despite the tendency for it to function in a more specific way. Moreover, to accept such a definition is to create a (poorly specified) synonym for 'political system'[75] best known from political science in terms of a set of arrange-ments 'through which values are authoritatively allocated for a society'.[76] This suggests something with inputs, gatekeepers, processes, outputs, feedback, etc. in a much more institutionalised sense, usually modelled on the modern pluralist state. This seems not very appropriate for something like a 'global polity' which is far less established. In another more minimalistic definition, for Hedley Bull a system of states is formed 'when two or more states have sufficient contact between them, and have sufficient impact on one another's decisions to behave – at least in some measure – as parts of a whole'.[77] If polity were used in this way, then any two states interacting enough to behave 'in some measure as a part of a whole' would make up 'a polity'. The US and Canada interact enough to take each other into account. But would we speak of a US-Canadian polity? China may be investing in Africa but could we speak of a Chinese-Angolan polity? Hardly. Something is missing. There is more to a polity than mere interaction. Additionally, such overarching definitions of polity stand in contrast to older definitions of polity, for example Aristotle's, in which polity denoted a specific system of rule in which many groups take turns to govern broadly in the interests of the whole community. But this latter definition resembles broadly what we today refer to as democracy.[78]

Rejecting both the hierarchy-based and the catch-all system definition and the Aristotelian idea of polity, polity can be reserved, along with anarchy and hierarchy, as a theory of political structure – how parts in a system relate to one another – while 'political system' can remain the overarching term for any situation in which units interact sufficiently to have to take each other into account.

The structure of polity

According to what principle are units in 'a polity' arranged, if not by relations of super and subordination? Looking at much current usage I have suggested that a

[73] Ferguson & Mansbach, *Polities*, p. 34.
[74] Claudio Cioffi-Revilla and Todd Landman, 'Evolution of Maya Polities in the Ancient Meso-american System', in *International Studies Quarterly*, 43 (1999), pp. 559–98.
[75] Cioffi-Revilla and Landman, 'Evolution'.
[76] David Easton, 'An Approach to the Analysis of Political Systems', *World Politics*, 9:3 (1957), pp. 383–400.
[77] Hedley Bull, *The Anarchical Society. A Study of Order in World Politics* (New York: Colombia University Press, 1977), p. 9.
[78] Aristotle like others at that time used 'democracy' to refer to rule by the poor in their exclusive interests. (Aristotle the *Politics*, IV).

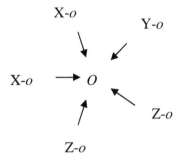

Figure 2. *Polity.*

polity is constituted not by the presence or absence of hierarchy between subjects but by their orientation towards a common governance-object. Speak of a polity signals not the presence of a hierarchy but the presence or absence of an object considered governable towards which a set of actors are oriented. This, I suggest, is what constitutes polities.

In formal terms a polity exists *whenever a set of actors are oriented towards the governance of one or more common governance-objects.* Figure 2 pictures a governance-object and X-*o*, Y-*o* and Z-*o* are different subjects oriented towards governing it. As will be explained, governance-objects may disappear or change over time, but without a common governance-object we can say that there is no polity. A polity thus conceived requires no common thick values or affinity between actors (and so is not identical to a society), or an ability for one agent to somehow coerce the others (and so is not defined by hierarchy) only a common interest in governing an object in some way. In contrast, an anarchy consists traditionally of units who define themselves in terms of governing their domestic spheres while they navigate in relation each other. Actors in anarchies and hierarchies do not necessarily have common governance objects.

Before considering more closely what, given this theory, a *global* polity might be, this basic definition of polity requires several points of clarification concerning: (i) what a 'governance-object' is; (ii) what governance-subjects are and why there needs to be a set of them; (iii) what the ordering principle of a polity is if not relations of super and sub-ordination, and finally, (iv) how polities relate to their environments, that is, how criteria of membership/non-membership of a polity can be conceived.

A 'governance-object' can be understood as an *'object' constituted as real, malleable and subject to attempts at steering.* Status as 'real' is an obvious necessary precondition, but is one that has often been taken for granted. While constructivist approaches have given much thought to the construction of identity, the construction of the object of steering has been largely ignored. One notable exception is Foucault's governmentality lectures. In them he points out that rulers in Machiavelli's time saw themselves primarily as rulers of 'territories' whereas in modern governmental states decision-makers view the managing of 'an economy' or the nurturing of 'populations' or society as their main governance-objects.[79]

---

[79] Michel Foucault, 'Governmentality', in *Essential Works. Power Vol. 3*, edited by James D. Faubion (London: Penguin, 2002 [1978]), pp. 201–22.

Secondly, logically the governability of an object implies also malleability. For example, a society may agree on the reality of 'the Earth beneath its crust' but no credible options for altering or governing such and object is perceived to exist. Thirdly, the availability of technologies of governing (technologies understood broadly and without prejudice as to who or what controls them) is also part of what makes a governance-object. The development of statistics and the new science of economics was one factor in transforming western states' object of governance from territory to society. 'The climate' has only very recently been successfully constructed as a global governance-object, (arguably a major one in a nascent global polity), by being constituted as; a) a meaningful object that b) can be manipulated for example, by regulating the mix of gasses in the Earth's atmosphere or by other kinds of geo-engineering.[80]

Governance-objects perhaps used to be defined primarily by governments and the term 'governance' used to be closely associated with state rule of a society or economy. However, governance has been loosened from its statist connotations now often denoting a more generic 'steering' regardless of who or what is doing that steering and whether it is done inside, outside or across states.[81] In fact in a post-international global governance discourse, governance came to denote steering involving non-state entities. Global governance literature largely defined governance in contradistinction to hierarchic power ('the regulation of interdependent relations in the absence of overarching political authority')[82] or in contrast to the antagonistic power politics traditionally associated with anarchy emphasising instead cooperation, solving common problems and generally dealing with transnational threats.[83] By defining governance negatively against the rule of a sovereign and the coercion of anarchy, a degree of technocratic consensuality and cooperation was imputed into 'global governance'. However, outside a post-international framework it is not necessary for 'steering' to be consensual or technocratic, and 'interdependent relations' need not be the sole object of governance.

The governance-subjects of a certain polity I suggest are therefore the ones who – within a specific social setting – are oriented towards somehow steering (consensually or antagonistically) a common governance-object. Many things will be construed as governable at any one time, but only a few come to define political relations. Global governance-subjects such as the 'global justice movement' constitute themselves as such through reference to the idea of a global society, 'globalization' or the implied object of 'global justice', for instance. Without such objects the identity of 'global movements' or actors would fall apart as coherent categories. There must be *a set of* actors because governance-objects as social constructions depend on social practices that define them intersubjectively.[84]

---

[80] Emery Roe, *Narrative Policy Analysis. Theory and Practice* (Durham NC: Duke University Press, 1994).

[81] Jon Pierre, *Debating Governance. Authority, Steering and Democracy* (Oxford;Oxford University Press, 2000), pp. 3–5.

[82] James N Rosenau, 'Toward an Ontology for Global Governance', in Martin Hewson and Timothy J. Sinclair (eds), *Approaches to Global Governance Theory* (Albany, NY: State University of New York, 1999).

[83] Ramesh Thakur and Thomas G. Weiss, *The UN and Global Governance: An Unfinished Journey* (New York: UN University Press, 2010).

[84] This is similar to the Copenhagen School securitisation theory that theorises securitised objects as socially constructed rather than objectively threatened or subjectively invented (see Buzan, Barry,

Constructs about what is governable need to be authorised by an audience, so this is not a free-for-all: for example, *Al-Qaeda* in Iraq refers to itself as '*Al-Qaeda* in Mesopotamia' (which can be seen as a polity-move), but 'Mesopotamia' is no longer consider a 'real' or governable entity in the same way that Iraq, Syria, Jordan, Lebanon, etc. now are. A subject can of course be oriented towards more than one governance-object since individual and group identity is typically multiple.[85] Most governance-subjects will, therefore, be members of more than one polity simultaneously. At the same time identity is structured and very often relatively stable and a governance-object will be of greater importance over time to some governance-subjects than others.[86] The Labour Party, for instance, has 'Britain' as its primary governance-object (without which Labour would not be Labour) but will also see itself in a different context as a party concerned with governing 'The Commonwealth' or global governance-objects such as 'climate', 'global economic stability', 'global society' or global public bads like 'poverty' or 'global terror'. Finally, it may be worth noting that political identities tend to be shaped in relation to governance-objects of a certain level of abstraction like 'Britain' or 'the global' rather than single issues like the building of a shopping centre, the Three Gorges Dam or global supply of financial credit. The politics of a prospective shopping mall would not be likely to constitute a polity in itself, if identities of actors are rarely dependent upon single issues (this explains why there are not polities literally 'everywhere').

The ordering principle of polity can be called 'object-orientation' because actors are structured into a polity through their common orientation towards a governance-object. Whereas actors in a hierarchy are arranged vertically and in anarchies they are arranged in terms of polarity, they are arranged concentrically in a polity in the sense of being oriented towards the same centre (though not necessarily with equal distance). 'Non-polities' are then situations where subjects are not dependent for their identities upon the same governance-objects. A collection of actors in world politics, say Venezuela, Egypt, the USA, UNRWA and General Motors taken together, for instance, may be part of a political*system* (because they interact enough ways to have to take each other into account), but they cannot be said to make up 'a polity' since they are not oriented towards a common governance-object, just as they do not make up a hierarchy (they are not a unit defined in terms of relations of super and subordination).

The acquisition of 'membership' will differ between hierarchies, anarchies and polities. The question of membership pertains to the relation between a political structure and its environment. The threshold of a hierarchy is ultimately guarded by the centre. In a state, for example, citizenship is conferred upon citizens by the state. Membership of an anarchic system is not centralised but is also not a free-for-all, since membership is in principle decided systemically through mutual recognition. In practice, recognition by the strongest units may be crucial, but the

---

Ole Wæver and Jaap de Wilde, *Security: A New Framework for Analysis* (London and Boulder, Colo.: Lynne Rienner, 1998).

[85] Social identity theory emphasises that what distinguishes social beings from isolated information processing machines is variable identity: 'the fact that we can vary our perspective on reality from the singular to the collective and between different social positions at each level'. See, Penelope Oakes, 'Psychological Groups and Political Psychology: A Response to Huddy's "Critical Examination of Social Identity Theory"', *Political Psychology*, 23 (2002), p. 814.

[86] This is referred to as 'identity salience' in Social Identity Theory. See, Oakes, 'A Response', p. 815.

principle of sovereignty is said to be reciprocal.[87] In the international system states recognise each other's sovereignty insofar as they recognise each other as states with equal formal status. In contrast, membership of a polity I will call *decentralised*. Instead of the centre determining the subjects, it is the subjects (in their structural and discursive contexts) that identify with and ultimately construct the centre. Exiled groups or terrorists are not necessarily citizens of the states which they seek to influence or terrorise, and neither are they recognised as legitimate or formally equal players by opposing actors in world politics. They thus fall outside both state hierarchies and anarchies. But they will be a part of a polity, insofar as they – as political agents – orient themselves (however perversely) towards the governance of an object, be that 'a nation', a region or a religious community.

This makes polities in principle open or 'permeable' structures and, in a mobile and mediated society in essence non-territorial (although polity members may happen to be within the same territory). Anybody who defines or enacts their identities in relation to a governance-object becomes *de facto* a member of the polity, irrespective of recognition from other members, and governance-subjects are therefore unlikely to be neatly limited to a certain geographical location.

Variations on the polity theme

Hierarchy and anarchy vary according to different subject-to-subject relations, for example, anarchy is unipolar or multipolar and hierarchy is dictatorial, oligarchic, or democratic. Looking through a polity-lens there are subject-to-object relations to consider too. Furthermore, both types of relations can also be considered diachronically over time. This results in four polity-variables: the *density* of a polity, level of *stability* over time, the level of *antagonism* and finally the degree of *institutionalisation* over time. These are not variations in structure, since they do not change the ordering principle of object-orientation (just as bi-polarity and multipolarity are variations on an anarchic structure). They are forms of interaction within the same structure.

Firstly, the *density* of a particular polity is not the same as *how strong* a polity is. The latter would violate the above definition by relying on an actor-oriented and hierarchy-based definition of a polity as an entity capable of mobilising resources.[88] Instead we may speak of density as a function of *how defining the governance-object is for the actors concerned*. To the extent at a global polity exists it is not particularly dense in the sense that global governance-objects are not central to most subject positions. Beyond this, polities can also be ranked from stable to unstable. In a stable polity it is the same identities that contest the governance of the same governance-object over time, whereas unstable polities would consist of changing subjects and/or governance-objects. Thirdly, polities may differ in terms of levels of conflict/cooperation. Actors may have a shared discourse and practices concerning the existence and governability of an object, but disagree on desired action regarding that governance-object. Actor-oriented definitions of polity

[87] Martin Wight, *Systems of States*, ed. Hedley Bull (Leicester: Leicester University Press, 1977), p. 135.
[88] This approximates James Rosenau's generic term for a hierarchy, namely 'Sphere of Authority'.

assume basic cooperativeness or order within the polity, a shared identity, thin community or the ability to command resources.[89] But such traits are not necessary in the terms set out here. A polity gains its identity as a polity by a set of actors sharing not values or 'agreed arrangements concerning expected behaviour (norms, rules, institutions)'[90] – but merely by them recognising the existence and importance of an object of governance of some kind. Hence a polity can be divided by friend-enemy relations or be relatively harmonious while being a polity in both cases. The Swiss and the Afghan polities could thus both be polities, albeit very different ones – one harmonious and peaceful, the other antagonistic and war-torn. Literature about international regimes and concepts such as International Society and World Society therefore refer to something *necessarily* involving shared norms or values. Polities can vary along the very variable that defines 'societies' and 'regimes', namely shared norms, values and expectations about behaviour. Fourthly, subjects in a polity may over time experience varying degrees of *institutionalisation* understood as '*explicit* principles, norms, rules and decision-making procedures around which actors' expectations converge in a given issue-area'.[91] Note that the institutionalisation-variable is not identical to level of cooperation, since even antagonistic polities can acquire explicit rules and norms, such as during the Cold War when an intricate system of arms negotiations, surveillance and arms control was established between the two superpowers, who were at loggerheads.

The differences between the structures of hierarchy, anarchy and polity are summarised in Table 1.

On a point of clarification, if 'political system' is the overarching term, and hierarchy, anarchy and polity are structural models, should they be regarded as mutually exclusive? Most people would see a polity as being a hierarchy also, for example. This statement confuses theory with ontology. The model of hierarchy is not the same as what it refers to. It is a truism that all social relations are somehow unequal, especially in world politics. This does not mean that only hierarchy exists. As pictures, mentally formed, that 'convey a sense of the unobservable relation of things' as Waltz has it,[92] hierarchy, anarchy and polity are abstractions that simplify reality in different ways. We may view global politics sequentially through each of these prisms to find evidence for or against a global hierarchy, a global anarchy or a global polity, picking out very different aspects of world politics as we go. In this sense they are analytically distinct concepts that pick out different objects. The international system as an anarchy (as defined by Waltz) is *by definition* not a polity of states since states in an anarchy are oriented primarily towards governing their own domestic spheres rather than a common governance-object. Likewise a hierarchy 'is' not a polity since a hierarchy is defined by relations of subordination between subjects rather than common orientation towards a governance-object. Inmates and prison warders may be part of a hierarchic system of subordination without them sharing a governance-object. Similarly, citizens

[89] See, for example, Ferguson and Mansbach, *Polities*.
[90] Buzan, *From International to World Society?*, p. 111.
[91] Stephen D. Krasner, 'Structural Causes and Regime Consequences: Regimes as Intervening Variable', *International Organization*, 36 (1982), pp. 185–205, at p. 185.
[92] Waltz, *Theory*, p. 9.

	Political systems (sets of units that interact enough to have to take each other's actions into account)		
	Hierarchy	Anarchy	Polity
Constitutive feature	Existence of a sovereign	Absence of sovereign power and absence of common governance-object	Existence of a common governance-object
Ordering principle	Super – and subordination between subjects	Coordination between subjects	Orientation towards common governance-objects
Organisation of political space	Vertical	Polar	Concentric
Principle of membership	Centralised inclusion/exclusion	Systemic mutual recognition	Decentralised identification
Variable dimensions	Centralisation/ Decentralisation of power	Unipolar/multipolar	Dense/dispersed

Table 1. *Summary of three different political structures*

within a state can be viewed as being part of a hierarchy by virtue of their subordination under the sovereign, not because their identities are dependent upon the same governance-object.

We can draw a parallel to 'nation', 'state' and 'society'. These have been taken to refer to things that have at times been fairly well aligned, particularly during the 'Westphalian moment'. This does not make them 'the same' in conceptual terms or mutually exclusive in empirical terms. What they each refer to may overlap in empirical terms but although a state may have a nation within it, we cannot say that a state 'is' a nation without muddling the concepts. Equally, a polity may have a distinct hierarchy or anarchy within it or *vice versa*, but this does not make them the same entities. All anarchies and polities will have an unequal distribution of power within them, but by characterising them as anarchies or polities we are defining them according to other features than their distribution of power.

A global polity?

While this article asks primarily *what* a global polity is rather than *whether* a global polity exists, a brief consideration of how the generic definition of polity could map onto global politics may help to clarify the ideas behind the model. The reader will appreciate that the limits of space will allow only a cursory glance at this potentially huge question, the main purpose of which is to point out the new research agenda opened up by the theory of polity. In particular global polity is compared in the following to two of the best developed existing accounts of global politics that seek to go beyond the state model.

Firstly, how should we understand the idea of 'global' governance-objects? While the term 'global' functions in many different ways, often as the opposite of 'local' or as a signal of transformation beyond internationalisation[93] it will be understood here as denoting substantial 'space-time compression' coupled with discourse supposing the world as one place. This follows the Roland Robertson's idea of globalisation as not simply shrinkage of geographical distance but also a growing consciousness of the world as a singular place of action.[94] Martin Shaw echoes this: beyond worldwide interconnectedness, 'to be Global now refers, maximally, to the self-consciously common framework of human society world-wide'[95] though this does not necessarily imply any form of cosy community. Thus a *global* governance-object is not inclusive of every single square inch of the globe nor simply an object that is 'cross-border'. Nor is it enough for subjects to utter the term 'global' for something to be constructed as a global governance-object as defined here. The construction of an object as 'global' will be an inter-subjective process constituting something in terms that reference the globe as a single place of human action, for example, 'global poverty', 'global financial stability' or 'the [human-influenced] climate'.

When did global governance-objects begin to arise in public discourse? This is highly debatable, but it is crucially a different debate to the usual one about when globalisation began. Increased commerce or the 'shrinking' of space and time do not necessarily imply the emergence of a discourse constituting something as global and governable. Deities believed since ancient times to be present in the 'whole world' and 'for all time' arguably referenced the globe as one place, but were not considered governable and nor, in fact, was 'globalisation' as depicted recently by globalist liberals in awe of global markets who saw it as a bottom up non-steerable process of social change.[96] Thus, although it would be foolish to venture a precise date for the emergence of a global polity, the definition of a global governance-object frames a new type of question concerning not just when globality arose but also when governability of an object referencing the globe became widely accepted. Finally, if we also ask at what point actors became politically oriented towards such global governance-objects this pushes the birth of the global polity even closer to the present, probably to the rise of global movements, governments and other actors who's identities make sense only in relation to the governance of global objects.

Such global polity questions have not been much posed, but one observer suggests that 'the global' has been 'constituted as a new object of thought and action' towards the end of the Millennium as the 'certainty about the factuality of the globalization process itself' became generally accepted.[97] Another points to the recent growth in discourse on global governance that 'tells us to act and to think

---

[93] Sabine Selchow, 'Language and "global" politics: Denaturalising the "global"', in Martin Albrow et al. (eds), *Global Civil Society 2007/8: Communicative Power and Democracy* (London: Sage, 2008).

[94] Roland Robertson, *Globalization: Social Theory and Global Culture* (Thousand Oaks, CA: Sage, 1992), p. 8.

[95] Martin Shaw, 'Contesting Globalisation', pp. 159–73 in Martin Shaw (ed.), *Politics and Globalizations* (London: Routledge, 1999), p. 160.

[96] John Micklethwait and Adrian Wooldridge, *A Future Perfect. The Challenge and Hidden Promise of Globalization* (London: William Heinemann, 2000); The Economist *Globalisation*, (London: Profile Books, 2001); Tomas Larsson, *The Race to the Top. The Real Story of Globalization* (Washington: Cato Institute, 2001).

[97] Jens Bartelson, 'Three Concepts of Globalization', *International Sociology*, 15 (2000), pp. 180–96, 191.

as if the world were already a virtual global polity simply waiting to be lived in and worked out, one way or another'.[98] Anthony Giddens implies something similar: 'The second globalization debate [after Seattle, 1999] is not about whether [globalisation] exists; it's about what globalization is, what its consequences are, and what kind of framework we can develop for the world to accommodate it'.[99] Building on the definition of globality given above, it can be argued that the emergence of the basis for a global polity began when the current human-dominated era of the Earth began to be recognised – what Paul J. Crutzen has controversially labelled the 'Anthropocene': the human dominated geological epoch supposedly taking over from the Holocene. While Crutzen dates the Anthropocene to the invention of the steam engine,[100] discourse constructing the globe as humanly governable has only recently become substantial and widespread.

Just how widespread discourse presupposing the existence of a global governance-object is a crucial question for global polity research but is beyond the scope of this article. Instead, the following examines two recent accounts of global politics that begin with an alternative conception of global politics and compares them to the theory of global polity advanced here.

According to Martin Shaw in his theoretical and historical exploration of the globalisation of state power, *Theory of the Global State*, globality involves a transformation of the national-international nexus rather than simply a tipping towards the international end of it: 'accounts of transnationalism hardly amount to theories of globality'.[101] Although states will remain and inevitably form an important part of global politics, in a global setting 'tensions [between national and international] reappear in novel terms, which are increasingly relativized by the greater consciousness of the global human whole'.[102] Within this emerging globality, Shaw argues that global state functions are gradually becoming globalised. This creates a nascent global state 'conglomerate' centred around the lone superpower of the US and shared institutions like NATO. The reorganisation of means of violence and legitimacy is at the heart of his notion of a global-Western conglomeration:

The globalized Western state-conglomerate, or global-Western state for short, is an integrated authoritative organization of violence which includes a large number of both juridically defined states and international interstate organizations.[103]

States within the Western bloc and NATO in particular have become so enmeshed in each others' military machines and political institutions that they are no longer able to be grasped as nation-states interacting but must be seen as constitutive parts of a global Western state. The global state has internal structures strong enough to redefine ideas about national interest and sovereignty while it acts outwardly as a partially hegemonic bloc: 'not only is western state power exercised world-wide, but it has a general (if strongly contested) global legitimacy'.[104] For

---

[98] Jean-François Thibault, 'As if the World Were a Virtual Global Polity: The Political Philosophy of Global Governance' (2000). Available at: {http://www.theglobalsite.ac.uk/press/108thibault.htm}.
[99] Anthony Giddens, 'A talk with Anthony Giddens: The Second Globalisation Debate' (2001). Available at: {http://www.edge.org/documents/archive/edge81.html} accessed on 2 December 2007.
[100] Paul J. Cruzen, 'Geology of mankind', *Nature*, 415 (2002), p. 23.
[101] Shaw, *Theory of the Global State*, p. 89.
[102] Ibid., p. 26.
[103] Shaw, *Theory of a Global State*, p. 199.
[104] Ibid., p. 200.

Shaw, other theories of global governance, international regimes or security communities focus on how sovereign states cooperate and tussle while underestimating the 'striking difference between nation-states within the West and outside it'.[105] A new distinction apart from the national-international is thus offered as a point of departure potentially fulfilling the aim of moving beyond post-internationalism.

Similarly focused on the politics of globalisation, though with a broader focus on more state functions than those related to violence and war-making, Morten Ougaard borrows concepts from historical materialism and state theory that have been refined in domestic analyses such as superstructure 'persistence function', and the reproduction of relations of power. Ougaard's project is also motivated by a wish to go beyond the model of the state system as a modified anarchy and he urges 'a holistic perspective on world politics as an integrated phenomenon'.[106] He too thus aims to go beyond the anarchy model. The result is also a powerful analysis of a growing global superstructure of institutions. Like Shaw's, Ougaard's analysis leads him to identify a global state-like construction based on the major Western powers and global institutions 'marked by dense contacts, routinized information exchange, mutual surveillance and peer pressure, strong analytical and statistical resources, and a capacity for development of joint strategies and policies'.[107]

For conceptual clarity I will refer to these as examples of *global state theory*, and reserve global polity theory for the version advanced here. The aim is not to comprehensively assess these two theories of global politics and the historical narrative they are explained by, but to glean the theory of political space behind them and compare it to the one on offer here at an equivalent level of analysis.

Firstly, they largely succeed in offering an alternative to standard accounts of modified international anarchy because they begin from the global level of analysis. However, they base their account on hierarchy instead positing a global state-agent with a (relatively) ordered and pacific inside and a relatively anarchic outside. Both theorists measure the 'global superstructure' in relation to the idea of a hierarchic state able to command resources, build institutions and secure loyalty. Ougaard's account of the global polity is openly based on a domestic analogy – something which he argues is legitimate, indeed indispensable, provided such domestic analogies are not used 'uncritically'.[108] Both emphasise the 'incomplete' nature of the global state which insulates somewhat against realist counterclaims about the primacy of state sovereignty but of course also suggests that the global revolution, over time, will or could be 'completed' into a proper global hierarchy.

This is perfectly legitimate and thanks to Marxist and state theory apparatus both are able to offer explanations and analysis of the globalisation of power structures often lacking in globalisation studies. But it does not fundamentally expand our repertoire of political morphologies beyond the two familiar ones of hierarchy and anarchy. Rather it transfers the morphology of hierarchy familiar from comparative politics and the methodological nationalism to the global level. Both warn against the uncritical use of concepts developed in a domestic setting. Yet transferred back down to the national level, it is hard to see how their global

---

[105] Shaw, *Theory of a Global Polity*, p. 202.
[106] Ougaard, *Political Globalization*, p. 5.
[107] Ibid., p. 199.
[108] Ibid., p. 4.

model of hierarchy would differ from standard state theory. The global state is by definition relatively pacific internally, institutionalised and possesses agent qualities, able to act towards an 'outside'. Thus, in terms of theoretical pluralism, global state theory has value as an alternative starting point to anarchy, but tips towards the opposite end of the anarchy-hierarchy dichotomy already at the heart of the international paradigm.

While measuring the global political realm in relation to a model of hierarchy sheds useful light on important questions concerning world politics, it also inevitably obscures other questions. Firstly with global state theory there will be a propensity to find internal cohesion and 'actorness' in a global state when envisaging it as a state writ-large. The plausibility of the global state argument depends on the internal cohesion of the bloc or the uniformity of the global superstructure and critics were quick to charge that the global state could easily break up, making it essentially a multilateral form of cooperation between states rather than a new state formation.[109] In contrast a global polity as defined here need not have agent qualities and is not necessarily made up of shared institutions and common identity. A global polity as defined here would logically include the radical opponents of the West if they too aspire to govern global objects, as some have claimed *Al-Qaeda* does.[110] The view of the existence and governability of the global would be shared by all members, but little else would necessarily follow.

Secondly and linked to this is the fact that the idea of a global society hovers above the notion of a global state. Ougaard and Higgott identify a 'growing sense of "community"' and note the 'recognition of the appropriateness of global discourse'.[111] as a central characteristic of the emerging global polity. Shaw's global state derives its cohesion in part from a common awareness of human society on a world scale ('society becomes global when this becomes its dominant, constitutive framework')[112] and externally has 'a general (if strongly contested) global legitimacy'.[113] In contrast, a global polity as defined above requires no shared values or consciousness, except for discursive agreement on the existence and governability of global objects.

Thirdly, global state theory gives priority to institutions, with institutionalisation and hierarchic bureaucracy being core connotations of the concept of a state. Shaw's emphasis on the shift towards consciousness of the world as one place is at the crux of his idea of 'global', but neither global consciousness nor global discourse figure prominently in the idea of a global Western state bloc which is rather based on means of violence. The same goes for Ougaard's global superstructure, which is conceived of mainly in terms of institutions and leverage over subjects. The polity approach offered here in contrast puts global discourse at the heart of the emerging global polity in terms of the social construction of global governance-objects and the way subjects put (or do not put) such objects at the heart of their political identities.

Finally global state and global polity (as defined here) are different in their conceptions of territoriality. For Ougaard, all political actors are analysed as being

---

[109] Hirst, book review.
[110] Oliver Roy, Globalized Islam. The Search for a New Ummah (Columbia University Press, 2007).
[111] Ougaard & Higgott, *Towards a Global Polity*, p. 3.
[112] Shaw, *Theory of a Global State*, p. 12.
[113] Ibid., p. 200.

part of a global polity which is planetary in scope, similar to Seyom Brown's idea of a world polity as the totality of local, national, regional and global political relations.[114] The 'global superstructure' is however, limited to roughly the same area as Shaw's global state, corresponding to a Western social transnational formation. The latter maintains a 'territorial base' defined by 'the areas controlled by its component state units'.[115] In contrast, the global polity as defined here would be defined neither as the system-wide entity (not all actors define themselves in relation to global governance-objects), nor as a geographically based entity. For instance, the US government and pressure groups based in the US, such as the internet-based Avaaz.org may define themselves in relation to governing global objects such as 'global peace and stability' or 'global justice' but other US actors such as unions or state legislatures are oriented towards other polities such as the US polity or that grouped around the governance of a particular federal state. Within the same geography, actors may or may not be a part of the global polity.

Conclusion

Polity will not replace hierarchy and anarchy as theories, nor the need for analyses of how far world politics deviates from anarchy or hierarchy. As simplifications with which we can compare a complex reality, they remain useful. Nor are post-international accounts of world politics useless, especially not in terms of showing the inadequacy or selective nature of the statist model. Nor does our model of polity provide a specification of power relations or a grand theory of what drives history like that delivered by historical materialism[116] or evolutionary functionalist theory.[117] But at the level of morphologies or pictures, mentally formed, that provide scaffolding for making sense of political space, it can provide an alternative way of identifying, characterising and describing hybrid political entities that are emerging in large numbers today in the global age. A different object of analysis is brought into focus generating a different set of research questions about the global polity: when did 'the global' come to be constituted in the eyes of a group of actors as both real and governable? How is globality constructed as a governance-object? Who defines themselves in relation to such an object and how? How does the current configuration of the global polity rate on the variables identified? That is, how dense, stable, antagonistic or institutionalised is the global polity? If global polity discourse is spreading, what courses of action or global governance technologies are made plausible or possible (for example, global taxes, climate geo-engineering projects?). This contrasts with more traditional (post-) international questions such as 'are states loosing or retaining power?' 'How many non-state actors are there and how significant are they (do they influence the international system)?' 'Are there shared values and norms in

[114] Seyom Brown, *International Relations in a Changing Global System. Toward a Theory of the World Polity* (Oxford: Westward View, 1996).
[115] Shaw, *Theory of a Global Polity* 2000, p. 201.
[116] Justin Rosenberg, 'Globalization. A Post-Morten', *International Politics*, 42 (2005) pp. 2–74.
[117] Alexander Wendt, 'Why a World State is Inevitable', *European Journal of International Relations*, 9 (2003) pp. 491–542.

world politics?' What are the prospects for a global state capable of wielding coercive power on a global scale?

Does the theory of polity presented allow us to identify when a polity has been established or dissolved? Yes and no. 'No', because it will always be difficult to draw the line. 'Yes', because with an analytical definition we know what to look for and how to argue about where to draw the line. Armed with a theory of polity, the question of the existence of a global polity becomes clearer, even if the answer to that question remains complex. As such polity differs little from other well-rehearsed analytical distinctions – such as the distinction between anarchical and hierarchical political systems: this too is an analytically clear distinction, but empirically often difficult to call either way.

Furthermore, polity improves the level of analytic leverage relative to some existing post-international conceptions that catch all transnational or non-state actors or processes. Notions such as the *nebuleuse*, 'complex multilateralism', 'unbundling' or 'assemblages' are evocative, but do not help us if we wish to go beyond deconstructions of the old organising principles and cut the analytical cake in a new way. The 'non-state' category itself initially lumps all non-state transnational actors together and as a consequence, concepts that build on that category such as 'global civil society',[118] and 'transnational civil society'[119] usually have to begin by throwing out certain non-state elements, for example, private companies, terrorists, mafia groups for reasons unrelated to the state/non-state distinction.[120] Seyom Brown's notion of a 'world polity' defined as the worldwide configuration of systems of enforceable societal relationships is also analytically relatively empty since such simple sum of enforceable relations would by the author's own admission have 'existed in one form or another throughout human history'.[121] In principle, a global polity could be dated to the emergence of a global governance object with importance for the identities of the governance-subjects.

Finally, the theory of polity here is also not bound to the idea of a 'global' polity and could be applied to other levels of analysis. A 'European polity', for example, would be a set of actors defined in relation to governance of 'Europe' or European governance-objects. A religious polity would be a group of actors who define themselves in relation to the governance of a particular religious object such as a community of believers. Polity thus has potential use outside IR in political geography, religious studies, anthropology and political science more widely.

---

[118] John Keane, *Global Civil Society?* (Cambridge: Cambridge University Press, 2003).
[119] Richard Price, 'Transnational Civil Society and Advocacy in World Politics', in *World politics*, 55 (2003), pp. 579–606.
[120] Mary Kaldor, *Global Civil Society: An Answer to War?* (Cambridge: Polity Press, 2003).
[121] Brown, *International Relations*, p. 6.

Review of International Studies (2010), 36, 181–200   © 2010 British International Studies Association
doi:10.1017/S0260210510001063   First published online 2 Sep 2010

Cosmological sources of critical cosmopolitanism

HEIKKI PATOMÄKI*

Abstract. Critical cosmopolitan orientation has usually been embedded in a non-geocentric physical (NGP) cosmology that locates the human drama on the surface of planet Earth within wide scales of time and space. Although neither a necessary nor a sufficient condition for critical cosmopolitanism, NGP cosmology provides a contrast to the underpinnings of centric cosmologies, such as those of Aristotle, which see the world as revolving around a particular observer, theorist and/or communal identity. NGP cosmology makes it plausible to envisage all humans as part of the same species. The connection works also through homology and analogy. An astronomic theory can be isomorphic with an ethico-political theory, that is, a structure-preserving mapping from one to the other is possible. Key cosmopolitan theorists have situated morality within a cosmic framework. However, the ethico-political implications of the NGP cosmology are ambiguous. Nietzsche was among the first to articulate its sceptical and nihilist implications. Various reactions have encouraged territorial nationalism and geopolitics. I suggest that critical cosmopolitical orientation should now be grounded on the notion of cosmic evolution, which is not only contextual, historical, pluralist and open-ended but also suggests that humanity is not a mere accident of the cosmos.

Heikki Patomäki is Professor of World Politics and the Vice Director of the Centre of Excellence in Global Governance Research at the University of Helsinki, Finland. He is also an Innovation Professor of Human Security – Globalisation and Global Institutions at the RMIT University in Melbourne, Australia. Patomäki's research interests include philosophy and methodology of social sciences, peace research, futures studies, global political economy, and global political theory. His most recent book is *The Political Economy of Global Security. War, Future Crises and Changes in Global Governance* (Routledge, 2008). Heikki can be contacted at: {heikki.patomaki@helsinki.fi}.

Introduction

There are two distinct ideal-typical forms of cosmopolitanism. The first is rooted in the context of separate communities and states and asks: do we have duties to others by assisting or civilising them or at least by preventing major maldevelopments – such as massive human rights violations – within their communities or states? Cosmopolitanism answers affirmatively, yes, we do have universal duties to everyone, including foreigners; whereas state moralists deny the wisdom of such universalism.[1] From a classical political realist viewpoint, this kind of universalism

---

* I am grateful to Pamela Slotte, Manfred Steger, Jennifer Gidley and the journal's anonymous referees for their very helpful comments; and to Jennifer also for her assistance in editing the text.
[1] In IR theory, the distinction between state-moralism and cosmopolitanism has been popularised by Chris Brown, *International Relations Theory: New Normative Approaches* (London: Harvester

comes close to moral imperialism. Hans Morgenthau discussed moral imperialism in terms of a general temptation to see oneself as the bearer and promoter of universal values: 'All nations are tempted – and few have been able to resist the temptation for long – to clothe their own particular aspirations and actions in the moral purposes of the universe'.[2]

In the second sense, however, cosmopolitanism has been used to take distance from any particular 'us' and criticise 'us' as a particular community, nation or state. Prior to the modern era, this criticism was usually confined to negative distance-taking, but since the late 18th century, critical cosmopolitanism has explored the possibility of creating better global institutions (becoming more political and transformative a century later). In this article, I leave the non-detached forms of both imperialism and cosmopolitanism aside and focus on explaining the possibility and emergence of detached – or what I also call critical – cosmopolitanism.[3] What is it that has made critical cosmopolitical thinking possible and plausible? From ancient proto-cosmopolitans to the 21st century transformative globalists, critics have challenged parochial ideas by re-contextualising particular histories, identities and moral understandings in broad, holistic terms. Somehow, at least since the 5th century BCE, human imagination has had the capacity to overcome its particular communal conditions and transgress existing divisions and boundaries. Does this mean that man is not a political animal in the Aristotelian sense? Is it not part of human nature to live in particular communities? Are ethical and political meanings not tied to specific languages, and thereby to specific human groups and communities? And has it not been risky, and often outright dangerous, to question the understandings and values of the community backed up by state-powers?

I argue that critical cosmopolitan orientation has usually been grounded on a non-geocentric physical cosmology (to be explained below) that locates the human drama on the surface of planet Earth within wide scales of time and space. The

Wheatsheaf, 1992). In this and related works Brown has assumed that cosmopolitanism usually comes in a rather parochial form: 'Most accounts of the universal values that might underlie a cosmopolitan ethic seem suspiciously like inadequately camouflaged versions of the first ten Amendments of the Constitution of the US of America'. Chris Brown, 'Cosmopolitan Confusions: A Reply to Hoffman', *Paradigms*, 2:2 (1988), p. 106, n. 2. For an analysis of how these two positions are defined negatively against each other, while circularly presupposing the other's position, see Heikki Patomäki, 'From Normative Utopias to Political Dialectics: Beyond a Deconstruction of the Brown-Hoffman Debate', *Millennium: Journal of International Studies*, 21:1 (1992), pp. 53–75. In that paper I argued, furthermore, that Hoffman's cosmopolitanism is at once too modest (it leaves many, perhaps most problems unanswered) and too strong (in some historical contexts Brown may well be right about the imperialist implications of Hoffman's view on human rights).

[2] Hans Morgenthau, *Politics Among Nations. The Struggle for Power and Peace*, 3rd edition (New York: Alfred A. Knopf 1961), p. 11.

[3] The two cosmopolitanisms are of course often intertwined. Many thinkers have oscillated between: (i) a view that justifies 'our' imperial interventions or expansion and, (ii) a view that denies that 'we' should have any specific position, rights or duties in the order, or city, of the universe. This applies of course to contemporary critical cosmopolitans as well. Even when arguing for just or democratic global institutions, cosmopolitans may still be embedded in a particular cultural and ethico-political context in a way that escapes their conscious attention. In other words, even the critical cosmopolitan sentiment may lack in self-reflexivity. For a recent attempt to carefully balance between the two distinct forms of cosmopolitanisms and elements of communitarianism or state-morality, see Toni Erskine, *Embedded Cosmopolitanism. Duties to Strangers and Enemies in a World of 'Disclosed Communities'* (Oxford: Oxford University Press, 2008). Also in this account, however, there are others who emerge as enemies (even when seen as 'fellow members of overlapping communities'); and thereby, the rules of just war becomes a key issue.

word 'cosmos' originates from a Greek term κόσμος meaning 'order, orderly arrangement, ornaments'. From Pythagoras onwards, the term has been applied to the visible, physical universe including planets and stars. This is of course not the only meaning of the term. There have been numerous mythical and religious attempts to understand the implicit order within the whole of being. Cultural theorists and social scientists discuss cosmologies in this sense, referring to the basic world views of various human groups (cultures, nations, civilisations).[4] Horizontal comparisons of cosmologies may easily lead to the conclusion that cosmologies are enduring cultural deep-structures that do not change easily. Furthermore, cosmologies may be depicted as being outside the realm of validity claims such as truth and good. This would imply a version of the thesis of cultural relativism.[5]

A non-geocentric physical (NGP) cosmology is built upon a scientific account of the distances and nature of the solar system and interstellar space, and of the cosmic conditions of life and society on planet Earth. NGP cosmology can of course be given meaning – framed and conceptualised – in a variety of ways.[6] My point is only that scientific NGP cosmology provides a clear contrast to the underpinnings of ego-, ethno – and geo-centric cosmologies, which see the world as revolving around a particular observer, theorist and/or communal identity.

A non-geocentric physical (NGP) cosmology may be neither a necessary nor a sufficient condition for critical cosmopolitanism. Yet I maintain that the two are closely related. Given a series of possible further assumptions (which I try to explicate below), NGP cosmology makes it plausible to envisage all humans as part of the same species. Humans have the shared potential for interbreeding, communication and learning. Furthermore, the connection works also through homology and analogy. There is an important similarity between the perspectives of NGP cosmology and cosmopolitanism. The similarity of perspectives explains their shared classical and modern ancestry. It also explains why an astronomic theory can be isomorphic with an ethico-political theory, that is, why a structure-preserving mapping from one to the other is possible. The connection works also through the substance of ethico-political theories, which give meaning to the NGP cosmology. Many cosmopolitan theorists have made explicit links between the two.

---

[4] For instance, Johan Galtung, *Peace by Peaceful Means, Peace and Conflict, Development and Civilization* (Oslo & London: PRIO & Sage, 1996), pp. 211–22; Juan M. Ossio, 'Cosmologies', *International Social Science Journal*, 49:4 (December 1997), pp. 549–62; Denise Martin, 'Maat and Order in African Cosmology A Conceptual Tool for Understanding Indigenous Knowledge', *Journal of Black Studies*, 38:6 (July 2008), pp. 951–67.

[5] From Giambattista Vico, we have learnt that myth – or cosmology in the cultural sense of the term – should not be opposed to abstract rationality or scientific truth; myths are narratives that can have truth-value and be based on the results of science, although myths themselves are not established scientific facts or theories. See Joseph Mali, *The Rehabilitation of Myth. Vico's New Science* (Cambridge: Cambridge University Press, 1992). For an explicit argument that modern scientific cosmology and big history of cosmic, biological and cultural evolution constitute a well-grounded and thus plausible modern creation myth, see David Christian, 'The Case for "Big History"', *Journal of World History*, 2:2 (Fall 1991), pp. 234–8; David Christian, *Maps of Time. An Introduction to Big History* (Berkeley, CA: University of California Press, 2005), pp. 1–5, 17–38.

[6] See, Helge S. Kragh, *Cosmology and Controversy: The Historical Development of Theories of the Universe* (Princeton, NJ: Princeton University Press, 1996); John North, *Cosmos. An Illustrated History of Astronomy and Cosmology* (Chicago: University of Chicago Press, 2008); Jayant V. Narlikar and Geoffrey Burbridge, *Facts and Speculation in Cosmology* (Cambridge: Cambridge University Press, 2008).

My discussion proceeds as follows. First, I summarise the difference between centric cosmologies and NGP cosmology in terms of Aristotle versus his opponents. I survey ancient proto-cosmopolitanism, and compare developments in ancient Greece with those in other main hubs of the Old World; and suggest a link between the first emergence of NGP cosmology and critical cosmopolitanism. Next, I explore early modern and Enlightenment cosmopolitanism in Europe, stressing the role of the new scientific framework of time, space and humanity; and then shed light on the nearly simultaneous emergence of the idea of world state in the 19th and early 20th centuries in Europe, Persia and China.

However, the ethico-political implications of the NGP cosmology are ambiguous. While enabling cosmopolitanism, it has also generated scepticism and nihilism, encouraging territorial nationalism and geopolitics. In the conclusion, I tentatively suggest that critical cosmopolitical orientation should now be grounded on the notion of cosmic evolution, which is not only contextual, historical, pluralist and open-ended but also suggests that humanity is not a mere accident of the cosmos.

Aristotle vs. cosmopolitans: two different cognitive perspectives

Aristotle (384 BCE–322 BCE) collected and synthesised the best astronomical theories of his day.[7] Following Plato's (427 BCE–347 BCE) teachings, it was clear to Aristotle that the Earth is a sphere. For Aristotle, however, the question was whether he should put the Earth or Sun at the centre of the planetary and, by implication, stellar system. From an empirical point of view, a key consideration was the lack of parallax. If Earth moved around the Sun, then one ought to be able to observe the shifting of the fixed stars in half-a-year cycle – say from spring to autumn – in relation to the background of other stars. The difference in angle from one side of the Earth's orbit around the Sun to the other side is called parallax. The shapes of star-constellations should change considerably over the course of a year; otherwise the stars are so distant that this motion remains undetectable.

Aristotle ignored the possibility of real cosmic-scale distances. As a matter of fact, the parallax angles are so tiny that they are measured in arc seconds where one second is 1/3600 of a degree (for Alpha Centauri, with a 4.3 light-years distance from the Earth, the parallax is 0.75 seconds). Therefore, stellar parallax was not detected until the early 19th century, when developments in optics and time-keeping created sufficient technological capacity for detecting effects so subtle. There were, however, other empirical anomalies in the Aristotelian system. For example, it could not explain the changes in brightness of the planets caused by a change in distance as they orbit the sun. Over time, some of Aristotle's and his

---

[7] Aristotle's astronomical theories were developed in his *On the Heavens* and to an extent in *Meteorological*, rather than in his famous *Physics* (which is about meta-physics). J. L. Stocks' translation of *On the Heavens* is available online at the Internet Classics Archive at: {http://www.classics.mit.edu//Aristotle/heavens.html} accessed on 20 July 2009). For a detailed account of Aristotle's cosmological system is J. L. E. Dreyer, *A History of Astronomy from Thales to Kepler*, 2nd edition (New York: Dover Publications, 1958), pp. 108–122; and also North, *Cosmos. An Illustrated History*, pp. 80–4.

followers objections to the heliocentric model started to appear increasingly superficial and confused.[8] The Copernican revolution occurred centuries before it was possible to detect and measure parallax empirically.

Arguably, Aristotle's and his followers' preference for a geo-centric model had roots in the cognitive perspective they took for granted. In short, Aristotle assumed that he has a privileged position to observe the world. The starting point is that the observer-theorist is at the centre of the world, and that the world revolves, literally or metaphorically, around him. In terms of figure-ground distinction, the observer-theorist forms the ground and everything else is figures that move, or are being caused, in relation to it. Sometimes, common sense misleadingly supports this assumption. If you stay awake overnight looking at the stars and planets, they indeed seem to revolve around you – even though this is merely an illusion of perspective caused by the rotation of the planet Earth.

By way of metaphoric extension, society too can be seen through an observer-centric cognitive perspective. Accordingly, Aristotle's geocentric astronomic theory is isomorphic with his ethico-political theory, that is, a structure-preserving mapping from one to the other is possible. There is a centre and a hierarchical system of layers. For Aristotle, natural slaves, women and lower-status men are essentially meant to serve the purpose of the good life of the aristocracy and free men (this is the centre, to which Aristotle himself belonged). And the outside world forms concentric circles of increasing barbarity. The further you go, the more barbarity you should expect to find.[9] Like the apparent rotation of planets and stars around the Earth, this kind of ethnocentrism is essentially an illusion of perspective stemming from being familiar with things that are close; from social practices that are structured to serve the purpose of a few and their sense of community; and from asymmetrical relations of power.[10] It is noteworthy that Aristotle did not support democracy – in our sense – even among the free male citizens, but rather argued for a compromise between what he called polity and aristocracy (*aristoi* means literally 'best persons'). For Aristotle, the true centre consists only of the central observer and of the few that are equal to him.

In the 4th and 3rd century BCE Hellenic world, Aristotle was not quite as dominant as he may now seem to us. Aristotle was arguing against distinguished thinkers who held different views. For instance, he was opposing the influential theory of Pythagoreans that the Earth is orbiting a central fire (which would explain day and night). He was also against the atomism of Democritus (c. 460

---

[8] North, *Cosmos. An Illustrated History*, pp. 82–4, 101–5, 429–31, 473–4; Dreyer, *A History of Astronomy*, pp. 310–412.

[9] For relevant passages about the nature of slaves (note that for Aristotle not all actual slaves are natural slaves), women, and barbarians, and differences among these categories, see Aristotle, *Politics*, trans. B. Howett (Mineola, NY: Courier Dover Publications, 2000), pp. 1252b, 1254b, 1255b, 1260b; and Aristotle, *Nicomachean Ethics*, 2nd edition, trans. T. Irwin (Indianapolis, IN: Hackett Publishing, 1999), pp. 1158b, 1160b–1161b, and 1177a. For a general discussion, see J. S. McLelland, *A History of Western Political Thought* (London: Routledge, 1996), pp. 59–67.

[10] Aristotle's perspective is in many ways structurally similar to world religions that assume a particular chosen people, or god's son, or the prophet, or anything equivalent, to have a special privileged place in the universe, that is, to constitute the ground around which everything else revolves. This explains the popularity of Aristotle among Christian and Islamic theologians. For an explanation of why Aristotle's theories did not allow him to look critically into his own conceptual metaphors and cognitive unconsciousness, see George Lakoff & Mark Johnson, *Philosophy in the Flesh. The Embodied Mind and Its Challenge to Western Thought* (New York: Basic Books, 1999), pp. 373–90.

BCE–c. 370 BCE), abhorred by Plato, but a possible a source of inspiration to the Cynics, the early cosmopolitans. Democritus held that the earth is spherical; and maintained that at first the universe comprised of nothing but separate tiny atoms, until they collided together to form larger units and structures, including the Earth and everything on it. Democritus also suggested that there are many worlds, some growing, some decaying; some with no sun or moon, some with several. Thus for Democritus, the Earth is just a world among many worlds. By a rather anti-Aristotelian implication, no Earthly observer of the universe can be privileged. No wonder Aristotle found this doctrine objectionable.

While the basic ethico-political sentiments of Democritus seem to have been more democratic than those of Aristotle, the evidence about his precise ethical and political views is scant. As far as we know, it was the Cynics (from the late 5th century BCE onwards) that challenged the importance of being a *politēs*, that is, of belonging to a particular *polis*, of being a member of a specific society with all of the benefits and commitments such membership entails.[11] For the Cynics, being a *kosmopolitēs* meant more than just being a citizen of the world; it meant also being a part of the natural order of the universe (cosmos). The Cynics took god-nature as a source of guidance – even as a norm – about how to live. This may now appear as a fallacy, but what is important is that the Cynics adopted a different cognitive perspective from the ego-, ethno-, and geo-centric perspective of Aristotle. For the first time, cosmos provided a non-privileging perspective on human societies and thus enabled critical and self-reflexive ethico-political conclusions.

Aristarchus of Samos (310 BCE–ca. 230 BCE) was probably the first to propose a fully-fledged heliocentric model of the planetary system. The later summary of Aristarchus' theory by Archimedes is our most direct evidence of it:

> [. . .] But Aristarchus of Samos brought out a book consisting of some hypotheses, in which the premises lead to the result that the universe is many times greater than that now so called. His hypotheses are that the fixed stars and the sun remain unmoved, that the earth revolves about the sun in the circumference of a circle, the sun lying in the middle of the orbit, and that the sphere of the fixed stars, situated about the same centre as the sun, is so great that the circle in which he supposes the earth to revolve bears such a proportion to the distance of the fixed stars as the centre of the sphere bears to its surface. Now, it is easy to see that this is impossible; [. . .].[12]

Aristachus' theory was tolerated but not accepted by his contemporaries – and in spite of Archimedes was soon all but forgotten until the Copernican revolution. Why did not a basically correct theory gain more popularity and support? The lack of adequate techniques to make sufficiently accurate observations was not the only reason. It was probably more decisive that the perspective of Aristachus' NGP cosmology had the potential to challenge the moral principles of societies built upon the observer-centric horizons of: (i) the relatively few free men of republican

---

[11] Georg H. Sabine, *A History of Political Theory* (New York: Holt, Rinehart and Winston, 1961), p. 130, interprets the rise of Cynics as a nihilistic but critical response to the decline of the Greek city-state. *Kosmopolitēs* would thus be a mere negation of membership in a city-state. But Cynics remained important for centuries in the Roman Empire, and shaped both Stoicism and early Christianity.

[12] *The Works of Archimedes*, ed. T. L. Heath (London: C. J. Clay and Sons, Cambridge University Press Warehouse, 1897), pp. 221–2. Freely available at: {http://www.archive.org/details/worksofarchimede029517mbp} accessed on 15 July 2009.

or oligarchic communities; or (ii) the privileged groups and strata within hierarchical empires; or, later, (iii) religious and political leaders of the communities founded on grand messianic religions such as Christianity and Islam that promised after-life redemption for believers.

Some scholars maintain that it was Stoicism, or the Stoic-Christian tradition, that first articulated universal moral principles in terms of laws of nature.[13] Stoicism was initiated by Zeno of Citium in the early third century BCE and subsisted until the collapse of the Roman Empire. However, Zeno's ideas were originally developed from those of the Cynics. Stoicism can be seen as a de-radicalised version of the Cynic idea that cosmos – the order of nature – provides guidance as to how to live and what the laws valid for all human beings are. The Stoics believed in something reminiscent of a NPG cosmology, but in more poetic-religious and compromised terms than the followers of atomists (and possibly Aristarchus). Occasionally, they delighted, or found comfort, in the idea of a city of all humankind, but the real, practical question for Roman Stoics was how far citizenship should be extended to the subjects of the Roman Empire. The ethics of Stoicism was based on the idea that wisdom is about simultaneous obligation to do one's duty and view one's consciousness and the world more or less as unchangeable, especially hierarchical relations of power.[14] It is no coincidence that Stoicism did not generate a research programme or develop a realist scientific theory of the cosmos and its true proportions, mechanisms and processes.

There were parallel developments in the other main hubs of the Old World. In India and China, there were sporadic atomists, heliocentrists, cynics, sceptics, democrats and cosmopolitans in various forms of manifestation, but hierarchical agrarian-military empires tended to adopt and enforce ideologies that were in important ways similar to the world-views of Plato, Aristotle and/or Stoics.[15] For

---

[13] Andrew Linklater's claim about a long-standing and unified 'Stoic-Christian tradition' that believes in the unity of mankind is based merely on one quotation from Sabine's dated history of Western political theory. Sabine, *A History of Political Theory*, pp. 148–51; Andrew Linklater, *Men and Citizens in the Theory of International Relations*, 2nd edition (London: MacMillan, 1990), p. 22; McLelland, *A History of Western Political Thought*, p. 85, gives some support by arguing that 'what Stoicism did was to connect the idea of individual character to the idea of *cosmos* '. For an argument that Roman Stoicism did shape Kant's thinking, see Martha Nussbaum, 'Kant and Stoic Cosmopolitanism', *The Journal of Political Philosophy*, 5:1 (1997), pp. 1–25.

[14] Hegel's famous discussion of Stoicism as 'unhappy consciousness' is *mutatis mutandis* applicable to much of classical Indian and Chinese philosophy as well. G. W. F. Hegel, *The Phenomenology of Mind*, trans. J. B. Baillie (Mineola, NY: Dover Publications, 2003), pp. 119–30. Roy Bhaskar has summarised and up-dated Hegel's analysis: 'The Stoic affects in-difference to the reality of the difference intrinsic to the power$_2$ relation in which she is held. The Sceptic even denies that it exists. The Unhappy Consciousness either (a) accepts the master's ideology and/or (b) compensates in a fantasy world of, for example, sport, soap or nostalgia'. Roy Bhaskar, *Plato Etc. The Problems of Philosophy and their Resolution* (London: Verso, 1994), p. 3.

[15] For similarities between Confucian schools and Roman Stoicism, see Warren W. Wagar, *The City of Man* (Boston, MA: Houghton Mifflin, 1963), pp. 18–22. For a general account of similarities, parallels and differences among the philosophies of the main hubs of the Old World, see Ben-Ami Scharfstein, 'Three Philosophical Civilizations: A Preliminary Comparison', in B-A. Scharfstein (ed.), *Philosophy East Philosophy West. A Critical Comparison of Indian, Chinese, Islamic and European Philosophy* (Oxford: Basil Blackwell, 1978), especially pp. 118–27. For an interesting contrast to Scharfstein's point that explicitly political thinking was mostly lacking in India, see Amartya Sen's argument about the relevance of India's ancient culture of disputation for democractic theory, 'Argument and History', *New Republic*, 233:6 (8 August, 2005), pp. 25–32, and Steve Muhlberger's somewhat speculative claim that in India in the Buddhist period, 600 BCE–200 CE, republican

instance, despite noteworthy differences between Greek and Chinese cosmologies, the Chinese too were tied to a geo-centric perspective. They depicted the Earth as being surrounded by heavens, including stars and planets, and then at times added an infinite space behind the heavens (they also talked about infinite time).[16]

Confucians have usually concurred with Plato and Aristotle in that everyone has a given, rightful place in society; and with the related ideas of applying the principles of freedom and tolerance to the privileged few, and of governance by virtue and practical reason rather than by force.[17] The characteristic Confucian emphasis on the authority of the ruler, father, and husband is similarly Aristotelian – *or vice versa*, whichever tradition should be seen as prior.[18] In these systems of thought, there is always a centre around which the whole world revolves and a hierarchy that places the centre at the top. The centre is occupied by the aristocratic (free) male who can read and write – literacy was still rare – and articulate speculative theories about nature, ethics and politics. Obviously, most ancient philosophers and scholars were beneficiaries of the rulers and aristocracy.

A cosmic perspective: the identity of human beings living on planet Earth

In 1543 CE, Nicholas Copernicus proposed to increase the accuracy and simplicity of astronomical theory by (re-)setting the Sun as the centre of the solar system. This implied a far-reaching shift of perspective: we are not observing the universe from a special position. However, the Copernican revolution – a starting point for the scientific revolutions of the 16th and 17th centuries – did not automatically generate cosmopolitanism. Rather the Copernican shift in perspective created a non-centric frame for reflexive self-observation. Moreover, by challenging the established tradition, it also constituted a space for spontaneous ethico-political learning that often resulted in tolerant cosmopolitanism.

Historically, the scientific revolution was a dialectical process. The Renaissance revival of ancient philosophies – including Stoicism – and the Atlantic voyages widened the prevailing terrestrial horizons, preparing the ground for both the new Copernican cosmology[19] and related planetary geography.[20] Although the

---

polities were common and vigorous; 'Democracy in Ancient India', available at the World History of Democracy site at: {http://www.infinityfoundation.com/mandala/h_es/h_es_muhlb_democra_frameset.htm} accessed on 8 May 2009.

[16] Joseph Needham, *Science and Civilisation in China Volume 7. Part II: General Conclusions and Reflections* (Cambridge: Cambridge University Press, 2004), pp. 24–35; and North, *Cosmos. An Illustrated History*, pp. 134–49.

[17] As pointed out, for instance, by Amartya Sen, *Development as Freedom* (Oxford: Oxford University Press, 2001), pp. 234–5.

[18] More interestingly, perhaps, the Confucian Golden Rule ('what you do not wish for yourself, do not do to others') echoes the teachings of Christianity, as do manifold debates on the real source of morality. As I have elsewhere argued, the realisation that there have been similar kinds of debates over language and reality in other times and places may also open up a more fruitful space for thinking about East and West. It is simplistic to imagine that it would be possible to synthesise either the East or the West into a coherent set of doctrines; rather there is global diversity of philosophical positions. Heikki Patomäki, 'From East to West. Emergent Global Philosophies – Beginnings of the End of Western Dominance?', *Theory, Culture & Society*, 19:3 (2002), especially pp. 100–1.

[19] Thomas S. Kuhn, *The Copernican Revolution. Planetary Astronomy in the Development of Western Thought* (Cambridge, MA: Harvard University Press, 1957).

Copernican cosmology was thus neither a strictly necessary nor a sufficient condition for cosmopolitanism, it provided a clear alternative to Aristotelian centrism. Obviously, also the meanings and values ascribed to the NGP cosmology are important.[21] The knowledge of basic physical laws and real cosmic dimensions and relations does not in itself impose cosmopolitanism; for instance that an object at rest tends to stay at rest and that an object in uniform motion tends to stay in uniform motion unless acted upon by a net external force; that $F = ma$ (force equals mass times acceleration); that the distance of the Earth from the Sun is 150,000,000 km; that the Sun is a main sequence G2 star that contains 99.86 per cent of the system's known mass and thus dominates it gravitationally; or that the Sun is only one of copious billions of stars in the galaxy and that galaxies themselves are equally numerous in the observable universe.

The new Copernican and Newtonian theories of the cosmic dimensions, laws and relations were enmeshed with various cultural and ethical assumptions that together formed an anti-centric myth about 'us' in the universe. Since then, this new planetary cosmology – in the cultural sense – has grounded criticism of the prevailing ego-centric imaginaries and related divisions and conflicts. Perhaps the best known revolutionary proponent of the Copernican cosmology was Giordano Bruno, who argued in the 16th century for an infinite universe in which every star is surrounded by its own solar system. Among other dissident ideas, Bruno also believed in cosmic pluralism, in the possibility and actuality of sentient life on other worlds, thus suggesting that humanity is a relatively insignificant part of the universe and thus creation. In 1600, in the aftermath of the French wars of religion, he was burnt at the stake as a heretic by the Roman Inquisition.[22]

However, the attitude towards the new science was soon reversed. Already in late 17th century Holland, Christiaan Huygens (1629–1695) crowned his celebrated career as a modern astronomer, mathematician and physicist by writing *Cosmotheoros. The celestial worlds discover'd: or, conjectures concerning the inhabitants, plants and productions of the worlds in the planets.*[23] In this book, which was published posthumously just months after Huygens' death, first in Latin and then in translations to several European languages, Huygens imagined a universe brimming with life both within our solar system as well as elsewhere. Humanity is not unique and Earth is just a planet among many. Among a few other works, this book paved the way for Kant's mid-18th century astronomical speculations and for the Enlightenment pluralist cosmopolitanism.

---

[20] Denis Cosgrove, 'Globalism and Tolerance in Early Modern Geography', *Annals of the Association of American Geographers*, 93:4 (2003), pp. 852–70.

[21] 'Men who believed that their terrestrial home was only a planet circulating blindly about one of infinity of stars evaluated their place in the cosmic scheme quite differently than had their predecessors who saw the earth as the unique and focal centre of God's creation. The Copernican Revolution was therefore also part of transition in Western man's sense of value.' Kuhn, *The Copernican Revolution*, p. 2. The importance of the consequences of the Copernican revolution are stressed also by Norbert Elias who distinguishes between the narrow scientific interpretation of the Copernican world-image and its impact on people's image of themselves and their place in the universe, especially in terms of emotional detachment. Norbert Elias, *Involvement and Detachment* (Oxford: Basil Blackwell, 1987), pp. 68–9.

[22] Dreyer, *A History of Astronomy*, pp. 351, 410–11, 416–7.

[23] Christiaan Huygens, *Cosmotheoros. The Celestial Worlds Discover'd: or, Conjectures Concerning the Inhabitants, Plants and Productions of the Worlds in the Planets*, trans. unknown (London: Timothy Childe, 1698). Available at: {http://www.phys.uu.nl/~huygens/cosmotheoros_en.htm} accessed on 17 June 2008.

A good example of the Enlightenment leaps of cosmic imagination is Voltaire's *Micromégas* (1752), a story of a 36,000-metre tall alien Micromégas who travels from a planet circling the star Sirius and almost by coincidence realises that there is life on our insignificant planet.[24] Through the perspective of Micromégas, Voltaire laughs at us silly humans who are killing each other in wars over religion. Voltaire's proto-science fiction satire thus takes moral distance from the Earthly disputes and wars. This kind of cosmic perspective enables and encourages distance from one's own identity and from the prevailing ideas and practices of one's own society. Of course, the cosmopolitanism of European Enlightenment was not based on merely a cosmic viewpoint, but also on the increasing familiarity with the existence and perspective of non-European others. Voltaire was influenced by the image of 'noble savages' by Baron de Lahontan's *Curious Dialogues Between the Author and a Savage of Good Sense Who Has Travelled* from 1703, on the one hand; and by invocation of China as an ancient and sophisticated civilisation, on the other.[25]

It is no coincidence that Kant the cosmopolitan started his intellectual pursuits as a cosmologist. In his *Universal Natural History and Theory of Heaven* (1755), Kant explains how one can explain the formation of the solar system from an initial state, in which matter is dispersed like a cloud, solely by means of the interaction of attractive and repulsive forces.[26] In essence, Kant's view is accepted by today's astronomy. Kant is also well-known for being one of the first to develop the concept of galaxy. Drawing on an earlier work by Thomas Wright, he speculated that a galaxy might be a rotating disk of a huge number of stars, held together by gravitational forces akin to the solar system but on a much larger scale.[27]

Cosmopolitanism is not only tied to the idea of order in nature but also to a very wide cosmic perspective on one's identity and place. Near Kant's tomb in Kaliningrad is the following inscription in German and Russian, taken from the 'Conclusion' of his *Critique of Practical Reason:* 'Two things fill the mind with ever new and increasing admiration and awe, the oftener and the more steadily we reflect on them: the starry heavens above me and the moral law within'.[28] In the *Critique*, Kant explains further that neither of these things is beyond his horizon.

---

[24] Voltaire, *Micromégas. Histoire Philosophique* (Paris: Firmin Didot, orig. probably 1752, but the precise date of publication uncertain). Available HTTP in French with the 1829 preface by Beuchot at the project Guthenberg {http://www.gutenberg.org/dirs/etext03/mcrmg10.txt} and an English edition revised by Blake Linton Wilfong {http://www.wondersmith.com/scifi/micro.htm] accessed on 22 September 2008. The tradition of science fiction novels that use a human from an alien culture or an alien stranded on Earth as a device for critiquing various aspects of society has continued since Voltaire, and Montesquieu, and Jonathan Swift. For social scientists, an especially interesting example is the humorous sci-fi book by the well-known socialist historian, social theorist and peace campaigner E. P. Thompson, *The Sykaos Papers* (London: Bloomsbury, 1988).

[25] Sankar Muthu, *Enlightenment Against Empire* (Princeton: Princeton University Press, 2003), pp. 24–7.

[26] Immanuel Kant, *Universal Natural History and Theory of Heaven*, trans. I. Johnston (Based on Georg Reimer's 1905 edition of the complete works of Immanuel Kant, orig. published 1755). Available at: {http://www.mala.bc.ca/~johnstoi/kant/kant2e.htm} accessed on 12 August 2008.

[27] For a detailed account of Wright's and Kant's contribution to our understanding of the Milky Way as a galaxy of stars, see North, *Cosmos. An Illustrated History*, pp. 444–9.

[28] Immanuel Kant, *Critique of Practical Reason*, trans. T. K. Abbott, in *Great Books of the Western World 42. Kant* (London: Encyclopædia Britannica, 1952; orig. published 1788), p. 360.

On the contrary: 'I see them before me and connect them directly with the consciousness of my existence'.[29] He also talks about 'universal and necessary connections'[30] between the starry heavens and moral law, thus maintaining that consciousness, morality and reason – far from being arbitrary – have cosmic grounds. But, may cosmically grounded morality fail on the planet Earth? Kant was at pains to show that although there is no guarantee since we cannot have certain knowledge about the future, world history *can* move towards perpetual peace and human perfection. It is possible, he argued, that in the future reason and universal moral maxims will be realised through human freedom.[31]

For a number of Enlightenment thinkers and their followers, the cosmic viewpoint puts the drama of life and human history on the planet in a very wide perspective. In one sense this is an optical effect: the longer the distance, the smaller the within-the-humanity differences appear. Moreover, distance and the non-centric Copernican perspective encourage judicious and at times ironic ethico-political sentiment towards one's own particular identity, and this sentiment is a key part of critical cosmopolitanism. In Kant's case, critical cosmopolitanism also opened up a new temporal horizon by constituting an interest in exploring possible futures that can be different – and perhaps better – than the current realities.

The cosmic vision also suggests that humans are not only dependent on each other but also on the physical processes of the planet, solar system and the universe as a whole; and on the thin sphere of life on planet Earth. Thus the new cosmological perspective encouraged scientists, philosophers, political theorists and novelists to think of all humans as part of an interdependent and fragile whole, the development of which has also given rise to consciousness, reason and morality. Awareness of the human interdependency and shared fate suggests widening the sphere within which the basic moral principles apply. Further, the idea of possible cosmic pluralism can also contribute to extending the variety of living and sentient beings with which we can identify. Any adequate form of morality has to do with the capacity to generalise normative claims in an acceptable way and, most importantly, with the ability to see things from others' point of view.[32]

---

[29] Ibid., pp. 360–1.

[30] Ibid., pp. 361.

[31] Immanuel Kant, 'Idea for a Universal History with a Cosmopolitan Intent' (1784) and 'On the Proverb: That May Be True in Theory But Is of No Practical Use' (1793), in Immanuel Kant, *Perpetual Peace and Other Essay*, trans. T. Humphrey (Indianapolis, IN: Hackett Publishing, 1988), pp. 29–40, 61–92. For an illuminating discussion, see Onora O'Neill, 'Historical Trends and Human Futures', *Studies in History and Philosophy of Science Part A*, 39:4 (December 2008), pp. 529–34.

[32] Kant's categorical imperative is critical of all forms of ego-centrism and thus treats *ego* and *alter* in strictly similar terms. Arguably, however, it still represents inadequate ethico-political learning because it cannot imagine others as different from oneself and sees no need for a democratic dialogue with concrete others. See Lawrence Kohlberg, 'The Claim to Moral Adequacy of a Highest Stage of Moral Judgment', *Journal of Philosophy*, 70:18 (1973), pp. 630–46; and Jürgen Habermas, 'Justice and Solidarity: On the Discussions Concerning "Stage 6"', in M. Kelly (ed.), *Hermeneutics and Critical Theory in Ethics and Politics* (Cambridge, MA: The MIT Press, 1990), pp. 32–52. Habermas' criticism of Kant's and Rawls' monological reasoning is in important ways similar to Jacques Derrida's discussion of the universal in terms of exemplarity that always inscribes the universal in the proper body of singularity and particularity, in Jacques Derrida, *The Other Heading. Reflections on Today's Europe*, trans. P-A. Brault & M. Naas (Indianapolis, IN: Indiana University Press, 1992).

Transformative cosmopolitanism: the rise of the notion of a world state

Probably the most radical idea of the French Revolution was that laws and institutions are man-made, not natural.[33] The Revolution demonstrated that new institutions can be created and old ones abolished. Solidarity acquired a new meaning: all together for social changes! But at that stage, very few people imagined global changes. Even Kant was basically envisaging a league of nations in Europe, realised through a constitutional treaty signed by the heads of states.[34]

While the prototypes, metaphors, framings and related conceptions of time and space stemming from the new Copernican science suggested critical cosmopolitanism, the social conditions were not favourable to their widespread distribution and adoption in their cosmopolitan form. One-way communication or transportation within Europe took weeks and across the planet months. Constant warfare – or at least threat of war – favoured the adoption of prototypes, metaphors and framings based on the category of the nation, especially during the French Revolutionary Wars (1792–1802) and Napoleonic Wars (1803–1815). Subsequently, in the nineteenth and twentieth centuries, various struggles against asymmetrical relations of power – not least those of the capitalist market economy –were framed in terms of rights and will of the people as a nation.[35]

Against all the odds, however, the idea of a global state formation emerged already during the Napoleonic wars. In 1811, an obscure German philosopher, Karl Krause proposed a world federation divided into five regional units of Europe, Asia, Africa, America and Australia. He renewed the proposal in his appeal for a united Europe in 1814. Krause was a romantic and mystical thinker that had some influence in the late-19th century and 20th century Hispanic world. Clearly, his ideal of Humanity and proposal for a Universal State extending over the whole planet stems from a cosmological framing of the human condition:

For although our earth is only a small part of the world, yet it is a complete image of the universe, and its dignity and beauty are founded primarily on its organism of life, the number and measure of its parts, and their reciprocal relation, and not on its mere individual magnitude.[36]

Bahá'u'lláh, the Persian founder of the Bahá'í Faith, developed similar ideas in the mid-19th century. While claiming to be a messenger of God, Bahá'u'lláh advocated religious freedom and fundamental unity of all religions. Bahá'u'lláh was familiar with the ideas of European radical and utopian writings and cultivated ideas of science, democracy and peace in the multicultural religious setting of the Ottoman

---

[33] This was of course ambiguous. A good example is the 1792 trial of Louis XVI, where the Jacobins, still in fear of the king's mystical persona, wanted to move quickly to execution, whereas the *de facto* more revolutionary Girondins were in favour of using legalistic method and argued that Louis was a citizen subject to ordinary justice. Alan R. How, 'Habermas, History and Social Evolution: Moral Learning and the Trial of Louis XVI', *Sociology*, 35:1 (2001), pp. 177–94.

[34] Hedley Bull, for instance, is sometimes read as suggesting that Kant was making an argument for an arrangement that in effect comes close to a world state, but also Bull clarifies that in *Perpetual Peace* Kant in fact turned to 'the negative surrogate of a league of republican or constitutional states'. Hedley Bull, *The Anarchical Society, A Study of Order in World Politics* (London: MacMillan, 1977), p. 244.

[35] See, Heikki Patomäki and Manfred S. Steger, 'Social Imaginaries and Big History: Towards a New Planetary Consciousness?', *Futures*, 41 (2009).

[36] Karl Christian Friedrich Krause, *The Ideal of Humanity and Universal Federation*, trans. W. Hastie (LLC: BiblioBazaar, 2009), p. 105.

Empire. What is especially noteworthy, however, is that he adopted cosmopolitanism and the idea of a world state.[37] For Bahá'u'lláh, humanity is a single race. Human improvement is dependent on the evolution of all humanity. It is time to start to unify humanity into a single society and state.[38]

The first one to develop a systematic account of a future world state was K'ang Yu-wei, a Chinese scholar and public intellectual who lived in the late 19th and early 20th century. Like Bahá'u'lláh, K'ang Yu-wei was a well-known moderniser, whose public mission originated in a mystical vision (that occurred to him during Buddhist meditation). However, K'ang's main book *Ta T'Ung Shu* is not a religious text, but combines autobiography, philosophy, science, social sciences and law. *Ta T'Ung Shu* – variously translated into 'The Book of Great Unity' or 'The One-World Book' – was first drafted in 1884–1885 and completed in 1902.[39]

K'ang developed a three-stage scheme for building a strictly egalitarian world federation ruled by a global parliament. In the first stage, 'The Age of Disorder at the Time the First Foundations of One World Are Laid', territorial states remain sovereign and law-making powers reside with them, yet 'the laws made by international conferences, being public law, are superior to the laws of the individual states'.[40] Functional cooperation has evolved in various issue areas, but some states may still decide to be out of any particular arrangements. There are global legal processes, however. 'All cases of international litigation are sent to the international conferences for litigation.'[41]

In stage two, in 'The Age of Increasing Peace-and-Equality, When One World Is Gradually Coming into Being', the states are gradually subsumed under the authority of global bodies. 'The laws made by the public parliament certify the laws made by the individual states'.[42] Parts of the world such as high seas – amounting to areas of the planet that Ambassador Arvid Pardo of Malta half a century later, in his 1967 speech at the UN, called 'the common heritage of mankind'[43] – would be at this point directly governed by global public bodies. Furthermore, 'there is the public government and the public parliament to deliberate on cases of undecided and divergent laws of the individual states, including cases in which the laws are defective or erroneous'.[44] K'ang's stage three, 'The Age of Complete Peace-and-Equality When One World has been Achieved' is a detailed description of a world state, run by a global parliament elected by means

---

[37] Juan R. I. Cole, *Modernity & the Millennium. The Genesis of the Baha'i Faith in the Nineteenth Century Middle East* (New York: Columbia University Press, 1998), especially chap. 4.

[38] A number of Bahá'u'lláh's sermon-like texts are available in English at: {http://www.bahaullah.com/} and {http://www.gutenberg.org/browse/authors/b#a6767} accessed on 2 July 2009.

[39] K'Ang Yu-Wei, *Ta T'Ung Shu. The One-World Philosophy of K'Ang Yu-Wei*, trans. and introduced by L. G. Thompson (London: Routledge, 2005); first published in Chinese partly in 1913 and fully in 1935; in English in 1958.

[40] Ibid., p. 107.

[41] Ibid., p. 122.

[42] Ibid., p. 107.

[43] Pardo's concept was embodied in the now ratified Law of the Sea Treaty. In the Preamble of the 1982 UN Convention for the Law of the Saw, it is stated: '*Desiring* by this Convention to develop the principles embodied in resolution 2749 (XXV) of 17 December 1970 in which the General Assembly of the UN solemnly declared *inter alia* that the area of the seabed and ocean floor and the subsoil thereof, beyond the limits of national jurisdiction, as well as its resources, are the common heritage of mankind, the exploration and exploitation of which shall be carried out for the benefit of mankind as a whole, irrespective of the geographical location of States.'

[44] K'ang Yu-wei, *Ta T'Ung Shu*, p. 109.

of universal 'one person-one vote' elections. K'ang envisages a Jacobinite world from which all borders and differences have been absolutely eliminated. All men would be equal, all property held in common, and all citizens cared for by the twenty ministries of the omnipotent world bureaucracy.[45]

What is especially interesting from the point of view of my main thesis, however, is the way K'ang frames his three-stage model of movement towards a unified world state. K'ang starts from an ethical discussion on how he has been touched by slaughters in wars ranging from a battle in the era of the Warring States to the Franco-German war of 1870–1871. He then moves on to a Confucian discussion how everything – Air, Heaven, Earth and Human – is connected. '[T]hey are all but parts of the all-embracing *ch'i* of the ultimate beginnings of the universe.'[46] The ensuing brief discussion is not only compatible with some readings of quantum mechanics (articulated as a scientific theory only decades after *Ta T'Ung Shu* was written), but K'ang's related account of the need for an ever widening horizon of moral identification is explicitly based on modern cosmology and also refers twice to the hypothesis of cosmic pluralism. K'ang was struggling with how to be able to act on his cosmic identification:

How about the living creatures on Mars, Saturn, Jupiter, Uranus, Neptune? I have absolutely no connection with them; they are too distant and obscure to expect it. I wish to love (*jen*) them, but they are so far off I have no way to do it. The size of the fixed stars, the numerousness of the galactic clusters, the nebulae and the globular clusters, the aspect of all of the heavens, my eyes themselves have seen, and my spirit has often roamed among (literally, with) them. Their states, men and women, codes of social behaviour (*li*), music, civilized pleasures, and their ways, must be vast and boundless. In the heavens as among men: although I have no way to see them; yet if they have creatures possessed of knowledge, then they will be no different in nature than we humans of this, our earth.[47]

In Victorian England, similar ideas were maturing, especially through the *persona* of H. G. Wells. From 1902 until his death in 1946, H. G. Wells preached the necessity of unifying the human species and building a world state.[48] In his 'scientific romances' of the 1890s such as *The Time Machine* (1895), *The Island of Doctor Moreau* (1896), *The Invisible Man* (1897), and *The War of the Worlds*

---

[45] Warren W. Wagar, *The City of Man*, p. 52, commented in 1963: 'K'ang's vision of world order may seem nightmarish in Western liberal eyes, but much of the Chinese way of life since 1950 under communist rule bears a startling, even a disquieting, resemblance.' Ironically, Wagar's own later scenario about a socialist democratic world state that would be established in the 2060s is not so dissimilar from K'ang's vision, yet appears as much less nightmarish – and in some ways even utopian – in his story, although it eventually collapses because of its inflexible bureaucracy and bigness. Warren. W. Wagar, *A Short History of the Future*, 3rd edition (Chicago, IL: University of Chicago Press, 1999).

[46] K'ang Yu-wei, *Ta T'Ung Shu*, p. 64.

[47] Ibid., pp. 66–7. K'ang refers to an experience of actually seeing the stars and (probably also) our planet from the outside. He may have interpreted this as a mystical experience, but in fact there are many pre-space age descriptions of how moons, planets and stars look from the space. The Copernican perspective and knowledge of the cosmic dimensions and relations enabled human imagination to envisage how things look from a cosmic viewpoint long before outer space photographs. See Ddenis Cosgrove, 'Contested Global Visions: One-World, Whole-Earth, and the Apollo Space Photographs', *Annals of the Association of American Geographers*, 84:2, (1994), especially pp. 272–3.

[48] In many of writings, Wells stressed that a world state does not have to resemble existing territorial states. Often Wells had in mind functionalist systems of global governance rather than a centralised state, although a key point was to transfer the legitimate monopoly of violence to a world body. For a good analytical discussion on Wells' political theory, see John S. Partington, *Building Cosmopolis. The Political Thought of H. G. Wells* (Aldershot: Ashgate, 2003).

(1898), Wells stretched out and expanded upon the prevailing sense of time, space and evolutionary and technological possibilities.[49] In *The Time Machine*, Wells takes his readers hundreds of thousands and, then, millions years ahead in time – in a setting of the solar system as a whole. *The Island of Doctor Moreau* discusses the ethics of biotechnologies; and *The Invisible Man* suggests the possibility of a fifth dimension. *The War of the Worlds* envisages a planetary invasion by desperate Martians whose own planet is dying.[50] These works popularised modern scientific ideas in an exciting and easily understandable way, by giving cultural meanings to the non-centric cosmology and evolutionary account of the planet.

But Wells did not write only fiction. His 1902 bestseller *Anticipations of the Reaction of Mechanical and Scientific Progress upon Human life and Thought* was probably the first work in systematic and analytical futures studies. While discussing manifold social and technological trends and possibilities, ultimately *Anticipations* was written for the political end of 'developing New Republic – a Republic that must ultimately become a World State of capable rational men, developing amidst the fading contours and colours of our existing nations and institutions'.[51] This became the key theme of the bulk of Wells' writings throughout the catastrophes of the 20th century. In *The Outline of History*, which was written immediately after, and in response to, the First World War, Wells summarised his vision of the philosophical and religious spirit of a world state, almost verging on desperation:

Our true state, this state that is already beginning, this state to which every man owes his utmost political effort, must be now this nascent Federal World State to which human necessities point. Our true God now is the God of all men. Nationalism as a God must follow the tribal gods to limbo. Our true nationality is mankind.[52]

After the Second World War, and after decades of trying his best to convince people about the necessity of a world state, Wells was giving up. He receded back to the Darwinist pessimism inherent in some of his early 'scientific romances'.[53] Talking about the divergence between his own aspirations and actual world

---

[49] All of these books are easily available in several different editions; moreover, they are in the public domain and can be freely accessed at: {http://www.gutenberg.org/browse/authors/w#a30} accessed on 17 June 2009.

[50] The story was an ambiguously ironic reversal of the fate of Tasmanians in the hands of the British colonialists. While the British were kind of Martians and Earthlings Tasmanians, in Wells' story viruses kill the 'British', not those being colonised. And yet there were elements of simplistic Manichean thinking in the story (the Martians as 'others'). For a discussion of the moral of the story, see Warren W. Wagar, *H. G. Wells. Traversing Time* (Middletown, CT: Wesleyan University Press, 2004), pp. 54–8.

[51] H. G. Wells, *Anticipations Of the Reaction of Mechanical and Scientific Progress upon Human life and Thought* (London: Chapman & Hall, 1902), available at: {http://www.gutenberg.org/etext/19229}.

[52] H. G. Wells, *(The New and Revised) Outline of History. Being a Plain History of Life and Mankind* (Garden City, NY: Garden City Publishing Company, 1931), p. 1157. The first edition was published in 1920; all together the book sold over two million copies. Characteristically, Wells explained in the revised edition that 'The *Outline of History* the writer would far prefer to his own would be the Outline of 2031; to read it and, perhaps with even more curiosity, to pour over its illustrations'; ibid., p. 6.

[53] In the early stories, evolution is seen as possibly implying the degeneration of the human species; the ultimate fate of the solar system is death as the sun becomes a red giant; and monsters, aliens and mad scientists run amok against the humanity. A gloomy section from the 11th chapter of the serial version of *The Time Machine* published in *New Review* (May 1895) was deleted from the book. This section, 'The Grey Man', is available at: {http://www.en.wikisource.org/wiki/The_Grey_Man}.

history, he declared that 'the more he weighted the realities before him the less he was able to detect any convergence whatever'.[54] Perhaps humanity is indeed just an accident that will be wiped out by its own stupidity and short-sightedness?

The reaction against the Copernican perspective: Nietzsche, etc.

The story of the cosmological sources of critical cosmopolitanism would be incomplete without at least a brief discussion on the 19th and 20th century reaction against critical cosmopolitanism and its interpretation of the meaning of the new Copernican horizon. Krause, Bahá'u'lláh, K'ang, and (most of the time) Wells, as well as Kant before them, ascribed positive and forward-looking cultural meanings and values to the NGP cosmology. They all agreed that humanity is a morally significant part of a very wide whole; that morality is not an accident but has somehow emerged from the cosmic evolution, as an essential part of it; and that our fate is shared and lies in the possibility of collective progress.

However, these meanings and values do not follow from empirical science. On the face of it, the value-neutral technical procedures of modern science would seem to entail thorough scepticism.[55] David Hume explained that we should trust only our sense-perceptions and be sceptical about anything else.[56] Friedrich Nietzsche was among the first to fully articulate the devastating impact of the positivist or empiricist sentiment (while being an empiricist himself, at least in the letter).[57] God is dead! We are alone on this insignificant planet. Nietzsche proclaimed, moreover, that no universal perspective is possible. Christianity, Kantianism, and utilitarianism are mere slave-moralities; we should be looking for something better. What is coming in the history of the next two centuries is the 'advent of nihilism'.[58]

However, Nietzsche took critical distance from the nihilism implicit in the new Copernican cosmology and the 19th century Darwinian framework of explaining the origins of humanity. A view of a planet orbiting sun in a huge void, in which

[54] H. G. Wells, *Mind at the End of Its Tether* (London: William Heinemann, 1945), p. 5.

[55] For an alternative account of the logic of science and scientific experimentation, see Roy Bhaskar, *A Realist Theory of Science* (London: Verso, 1975).

[56] According to a common interpretation, Hume mounted a sceptical attack on all forms of design arguments and teleological reasoning, in effect denying that the universe would have any meaning or purpose whatever; it just happens to be; see, for example, John D. Barrow and Frank J. Tipler, *The Anthropic Cosmological Principle* (Oxford: Oxford University Press, 1988), pp. 69–72. However, Hume was not consistent on his attitude towards objective morality or religion and also wrote things like 'the whole frame of nature bespeaks an intelligent author'; quoted in J. C. A. Gaskin, 'Hume on Religion', in D. F. Norton (ed.), *The Cambridge Companion to Hume* (Cambidge: Cambridge University Press, 1993), p. 320. Although the fear of censorship and consequences might have made Hume write contradictory statements, it seems clear that as a consistent sceptic Hume was unable and unwilling to deny the existence of God. It should be noted that for the same reason he was far less opposed to causal realism than what is often thought (for a provocative discussion of Hume as a causal realist, see John P. Wright, 'Hume's Causal Realism. Recovering a Traditional Interpretation', in R. Read and K. A. Richman (ed.), *The New Hume Debate. A Revised Edition* (London: Routledge, 2007), pp. 88–99.

[57] For a detailed analytical overview of Nietzsche's three phases and his diverse and ambivalent pursuits, see Maudemarie Clark, 'Nietzsche, Friedrich', in E. Craig (ed.), *The Shorter Routledge Encyclopedia of Philosophy* (London: Routledge, 2005), pp. 726–41.

[58] Friedrich Nietzsche, *The Will to Power*, trans. W. Kauffman and R. J. Hollingdale (New York: Vintage, 1968), p. 3.

the sun itself is located and moving, makes us lose our sense of direction and place. This is spatial nihilism. 'Are we not straying as if through an infinite nothing?'[59] At times Nietzsche displayed nostalgia for the world of ancient Greece; at other times he was suggesting the possibility of new values of life and vitality and introducing concepts such as 'overhuman', and 'will to power'.

Either way, Nietzsche's reaction was basically about going back to the ego – and geo-centric perspective of Aristotle, albeit in a more desperate way and at a new level of critical reflexivity. Nietzsche's reflections centered on the vitality, values and will-to-power of the *aristoi* ('best persons'). The perspectives of those who can differentiate themselves from the 'herds' must define relevant knowledge. Moreover, by being critical of the 'spatial nihilism' of the NPG cosmology, Nietzsche evoked a desire for a concept of worldliness, or being-in-a-place, which would overcome that nihilism. In the 20th century, this idea has been explored by various phenomenologists, Heidegger, later Wittgenstein and their followers. These explorations have at times resulted in the construction of a terrestrial ontology of earthliness that involves a territorial conception of politics.[60]

The effects of the implicit nihilism of Copernicus and Darwin have not been confined to those who have read and reflected upon Nietzsche. Rather, Nietzsche has provided a genuine insight into the cultural undercurrents of modernity. The subjectivist value-theory of neo-classical economics, for instance, comes close to what Nietzsche meant by nihilism (the marginalist theory was articulated at the time of Nietzsche).[61] Another illuminating example of the sense of nihilism is Louis Althusser, a key ideologue of the French Communist Party in the 1960s and 1970s, whose life turned into a disaster when he killed his wife in Paris in 1980. Althusser's commitment to the true meaning of Marx's theory, his 'anti-humanism', and his loyalty to the Communist Party[62] despite its hierarchies, exclusions and violence can be plausibly read as a desperate existentialist ethico-political commitment in an otherwise nihilist world.[63] Althusser's life-struggle was about trying to sustain hope by cultivating a rather orthodox, scientistic Marxian reading of societal developments that will inevitably lead to socialism and communism – to be realised through the institutions of a territorial state.

---

[59] Friedrich Nietzsche, *Thus Spoke Zarathustra*, trans. R. J. Hollingdale (Harmondsworth: Penguin Classics, 1961), p. 14.

[60] Neil Turnbull, 'The Ontological Consequences of Copernicus. Global Being in the Planetary World', *Theory, Culture & Society*, 23:1 (2006), pp. 125–39.

[61] The originators of marginalism tended to have progressivist ethico-political ideas, but the implicit Humean scepticism of neo-classical economics started to take over in the 20th century. See Milja Kurki, Jamie Morgan and Heikki Patomäki, 'Towards a New Political Economy: A Critical Dialogue with Léon Walras and Alfred Marshall', a paper in progress.

[62] See 'To My English Readers' and 'Introduction: Today', in Louis Althusses, *For Marx*, trans. B. Brewster (London: Verso, 1969), pp. 9–15, 21–39.

[63] Five years after killing his wife, Althusser wrote his memoirs where he repeats, in a Freudian language, many of the points made by Nietzsche. 'Does one have to point out that, in addition to the three great narcissistic wounds inflicted on Humanity (that of Galileo, that of Darwin, and that of the unconscious), there is a fourth and ever graver one which no one wishes to have revealed (since from the time immemorial the family has been the very site of the *sacred* and therefore of *power* and of *religion*). It is an irrefutable fact that the Family is the most powerful ideological State apparatus.' Louis Althusser, *The Future Lasts Forever. A Memoir*, trans. R. Veasey (New York: The New Press, 1993). In many ways, these memoirs constitute a tragic story of modern Europe in 1914–1989.

Conclusion: towards a new cosmological imaginary?

In the early twenty-first century, popular imagination is filled with metaphors that envisage the human world as a whole – from the 'global shopping mall' or 'global village' to the 'spaceship Earth'. The emergence of planetary dimension to everyday life of many makes it increasingly easy to identify with the cosmopolitan interpretation of the NPG cosmology. Outer space pictures of the Earth are now routinely used to stress the global nature of products, corporations and ideologies. Nietzsche, Heidegger and other sceptics notwithstanding, the blue planet 'straying as if through an infinite nothing' can be, and often is, conceived of as a home. Moreover, global warming has made it clear that the planet's cultural and ecological elements form a singular and vulnerable cosmological embrace.[64]

And yet, the permeation of the popular mind with commodified images of the planet does not resolve the underlying scientific, philosophical and ethico-political issues. What are the meanings and values that should be ascribed to the NGP cosmology? The precise nature and meaning of the NGP cosmology is something that scientists are also hotly debating. For instance, the Copernican principle that we are not observing the universe from a special position has been challenged. No scientist is arguing for a return to Aristotelian cosmology. Nothing except the moon and a few artificial satellites are revolving around the Earth. Our planet is but a tiny speck in the vastness of the cosmos.

However, there are senses in which our position is special and in which life and our consciousness can be quite central to the cosmos.[65] Already in the early 1960s, Robert Dicke noted that the age of the universe as seen by living observers is not random, but is constrained by biological factors that require it to be roughly a 'golden age'.[66] For life to evolve, the cosmos and many of its basic laws and mechanisms must have been stable for a long time. For billions of years the early universe was too simple for life as we know it to evolve, but much later the main sequence stars and stable planetary systems would have already come to an end.

The term 'anthropic principle' was first coined by the theoretical astrophysicist Brandon Carter, in his contribution to a 1973 Kraków symposium honouring Copernicus's 500th birthday. Carter articulated the Anthropic Principle as a reaction to over-reliance on the Copernican Principle, which states that we are not in a special position in the Universe. 'Although our situation is not necessarily *central*, it is inevitably privileged to some extent.'[67] Carter defined two forms of the

---

[64] Turnbull, 'The Ontological Consequences', pp. 135–7; see also, Manfred B. Steger, *The Rise of the Global Imaginary: Political Ideologies from the French Revolution to the Global War on Terror* (Oxford: Oxford University Press, 2008).

[65] This is too vast an issue to even try to list relevant references, but it consists of two parts: quantum mechanics and cosmic evolution. Quantum mechanics implies that either reality is somehow dependent on consciousness, or that the universe is intra-connected way beyond the confines of local causality. Cosmic evolution, in turn, re-raises the question of formal and teleological causality. For a tentative discussion on both issues, see Heikki Patomäki, 'After Critical Realism? The Relevance of Contemporary Science', *Journal of Critical Realism*, 9:1 (2010).

[66] Robert Dicke, 'Dirac's Cosmology and Mach's Principle', *Nature*, 192 (1961), pp. 440–1.

[67] Brandon Carter, 'Large Number Coincidences and the Anthropic Principle in Cosmology', in M. S. Longair (ed.), *Confrontation of Cosmological Theories with Observational Data* (International Astronomical Union, 1974), p. 291, available at: {http://www.adsabs.harvard.edu/abs/1974IAUS... 63..291} accessed on 14 March 2008.

anthropic principle, a weak one which referred only to anthropic selection of privileged space-time locations in the universe, and a more controversial strong form which referred to the fundamental parameters of physics. According to the strong principle, supported by many apparent large-number coincidences, the universe must be such as to admit the creation of observers within it at some stage.[68] On this basis, it is possible to build new metaphors and symbols to make sense of our special place in the universe.[69]

Similarly, the standard Darwinist interpretation of the evolution of life has been challenged. Charles Darwin himself gave some credence to the Lamarckian theory and qualified his theory by arguing that 'I am convinced that Natural Selection has been the main but not exclusive means of modification'.[70] When read from the perspective of the new theories of complexity, Darwin seems to have concurred that in addition to the blind mechanisms of short-term natural selection, also a generative diversity- and order-building mechanisms seem to have been at play, co-responsible for the order that is not accidental in terms of large time-scales and wide categories and layers of emergence of order upon order. Randomly mutating genome is unlikely to have been able to produce viable complex organisms within the known time-frames.[71] The search for causal forces and mechanisms of complexity and emergence in open systems is now on.[72]

In some ways, the early 21st century science seems to be moving towards the world views of Kant, Krause, Bahá'u'lláh, K'ang, and Wells. There is more coherence and connectedness to the universe than previously appreciated.[73] Morality has emerged from the process of cosmic evolution. In philosophy and social theory, ethics and normative theory are back. Post-Kantian critical theories are practised and taught widely. Moreover, since the 1980s, globalisation has been a key area of research and public discussion. There is a lot of talk about global

---

[68] Ibid., p. 294. The most thorough analysis of different versions of the anthropic principle is Barrow and Tipler, *The Anthropic Cosmological Principle*. See also the very different accounts of Eric J. Chaisson, *Cosmic Evolution. The Rise of Complexity in Nature* (Cambridge, MA: Harvard University Press, 2001); James N. Gardner, *Biocosm. The New Scientific Theory of the Universe: Intelligent Life is the Architect of the Universe* (Inner Ocean: Makawao, 2003); Paul Davies, *The Goldilock's Enigma. Why Is the Universe Just Right for Life?* (London: Allen Lane, 2006); and Jacob Klapwijk, *Purpose in the Living World. Creation and Emergent Evolution* (Cambridge: Cambridge University Press, 2008).

[69] This is the project of Joel Primack and Nancy Ellen Abrams, *The View from the Centre of the Universe. Discovering our Extraordinary Place in the Cosmos* (London: Fourth Estate, 2006); and, from a rather different but parallel perspective, Jennifer Gidley, 'Spiritual Epistemologies and Integral Cosmologies: Transforming Thinking and Culture'. In S. Awbrey, D. Dana, V. Miller, P. Robinson, M. M. Ryan & D. K. Scott (eds), *Integrative Learning and Action: A Call to Wholeness*. Vol. 3 (New York: Peter Lang Publishing, 2006), pp. 29–55.

[70] Charles Darwin, *The Origin of Species* (Oxford: Oxford University Press [World's Classics], 1998, originally published in 1859), p. 7.

[71] This is one of the numerous points made by Ervin Laszlo in favour of what he calls an 'integral' cosmology; Ervin Laszlo, *Science and the Reenchantment of the Cosmos. The Rise of the Integral Vision of Reality* (Rochester, VT: Inner Traditions, 2006), pp. 16–7.

[72] Stuart Kauffman, *At Home in the Universe. The Search for the Laws of Self-Organization and Complexity* (New York: Oxford University Press, 1995); Stuart Kauffman, *Investigations* (New York: Oxford University Press, 2000).

[73] For a full, critical discussion of this and related ideas, see Heikki Patomäki, 'After Critical Realism?', and my rejoinder to Nick Hostettler in the same issue of the *Journal of Critical Realism*. Furthermore, in *Global Futures. On the Temporality of the Human Condition*, a book in progress, I explore and develop the idea of Vicoan and Gramscian re-appropriation of myth for re-constructive purposes from a critical, scientific realist perspective.

governance, sustainability, justice and democracy. While the future is of course open, these developments have created a space for the re-articulation of cosmo-political visions of change in dialogical, pluralistic and open-ended terms.

Review of International Studies (2010), 36, 201–223   © 2010 *British International Studies Association*
doi:10.1017/S0260210510000902   *First published online 31 Aug 2010*

Ancient cynicism: a case for salvage

PIERS REVELL

Abstract. Taking a quote from President Obama as its starting point, this article examines the usages of the word cynicism in politics, business and International Relations. It distinguishes five different forms: accusative; reflexive; projective; cathartic and ancient. When used accusatively, the cynic is an archetype we see in others whose character or actions we wish to reproach. When used reflexively, the cynic is a social archetype we identify with ourselves. Projective cynicism is the means by which an impertinent discourse may be playfully distanced. Cathartic cynicism is a means by which mental conflict is mediated. Ancient cynicism was a utopian attempt to negotiate the contradiction between cosmopolitanism and the overwhelming reality of slavery. The article concludes that it may be worthwhile comparing and contrasting all these forms of cynicism out in the public sphere.

Piers Revell is an Associate Lecturer at the University of Plymouth where he teaches International Political Economy, Environmental Politics and International Political Theory. He took his PhD in International Relations at the LSE in 2007.

Some people will tell you that I've got my head in the clouds, that I'm still offering false hopes, that I need a reality check, that I'm a hope-monger [. . .] Nothing worthwhile in this country has ever happened unless somebody somewhere is willing to hope, when somebody is willing to stand up, somebody who's willing to stand up when they're told 'no you can't' and instead say 'yes we can'. That's how this country was founded [. . .] That's how slaves and abolitionists resisted [. . .] That's how women won the vote, how workers won the right to organise [. . .] and sit in, and go to jail, and some were beaten, and some died for freedom's cause. That's what hope is. That's what hope is, Madison, that moment when we shed our fears, and our doubts, when we don't settle for what the cynics tell us we have to accept, because cynicism is a sorry kind of wisdom.[1]

The purpose of this article is to set aside some time to reflect upon the sorry kind of wisdom referred to so powerfully by Barack Obama during his campaign for the presidency of the US. It is with some trepidation that we set out on this course, because cynicism is a word that can evoke deep emotions in people that can be hot to handle. The decision to go ahead is based upon the observation that cynicism is where a lot of the action appears to be when it comes to contemporary popular consciousness about problems of structure and agency in politics and International Relations. Therefore, at least in principle, cynicism has the potential to help us rethink some very old problems in international political theory using a vernacular that should be readily accessible to a wide audience in global civil society. The plan of what follows is first to survey the semiotics of contemporary cynicism and then juxtapose this with a case for the salvage of ancient cynicism.

---

[1] Barack Obama, 'Remarks on February 12th Primaries', Wisconsin University: Madison (12 February 2008).

What do people mean when they use the word cynicism? Perhaps the first thing to note about the words cynic, cynicism and cynical is that they are polysemous. That is to say, in modern discourse these words have a variety of possible meanings that may ostensibly seem inconsistent. That does not mean that these meanings are utterly discrete, in fact, the whole point of this article is to reflect upon the ethics of cynicism in a holistic manner.[2] When words are polysemous, careful interpreters will look for the context of the discourse within which a word is embedded in order to determine meaning. I find it useful to break these contexts down into five groups:

1) Accusative;
2) Reflexive;
3) Projective;
4) Cathartic;
5) Ancient.

Obviously this typology is not necessarily meant to be exhaustive. Other people might wish to cut the cake differently.

1. Accusative

When the words cynical and cynicism are used in an accusative context the cynic is a social archetype we see in others whose character or actions we hold up for deep reproach or condemnation (for example, 'they're so cynical', 'the cynicism of this decision beggars belief', 'this example of negative campaigning is pure cynicism', etc.).

A cynical character is often evoked when people want to conjure up an image of the misanthrope who has a disposition to find fault or see the worst in somebody, or the worst in humanity in general. This individual has an unattractive propensity to disbelieve in the possibility of human sincerity or goodness, particularly when it comes to the conduct of politics, business and International Relations. This is allied with a tendency to sneer or snipe at those who are greater than oneself, or those who are attempting something greater than oneself. In this manner, the great and the good amongst us are brought down by the small and the mean.

On the right the cynical character often appears as the enemy within, who has a propensity to turn national and international self images, identities, institutions and principles into objects of ridicule:

What is that threat? It is the New British Disease: the self destructive sickness of national cynicism. It is spread by so called opinion formers within the British elite. The disease shows itself in a readiness to denigrate our country and praise others; to devalue our achievements, and envy others, to hold our national institutions in contempt, to deride every one of our national figures [...] Too many politicians, academics, churchmen, authors, commentators and journalists exhibit the full-blown symptoms of this disease.[3]

---

[2] To my knowledge, the first person to attempt this in a systematic manner was Peter Sloterdijk, *Critique of Cynical Reason*, trans. Michael Eldred (London: Verso, 1988).

[3] Michael Portillo, 'Cynicism, the new British disease', *The Observer* (16 January 1994).

The cynic is not just a negative irritant, but a clear and present danger to national security. He is a disease in the body politic. He is a perennial problem for political authority because he undermines that essential bond of trust between the statesman and the people upon which authority and government is based.

On the left the cynical archetype will usually appear as an apostle of apathy, with a formidable talent for persuading humanity to submit to the overwhelming power of circumstances. One of his habitual vices is mockery toward those who seek to make things better by tilting at the way things are. This makes the cynic a natural ally of the *status quo*. The task of the progressive modern prince is thus to isolate and cast out the mocker:

> It's the same message we had when we were up, the same message when we're down, that out of the many, we are one, that our destiny will not be written for us, but by us, and that we can cast off our doubts and fears and cynicism because our dreams will not be deferred, and our future will not be denied, and our time for change has come.[4]

Ah yes, that sorry kind of wisdom. Cynicism may be a kind of wisdom, but it is sorry wisdom in that its only contribution is to work upon doubts and fears that induce incredulity toward hope for positive change. It is sorry because its highest ambition can only ever be to be a counsel of despair:

> We must awaken and ignite in our people the hope that change can bring, because the last weapon the Tories have, you know their final weapon, is despair and cynicism. It's telling people well it doesn't matter who's in power 'cos they're all the same, it'll make no difference, nothing can ever change. Rubbish. Of course things can change. When they say 'don't let Labour ruin it' I say to them 'Britain can be better than this.'[5]

In such discourses, the cynic is thus a perennial problem for progressive politics because he always threatens to sap the strength of will for collective action for the common good. Major victories against him thus deserve to be celebrated. This mood was evident, for example, in the early 'new dawn has broken' salad days of the Blair government:

> On the 1st May 1997, it wasn't just the Tories who were defeated. Cynicism was defeated. On the 1st May 1997, fear lost. Hope won. The giving age began.[6]

But evidently, cynicism can never be defeated decisively, once and for all, because fighting cynicism became a perennial theme of the Blair government. When campaigning for Africa, Blair was fighting 'the cynics back home'.[7] When speaking in the Commons in favour of military intervention in Iraq, Blair was defending the 'coalition of the willing' against European cynicism about its motives.[8] And then, in his last speech as Prime Minister, came that final plaintive appeal:

> We devote reams of space to debating why there is so much cynicism about politics and public life. In this, politicians are obliged to go into self-flagellation, admitting it is our own

---

[4] Barack Obama, 'Remarks on February 12th Primaries', Wisconsin University: Madison (12 February 2008).

[5] Tony Blair, excerpt from a Labour Party general election broadcast (24 April 1997).

[6] Tony Blair, 'Speech to the Labour Party Annual Conference', Brighton (September 1997).

[7] Jackie Ashley, 'Party Chiefs to Tackle Cynicism', *The Guardian* (11 February 2002).

[8] Blair's PM speech in the debate over the House of Commons amendment approving the use of 'all means necessary to ensure the disarmament of Iraq's weapons of mass destruction', *Hansard* (18 March 2003), column 771.

fault. And, believe it or not, most politicians come into public life with a desire to do the right thing not the wrong thing.[9]

This common desire of all politicians to do the right thing, the virtue ethics imperative, brings us neatly to the question of cynical action. When it comes to action, the cynic stands accused as the agent who can transcend the inhibitions of public shame or private conscience. The cynical agent acts against better knowledge. The cynic is someone who has done wrong knowingly, or is capable of doing wrong knowingly ('they know what they do'). This conception of cynicism is deeply embedded within the psychological engine room of Western norms about political agency.

For example, the convention of ministerial responsibility, a central plank of British constitutional theory, holds that governments are made accountable through its ministers to Parliament. In order to hold ministers accountable to Parliament we have an agreed set of rules known as the *Ministerial Code*.[10] Under section 1 of this code principle 3 states that:

It is of paramount importance that Ministers give accurate and truthful information to Parliament, correcting any inadvertent error at the earliest opportunity. Ministers who knowingly mislead Parliament will be expected to offer their resignation to the Prime Minister.[11]

The 'unwelcome adverb' *knowingly*, as Tomkins calls it, was inserted by John Major in a deft response to the Nolan Committee on *Standards in Public Life*.[12] In politics it is not necessarily fatal if you do wrong in error or ignorance (in fact to admit this will sometimes get you off the hook), but if you are successfully accused of doing wrong knowingly you are usually in trouble, because you have been caught committing a *cynical act*.

It is around the subtle adverb *knowingly* that the Scott, Hutton and Butler inquiries all danced around the controversy over democratic accountability in British foreign policy. Scott perhaps came closest to the accusative, stating that a minister had been 'designedly uninformative' to Parliament about the decision to sell various components of weapons of mass destruction to Iraq, but then undermined this with the paradoxical conclusion that he had no 'duplicitous intention'.[13] With Lord Hutton, the judgement was that the Government did not knowingly add false claims to the JIC dossier on Iraq. Famously, a psychoanalytical distinction between the conscious and the unconscious was used to account for some of the evidence which might have led to an alternative judgement. Hutton considered that the 'possibility cannot be completely ruled out' that the Prime Minister had:

subconsciously influenced Mr Scarlett and the other members of the JIC to make the wording of the dossier somewhat stronger than it would have been if it had been contained in a normal JIC assessment.[14]

[9] Tony Blair, 'Our Nation's Future – On Public Life', Speech delivered at Reuters on Canary Wharf, London (12 June 2007).
[10] *Ministerial Code: A Code of Ethics and Procedural Guidance for Ministers*, published by the Cabinet Office, July 2005. Available at: {http://www.cabinetoffice.gov.uk}.
[11] Ibid., p. 1.
[12] Adam Tomkins, *The Constitution After Scott: Government Unwrapped* (Oxford: Oxford University Press, 1998), pp. 41–5.
[13] Sir Richard Scott, *Report of the Inquiry into the Export of Defence Equipment and Dual Use Goods to Iraq and Related Prosecutions* (London: HMSO, 1996), see paras D3.107 & D3.124.
[14] Lord Hutton, *Report of the Inquiry into the Circumstances Surrounding the Death of David Kelly* (London: HMSO, 2004), para. 467, pp. vi & vii.

In some dark recess of his unconscious mind then, the Prime Minister may have half suspected that he was attempting to cajole the nation into an unpopular war through the misuse of unreliable intelligence about weapons of mass destruction, but in this clarification of the convention of ministerial responsibility it is only the conscious mind that can be held to account. Meanwhile, for Butler, it is acknowledged that the intelligence released to the British public was misleading, but this was due to collective errors of government and there is no evidence of deliberate distortion.[15] In short, in order to commit a cynical act you have to be conscious that you are acting against better knowledge when you are doing it.

2. Reflexive

When the words cynical and cynicism are used within a reflexive context the cynic is a social archetype who, in contrast to the accusative sense above, we claim to recognise in ourselves, or with whom we can identify strongly ('I am cynical', 'we are cynical', or 'they have reason to be cynical'). Often this reflexivity is used rather crudely as a counter-accusative position. If we pick up the example of debate over British foreign policy again, for example, it was common for people to admit that they were cynical, but then argue that responsibility for this lay with the cynicism of those who took Britain into war. 'Cynicism breeds cynicism' is generally the message. But the internalisation of cynicism, once initiated, does tend to take people on a journey, and thus what was once just a simple reflex can quickly become rather more complex.

Let us follow this journey for a short while.

Experience of life somehow drives the cynic to the conclusion that hypocrisy matters a lot and this compels him to draw attention to any evidence of it. Suggestions that the motivation behind this is a desire to tear down the authority of morality are not quite right. Rather, ethics has become a serious business, perhaps too serious, and cannot live easily within its own contradictions. The reflexive cynic tends to profess contempt for the promulgation of ethics with limited liability. Reflexive cynicism involves an irresistible temptation to observe contradictions between words and actions – between what is said and what is done. In reflexive cynicism, the conscious mind is always already on the lookout for betrayal by the unconscious, being only too alive to the human capacity for self-deception.

The reflexive cynic will often be the conscious subject of alienation and disillusionment. Surprise! The gap between words and actions is more universal than we had previously thought. The gap also exists for people on my own side. This is a road that leads to many destinations of disillusion. Once bitten, twice shy, the cynic begins to develop a stance of incredulity toward countless national and transnational self-images, identities, institutions, organisations and values. The cross she has to bear is that of being the perpetual party pooper, with a compulsion for blurting out truths that are not welcome. One way of offsetting this, of course, is playful self-deprecation about the contradiction between one's own words and actions.

[15] Lord Butler, *The Review of Intelligence on Weapons of Mass Destruction* (London: HMSO, 2004).

The reflexive cynic becomes a world weary advocate for experience over hope and has an acute sensitivity to the human capacity for making things worse by trying to make things better. He will frequently invoke the law of unintended consequences. The default disposition is to question the wisdom of action, and of course the deeper motives behind seeking to act. The reflexive cynic becomes wary of the call to arms for progress. Watch out, this could be bad for your health! He will also warn you against the futile gesture. Stand up and be counted? Don't be a fool! Keep your head down and wait 'til all the fuss has blown over. There is a corresponding intolerance toward facile optimism. Pessimism of the intellect allied with optimism of the will? Give me a break!

The way reflexive cynicism translates into action is not always predictable. Sometimes it can lead, as has previously been argued, towards a conscious stance of inaction: apathy rules ok! Why bother to do anything when it only encourages them? Baudrillard once lambasted righteous indignation about this form of political action and toyed with its possibilities.[16] The mass withdrawal into the private sphere and the ensuing collapse in participation produces a silence that refuses to be spoken for in its name. The game of political representation consequently implodes into the TV centre studios. The story starts to become about how well the political parties are presenting their story in their reality game-show. Baudrillard's armchair gambit was that there comes a tipping point where apathy ceases to be an asset to the powerful and starts to mature into a crisis of legitimacy.

On the other hand, reflexive cynicism can often express itself as agency with stamina. This archetype is the reflexive cynical activist who has 'seen them come and go' and somehow survived the relentless disappointments of active service. The survival of cynical agency amidst disillusionment thus becomes a daily anti-heroic act. The health of civil society relies on this psychological strategy for survival in action perhaps more than most people seem to realise. After all, who would you rather have fighting on your side: the naïve idealist who may not turn up tomorrow or the hardened veteran who has learned to 'expect the worst' and 'be ready for anything'?

Most of us cannot afford to give up the day job though, and so a lot of reflexive cynicism tends to express itself at work. Cynicism in the workplace will often be low level disillusionment with what one is doing. Reflexive cynicism can occur where we know what we are doing and can see where it will all lead us in the end, but we still do it because:

in the short run, the force of circumstances and the instinct for self-preservation are speaking the same language, and they are telling us that it has to be so. Others would do it anyway, perhaps worse.[17]

Take the new initiative that comes from the top that everybody knows will end in chaos but has to be implemented anyway. Together we boldly strive to go through the motions of compliance whilst struggling to contain that burgeoning bubble of disbelief. Take the dodgy dealings we might be asked to overlook or the exploitative relations that must be tolerated until we might be able to manoeuvre ourselves into a position to do something about it. In order to survive at work,

---

[16] Baudrillard, *In the Shadow of the Silent Majorities* (New York: Semitext, 1983).
[17] Peter Sloterdijk, *Critique of Cynical Reason* (London: Verso, 1988), p. 5.

people have to choose their fights carefully. Together we learn how to cope with the psychic fallout that comes with the pragmatic compromise of making such calculations in everyday life. This is all fruitful ground for the formation of reflexive cynicism.

Other reflexive cynical actors tend to flourish in jobs where people are employed to mop up and pick up the pieces shattered by a crazy world. The classic film MASH played upon this phenomenon. As the characters demonstrate in action, cynicism can be a healthy tactic for dealing with the grotesque absurdity of certain extreme situations, like trying to provide healthcare in a war zone. Some employees of NGOs are perhaps amongst the most thoughtful reflexive cynics one could ever have the pleasure to meet. Reflexive cynics in action often like to think they will be the ones left behind to 'keep the show on the road' when 'the shit hits the fan' and 'all the optimists have gone off to be optimistic somewhere else'.

3. Projective:

Here the cynic is neither the object of condemnation nor identified with the self, but an imaginary other who gives voice to scurrilous thoughts. The cynic becomes an anonymous citizen upon whom insolent observations may be safely projected. This is common in the media where the interlocutor has half a mind on the private thoughts of his viewer or listener, but the habit is a hardy perennial at all levels of civil society. Projective cynicism is the means by which an impertinent discourse may be playfully distanced (for example, 'I suppose a cynic would say you are just [. . .]', 'a cynical friend of mine said to me the other day that this is all about [. . .]'). The projective cynic is the hypothetical nobody who, because he only exists in the inter-subjective ether, can tell the emperor what many are thinking in private but which few are prepared to tell him directly. The clever emperor will often tolerate or even play along with this up to a point, partly because this information is useful (how else is he going to find out?), and partly because the news is sugared by the playful humour of distance. Every emperor needs to patronise a joker in his court. But the spell is broken if the joker lets the pretence of anonymity slip, because that is a direct challenge and thus a potential threat.

4. Cathartic

With cathartic cynicism the stakes have been raised markedly, because it is the flip side of 'they know what they do'. Once sensitised, one can also learn to listen out for 'I know what I do'. Here we are usually talking about people with real power over real lives, where reflexive cynicism is burdened with a much heavier caseload.

Sometimes it is best here to see the cathartic cynic as a mediator in a mental conflict, where all those years of power have brought changes that have divided the mind against itself:

In mental conflict a mind is divided against itself, and becomes a battleground of opposing beliefs or desires. The conflicted mind is characterised by relations not just of difference and divergence, but of contention and confrontation. It feels not so much attracted from outside by incompatible alternatives between which it has to make a choice, as torn within itself by hostile forces between which it cannot make peace. It is aware not just of contrasting considerations that need to be brought together in an exercise of judgement, but of colliding tendencies that refuse to co-exist within a single perspective.[18]

The mind splits, but the two rival parties still somehow have to live under the same roof. It is like an old couple who cannot bear to speak to each other anymore but use their children in order to communicate. In politics, business and war, 'it is easy to get one's hands dirty and it is often right to do so'.[19] But an occupational hazard for those whose profession is to shoulder responsibility for the 'dirty work' is the compulsion to be frank. The problem of course is that in mental conflict, as in any conflict, truth is the first casualty of war, but sometimes the dissonance reaches levels of such intensity that a desire grows to turn the truth back into a simple concept again.[20] The low ethics puts out a feeler toward the high ethics and seeks an armistice in order to talk. Rival parties within a mental conflict then meet to be frank with one another under the supervision of a trusted third-party. In this instance of cathartic cynicism the cynic often acts as if he is speaking to you, the third party, but slowly it becomes obvious that he is actually talking to a rival part of himself.

In other cases cathartic cynicism is rather looking for confirmation in another. That is to say, a low ethics seeks conspiratorial release with the low ethics of a fellow subject. The first tentative moves toward this kind of catharsis are often subtle, humorous and deniable (did he really mean that or didn't he?). But then, if a cynical signal is reciprocated, the game of mutual disinhibition can begin. The wry observations, witticisms and confidences of a governing consciousness that has learned 'how not to be good' starts to flow, maybe after a couple of drinks:

For there is such a gap between how one lives and how one ought to live that anyone who abandons what is done for what ought to be done learns his ruin rather than his preservation: for a man who wishes to make a vocation of being good at all times will come to ruin among so many who are not good. Hence it is necessary for a prince who wishes to maintain his position to learn how not to be good.[21]

Cathartic cynicism could thus be seen as a habitual discourse for dealing with the cognitive dissonance that takes place when principles and norms encounter the necessity of their violation. Usually this takes place in confidence within the private sphere, which is why it is not easy to gather concrete evidence to ascertain how widespread cathartic cynicism is. It is usually best represented in fictional literary characters whose words somehow capture the essence of people's own private encounters with cathartic cynicism. One indicator of the prevalence of cathartic cynicism can thus be judged by the literary success of a cathartic cynic in fiction – by the zeitgeist that he personifies. Think the Grand Inquisitor. Think Harry Lime. Think Gordon Gecko.

[18] A. W. Price, *Mental Conflict* (London and New York: Routledge, 1995), pp. 1–2.
[19] M. Walzer, 'Political action: the problem of dirty hands', *Philosophy and Public Affairs*, 2 (1973), quoted in C. A. J. Coady, 'Politics and the Problem of dirty hands', in Peter Singer (ed.), *A Companion To Ethics* (Oxford: Blackwell, 1991).
[20] As Iain McDonald, head of the Ministry of Defence's Defence Sales Secretariat wistfully put it in oral evidence to the Scott Inquiry, 'Truth is a difficult concept'. See Richard Norton-Taylor, *Truth is a Difficult Concept: Inside the Scott Inquiry* (London, Fourth Estate, 1995).
[21] Machiavelli, *The Prince*, ch. XV.

Sometimes though, the low ethics becomes so confident of its position in the structure of things that the high ethics feels like a cumbersome mask, and so it is allowed to slip – a holiday is taken away from the tiresome obligation to legitimate. So you really want the truth? Well here it is. How do you like it?

In its cynicisms hegemonic power airs its secrets a little, indulges in semi- self-enlightenment, and tells all [. . .] The more a modern society appears to be without alternatives, the more it will allow itself to be cynical. In the end, it becomes ironical about its own legitimation.[22]

Where there is only one game in town, cathartic cynicism often feels it can afford to be less careful about its confidences. At last! The low ethics can come out of the closet, flaunt its amorality and tell the truth about itself – often dressed as wit. We can sometimes identify it as cathartic when it makes us laugh and then, momentarily, we pause with shocked wonder at our laughter.

5. Ancient cynicism

A fascinating thing about ancient cynicism is that it has semantic links to all the disparate meanings of cynicism above – the root of them all. Of course we have to acknowledge Saussure's point that the history of a word does not necessarily mean everything and that each word in any given language has a valid existence apart from its etymology.[23] Nevertheless, juxtaposing modern cynicism with ancient cynicism is, I would argue, an important step for transforming our 'sorry kind of wisdom' into a more life-affirming one.

The first thing we need to understand is that ancient cynicism was about inclusion and exclusion in the classical *polis*. The word cynic is derived from the Greek word for dog (*kun*). It was applied to a social movement that began in the 4th century BC and persisted late into the Roman Empire until it was crowded out by the rise of Christianity. To be a cynic was to be a dog. To be cynical (*kunikos*) was to be 'dog-like'.[24]

In human thought, the perceived traits and characteristics of animals have often been used to describe or express normative judgements about people. If we think someone is greedy, we might call him a pig. If we think someone is lazy, we might call him a sloth. If we think someone is crafty, we might call him a fox. And so it goes. Nowadays, most of us are aware that these metaphors are anthropomorphic even as we use them, and that they say more about our feelings toward human nature than they do about the animals themselves. We know that the pig is not really greedy, the sloth is not really lazy, the fox not crafty, etc. Rather, animals often represent aspects of ourselves.[25] So, what aspects of the human condition were the people of classical antiquity referring to when they classified the adherents of a particular social movement as 'dog-like'?

[22] Peter Sloterdijk, *Critique of Cynical Reason* (London: Verso, 1987), pp. 111–2.
[23] Terence Hawkes, *Structuralism and Semiotics* (London: Methuen, 1977), p. 20.
[24] C. T. Onions (ed.), *The Oxford Dictionary Of English Etymology* (Oxford: Oxford University Press, 1966), p. 240.
[25] James Serpell, 'From paragon to pariah: some reflections on human attitudes to dogs', in James Serpell (ed.), *The Domestic Dog: its evolution, behaviour and interactions with people* (Cambridge: Cambridge University Press, 1995), p. 254.

From the extant literature, it would seem that Hellenic attitudes toward the dog strongly resemble those of many other societies since human beings first struck up an alliance with it back in the Upper Palaeolithic, including our own. Sometimes the dog is a paragon amidst the animal kingdom, at other times a pariah and outcast.[26]

On the plus side, the dog was an important guardian within a human society where security was an important value. The barking of dogs gave the *polis* and the *oikos* advance warning of the approach of the potentially predatory foreigner. At the micro-political level of the *oikos*, they could also be bred and trained to be an effective deterrent in themselves. In Homer's *Odysseus*, for example, we find an instance where 360 fatted hogs are guarded at night by:

four dogs, as savage as wild beasts, trained by the master swineheard.[27]

The dogs fly toward Odysseus when they catch sight of him approaching, and the swineherd has to call them off:

'Old man, that was a narrow escape! The dogs could have almost torn you to pieces in a moment'[28]

360 fatted hogs is an awful lot of money in Homer's world, and the poet himself assures us in the narrative that Odysseus might have suffered a savage attack. Security was a serious business and these dogs were trained to maim or even kill.

Secondly, dogs often made a contribution to the wealth of the Greek household. The hunting dog actually helped to put food on the table. Some have argued that the human and the wolf domesticated each other through a mutually beneficial hunting alliance between the two species.[29] When Odysseus returns to his homestead after twenty years of exile he meets Argus his old hunting dog who, in his prime, had gone after wild goats, deer and hares:

'you'd be astonished at his speed and power. No game that he gave chase to could escape him in the deepest depth of the forest. He was a marvel too at picking up the scent.'[30]

Thirdly, the dog was the master's loyal companion and friend. When Argus sees Odysseus he pricks up his ears and wags his tail. He is the only sentient being that can still spontaneously recognise the master of the household despite his beggar's rags and the ravages of time. The faithful dog is always pleased to see his master, will always provide the affection that is not contingent upon worldly success or outward appearance, and the master will usually be delighted to receive it because it provides him with feelings of unconditional acceptance.[31] In this respect the dog may often be closer to its master than any other member of his household. Argus can remember Odysseus better than the archetypal loyal son Telemachus, quicker even than his own wife Penelope. The feeling seems to be mutual. As Argus dies, Odysseus the sacker of cities, archetypal hard man of the Western world, brushes 'away a tear'.[32] Our master loves his dog.

[26] Serpell, 'Paragon to pariah', pp. 246–7.
[27] Homer, *The Odyssey*, trans. E. V. Rieu (London: Penguin, 1991), p. 207.
[28] Homer, *Odyssey*, p. 208.
[29] James Serpell, 'Paragon to pariah', p. 247.
[30] Homer, *Odyssey*, p. 263.
[31] Lynette A. Hart, 'Dogs as human companions: a review of the relationship', in James Serpell, 'Paragon to pariah', p. 164.
[32] Homer, *Odysseus*, p. 263.

On the other hand, the ability of the Greek dog to inveigle his way into the heart of his master was also capable of inspiring human suspicion, denigration and hostility. Ever since his first alliance with hunter-gatherers some 12,000 years ago, the dog has patrolled that uncertain boundary line that divides nature and man.[33] The dog is thought to be the first animal to be domesticated by man and as such, represents the domestication of nature and the domestication of the human subject himself. Consequently, when the dog absentmindedly reveals too much of his animal nature and fails to live up to his quasi-human status (for example when he shits or shags in public, sniffs or licks his genitals) he reminds humanity of the animal within man. Sometimes, the dog also represents the beast lurking under the skin of domesticated nature waiting to exploit the fragility of civilisation. In the *Iliad*, whenever Homer really wants to drive home the pathos of human conflict, he begins to talk about the eating habits of dogs in times of war.[34]

The dog's loyalty, its boundless affection, its eagerness to please, its readiness to accept the master as the dominant partner, also appears to have provoked mixed feelings. As in our own society this was part of what made the Greek dog so therapeutic and appealing, but on a bad day such behaviour might be construed as fawning, sycophantic and obsequious.[35] Sometimes friendship between the unequal can begin to cloy. On other bad days the faithfulness of the dog might also begin to press ethical claims upon its master that engenders a burdensome sense of guilt when it comes to treating him just like any other domesticated animal. If times were hard a good dog might have to be sold, abandoned, killed or even eaten. Cynicism is partly about the fact that humans are capable of constructing complex psychological defence mechanisms to protect a divided mind from conflict. Perceiving dogs in an ambivalent light made it easier to both love them and dispose of them with a clear conscience. The Greek word for dog, when projected onto humans, thus logically accumulated insulting or disparaging connotations, denoting baseness, illegitimacy, shame or inferiority.[36]

In ancient Greece, there were also populations of feral dogs, without any owner or a home to go to. As with modern feral populations, such dogs had to fend for themselves, scavenging off the carrion and the rubbish thrown out by the *oikos* and the *polis*. According to Serpell, feral populations of dogs were commonplace just beyond the walls of the classical *polis*. The word dog could thus also be used as an insult when a group of people were getting ready to *other* someone into a human outcast, exile, refugee or migrant. This person would thus have to live a dog's life of scavenging and begging along the margins of Hellenic society.

We have tried to convey something of the ambivalence that the Greek word for 'dog' signified when applied to the human subject. What remains to be described is why a social movement might be prepared to step forward and actually call itself 'doglike' with pride and self-assurance. What did the Greek think he was doing

[33] James Serpell, 'Hair of the dog', *The Domestic Dog*, p. 261.

[34] For example, when Priam contemplates defeat in the Trojan war, he forecasts that: 'the dogs I reared in the house and at my own table to guard the doors will lie in the gateway with their hearts excited by gnawing my bones [...] when an old man has been killed and the dogs are mutilating his grey head and grey beard and private parts, this is the most pitiful sight that poor mortals can see.' Homer, *The Iliad*, trans. Martin Hammond (London: Penguin, 1987), pp. 352–3.

[35] James Serpell, 'From Paragon to Pariah', p. 252.

[36] Martha Nussbaum, *The Fragility of Goodness: luck and ethics in Greek tragedy and philosophy* (New York: Cambridge University Press, 1986), p. 414.

when he agreed to collude with and even encourage the identification of himself as a cynic?

All social movements are complex things that contain a large number of individuals with a huge variety of sometimes contradictory desires, motivations, and objectives. To abstract is to vulgarise, to fail to do justice to the richness of social movements, all the characters who participate in them, and all the scholars who write about them. Ancient cynicism is no exception to this rule, but if I had to put my head on the block and sum it up in one sentence I would say it was a utopian attempt to find a resolution to the mental conflict which arose from the contradiction between the concept of the unity of mankind in Greek thought and the overwhelming reality of slavery.

This assertion is contestable on two counts. Firstly, it is generally accepted that a concept of the unity of mankind did emerge in antiquity, germinating out of Homer and the pre-Socratics, and evolving into a more mature stage in the thought of the Stoics.[37] But it is not always accepted that the development of the idea of the unity of mankind prompted any critique of the ancient institution of slavery. Indeed, a more common view is well articulated by Fogel:

> For 3,000 years – from the time of Moses to the end of the 17th century – virtually every major statesman, philosopher, theologian, writer and critic accepted the existence and legitimacy of slavery. The word 'accepted' is chosen deliberately, for these men of affairs and moulders of thought neither excused, condoned, pardoned, nor forgave the institution. They did not have to; they were not burdened by the view that slavery was wrong. Slavery was considered to be part of the natural scheme of things.[38]

Such views are not so very difficult to counter. The classic reference is to Aristotle's *Politics* (1253b20–23). Here Aristotle candidly states that he *has* been burdened by arguments suggesting that slavery is wrong:

> Others say that it is contrary to nature to rule as master over slave, because the distinction between slave and free is one of convention only, and in nature there is no difference, so that this form of rule is based on force and is therefore not just.[39]

Aristotle was clearly convinced that such arguments were worthy enough for him to have to pick up the challenge. He then sets about his famous defence of slavery, arguing that it is not only necessary but natural and just. The game of critique and counter-critique seems to be well under way, and the opening moves have already been worked out for Aristotle's students to learn and practice.

Unfortunately, Aristotle does not tell us who the critics of slavery were. The second reason why my assertion that ancient Cynicism was an attempt to resolve the mental conflict arising from the contradiction between the emergence of cosmopolitan thought and the existence of slavery is contestable is that modern classical scholarship usually identifies the Sophists as the prime suspects.[40] In

---

[37] The classic narrative is H. C. Baldry, *The Unity of Mankind in Greek Thought* (Cambridge: Cambridge University Press, 1965).

[38] R. W. Fogel, *Without Consent or Contract*, p. 201. Quoted in Peter Garnsey, *Ideas of Slavery from Aristotle to Augustine* (Cambridge: Cambridge University Press, 1996), p. 9.

[39] Aristotle, *The Politics*, trans. T. A. Sinclair (London: Penguin, 1962, p. 63.

[40] See, Robert Schlaifer, 'Greek theories of slavery from Homer to Aristotle', in M. Finley (ed.), *Slavery in Classical Antiquity* (Cambridge: Heffer, 1960); Giuseppe Cambiano, '*Aristotle and the anonymous opponents of slavery*', in M. Finley (New Jersey: Totowa, 1987); Joseph Vogt, *Ancient Slavery and the Ideal of Man* (Cambridge: Harvard University Press, 1975).

support of this a fragment known to be written by a Sophist called Alcidamas is usually cited:

God has set all men free; nature has made no man a slave[41]

Sometimes this is backed up with another fragment from the Sophist Antiphon:

By nature we are born alike in all respects, barbarians and Greeks[42]

These may then be compared with quotes from the tragedian Euripides, who was said to have associated with and been influenced by prominent Sophists, and whose plays furnish a wealth of instances where the victims of slavery appear to be represented in a sympathetic manner. On top of this it has been pointed out that the arguments cited by Aristotle bear the tell tale signs of an Older Sophist at work. The distinction between nature (*physis*) and convention (*nomos*), for example, were classic Sophistic terms used for debating matters ethical and political.

I certainly would not care to dismiss the view that the Sophists made a major contribution to the development of Cosmopolitan thought and that they may have been the first to express profound doubts about the legitimacy of slavery. However, what I would like to suggest is that by the time Aristotle was sitting down to write the *Politics*, he would have been aware of two philosophers who had both the motivation and the ability to take the critique of slavery to a new level of sophistication. The first of these was Antisthenes and the second was Diogenes.

We don't know much about Antisthenes, but what we do know is suggestive. We know that he was first a student of Gorgias, one of the most eminent Sophists after Protagoras, which would have made him a fellow student of Alcidamas, whose anti-slavery fragment we have already mentioned.[43] After this Antisthenes was said to have become a follower and close companion of Socrates. In the *Phaedo*, Plato is happy to relate that Antisthenes was with Socrates in prison in the last few hours of his life. We know that he was the bastard son of an Athenian and a Thracian slave, and was thus not entitled to register as an Athenian citizen.[44] This is an interesting contradiction between the historical Socrates and the Platonic Socrates, because in the *Republic* Plato repeatedly has Socrates warn that bastards should not be admitted into higher education.

Why is the foundation stone of Western political theory so keen to exclude the bastard? One possibility is that it was because the Athenian bastard sits at the nexus between politics and International Relations. Therefore, an educated bastard might prove to be a very volatile agent in a society structured according to the division between the foreign slave and the native master. Being the fruit of a power relationship between his master father and his slave mother Antisthenes, like all Athenian bastards, would have contained the primary contradiction of Hellenic society at the very core of his being.

Sometimes fate would determine that the bastard would fall into the slave side of the Greek household. In other cases fate would smile on the bastard and he

---

[41] Quoted in Giuseppe Cambiano, 'Aristotle and the anonymous opponents of slavery', p. 24.
[42] Cambiano, 'Aristotle and the anonymous opponents of slavery', pp. 30–1.
[43] Guthrie, *The Sophists* (Cambridge: Cambridge University Press, 1971), p. 305.
[44] Diogenes Laertius, *Lives of Eminent Philosophers*, vol. 2, trans. R. D. Hicks (London: Heinemann, 1925), trp. 3.

might actually become the object of paternal love, though this love, like the master's love for his favourite dog, would inevitably be mixed with feelings of ambivalence. Out of such prospects some bastards were able to eke out a relatively comfortable existence. There are characters in Greek tragedy, for example, where the bastard son does find a *niche* within the classical *polis*. As for the bastard's feelings toward his mother, this must surely have been the wild card of antiquity. Most would surely have taken the easier option of disowning the shameful status of the breasts at which they had once so eagerly suckled. But what if an upwardly mobile bastard was capable of retaining this love for his mother as well as developing a genuine respect for his father? And what if such a man subsequently falls into a circle like the one led by Socrates and is given the tools of logical reflection? What on earth is such a consciousness going to make of the society that made him?

It does seem that there was a critical mass of bastards in Athenian society which might thus have been capable of generating such an aberration. Various sources report that Antisthenes was in the habit of teaching philosophy at a venue called the 'white dog', which was a gymnasium and temple reserved especially for Athenian bastards.[45] In ancient Greece, white dogs were synonymous with 'mongrels'. In the Platonic dialogues the dialectic takes place between sovereign minds. Knowledge is generated through interpersonal debate. But in Antisthenes it appears that an internal dialectic was going on between two halves of the self and self knowledge is generated through intrapersonal debate. Thus one anecdote about him that has survived is that he was once asked what advantage had accrued to him from his studies in philosophy. His reply was 'the ability to hold conversation with myself'.[46] Of his writings, none of which have survived, one of them was said to have been entitled 'Of freedom and slavery'.[47]

We don't know much about Antisthenes' philosophy. What we do know is pieced together from references to him by other ancient authors whose works have survived. Navia suggests that as with Plato, the manner of the death of Socrates must have had a profound effect upon Antisthenes.[48] Like Plato, the initial reaction seems to have been disillusionment and withdrawal from public life. Given that Antisthenes was a bastard non-citizen, this probably didn't mean much as far as Athenian politics was concerned. What it probably meant was that he finally gave up on his ambition to earn a living as a Sophist, or in other words a higher education teacher of excellence to rich students aiming for a public career in law and politics. He became impatient with preachy lectures about the principles of virtue without practical attempts to embody them. He began to define virtue as a rhetoric communicated through body-acts rather than speech-acts or, to be less obscure, Antisthenes began to adopt a stance of 'do as I do' not 'do as I say'.[49] In this respect, he began to behave in a manner that would later be interpreted as 'doglike', experimenting with the idea of living a life outside the *oikos*. The idea of

[45] Luis Navia, *Classical Cynicism: a critical study* (Westport: Greenwood Press, 1996), p. 15.
[46] Diogenes Laertius, *Lives*, p. 9.
[47] Ibid., p. 17.
[48] Navia, *Classical Cynicism*, pp. 53–6.
[49] R. Bracht Branham, 'Defacing the currency: Diogenes' rhetoric and the invention of cynicism', in R. Bracht Branham & Marie-Odile Goulet-Gaze (eds), *The Cynic Movement in Antiquity and its Legacy* (Berkeley and Los Angeles: University of California Press, 1996), p. 83.

living a life outside the *oikos* was important because, as Aristotle makes clear in the *Politics*, the *oikoi* were the primary economic units within which slave ownership and production was organised.[50] In other words, Antisthenes was attempting to embody a break with surplus accumulation through slavery to well being through sufficiency.

We move on now to Diogenes about whom we know a little more than Antisthenes. Diogenes was born in Sinope, a Greek colony lying along the northern coast of Turkey on the Black Sea, probably around 413 BC.[51] Diogenes thus came from the eastern margins of Greek settlement, traditionally looked down upon by the Greeks on the Western coast of the Aegean. Sinope was an important trading post between the ancient West and East, an alternative to the shipping routes along the Levant. Like Antisthenes, Diogenes' mother was probably a woman of uncertain origin:

Snubbed by a man of noble descent for the lowly origins of his mother, Diogenes replied: 'In my case, the line of my nobility begins with me, whereas in yours it ends with you.' [52]

According to the legend, the philosophical career of Diogenes began after a scandal at the mint of Sinope. For some reason that is unknown Diogenes, who worked at the bank under the supervision of his father, took the rap for the deliberate defacing of the currency. The precise interpretation of this act is a matter for debate, because in antiquity coins were often clipped or adulterated for personal gain, but in other cases the faces of coins were struck through in such a way as to represent some sort of challenge to the authority of those who had assumed power over the issue of money and credit. Either way, in this case the act ended badly for those who committed it and, like the endearingly loyal Greek dog perhaps, Diogenes was disposable when it came to the crunch. He was prosecuted after an inquiry into the affair, convicted, and banished from the city of Sinope. The young man then drifted toward Delphi to ask the Oracle what he should do with his life now that the bottom had dropped out of it, whereupon the Oracle told him that he should 'devalue the currency'.

Conviction and exile seems to have been a life changing experience that alienated Diogenes from the values of the city he had been brought up in. He had participated in an attempt to deface the city's primary measure of value, but the subsequent disgrace had brought him in despair to Delphi. Later on in life, when taunted with the fact that he had been exiled for defacing the currency his reply was:

'Nay it was through that, you miserable fellow, that I came to be a philosopher.'[53]

Taking the cue from the oracle, Diogenes thus set out on a philosophical odyssey to devalue the currency of norms and values upon which his society was based and replace them according to alternative conceptions of well-being.

His journey takes him to Athens, where he begins to rub shoulders with the philosophers there. After seeing, hearing or reading about the example of

---

[50] Doyne Dawson, *Cities of the Gods: Communist Utopias in Greek Thought* (Oxford: Oxford University Press, 1992), ch. 2: 'The cynic way: a life without the household'.

[51] Navia, *Classical Cynicism*, p. 85.

[52] Dimitri Gutas, 'Sayings by Diogenes preserved in Arabic', in M. O. Goulet-Caze & R. Goulet (eds), *Le cynisme ancien et ses prolongements: Actes du Colloque international du CNRS* (Paris, 1993).

[53] *Gutas*, 'Sayings by Diogenes', p. 51.

Antisthenes, Diogenes begins to emulate his lifestyle and makes a virtue out of his fate. He claims that his ostracism is a blessing because it has forced him to construct an autonomous life that is free of the *polis*. When reminded of his fall from grace when Sinope had condemned him to exile, Diogenes replied:

'And I them, to home-staying.'[54]

The citizens of Sinope, enclosed within the culture of communitarian life, are thus condemned to the unhappiness of a life lived without reflection. His alienation from Sinope leads, according to Diogenes, to his emancipation.

As with Antisthenes, the thought of Diogenes is communicated through the rhetoric of acts rather than through dialectic. But his acts seem more 'dramatic'. He seems to turn his life into a performance that borrows ideas from the tragicomedy of Greek theatre. He draws our attention to this in yet another act:

He was going into a theatre, meeting face to face those who were coming out, and being asked why, 'this', he said, 'is what I practise doing all my life.'[55]

When the people come out of the theatre, Diogenes goes into the theatre. In other words he brings theatre out onto the streets of Athens. He is a thinker who has turned his life into a stage. Upon this stage Diogenes enacts dramas that, like the comedies of Aristophanes, attempt to use wit to convey a serious message. His favourite costume is that of the homeless beggar, using props that the Athenians would have recognised from the Homeric character of Odysseus when testing the ethical patience of the people of Ithaca.

There is insufficient space here to present enough of these little dramas to do proper justice to the philosophy of Diogenes, but let us unwrap just a few. Firstly, we should note that Ancient Cynicism initiates a Western tradition of contempt for the follies of great power rivalry and predatory hegemony. Diogenes lived his adult life in the immediate aftermath of the tragic disaster of the Peloponnesian war – the consequence of a break up in the *original* Western Alliance as depicted by Thucydides. The disillusionment with power politics that this wrought in Athens, Corinth, and all the other cities Diogenes visited must have made many of its people receptive to his cynical message, and that is presumably why so many anecdotes about him survived through word of mouth. The response of Diogenes to the tragedy of great power politics was a conscious attempt to turn Greek tragedy on its head. In the tragedies of Aeschylus, Sophocles and Euripides, exile and homelessness is shown to be a disaster. To lose your *polis* and your *oikos* means social death and slavery. But Diogenes makes the utopian point of showing that he thinks that the *polis* and the *oikos* are things that humanity can do without. He is a poor homeless beggar, but he believes himself to be happy, because he is free from the tyranny of the *polis*.

The fact that the city state system was in decline and was giving way to the empire building of Alexander probably made it easier for Diogenes to promote his message of indifference toward communitarian values. The retreat of the city state in terms of wealth and power in the political economy of antiquity must have had some impact on tolerance toward philosophers promoting alternative identities.

[54] Diogenes Laertuis, *Lives*, p. 17.
[55] Ibid., p. 67.

The identity flaunted by Diogenes though, was revolutionary. When asked where he came from, Diogenes replied:

'I am a citizen of the cosmos'[56]

Diogenes lifted the term cosmos from the astronomical speculations of the pre-Socratic philosophers and applied it to the realm of human society. He thus became the first person to call himself a cosmopolitan.[57] But the cynicism of Diogenes was very clearly advocating a 'cosmopolitanism from below' which was very consciously opposed to the *cosmopolis* from above that Alexander had just set out to build through his campaign of imperial war and coercion.

The anecdotes which most people remember, if they have ever heard of Diogenes at all, are from when the lives of Diogenes and Alexander crossed at Corinth. When Alexander arrived at Corinth, its public officials and philosophers came in 'from all parts' to pay court to him, but to Alexander's disappointment Diogenes did not bother and remained where he was in the 'suburb called the Craneum' sunning himself. Alexander went to the district and sought Diogenes out:

Alexander came and stood next to him and said, 'I am Alexander the great.' 'And I', said he, 'am Diogenes the Dog.'[58]

The humour of this was not lost on their contemporaries. The meeting dramatises the gulf between two different worldviews. On the one side we have the Western man whose cosmopolitanism is personified in an unquenchable thirst for power. On the other we have the Western man whose cosmopolitanism is much better served by loafing around like a dog in the sun:

Alexander came and stood over him and said, 'ask of me any gift you like.' To which Diogenes replied 'stand out of my light.' [59]

The encounter illustrates the indifference of Diogenes to the political changes which were about to sweep across the ancient Mediterranean and the Near East. Alexander is setting out to be king of the world. Meanwhile, the old man Diogenes has begun to set out his stall as the king of everyday life.

Some people have tried to characterise the philosophy of ancient cynicism as a kind of apathetic hedonism, a lifestyle which shrinks from the sphere of the political. This is why it is important to highlight some of the anecdotes which dramatise the cynical position on slavery – the institution which was the primary contradiction of classical political economy. As we have already intimated, the rationalist philosophers of Greece had a problem. They had a contradiction on their hands which, if repressed into the unconscious, could easily turn into protracted mental conflict. This is the 'weakening' of the Western spirit which the more reactionary side of Nietzsche the classicist railed against. On the one hand there was a common belief in the principle of the unity of mankind, and on the other there was the empirical observation that a lot of wealth accumulation in Greece was based upon the international institution of slavery. The cynical solution

---

[56] Ibid., p. 65.

[57] This point is pursued further by John L. Moles, 'Cynic Cosmopolitianism', in R. Bracht Branham & Marie-Odile Goulet-Gaze (eds), *The Cynic Movement in Antiquity and its Legacy* (Berkeley and Los Angeles: University of California Press, 1996).

[58] Diogenes Laertius, *Lives*, p. 60.

[59] Ibid., p. 41.

to this problem was very simple and pragmatic. It might be summarised as the art of communicative action by seizing opportunities to make public spectacles out of inconvenient truths.

For example, in the early days of his exile Diogenes was accompanied by his slave Manes but, seeing the plummeting socio-economic status toward which Diogenes was heading, Manes decided to cut and run. When asked why he does not pursue the runaway slave Diogenes replies:

'It would be absurd if Manes can live without Diogenes, but Diogenes cannot get on without Manes.'[60]

The political ideology behind the slave-master relationship in classical antiquity is overturned. The legitimation of slavery was based on the principle that it was natural for slaves to need a master. As Orlando Patterson notes, Diogenes made an important contribution to the value of freedom in Western culture, because he consciously tried to demonstrate that it could not rationally be based on the institution of slavery:

With his notorious sense of irony, Diogenes saw, millennia before Hegel, that in the domination of the slave the master exposes himself to a kind of slavery more real than that of his slave, because he ends up being dependent on him.[61]

On seeing a master whose shoes were being put on by his slave, Diogenes remarks:

'You will never be truly happy until he wipes your nose as well; and that will come, when you have lost the use of your hands.'[62]

The critique of slavery then takes another twist when, on a short voyage to Corinth Diogenes is captured by pirates and put up for sale. When asked what he can do so that he may be found a buyer Diogenes replies:

'Govern men.'[63]

He then tells the crier to ask if anyone would like to purchase a master for himself, and someone does buy him, for the purpose of educating his two sons. The new slave is put in charge of the curriculum. Amongst other things, Diogenes teaches them to wait on themselves.

Ancient Cynicism is often depicted as a rather ascetic creed, promoting a monkish life of austere abstinence. But this is not quite right:

When someone declared that life is an evil, Diogenes corrected him: 'Not life itself, but living ill.'[64]

The story is rather of someone who, by force of circumstances, has had to embark upon a rapid downsizing of expectations. For Diogenes, perhaps to his surprise, this appears to have become a very liberating experience. Losing his property in Manes the slave turns out to be not so bad. Diogenes is relieved to discover that he can free himself from his dependency upon Manes. When he arrives in Athens, Diogenes latches on to Antisthenes' conception of sufficiency and applies it with rigour:

[60] Ibid., p. 57.
[61] Orlando Patterson, *Freedom: Freedom in the Making of Western Culture*, vol. 1 (London: Tauris, 1991), pp. 185–6.
[62] Diogenes Laertius, *Lives*, p. 47.
[63] Diogenes Laertius, p. 31.
[64] Diogenes Laertius, *Lives*, p. 57.

Through watching a mouse running about [. . .] not looking for a place to lie down in, not afraid of the dark, not seeking any of the things which are considered to be luxuries, he discovered the means of adapting himself to circumstances.[65]

For accommodation, Diogenes begins by improvising a rather dangerously secular joke about a vacancy in its temples by pointing to the portico of Zeus and the Hall of Processions, declaring the Athenians had built him places to live in. It is a play upon his name, meaning 'from Zeus'. After squatting in these for a while, Diogenes takes up residence in an old tub.

These anecdotes should be seen as dramatic performances which convey the ideal of sufficiency rather than the piety of poverty. He likened his example to the trainers of choruses who set the note a little high to ensure the rest hit the right note.[66] Moving toward the cynical goal of sufficiency was more about the feeling of release that comes with shedding wealth which has become an obstacle to happiness than about abstinence.

It is also worth emphasising that Diogenes advocated sufficiency and not 'self-sufficiency'. He was in no position to fall into the trap of believing that human security could be achieved by some sort of collective withdrawal from our common fate of interdependence. Diogenes was all too aware of his dependency upon the fragile Mediterranean political economy, as the many anecdotes about his recourse to beggary in order to pursue his philosophy testify. These anecdotes have often prompted some to allege that cynicism was in denial of the old nostrum that there 'is no such thing as a free lunch' – in effect that it was a school for scroungers. The response of Diogenes needs to be seen in the context of an old debate in Greek antiquity about the political economy of knowledge. Ever since Aristophanes and probably before, scepticism had been expressed about whether knowledge could ever be bought and sold as a commodity. The charge was that men gave money to the sophists simply in order to find out how to win in the assembly, the law courts and in the diplomatic and military affairs of state, not for their philosophy. Plato's Socrates also spends much of his time joshing at contemporary Sophists who claimed to be in the business of selling wisdom. The prevailing view seems to have been that to really fall in love with knowledge one had to be an aristocrat with independent means, thus free of the pressure to take it to market. Needless to say, this option was not available to the likes of Diogenes, and his improvised solution added a delightfully ironic twist to this debate that reminds us of Rawls' contemporary gambit of the 'veil of ignorance':[67]

Being asked why people give to beggars but not to philosophers, he replied 'because they think they may one day be lame or blind, but never expect that they will turn to philosophy.'[68]

Up until his fall into slavery at least, the philosophy of Diogenes appears to have survived by embedding itself within an informal social economy that supplemented the logic of the *oikos*, the *polis* and the *agora:*

He was begging of a miserly man who was slow to respond, so he said 'my friend, it's for food that I'm asking, not for funeral expenses.'[69]

[65] Ibid., p. 25.
[66] Ibid., p. 37.
[67] Rawls (ed.), *A Theory of Justice* (Cambridge Mass: Harvard University Press, 1971), pp. 136–42.
[68] Diogenes Laertius, *Lives*, p. 57.
[69] Ibid., pp. 58–9.

This, together with other examples of unabashed chutzpah in the beggary of Diogenes suggests a self-confidence that comes from a well worked out position. He really thought he was providing a service by offering the citizens of Athens and Corinth an alternative philosophy, funded by demands for evidence of common humanity upon which his *cosmopolis* would have to be built, if it were ever to be built.

This brings us to the question of hope in ancient cynicism. Antisthenes and Diogenes were evidently able to cast aside their fears and doubts to think, say and do some brave things, given the prevailing structure of everyday life in which they lived. What kind of hopes for the future were these acts of courage based upon? Well, they did have a utopian conception of cosmopolitan society to cling to, but it was only a highly ironical, almost surrealist folk utopia, inspired by the music of festivals popular amongst the *demos* of cities like Athens and Corinth at the time.

In the *Works and Days* of Hesiod, his song lays out a myth of the ages of men in which the prospects for humanity just keep on getting worse and worse. But a bygone early age in the ages of men was the age of Cronos, a great age for human well-being. The sons of Cronus then go to live 'with a carefree heart in the Isles of the Blessed', where the 'grain giving soil bears its honey sweet fruits thrice a year'.[70] Ostensibly, this is not a particularly promising point of origin for hope, given that it springs from a myth that is the very antithesis of our modern conception of progress. Nevertheless this fantasy of the age of Cronos and the Isles of the Blessed thrived, for example at the harvest time festival of Cronia in Attica, where masters and slaves would playfully exchange places for a day in some sort of homage to the mythical equality of Cronus' time.[71] Then there are the fragments from Greek comedy during the festival of Dionysus, that contain passages about the age of Cronus, when rivers would run with barley-cakes and the fish would jump out onto pans in order to fry themselves.

When the cynics started to call themselves 'the sons of Cronus' they were clearly trying to evoke this tradition. Cynical utopianism was thus leavened heavily with the surreal humour of the carnival day and the satyr tragedy, embedding itself in a culture within which it could survive the overwhelming power of prevailing circumstances by making humour out of its lack of realism. In this way, by invoking the satyr 'fools privilege' that the Athenian demos had learned to internalise through their festival traditions such as the City Dionysia, the cynics discovered a means to publicise their critique of slavery that would have been effortlessly crushed and then forgotten if it had been expressed otherwise. If this was hope, it was a rather sorry kind of hope, but impressive enough when one considers the legitimate fears and doubts it must have had to overcome. It was impressive enough too, if our thesis is correct, for Aristotle to find himself having to acknowledge it and thus preserve it for posterity in the *Politics*.

The fact that they called themselves the 'sons of Cronus' begs another question. Evidently, ancient cynicism was not quite so easy to sustain with the responsibilities of fatherhood or motherhood. This is perhaps the Achilles heel of ancient cynicism, where we start to deal with the question of its gendering. Of course we

[70] Hesiod, *Works and Days*, lines 169–70.
[71] Doyne Dawson, *Cities of the Gods* (Oxford: University Press, 1992), pp. 13–4 & 146.

have already reasoned that cynicism was the fruit of a power relationship between master fathers and slave mothers. This possibly explains why Diogenes also became famous for his disavowal of a main plank of Hellenic patriarchy, advocating:

a community of wives, recognizing no other marriage than a union of the man who persuades with the woman who consents.[72]

Uncharacteristically, however, there is no anecdote suggesting that Diogenes ever embodied this argument himself. And though the shamelessness of the cynics when it came to sexual mores scandalised and titillated antiquity in equal measure, their existential position generally appears to have condemned them to a defiant loneliness that excluded the possibility of partnership and family. This left their political philosophy open to the charge of being great for youthful bohemians, but not quite so brave when it came to the frailty of age and experience. In exchange for the joys of the family, the proud cynic must surely have to crawl back with some humility under the communitarian security of the *polis* and the comforting wealth of the *oikos*? This point was made very early by Epictetus. When the cynic marries:

he must get a kettle to heat the water for the baby [...] wool for his wife [...] oil, a cot, a cup, and many other pieces of crockery [...] What then will become of our Cynic-King, whose duty it is now to be overseer over the rest of mankind – who have married; who have had children: who is treating his wife well, who ill: who quarrels: which house stands firm, which does not; making his round like a physician feeling pulses. See what straits we are reducing our Cynic, how we are taking his kingdom away from him.[73]

How the mighty are fallen! Which is why, perhaps, classical cynicism had to invent Crates and Hipparchia. Or were they invented? Can it really have been possible for a young woman from the patriarchal aristocracy to fall in love with a cynic, defy the wishes of her parents and demand marriage to Crates, and then become accepted as the only female philosopher of antiquity whilst giving birth to three children? Was it really possible for such an eccentric couple to bring up three children on a shoestring, maintain the cosmopolitan idyll of well-being and yet retain the famous cynical sense of humour too? No, surely this is stretching our credulity much too far...[74] There were rumours that the happy couple took one or two hand-outs from father. And so we begin the passage toward all the compromises of Stoicism.

Conclusion

So what have we learned then, about Obama's sorry kind of wisdom? Now that we have endured our tour of some of its primary twists and turns, what can be done with it? What might it contribute? What might come next?

One thing that will be avoided here is any attempt to set out some sort of 'research programme'. Anyone who could seriously contemplate that hasn't really got it yet. Many of the cynicisms described above would doubtless make great

---

[72] Diogenes Laertius, *Lives*, p. 75.
[73] Donald R. Dudley, *A History of Cynicism* (London: Bristol Classical Press, 1998), p. 51.
[74] Diogenes Laertius, *Lives*, pp. 89–108.

mirth out of such academic earnestness. Cynicism could never really be something
we set out in search of, with all our epistemological and methodological butterfly
nets. Rather, cynicism is something that comes searching for you, usually
unsolicited, and so the question is more about how best to handle our cynicism
when it finally catches up with us.

Another thing that must be avoided at all costs is any attempt to present
cynicism as some kind of 'new perspective'. Lord knows, we probably have enough
of them in international political theory already. Cynicism is not so much a way of
seeing the object of international studies, more about the well-being of the subject
who is doing and seeing. More often, curiosity about cynicism is not aroused in
order for it to ossify into a perspective, but to turn the page and move on.

Perhaps a better way would be to see Cynicism (with a capital C) as a potential
resource for the cynical (with a lower case c). Those who have never been touched
by it, obviously, would not need to draw upon such a resource. But for those who
have, there may be some value in bringing the various forms of cynicism together
out into the public sphere. Precisely because it perceives itself as 'a sorry kind of
wisdom', it is often reproduced as a private disposition that reveals itself only with
discretion.[75] This explains why the different meanings of the word are often used
in apparent innocence of their coexistence with other meanings, to the extent that
misunderstanding is not uncommon. This furtiveness is potentially harmful in that
it forecloses debate about the diversity of options for when hope becomes tempered
by disillusionment. Therefore, it may be worth challenging the assumption that
cynicism is somehow beyond the pale.

As Obama has recognised so eloquently, hope has always been the animating
principle behind any collective political action that has achieved positive change.
Hope has always been that endearing trait in human nature that insists upon
taking a wrecking ball to some of the most painstaking calculations of our
brightest rational choice theorists. It also happens to be a motivating principle
behind much critical international theory. Whenever hope fails to turn up, it
immediately becomes apparent how incredibly boring international political theory
can be.

Nevertheless, the sad fact is that it is inherent in the structure of things that the
odds are usually stacked against hope, and so hope loses more often than many
would care to admit.[76] Where there is hope, there will be casualties, and so the
question then becomes: how do we cope with the wounded? For those who have
been there but who have somehow managed to avoid the most *clichéd* path ('if you
aren't a liberal when you are young you haven't got a heart – if you aren't a realist
when you are old...etc.), it is irresponsible not to think about this question at all,
especially when one considers how dangerously bitter the fallout can often become
for old friends who once seemed so much more radical than ourselves. Arguably,
some of the most destructive reactionaries emerge from the ranks of wounded
idealists, so this question has a tactical aspect too. Now, with the incipient decline
and fall of neo-liberalism, and the ideological vacuum that arises as a consequence,
these lessons may have to be learnt all over again.

[75] Sloterdijk, *Critique of Cynical Reason* (London: Verso, 1988), p. 7.
[76] As a young student in an international theory seminar once remarked: 'Critical Theory is for losers!'
– which made everyone laugh.

As was intimated in our opening paragraph, cynicism is where the action appears to be when it comes to popular consciousness about problems of agency and structure. This is the common thread that links its great diversity of expression. So in a sense, Obama hit the nail on the head when he called it 'a sorry kind of wisdom'. But as the example of ancient cynicism demonstrates, we have choices when the structure of things confronts us with commensurable experiences of disillusionment. Some choices made within cynicism appear to be self-inhibiting or even self-destructive, whilst others exhibit rude health. The oldest of them all unleashed a cosmopolitan perspective that has had the stamina to inspire courage for two and a half millennia. Maybe, armed with our knowledge of all these, we can hope to trump the former with the latter.

Review of International Studies (2010), **37**, 225–248   © 2010 British International Studies Association
doi:10.1017/S0260210510001580   First published online 28 Jan 2011

Journeys beyond the West: World Orders and a 7th century Buddhist Monk

L. H. M. LING*

Abstract. Novice Lee ('Frank') seeks world peace and thinks he has found it in the Liberal world order. He informs the Learned One, head of the monastery. Through their discussions, Frank discovers that the Liberal world order, despite its promises, offers neither 'democracy' nor 'peace'. Turning to the Confucian world order of 'all-under-heaven' (*tianxia*), they find it similarly top-down and one-way. Finally, Frank and the Learned One, now joined by their brother monks and sister nuns, consider the life of the 7th century monk, Xuanzang. He inspires Frank to imagine a 'worldly world order' where humility and learning drive one's engagements with others, rather than what we have today: hegemony and imperialism.

L. H. M. Ling (PhD, MIT) is an Associate Professor in the Graduate Program in International Affairs (GPIA) at The New School in New York City. Her research agenda focuses on developing a post-Western, post-Westphalian understanding of and approach to International Relations/World Politics. Dr. Ling is the author of three books: *Democratizing International Relations: Culture as Method* (Routledge, forthcoming), *Postcolonial International Relations: Conquest and Desire between Asia and the West* (Palgrave Macmillan, 2002), and *Transforming World Politics: From Empire to Multiple Worlds* (Routledge, 2009), co-authored with Anna M. Agathangelou (York University). Additionally, Dr. Ling is developing a textbook, *Learning World Politics: A Wanderer's Guide to Global Traditions, Volume I: Confucianism, Hinduism, Islam*, for advanced undergraduates and entry-level graduate students. From 2008–2010, Dr. Ling was a Faculty Fellow with the India China Institute (ICI) at The New School. She is working on a manuscript with other ICI Fellows titled, *Rethinking Borders and Security, India and China: New Connections for Ancient Geographies*. Dr. Ling's articles have appeared in various journals and anthologies.

Cast

THE LEARNED ONE ....Head of the Monastery
NOVICE LEE/FRANK ....A New Recruit
MONKS & NUNS...Members of the Monastery
ELDERLY MONK...Expert on Xuanzang

* I am grateful to Payal Banerjee, Martha Bonham, Stephen Chan, Boyu Chen, Erica Dingman, Gavan Duffy, Christopher Goto-Jones, Kathleen Maloney, Yumiko Mikanagi, Binod K. Mishra, Tim Pachirat, Patricia J. Robertson, Everita Silina, Tan Chung, Jishnu Shankar, and Hong Anh Thi Vu, as well as two anonymous reviewers, for their contributions to this article. Nevertheless, I retain all responsibility for the contents herein. This article was first presented at the 'After Liberalism?' conference for *Millennium: Journal of International Studies*, London School of Economics, 17–18 October 2009.

Introduction

Curtains rise. The stage is empty and dark except for a single shaft of light on a lone figure, a monk in saffron robes sitting crossed-legged on a prayer mat. It is the Learned One.[1] A screen above the stage shows an image of a 'sea of clouds' at dawn, indicating we are high up in the Himalayas. All is quiet and peaceful. We hear crickets and chanting in the background.

Suddenly, an eager voice calls from Stage Right. Lights turn on. Enter Novice Lee, panting. He carries a heavy computer bag slung across a shoulder.

NOVICE LEE: Learned One, Learned One! I've found it!

LEARNED ONE (opening one eye): Found what, my child?

NOVICE LEE (still panting): The plan for world peace!

LEARNED ONE (returning to meditative pose, keeping both eyes closed): Remarkable. And where, may I ask, did you find it?

NOVICE LEE: On the Internet! It is truly the fount of all things. See, it gave me this document and for free!

(He waves a thick slab of paper.)

LEARNED ONE: Please, tell me more.

(The Learned One gives up trying to meditate and turns to the novice. He is a bright, earnest young man with great aptitude but little discipline so far. The Learned One likes him dearly and wishes him well, whatever he may choose for his future. Still too recent a recruit, Novice Lee is far from being ordained.)

NOVICE LEE: It's called 'The Princeton Project on National Security'. It's from that great university in America by the same name![2]

LEARNED ONE (smiling slightly): I know Princeton. I spent some time there in my youth. (*The novice's eyes widen with wonder.*) Still, Novice Lee, how do you know this Project is important?

NOVICE LEE: The sponsors and authors of this Project are all famous and important people![3]

LEARNED ONE: Ah. . .

NOVICE LEE (pausing slightly): Before we continue, Learned One, may I beg an indulgence?

---

[1] This is a fictional title. I use it to convey the sense of respect usually accorded to the head of a monastery. In India, this person is called *gurudeva* ('immortal master'); in Tibet and Nepal, *rinpoche* ('incarnate'); in China, *fa shi* ('*dharma* teacher/master'); in Japan, *jushoku* ('resident minister'); in Vietnam, viện chủ ('institute owner'); in Thailand, *luang paw* ('grand' or 'royal father'). Although this person is typically a man, it is not always so. For this reason, I refrain from giving 'the Learned One' a specific gender identity.

[2] G. John Ikenberry and Anne-Marie Slaughter, Co-Directors, *Forging A World of Liberty Under Law: US National Security in the 21st Century*, Final Report of the Princeton Project on National Security (Princeton: Woodrow Wilson School of Public and International Affairs, 2006). Available at: {http://www.princeton.edu/~ppns/report.html} accessed on 13 September 2009.

[3] They include a former Secretary of State (George Shultz), former National Security Advisor (Anthony Lake), a Director of Policy Planning (Anne-Marie Slaughter) in the State Department under Hillary Clinton, and a Professor of Politics and International Affairs (G. John Ikenberry) at Princeton University.

LEARNED ONE: Of course.

NOVICE LEE: Please call me by my new name, Frank.

LEARNED ONE: Frank?

NOVICE LEE/FRANK: Yes. I've decided to take a modern, outward-reaching name – to be more compatible with our times. This way, I could communicate with others more easily from across the valleys and over the seas. I found this name on the Internet also. It belonged to a famous American singer.

(*Faint echoes of 'doo bee doo bee doo' in the background. Frank adds quickly –*)

He's passed on so he wouldn't be offended by my using his name. (*quietly and shyly*) Music and song are good metaphors, I think, for my purpose.

LEARNED ONE: Why an *American* singer, if you don't mind?

FRANK: America and its culture seem most universal – that is, popular – in the world today. So I thought this name would be most useful.

LEARNED ONE: Very well, Novice Frank –

FRANK: Er, if you please, Learned One, just Frank will do.

LEARNED ONE: Frank, it is. Please tell me about the Princeton Project.

Act I: The Princeton Project

FRANK (enthusiastically): It says we need a Liberal world order.

LEARNED ONE: What does this mean?

FRANK: Democracy, individual liberty, and 'a framework of order established by law'.[4]

LEARNED ONE: And its relation to world peace is ..?

FRANK: A set of fair and just rules for all.

LEARNED ONE: How does it work?

FRANK: A Concert of Democracies will ensure a Democratic Peace.[5]

LEARNED ONE: Democratic Peace?

FRANK: It's the idea that democracies don't fight one another. The German philosopher, Immanuel Kant, originated this notion of a 'perpetual peace' among like-minded republics.[6]

---

[4] Slaughter and Ikenberry, *Forging A World of Liberty Under Law: US National Security in the 21st Century*, p. 6.
[5] '[The purpose of a "Concert of Democracies"] would be to [...] serve as the institutional embodiment and ratification of the "democratic peace"', Ibid., p. 25.
[6] For a critical review of this literature, see Andreas Behnke, '"Eternal Peace" as the Graveyard of the Political: A Critique of Kant's *Zum Ewigen Frieden*', *Millennium: Journal of International Studies*, 36:3 (2008), pp. 513–31.

LEARNED ONE: And the Concert of Democracies?[7]

FRANK: These are states that measure up to PAR – that is, (*reads*) 'Popular, Accountable, and Rights-regarding'.[8] Clever, isn't it?

LEARNED ONE: Uh, yes ... How does the Project propose to bring every state up to PAR?

FRANK: Through linkages and networks. Connecting *international* institutions with *domestic* ones will spread Liberalism throughout the globe.[9]

And the economy plays an important role. Together, capitalism and democracy can 'manag[e] crises', 'provid[e] incentives], and 'enhance the power of attraction of the world of liberal democracies'.[10]

LEARNED ONE: Tell me, what does the Project say about culture?

FRANK (eagerly): Oh, it's in favour of it! The Project wants to promote 'liberty under law' in accordance with the different histories, cultures, and stages of development that exist in the world. This will prevent 'growing resentment, fear, and resistance'.[11]

LEARNED ONE: Even on military matters?

FRANK: On military matters ... (*searches the text*) ... the Project quotes former US Secretary of State, Henry Kissinger:[12]

[I]n many ways several geopolitical worlds coexist, with Western Europe and North America in the 21st century, East Asia in the 19th, and the Middle East rooted in the 17th.

Hmm ...

LEARNED ONE: Something wrong?

FRANK: This quote suggests that the West leads – or should lead – because it represents the Future. Everyone else is just catching up.

LEARNED ONE: Speaking of catching up, what about China? Does the Project mention it?

FRANK: Yes, it identifies China as one of the 'Major Threats and Challenges' to world order.[13]

---

[7] '[It] would be selective, but self-selected. Members would have to pledge not to use or plan to use force against one another; commit to holding multiparty, free-and-fair elections at regular intervals; guarantee civil and political rights for their citizens enforceable by an independent judiciary; and accept the responsibility to protect.' Ibid., p. 7.

[8] Ibid., p. 6.

[9] '[W]e need to build, or rebuild, not simply an international order but a liberal international order [. . . with] international institutions [. . .] integrally connected to the domestic conditions necessary for liberty under law [. . .]'. Ibid., p. 23.

[10] Ibid., p. 23.

[11] Ibid., p. 19.

[12] Ibid.

[13] The full list includes: '(1) the collapse of order in the Middle East, (2) global terror networks, (3) the proliferation and transfer of nuclear weapons, (4) the rise of China and order in East Asia, (5) global pandemics, (6) energy, and (7) the need for a protective infrastructure within and around the US.' Ibid., p. 23.

LEARNED ONE: Why?

FRANK (reads):

The rise of China is one of the seminal events of the early 21st century. America's goal should not be to block or contain China, but rather to help it achieve its legitimate ambitions within the current international order and to become a responsible stakeholder in Asian and international politics.[14]

LEARNED ONE: How kind of America to help. But is China an *irresponsible* stakeholder at present?

FRANK (laughing): O Learned One, I hope you don't mind my saying so, but you are most hilarious when you joke! Of course the Project wants China to be a responsible stakeholder *in* the Liberal world order.

LEARNED ONE: Nothing escapes you, I see! But, seriously, isn't China already part of the Liberal world order? How else did its economy grow so fast in recent years?[15]

FRANK: The Project probably sees it as economic integration, not political or cultural.

LEARNED ONE: Ah, so the Project distinguishes between these domains of activity?

FRANK: Yes and No. The Project fears that China will remain politically and culturally 'alien' *despite* increasing globalisation.

At the same time, the Project expects China to adjust to the West, given the 'soft power' of the US and other Liberal democracies.[16]

LEARNED ONE: What do you think of this proposition?

FRANK (ruminating): Sounds like a one-way street. First, the Project wants everybody to 'come up' to PAR.

Then, the Project wants to 'manage' China.

And, if force is necessary, so be it.[17] The Project is quite open about keeping US military superiority,[18] even pre-emptive war as an option![19]

---

[14] Ibid., p. 9.

[15] The Chinese government announced its economy grew by 8 per cent in 2009. See *BBC News* (22 October 2009), available at: {http://news.bbc.co.uk/2/hi/business/8319706.stm} accessed on 22 October 2009. The global economy, in contrast, is facing the 'worst crisis since the 1930s', *BBC News* (10 March 2009), {http://news.bbc.co.uk/2/hi/7934920.stm} accessed on 12 December 2009.

[16] '[. . .] Chinese officials and institutions [will have to] develop a degree of transparency and integrity comparable to the level of other participants in the network. Further, collective regulations and practices agreed on by network members will have to be enforceable through local administrative agencies or courts. Similar networks in areas such as securities regulation or antitrust enforcement routinely collect and disseminate best practices, which serve to transmit the values and practices of rights-regarding governments to other governments.' Ibid., p. 6.

[17] '[B]uilding and maintaining a world of liberty under law requires a mix of sticks and carrots. Liberty requires order, and order, at some level, must be able to harness force.' Ibid., p. 20.

[18] 'The US should aim to sustain the military predominance of liberal democracies and encourage the development of military capabilities by like-minded democracies in a way that is consistent with their security interests.' Ibid., p. 31.

LEARNED ONE: What about the Democratic Peace?

FRANK: Now I'm unsure how democratic or peaceful it is ... The Project offers no principles or guidance on what happens when systems mix. It presumes only that total conversion is both possible *and* desirable.

LEARNED ONE: Would conversion be so bad?

FRANK (agitatedly): For those outside the Concert, conversion means not perpetual peace but a perpetual pox!

This Liberal world order claims to protect and promote individual liberty through democracy. But, really, the Concert seeks to turn all those who do not measure up to PAR – and that covers a majority of the globe – into disciples, servants, and lackeys, at best, or ...

LEARNED ONE: Or ..?

FRANK: Rogues, revolutionaries, and terrorists, at worst![20] And sometimes, the former turns into the latter while the latter often remains yoked to the former.

LEARNED ONE: How do you mean?

FRANK: The Philippines, for example, was annexed by the US in 1899 and granted independence in 1946. From its very beginning, then, the Philippines has been tethered to America's interests and power in Asia.[21] To secure this compliance, Washington's representatives allied with those in charge in Manila – who are primarily Catholic and landowning – to isolate and marginalise 'rebel' groups like the Muslims or Moro people in Mindanao, a land rich in minerals and resources. The government in Manila now links the Moro to other terrorist groups like *Al-Qaeda*.[22]

So Manila's external servitude to Washington exacerbates and perpetuates an internal rebellion that justifies greater expenditures of blood and treasure to fight so-called terror, just so elites, in Washington and Manila alike, could claim they are working hard to preserve stability and prosperity for all.[23]

---

[19] 'As a matter of strategy, it is unhelpful either to rule the preventive use of force out completely or to identify it as the policy of choice.' Ibid., p. 8.

[20] Pinar Bilgin and Adam D. Morton, 'Historicising Representations of "Failed States": Beyond the Cold War Annexation of the Social Sciences?', *Third World Quarterly*, 23:1 (2002), pp. 55–80; Samir Amin, *The Liberal Virus: Permanent War and the Americanisation of the World* (New York: Monthly Review Press, 2004).

[21] See, for example, Roxanne L. Doty, *Imperial Encounters: The Politics of Representation in North-South Relations* (Minneapolis: University of Minnesota Press, 1996).

[22] Raymond Bonner, 'Philippine Camps Are Training Al Qaeda's Allies, Officials S', *New York Times* (31 May 2003), {http://www.hvk.org/articles/0603/49.html} accessed on 8 March 2010; Preeti Bhattacharji, 'Terrorism Havens: Philippines', Council on Foreign Relations, (updated 1 June 2009), {http://www.cfr.org/publication/9365/} accessed on 13 March 2010.

[23] For a critique of this rationale from a Muslim woman's perspective, see Amirah Ali Lidasan, 'Moro Women's Struggle for Human Rights in the Philippines', paper presented at the Regional Conference on Advancing Gender Equality and Women's Empowerment in Muslim Societies, (11–12 March 2009), Jakarta, Indonesia, sponsored by the UN Development for Women (UNIFEM), Canadian International Development Agency (CIDA), and International Center for Islam and Pluralism (ICIP). {http://unifem-eseasia.org/docs/agewems/11.Amirah%20Lidasan.pdf} accessed on 16 March 2010.

LEARNED ONE: You have an excellent point, my child – er, Novice – Frank. Does your Liberal world order still seem like a good idea?

FRANK (sounding depressed): I'm beginning to wonder ...

LEARNED ONE: Doesn't this proposition sound familiar, though?

FRANK: Yes! Critics call it 'hegemony'.

LEARNED ONE: Is it a recent phenomenon?

FRANK: Today's hegemony, of course, was yesterday's 'white man's burden'.[24] In both cases, the same group wants to be in charge.

LEARNED ONE: Is the West alone in perpetrating a top-down, one-way world order?

FRANK (eyes lighting up): Seems like the West and China have more in common than each realises. Are you referring, Learned One, to the Confucian world order of 'all under heaven' or *tianxia*?[25]

LEARNED ONE: Why do you think that, Frank?

FRANK: There are important distinctions, of course, but also striking similarities between the two!

LEARNED ONE: Intriguing. But first, how about some tea? Let's invite other members of our monastery to join in. They would have much to contribute, I'm sure.

(*The Learned One rolls up his prayer mat. He and Frank leave Stage Left. We hear the monastery's bells ringing in the background. It is tea time.*)

Act II: Tianxia

Curtains rise. We are in the monastery's spacious Hall of Meditation. The overhead screen shows a teapot with steam streaming out the spout. We hear the slurp and splash of tea drinking and pouring.
 In the middle of the Hall is a 4' × 4' box of sand for meditative and illustrative purposes. The Learned One sits, cross-legged, on a large, flat cushion in saffron silk at one end of the sandbox. The rest of the monastery is similarly seated —monks on one side, nuns the other – around the sandbox, on cotton cushions of brown, red, yellow, purple, and other colours. There are about twenty of them altogether.
 Before each group of five is a long, low table of dark, lacquered teak. A large, earthen pot of steaming, fragrant tea centres each table, surrounded by tiny, round, ceramic cups. Also displayed are small bowls of nuts and fruit.
 The Learned One addresses the gathering.

LEARNED ONE: Novice Lee – uh, Frank – and I are having the most interesting discussion: the Princeton Project, democratic peace, hegemony and

---

[24] See Chapter Four of Anna M. Agathangelou and L. H. M. Ling, *Transforming World Politics: from Empire to Multiple Worlds* (London: Routledge, 2009).
[25] *Tianxia* is pronounced 'tian-shia'.

imperialism. We've come to a comparison between a Liberal world order and a Confucian one.

(*The gathering murmurs interest and approval.*)

Frank suggests that the Liberal and Confucian world orders are alike despite obvious differences in philosophy, time, and place. What say you?

NUN #1 (inquiringly): How are they alike?

FRANK: Both offer a grand and unified vision of order for all peoples and societies.[26]

MONK #1 (loudly): *Tianxia* may have ruled as a concept for two millennia but it was never realised. And, in modern times, it hasn't even served as a concept. Why is it relevant for us today?

(*This question seems a little too direct, too bellicose. Everyone steals a glance at Monk #1. Perhaps he is suffering from indigestion or some other discomfort?*)

FRANK: Actually, Brother Monk, that is not quite accurate.

Tianxia has always been an active concept in Confucian Asia.[27] Even until the last world war, scholars and officials were debating it from Beijing to Hanoi, Singapore to Tokyo.[28] And today, *tianxia* is regaining attention as the Chinese Communist Party (CCP) presents a related concept, a 'harmonious world', for international affairs.[29]

MONK #1: Some say *tianxia* is just a rhetorical ploy by the Chinese government to resist US pressures to liberalise rather than an actual prescription for foreign policy.[30]

FRANK: That may be true but who knows for sure? Moreover, this tactic makes *tianxia* more, not less, appealing. A scholar from China, for example, suggests

[26] Tingyang Zhao, 'Rethinking Empire from a Chinese Concept "All-under-Heaven" (Tian-xia)', *Social Identities*, 12:1 (January 2006), pp. 29–41; Huang Yiehwei, '*Lun "tianxia weigong" sixiangde chuantong neihan yu xianshi yiyi*' (On the Implicit and Practical Meanings of the *tianxia* Tradition), *Chongqing gongxueyuanbao (Journal of Chongqing Institute of Technology, Social Science Edition)*, 21:8 (August 2007), pp. 196–8; Shih Chih-yu and Hsieh Ming-Shan, '*Xifang bu zai xibian: xifangzhuyide ziwuorenshi fangfa*' (The West that is not Western: Self-Identification in the Oriental Modernity), *Dongya yanjiu (Studies of East Asia)*, 39:2 (2008), pp. 1–32.

[27] Throughout Japan's Tokugawa period (17–19th centuries), for example, various Confucian and neo-Confucian scholars debated what they called *tenka*, the Japanese version of *tianxia*. (I thank Chris Goto-Jones for this reminder. See also, Shih and Hsieh, '*Xifang bu zai xibian: xifangzhuyide ziwuorenshi fangfa*', for how *tenka* differed from *tianxia* when filtered through Shintoism). In China, Sun Yatsen rallied republican forces against the dying Qing dynasty in 1911 with the slogan of 'justice under *tianxia*' (*tianxia weigong*).

[28] For example, Imperial Japan's proclamation of a Greater East Asia Co-Prosperity Sphere in 1940 combined elements of *tianxia* with European imperialism. {http://www.worldfuturefund.org/wffmaster/Reading/Japan/Japan-1940.htm} accessed on 26 January 2010.

[29] See, for example, Qing Cao, 'Confucian Vision of a New World Order? Culturalist Discourse, Foreign Policy and the Press in Contemporary China', *The International Communication Gazette*, 69:5 (2007), pp. 431–50; Jiang Xiyuan, '*Cong tianxiazhuyi dao hexie shijie: zhongguo waijiao zhexue xuanze jiqi shijian yiyi*' (From Tianxiaism to a Harmonious World: The Significance of China's Choice in Foreign Relations Philosophy and Practice), *Waijiao pinglun* (Foreign Affairs Review), 97 (August 2007), pp. 46–53.

[30] William A. Callahan, 'Chinese Visions of World Order: Post-Hegemonic or a New Hegemony?', *International Studies Review*, 10:4 (December 2008), pp. 749–61.

that the CCP is in a better position than at any time in Chinese history to realise *tianxia*'s goal of a harmonious world.[31]

MONK #1 (gruffly): Still, what makes *tianxia* worthy of our attention?

(*Monk #1's neighbour pours him some tea, hoping that will help. The Learned One notices the gesture and bows slightly to the kind neighbour in acknowledgement. Monk #1 sees this exchange and senses he may have acted out of turn.*)

NUN #1: To answer this question, we must review what *tianxia* means.

FRANK: Quite right, Sister Nun! (*whips out laptop*) According to one, authoritative source, *tianxia* has three meanings: (1) 'the universe' or 'the world'; (2) the 'hearts of all peoples' or the 'general will of the people' and, (3) 'a world institution, or a universal system for the world, a utopia of the world-as-one-family'.[32] Altogether, these convey a sense of 'world-ness' under *tianxia*.

LEARNED ONE: Liberalism accounts for the Liberal world order. What is *tianxia*'s organising ideology?

NUN #2: *Ren*.

LEARNED ONE: Ah, what the Confucian classics refer to as 'humaneness' or 'sociality'?[33]

NUN #2: Yes. My knowledge, of course, is incomplete. But please allow me to share what I know.

The *Analects* defines *ren* as the ability 'to love *all* men'.[34] *Ren* is composed of two 'radicals' or roots. One refers to 'person'; the other, the number 'two'. Thus *ren* means, literally, a society of two or more persons.

(*She writes the Chinese character for* ren *on the sandbox. It shows on the screen over the stage.*)

Hence, *ren* cannot conceive of anything – whether person, institution, society, or state – outside of community. One is *necessarily* and *always* enmeshed with others.

---

[31] Huang Yiehwei, '*Lun "tianxia weigong" sixiangde chuantong neihan yu xianshi yiyi*' (On the Implicit and Practical Meanings of the *tianxia* Tradition).

[32] Zhao, 'Rethinking Empire from a Chinese Concept "All-under-Heaven" (Tian-xia)'.

[33] Hwa Yol Jung, 'Confucianism and Existentialism: Intersubjectivity as the Way of Man', *Philosophy and the Phenomenological Research*, 30:2 (December 1969), pp. 193–4.

[34] *Analects* quoted in Ibid., p. 191, emphasis in original.

From *ren* comes a sense of multiplicity. The Grand Historian, Sima Qian,[35] drew on what he called 'mutual illumination' to extract 'truth in plurality'.[36] He would record an assassin, for instance, as a 'romantic avenger' in one passage and 'bandit', in another.[37] From their juxtaposition, it is suggested, we may get at the 'truth' of this character.

Su Shi, the famous Song Dynasty poet, put it another way. One could relate differently to the same object, he said, even if it is inanimate, depending on one's relationship to it (*recites*):

> *Mornings I view Wu Mountain's breadth,*
> *Evenings I view its distant reach;*
> *Wu Mountain assumes many appearances*
> *Turning about to pose for its lover.*[38]

Such is the extent of my knowledge of *ren*.

(*Nun #2 bows, lowering her eyes demurely.*)

LEARNED ONE: Thank you, Sister Nun, for such a, *ahem*, learned exposition. (*turning to general gathering*) How is *ren* expressed or exercised?

MONK #2: Through 'exemplary power' or *de*.[39] The Confucians believed that power comes from an ethical order, not just political institutions or military might.

FRANK: Sorry to interrupt but this concept of *de*, it seems to contrast completely with the notion of state power in the Liberal world order.

MONK #2: That's right. *De* requires no fixities like borders or sovereignty or even a national body like a government to give it meaning.

Rather, *de* emanates from a leader's proper cultivation. This depends on how the leader relates to family, community, state, and the universe. The reverse applies as well: that is, how the universe, the state, the community, and the family relates to oneself.[40]

The idea is that if a society's leader is able to set such an admirable standard of virtue, then the rest of society cannot help but follow.

Each element depends on the others. Each also determines the others. All contribute to *de*. That is *tianxia*.

---

[35] Sima Qian is pronounced 'sima chien'.
[36] Wai-Yee Li, 'The Idea of Authority in the Shih chi (Records of the Historian)', *Harvard Journal of Asiatic Studies*, 54:2 (December 1994), p. 395.
[37] Ibid., p. 400.
[38] Ronald C. Egan, *Word, Image, and Deed in the Life of Su Shi* (Cambridge: Harvard University Press, 1994), p. 185.
[39] *De* is pronounced 'duh'. I take this translation from James Anderson, *The Rebel Den of Nùng Trí Cao: Loyalty and Identity Along the Sino-Vietnamese Frontier* (Seattle: University of Washington Press, 2007), p. 15.
[40] For elaboration on this notion of Confucian interrelationality and world politics, see L. H. M. Ling, *Postcolonial International Relations: Conquest and Desire between Asia and the West* (London: Palgrave Macmillan, 2002). For a translation of the original text in the *Great Learning* (*daxue*), see James Legge, *The Four Books* (Taipei: Culture Book Co., 1992), pp. 2–7.

LEARNED ONE: How does *tianxia* govern, then?

MONK #3: As a world-family.

Tianxia calls for 'cherishing men from afar'.[41] Typically, the Chinese Emperor, as the Son of Heaven and centre of the Confucian world order, would pacify 'barbarians' by offering a marital alliance between one of his sisters or concubines with a tribal chieftain. In this way, all become members of the Emperor's family, both literally and politically.

FRANK: What about the role of the economy?

MONK #4: People must live well, that's all.[42] This means having adequate food, clothing, and shelter. Moreso, the people should be able to *enjoy* their lives and not just trudge from one chore to another.

FRANK: And military matters?

MONK #5: A good example comes from Sunzi's *The Art of War*.[43] Many today mistake it for a Chinese version of Machiavelli's *The Prince* or a manual for cut-throat strategies in war or business.

These overlook Sunzi's own purpose, philosophy, and worldview.[44] Sunzi preferred diplomacy, negotiations, and even deception over war. His perfect scenario was to win war without spilling blood or wasting treasure. But if war was inevitable, then he urged caution by minimising its costs.

Sunzi was not just being prudent or humane. He believed that opposites complemented each other, thereby producing the possibility of change at all times. Where there is hardness, for example, there is also softness; fixity, mobility; bravery, cowardliness; victory, defeat.[45]

Everything is subject to change. Nothing can be taken for granted.

LEARNED ONE: What about relations with others? What does *tianxia* propose in this regard?

MONK #6: Transformation.[46]

LEARNED ONE: From what to what?

---

[41] James L. Hevia, *Cherishing Men from Afar: Qing Guest Ritual and the Macartney Embassy of 1793* (Durham: Duke University Press, 1995); Xue Jieling, *'Chunquiu bangjiao sixiang xulun'* (Discussion of Texts on Thoughts about Diplomatic Relations during the Spring and Autumn Period), *Qiushi xuekan (Seeking Truth)*, 30:1 (January 2003), pp. 106–10.

[42] This was the *fumin* policy. See, for example, Huang Yiehwei, *'Lun "tianxia weigong" sixiangde chuantong neihan yu xianshi yiyi'* (On the Implicit and Practical Meanings of the *tianxia* Tradition).

[43] 544–496 BCE.

[44] Ching-Chane Hwang and L. H. M. Ling, 'The Kitsch of War: Misappropriating Sun Tzu for an American Imperial Hypermasculinity', in Bina D'Costa and Katrina Lee-Koo (eds), *Gender and Global Politics in the Asia Pacific* (London: Palgrave Macmillan, 2009), pp. 59–76.

[45] Ping-ti Ho, *Youguan sunzi laozi de sanpian kaocheng* (Three Studies on Sun Tzu and Lao Tzu) (Taipei: Institute of Modern History, Academica Sinica, 2002).

[46] This was the *xianghua* (pronounced 'shiang-hua') policy. See James L. Hevia, *Cherishing Men from Afar: Qing Guest Ritual and the Macartney Embassy of 1793*.

MONK #6: Foe to friend, stranger to family. It's the other side of 'cherishing men from afar'.

LEARNED ONE: Is this fundamentally different from the Liberal world order?

MONK #6: Yes and No. The Liberal world order demands assimilation ('come up to PAR'); whereas, *tianxia* seeks transformation ('be my friend/family').

But they overlap in one area and that is the direction of change. Like the Liberal world order, transformation under *tianxia* is one-way only. It seeks always to turn the 'barbarian' toward the Confucian; the periphery, to the centre. But unlike the Liberal world order, Confucian transformation does not 'discipline' or 'reform' others should transformation fail to take place. They are seen, simply, as mired in barbarity.[47]

MONK #1 (wishing to amend his previous bellicosity): Perhaps we could sum up the discussion so far.

Let us draw a comparison between the Liberal world order and *tianxia*. Everyone, please, help me with your suggestions.

(*He begins drawing on the sandbox. Everyone pitches in. The final product looks like Figures 1 and 2. Everyone approves.*)

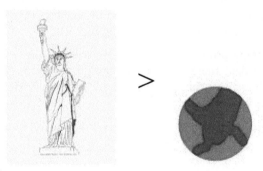

Figure 1. *The Liberal world order.*

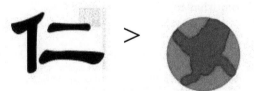

Figure 2. *Tianzia.*

---

[47] In this sense, Confucianism is a non-universalistic doctrine. Zhang Xiangiong, 'The Philosophical Feature of Confucianism and its Position in Inter-Cultural Dialogue: Universalism or Non-Universalism?', *Frontiers in Philosophy from China*, 4:4 (2009), pp. 483–92.

LEARNED ONE: Given all this, could one conclude that Confucians and Liberals alike offer a world order of top-down, one-way power?

MONK #7: One would have good reason to. Sunzi himself may have preferred peace over war, diplomacy over defence, and strategy over brute force but Chinese history is full of wars, conquests, killings, and enslavements. Sunzi himself lived in one of the bloodiest eras in Chinese history.[48]

But we need not rely on ancient times for evidence. Just look at Chinese policies toward our neighbours, the Tibetans[49] – or the Uighurs, for that matter[50] – and we get a sense of Confucian transformation in practical terms.

Moreover, the family serves as a poor model for world politics. We all know that families are capable of all kinds of abuses and humiliations, exploitations and vice. Even where abuses may not occur, patriarchy still defines the Confucian family.[51] Where is *ren* in this case?

(*The nuns nod approvingly. Their brother monks have come a long way.*)

NUN #3: Aren't China's current controversies with Tibetans and Uighurs as much a product of Liberalism as Confucianism? After all, why are the Tibetans agitating for 'sovereignty' and the Uighurs for 'civil rights'?[52]

MONK #7: No doubt, Sister Nun. For this reason, many in Asia today seek to 'de-colonize', 'de-imperialize', and 'de-Cold War' the region.[53]

It's not that they are against 'sovereignty' or 'civil rights'. Rather, they want to define these concepts on *their* own terms from *their* own circumstances, rather than the West's. They ask: what is 'Asia' anyway?[54]

---

[48] Sunzi's lifetime shaded from the Spring and Autumn period (722–481 BCE) to the Warring States period (475–221 BCE).

[49] Wang Lixiong, *Tianzang: Xizang the mingyun* (The Destiny of Tibet) (Taipei: Locus Publishing, 2009).

[50] Andrew Jacobs, 'China Fears Ethnic Strife Could Agitate Uighur Oasis', *New York Times* (22 July 2009), {http://www.nytimes.com/2009/07/23/world/asia/23kashgar.html} accessed 3 August 2009); Huma Yusuf, 'Effects of Uighur Unrest', *Dawn.com* (13 July 2009), {http://www.dawn.com/wps/wcm/connect/dawn-content-library/dawn/news/world/16-effects-of-uighur-unrest-hs-06} accessed on 3 August 2009.

[51] Timothy Brook and Hy V. Luong (eds), *Culture and Economy: The Shaping of Capitalism in Eastern Asia* (Ann Arbor: University of Michigan Press, 1997); Jongwoo Han and L. H. M. Ling, 'Authoritarianism in the Hypermasculinized State: Hybridity, Patriarchy, and Capitalism in Korea', *International Studies Quarterly*, 42:1 (March 1998), pp. 53–78; Thanh-Dam Truong, 'The Underbelly of the Tiger: Gender and the Demystification of the Asian Miracle', *Review of International Political Economy*, 6:2 (1999), pp. 133–65.

[52] See, for example, 'Tibetan Sovereignty has a Long, Disputed History', *National Public Radio* (11 April 2008) {http://www.npr.org/templates/story/story.php?storyId=89552004} and Rebiya Kadeer, 'A Civil Rights Movement for Uighurs', *Guardian* (14 July 2009), {http://www.guardian.co.uk/commentisfree/2009/jul/14/china-uighur-equality-xinjiang} accessed on 15 March 2010.

[53] Chen Kuan-Hsing, *Qudiguo: Yazhou zuowei fangfa* (Towards De-Imperialization: Asia as Method) (Taipei: Flaneur Publisher, 2007).

[54] Sun Ge, 'How Does Asia Mean?' and Wang Hui, 'The Politics of Imagining Asia: A Genealogical Analysis', in Kuan-Hsing Chen and Chua Beng Huat (eds), *The Inter-Asia Cultural Studies Reader* (London: Routledge, 2007), pp. 9–65 and 66–102; Wang Yimen, 'Screening Asia: Passing, Performative Translation, and Reconfiguration', *Positions: East Asia Cultures Critique*, 15 (2007), pp. 319–43.

In fact, the continent of Asia has always been dynamic, fluid, and multiple. The Silk Road, after all, mixed peoples, languages, cultures, and religions for fifteen centuries![55]

FRANK (despairingly): All this is very nice but what about world order? It seems we have decided that though the Liberal world order and *tianxia* may each have worthy elements, both remain hegemonic and imperialistic. Consequently, neither offers a sustainable order for the world.

LEARNED ONE: Is a world order necessary?

FRANK: We can't escape having one since globalisation entwines us all, for good or ill. And given the amount of suffering that passes for daily life in too many parts of the world today, is it not better to have a world order by design than by default?[56]

MONKS & NUNS (chant): *Emituofo!*[57]

FRANK: What to do, Learned One? How should one proceed?

LEARNED ONE: What if, as the Silk Road reminds us, we were to turn to our own long and venerable traditions for inspiration and insight?

MONK #8 (slapping his knee): Excellent idea, Learned One! After all, our monastery stands in testament to one who has given us a legacy of worlds and how to find order within them.

FRANK (curiously): Who is that?

MONK #8 (laughingly): Why the 7th century monk, Xuanzang,[58] of course!

FRANK: You mean the monk who was immortalised in the 16th century Chinese classic, *Journey to the West*?

MONK #8 (nodding): In those days, 'the West' meant India. Today, our Prior Brother Monk is remembered throughout the Buddhist world.[59]

FRANK (admiringly): Well ..!

LEARNED ONE: We have arrived at a momentous juncture in our discussion. I'm sure we'll progress with greater vigour after our noonday repast, prayers, and daily chores. Shall we?

(*The Learned One rises. Everyone repairs to the Dining Hall.*)

---

[55] The Silk Road lasted from 1 BCE-14 AD. See, for example, Susan Whitfield, *Life Along the Silk Road* (Berkeley: University of California Press, 1999) and D. Devahuti, *Ancient Central-Asia and India* (New Delhi: Oxford University Press, 2002).

[56] See, for example, the *Human Development Report* (2009), {http://hdr.undp.org/en/media/HDR_2009_EN_Summary.pdf} accessed on 12 October 2009.

[57] This utterance means a 'sigh' or 'purification' in response to a horrifying violation of taboos and norms. *Emituofo* is the sinicised version of Amitābha, the Buddha of infinite qualities. Tan Chung and Geng Yingzeng, 'India and China: Twenty Centuries of Civilizational Interaction and Vibrations', D. P. Chattopadhyaya (General Editor), *History of Science, Philosophy, and Culture in Indian Civilization*, Vol. III, Part 6 (New Delhi: Centre for Studies in Civilizations, 2005), p. 62.

[58] Xuanzang is pronounced 'shuan-tsang'.

[59] In Japan, for example, the monk is known as Genjō-sanzō (it also signifies a title given to a learned and devoted monk); in Korea, as Hyeon Jang; in Vietnam, people call him Đường Tăng, although official texts refer to him as Huyền Trang (many thanks to Hong Anh Thu Vi for this information); and in India, he is known as Hiuen Tsang.

Act III: Xuanzang's worlds

Curtains rise. We are back in the Hall of Meditation. Lighting is muted to show it is late afternoon, a time for rest and tea. Everyone is seated as before. The screen overhead shows an image of the monk, Xuanzang.

LEARNED ONE: To continue with this morning's discussion, I have asked our resident archivist and temple historian to tell us about our Prior Brother Monk, Xuanzang.

(*The Learned One motions to an elderly monk. He rises to narrate the history of Xuanzang, which he knows by heart.*)

ELDERLY MONK (in a sing-song voice):[60]

In the year 629 AD, a young monk by the name of Xuanzang stole out in the middle of night to embark on his travels. The Tang Emperor Taizong, an unbeliever at the time, had expressly forbidden anyone to venture into what was known then as the 'western regions'. But Xuanzang was determined. Dissatisfied with the confusing and vague nature of Chinese translations of the *sutras*, he was determined to journey to India to learn from the source and bring back better knowledge to his homeland.

It took him 16 years. He trekked 10,000 miles from China to India, and back again, across mountains and deserts, jungles and rivers, in the heat and the cold, through thirst and hunger, robbery and assault. More than once, Xuanzang faced mortal danger. But he persevered, never losing sight of his purpose or vision. (*Emituofo!*)

By the time of his death, Xuanzang had left a legacy of brilliance to last all time. It ranged from the archaeological[61] to the anthropological[62] to the artistic[63] to the religious[64] to the literary[65] to his original motivation: that is, translation of over 1,000 scrolls.[66]

We know of these deeds, events, and accomplishments from Xuanzang's own journals, fastidiously kept despite the hardships of his travels, and later remembrances by his disciples.

(*The elderly monk bows upon finishing and sits down.*)

LEARNED ONE: We are most grateful for your recitation, Senior Brother Monk. What would you say was Xuangzang's motivation for undertaking what he did?

---

[60] This passage is drawn from Sally Hovey Wriggins, *The Silk Road Journey with Xuanzang* (Boulder: Westview Press, 2004).
[61] For example: locations of principal Buddhist cities and monuments.
[62] For example: documentation of life in the oases, sacred cities like Bamiyan, quasi census of monks and monasteries in India and Central Asia.
[63] For example: Buddhist paintings, sculptures, statues, architecture like *stupas*, monasteries, the Asoka pillar at Sarnath, collection of Gupta images that so affected Tang art.
[64] For example: records of Buddhist beliefs, practices, iconography, pantheon, and legends.
[65] For example: the Monkey King, a Chinese counterpart to India's Hanuman.
[66] These include the *Heart Sutra*, *Diamond Sutra*, *Thirty Verses*, *Treatise on the Stages of Yoga Practice*, and *Master of Lapis Lazuli Radiance Tathagatha*.

ELDERLY MONK: Perhaps 'co-dependent arising' or *pratītyasamutpāda*.[67] It teaches that our sense of who we are arises from reverberations with others. These lead to insight and connections where previously ignorance and divisions reigned. From this basis, we may begin to share in something larger than ourselves and approach that infinite ideal of love and compassion.

Such becoming involves the heart, not just the mind; and it requires a journey inside as much as outside. That is: through others, we may discover 'the genius that is already there'.[68]

Our brother monk, Thich Nhat Hanh, puts it pithily:

A teacher cannot give you the truth. The truth is already in you. You only need to open yourself – body, mind, and heart – so that his or her teachings will penetrate your own seeds of understanding and enlightenment.[69]

FRANK (excitedly): In other words, emancipation or enlightenment comes from two, simultaneous processes: (1) an internal interrogation of one's anger, fears, or prejudices that shackle us and, (2) an external engagement of discourse and disputation, care and mindfulness, with all forms of life, including Nature.

(*The other monks and nuns look at Frank, thinking: Doesn't he know this already?*)

ELDERLY MONK (patiently): This is called the process of 'interbeing'.[70] Once on this journey, we may aspire to the transcendent condition of 'no-mind'.

'No-mind' does not mean a mental emptiness but a spiritual fullness. It emerges when one lets go of false cravings, desires, and anxieties. Only then, could one be more responsive to the world.

Let me illustrate with another poem from Su Shi. He drew on the image of a 'thousand arms and eyes' to describe the condition of 'no-mind' (*recites*):

> *If a single person had a thousand minds,*
> *They would fight with each other inside him,*
> *What time would he have to respond to things?*
> *But when a thousand arms have no single mind,*
> *Every arm attains its proper place.*
> *I bow to the Revered One of Great Compassion,*
> *Desiring also to save all living beings.*
> *May each actualize the way of no-mind*
> *And each acquire a thousand arms and eyes.*[71]

To allow a 'thousand arms and eyes' each to attain its 'proper place' does not mean retreating into a discrete insularity. Rather, this image suggests that when one is freed of false fears and desires –

---

[67] Similarities also exist between *pratītyasamutpāda*, *ren*, and the ancient Greek concept of *poisies*. Agathangelou and Ling, *Transforming World Politics*.

[68] I am grateful to Patricia Robertson for these words.

[69] Thich Nhat Hanh, *The Heart of the Buddha's Teaching* (New York: Broadway Books, 1998), pp. 12–13. I am grateful to Jishnu Shankar for this reference.

[70] See, for example, Thich Nhat Hanh, *Interbeing* (Berkeley: Parallax Press, 1998).

[71] Su quoted in Egan, *Word, Image, and Deed in the life of Su Shi*, p. 151.

FRANK (impishly): Like a 'clash of civilizations'![72]

ELDERLY MONK (calmly continuing): – each 'arm' and 'eye' can find its own path to contentment. This is much-needed since the 'thousand arms and eyes' all come from and depend on one body – just like us, the peoples and societies of this Earth.

FRANK (slowly): So … a 'thousand arms and eyes' convey another kind of democracy, doesn't it? Unlike the Liberal understanding of freedom, independence, and autonomy, which is based on an individual's struggles against or despite others, a 'thousand arms and eyes' tell us we can achieve the same in *harmony* with others. That is, if we remain respectful of and responsive to one another.

ELDERLY MONK: This is no abstract goal. It requires an active *working through* of conflicts and contradictions by recognising their underlying connections and complements. This is the genius within.

Equally important, a 'thousand arms and eyes' exhort us to recognise the other side of democracy and that is complicity. None of us is innocent of power or what makes it possible.[73] For this reason, we are always responsible for our thoughts and actions – even our non-thoughts and non-actions.

FRANK: What about social and political institutions? Don't they hold us accountable as members of a society?

ELDERLY MONK: Yes and No. It mattered little to Xuanzang whether he was dealing with the state, the temple, the ashram, or the household. Each had its role yet was limited on its own. Rather, Xuanzang sought integration as a happy reconciliation of difference, as demonstrated by his journeys, discourses, debates, translations, and documentations.

In other words, society as a whole needs to value accountability in its institutions for them to have credibility with individuals, and for individuals to *own* this sense of accountability in order to demand it of their institutions.[74] Otherwise –

FRANK: Even democracies could turn fascist, like Nazi Germany in the 1930s![75]

LEARNED ONE: What about the economy? What role does it play?

ELDERLY MONK: As a matter of belief, Xuanzang treated the material world as an illusion. For daily survival, however, he depended on the generosity of

---

[72] Samuel P. Huntington, 'The Clash of Civilizations?', *Foreign Affairs*, 72:3 (1993), pp. 22–49.

[73] For an elaboration of how complicity worked in colonial power relations, see Ashis Nandy, *The Intimate Enemy: The Psychology of Colonialism* (Delhi: Oxford, 1988). For how complicity can be theorised into a model of 'multiple worlds', see Agathangelou and Ling, *Transforming World Politics*.

[74] See, for example, Nidhi Srinivas, 'Gender Rights and Women's Leadership: The Right to Information Act in India', paper presented at a conference on 'Gender, Peace, and Security', hosted by the Gender Policy Working Group, School of International and Public Affairs (SIPA), co-sponsored by UNICEF/UNIFEM, Gender Policy Program, Economic and Political Development Concentration, CUPID, GLIPA the Conflict Resolution Working Group, Center for International Conflict Resolution, Columbia University, New York (23 October 2009).

[75] William Allen, *Nazi Seizure of Power: The Experience of a Single German Town, 1922–1945* (Danbury, CT: Franklin Watts, 1984).

others since he only possessed the pilgrim's 'triple jewels' of a frugal robe, a walking stick, and a begging bowl.[76]

Nonetheless, our Prior Brother Monk exercised independence and autonomy, innovation and *self*-possession. Xuanzang not only defied the Tang Emperor's orders but also engaged in passionate debates and disputations with many kings and *gurus* during his travels, including the almighty King Harshavardhan of northern India and the Tang Emperor Taizong himself.

Ultimately, it was humility and a thirst for knowledge that impelled the Monk. He wanted to learn and engage, not to preach or convert or transform.

NUN #2 (pipes up): I believe India's poet laureate, Rabindranath Tagore, captured this spirit in his poem, 'To the Buddha'. It reads, in part (*recites*):

> *O Serene, O Free,*
> *in thine immeasurable mercy and goodness*
> *wipe away all dark stains of the heart*
> *of this earth.*
>
> *Thou giver of immortal gifts,*
> *give us the power of renunciation,*
> *and claim from us our pride.*[77]

FRANK (moved): Beautiful ... Xuanzang may have come closer to what both the Confucians and the Liberals desire but cannot attain: that is, a worldly world order.

(*Everyone is stunned.*)

Act IV: a worldy world order

NUN #3 (curiously): 'Worldly'? How could it be so for one whose life and work removed him from the world?

FRANK: I mean worldly in the sense that, like a 'thousand arms and eyes', multiple worlds make us who we are.[78] A 'bandit', after all, can also be a 'romantic avenger'!

By recognising such worldliness, our judgments, prejudices, and hostilities begin to thaw. The dazzle and fear of a 'thousand arms and eyes', each fighting against the other, fade in comparison to the underlying connections that bind them so that we perceive, finally, their refuge in a common, single body.

LEARNED ONE: What would your worldly world order look like?

---

[76] Tan and Geng, *Twenty Centuries of Civilizational Interaction and Vibrations*, p. 76.
[77] Rabindranath Tagore, *Poems*, ed. Krishna Kripalani (Calcutta: Visva-Bharati, 2003), pp. 129–130 (poem #88). Many thanks to Tan Chung for this reference, and Binod K. Mishra and Uma Dasgupta for helping me find the Bengali version of it.
[78] Ling, *Postcolonial International Relations*, and Agathangelou and Ling, *Transforming World Politics*.

FRANK (turning to Monk #1): Brother Monk, if you wouldn't mind drawing another figure for us?

(*Monk #1 is only too happy to oblige.*)

This is purely a thought experiment. But our Xuanzang-inspired, worldly world order would look something like this.

(*Monk #1 produces Figure 3 under Frank's instructions. Everyone 'Aahs!'*)

Figure 3. *A worldly world order.*[79]

LEARNED ONE: Could you elaborate, please?

FRANK: Certainly.

Linking the circle, square, and triangle signifies *pratītyasamutpāda*. No matter how different we think our worlds may be – like a circle to a square to a triangle – each world comes into being from interactions with other worlds. We see this happening precisely where they intersect or overlap,[80] bringing challenges as well as benefits – sometimes with one producing the other.

For example, our multiple worlds could lock into one another through patriarchy or some other hooks of power.[81] This may enable multiple worlds to function smoothly but it also allows oppression.

---

[79] Painting by Sengai Gibon (1750–1838) titled, 'Universe'. {http://www.raisethehammer.org/static/images/sengai.jpg} accessed on 18 January 2010.

[80] For examples of such cultural co-productions, see Martin Bernal, *Black Athena: the Afroasiatic Roots of Classical Civilisation* (The Fabrication of Ancient Greece 1765–1985, Volume 1) (New Jersey: Rutgers University Press, 1987); Paul Gilroy, *The Black Atlantic: Modernity and Double-Consciousness* (Cambridge: Harvard University Press, 1993); Arturo Escobar, *Encountering Development: The Making and Unmaking of the Third World* (Princeton: Princeton University Press, 1996); John Hobson, *The Eastern Origins of Western Civilisation* (Cambridge: Cambridge University Press, 2004); Pinar Bilgin, 'The International Political "Sociology of a not so International Discipline"', *International Political Sociology*, 3:3 (2009), pp. 338–42; Geeta Chowdhry and Shirin Rai, 'Geographies of Exclusion and the Politics of Inclusion: Race-Based Exclusions in the Teaching of International Relations', *International Studies Perspectives*, 10:1 (2009), pp. 84–91.

[81] See, for example, Bina D'Costa and Katrina Lee-Koo (eds), *Gender and Global Politics in the Asia Pacific* (London: Palgrave Macmillan, 2009).

Other times, our multiple worlds may conflict. This could lead to wars, rebellions, 'regime change', and other sources of violence. But, at another level, differences among multiple worlds can also keep each world honest about itself as well as others, enabling all to evolve over time.

For instance, Confucian *ren* can help to cosmopolitanise Liberal governance. Who gets to set these 'fair' and 'just' rules for all, anyway?[82]

Similarly, Liberalism can help to dislodge *tianxia*'s complacency. Notions of 'democracy', 'individual liberty', and 'a framework of order established by law' would compel transformation on *all* sides, not just one.

The concept of 'no-mind' guides us here. It urges mutual respect within and among all worlds. This does not mean non-interference so tyrants could do what they will with impunity. What 'no-mind' encourages, instead, is being responsive to others, not telling them what to do or how to think, but learning from them just as they can learn from us.

LEARNED ONE: What enables such communication across worlds, Frank? Where does the common vocabulary of inter-civilisational discourse come from? (*Frank hesitates. He has not anticipated this question.*)

Nun #4 (intercedes): Everyday living.[83] Much is made of the difficulties of multiple worlds to talk to one another. The presumption is that different norms, power, and interests, especially when embedded in contending worldviews, cannot reconcile or even meet. This is the 'clash of civilizations' perspective. Yet people cross such borders all the time, whether it is to survive colonialism, imperialism, and other forms of hegemony, or because it is fun and they're curious.[84] And the locus of such border crossings can range from the mundane (food, dress, shelter, trade) to the sublime (music, art, religion).[85] Indeed, Xuanzang wouldn't have been able to accomplish all that he did had he not crossed all sorts of borders. (*Frank bows gratefully to Nun #4. She nods back with a smile.*)

LEARNED ONE: So we've been looking at all the wrong places for inter-civilisational dialogue?

FRANK: Yes and No. We need to look at discourse but we've set our sights too high when evidence lies right beneath our noses.

NUN #5: 'Exemplary power' takes on a new meaning, in this case. It comes from 'the layperson' as much as 'the expert', 'local knowledge' as much as 'scientific

---

[82] See, for example, Brooke A. Ackerly, 'Is Liberalism the Only Way toward Democracy? Confucianism and Democracy', *Political Theory*, 33:4 (August 2005), pp. 547–76.

[83] See, for example, John M. Hobson and Leonard Seabrooke (eds), *Everyday Politics of the World Economy* (Cambridge: Cambridge University Press, 2007) and Oliver P. Richmond, *A Post-Liberal Peace* (forthcoming).

[84] For a sample of this literature, see Geeta Chowdhry and L. H. M. Ling, '(Race)ing Feminist International Relations: A Critical Overview of Postcolonial Feminism in International Relations', in Robert A. Denemark (ed.), *The International Studies Encyclopedia* (London: Blackwell Publishing, 2010), pp. 6038–57.

[85] See, for example, M.I. Franklin, *Resounding International Relations: On Music, Culture, and Politics* (London: Palgrave Macmillan, 2005); Roland Bleiker, *Aesthetics and World Politics* (London: Palgrave Macmillan, 2009).

discoveries', 'tradition' as much as 'modernity'.[86] Each relates to the others. Each determines the others. All contribute to a worldly world order.

FRANK: That's right, Sister Nun. Strict adherence to certain principles or ideology cannot determine how we organise ourselves. We could choose to borrow PAR elements or not, a family structure or not. Or aspects of each! Such formalities matter little so long as we are able to improve society's responsiveness to its people, and the people to one another.[87]

NUN #6: This is an example of the 'other kind of democracy' that Brother Frank mentioned earlier. (*Frank beams.*) In recognising that *everyone* – Liberals and Confucians, men and women, masters and servants – has a role in producing us, we realise there is no need to assimilate or convert anyone. A world order or world-ness is already in place!

LEARNED ONE: What about practical matters like the economy?

FRANK: Xuanzang showed that these are as much social and spiritual as material.[88] Most important is that ordinary folks are able to live well and without undue stress or grind. Because nothing stays the same and reversals are always imminent, cooperation can, does, and *must* coexist with competition.[89] A 'zero-sum' attitude, in other words, does not work nor is it necessary. It merely jeopardises all forms of sentient life, including the Earth itself.

LEARNED ONE: Does this apply to military affairs as well?

FRANK: Definitely. It's not enough to wage a humane war as Sunzi recommended. Citizens need to speak up, also, *across* national boundaries *and to one another*.[90] Too often, dissent stops at the water's edge due to concerns about 'national security' when it has long been internationalised.[91] We need to shatter

---

[86] For an articulation of this perspective in environmental terms, see Vandana Shiva, 'Reductionist Science as Epistemological Violence', in Ashis Nandy (ed.), *Science, Hegemony and Violence: A Requiem for Modernity*, 4th edition (Tokyo: UN University, 1996), pp. 232–56.

[87] Note, for example, the generational nature of precedential learning with regard to capitalism and the Westphalian inter-state system in Asia. See Ling, *Postcolonial International Relations.*

[88] Agathangelou and Ling refer to this as 'relational materialism'. Agathangelou and Ling, *Transforming World Politics.*

[89] The notion of 'cooperative competition' is not new, especially in the development of what is known as 'Asian capitalism'. See Ling, *Postcolonial International Relations.* For applications of 'cooperative competition' in other contexts, see John Rawls, *A Theory of Justice* (Cambridge: Harvard University Press, 1970); Charles Sabel and Michael Piore, *The Second Industrial Divide: Possibilities for Prosperity* (New York: Basic Books, 1984); and Amartya Sen, 'Gender and Cooperative Conflicts', in Irene Tinker (ed.), *Persistent Inequalities: Women and Development* (Oxford: Oxford University Press, 1990), pp. 123–49.

[90] There is an increasing recognition of this need for inter-civilisational dialogue in world politics. In 1998, the UN (UN) named 2001 as the 'UN Year of Dialogue among Civilizations'. Despite the attacks on New York and Washington, DC on September 11 of that year, other nations have taken up the banner. Under the auspices of the UN and supported by the EU and the Vatican, first Spain then Turkey formed an 'Alliance of Civilizations' to enhance exchanges between 'Islam' and 'the West'. See, also, Fred Dallmayr and Abbas Manoochehri (eds), *Civilizational Dialogue and Political Thought: Tehran Papers* (New York: Lexington Books, 2007); Peter J. Katzenstein (ed.), *Civilizations in World Politics: Plural and Pluralist Perspectives* (London: Routledge 2009); Arlene Tickner and Ole Wæver (eds), *International Relations Scholarship Around the World: Worlding Beyond the West* (London: Routledge, 2009); Takashi Shogimen and Cary J. Nederman (eds), *Western Political Thought in Dialogue with Asia* (Lanham: Lexington Books, 2009).

[91] Anna M. Agathangelou and L. H. M. Ling, 'Power, Borders, Security, Wealth: Lessons of Violence and Desire from September 11', *International Studies Quarterly*, 48:3 (September 2004), pp. 517–38.

the illusion that what happens inside one set of borders has nothing or little to do with others elsewhere.[92]

LEARNED ONE: These are admirable principles, Frank, but do they have any practical import?

FRANK: Yes. Take terrorism, for example. Current policies tend to drive terrorism underground for they seek only to annihilate, subordinate, or conquer.[93] With a worldly world order in mind, we ask: how can we convince an ideologue *not* to kill innocents, especially children, for a political ideal?

NUN #7: Here, we can draw on the concept of 'interbeing' mentioned earlier, where a simultaneous process of internal interrogation supported by external engagement could help emancipate terror from the terrorist, ideology from the ideologue.

FRANK: And by 'terrorist' and 'ideologue', we mean those who decide the fate of others in fancy offices as well as barren caves. As for 'we', that refers to *all* of us including victims, bystanders, and the so-called removed or uninvolved.

(*Some monks and nuns exchange sheepish glances.*)

Such intervention requires input from inside and below, outside and above. Here, Xuanzang teaches us most directly. Like him, we need to learn about one another collectively and mutually, for extended periods of time, and through local institutions.

LEARNED ONE: How could we follow in his footsteps today?

FRANK (paces back and forth, rubbing his chin, then snaps his fingers): Mobile centres of learning! Instead of scholars, practitioners, and students gathering in one centre to study the world – which is the current model – they could journey from one location to another. And I don't mean short-term, student exchanges or government commissions to gather 'data' about 'others'. Our mobile centres of learning would be premised on *mutual* learning, in the localities, and for sustained durations.[94] With such, we may continue Xuanzang's tradition of nurturing future 'worldizers'.

NUN #8: What about the Internet? Doesn't it already 'worldize' us without the need for physical travel?

FRANK: The Internet is useful for many things but it can't replace actual, personal contact. We must see, smell, touch, hear, eat, drink, and discourse with a locality to know it.

---

[92] Tarak Barkawi and Mark Laffey, 'The Postcolonial Moment in Security Studies', *Review of International Studies*, 32:4 (2006), pp. 329–52.

[93] For one example, see Petra Bartosiewicz, 'The Intelligence Factory: How America Makes its Enemies Disappear', *Harper's Magazine* (November 2009), {http://harpers.org/archive/2009/11/0082719} accessed on 17 December 2009. I thank Everita Silina for this reference. For a deeper analysis of why such strategies are taken, see Sankaran Krishna, *Globalization and Postcolonialism: Hegemony and Resistance in the Twenty-First Century* (Lanham: Rowman & Littlefield.)

[94] For one attempt at this model of learning, see: {http://ici.parsons.edu/institutions/india-china-institute/}.

This acknowledgement leads us to relate to others, as Xuanzang did, with humility and a thirst for learning. From power and wealth, we may begin to shift to a worldly world order of knowledge and sustainability that, over time, could culminate into love and compassion. And like Xuanzang, we embark on this journey knowing, all the while, that we may never, ever reach its shores.

MONKS & NUNS (chant): *Emituofo!*

Act V: Conclusion

Curtains rise. The screen overhead shows a pagoda in moonlit shadow. Lighting is muted. Off-stage, we hear the monastery's bells ringing again, signalling time for the evening meal and prayers. We also hear plates of food being put on tables. The stage is empty except for Frank and the Learned One.

FRANK: I've learned much today, Learned One. Thank you. (*He bows.*)

LEARNED ONE: Not at all, Frank. I've learned a lot, too. Isn't that the point?

FRANK (nodding): Yes ... Um, Learned One, I've come to another decision. I'm keeping my old name.

LEARNED ONE: You're giving up Frank?

FRANK: Oh no. I will keep Frank for communication with those from across the valleys and over the seas. But I will remain Novice Lee here, especially with my brother monks and sister nuns.

LEARNED ONE: Why, Fr – uh, Novice Lee?

NOVICE LEE/FRANK: Well, as we have learned from Xuanzang, there's no need to be absolute, is there?

Moreover, I cherish the friendships that make me Novice Lee with all of you here, just as I'm sure I'll value the friendships that will make me Frank with others elsewhere. In fact, I think we should all have many names in many languages so we could have many friendships! You know what Shakespeare said –

LEARNED ONE (smiling): Yes, yes. Roses and names smelling sweet and all that.[95] Excellent, my child.

(*The Learned One turns to go.*)

NOVICE LEE/FRANK (keeping pace): Uh, Learned One, just one more thing, if you don't mind. I can't help but notice that throughout our discussions, you asked questions only. Why is that?

---

[95] The line comes from *Romeo and Juliet* (1594): 'What's in a name? That which we call a rose/By any other name would smell as sweet' (II.2).

LEARNED ONE (eyes twinkling): How do you think I got to be the Learned One?[96]

(*Lights out. Curtains down. Collective chanting of 'Om!' fills the theatre.*)

THE END

[96] On the role and significance of asking questions in International Relations, see L. H. M. Ling, 'The Fish and the Turtle: Multiple Worlds as Method', in Michael Brecher and Fred Harvey (eds), *Critical Perspectives in International Studies* (Ann Arbor: University of Michigan Press, 2002), pp. 141–7.

For EU product safety concerns, contact us at Calle de José Abascal, 56–1°,
28003 Madrid, Spain or eugpsr@cambridge.org.

www.ingramcontent.com/pod-product-compliance
Ingram Content Group UK Ltd.
Pitfield, Milton Keynes, MK11 3LW, UK
UKHW030900150625
459647UK00021B/2701